High Praise for
Aircraft Finance

In this insightful book, authors Bijan Vasigh, Reza Taleghani, and Darryl Jenkins bring the financial aspects of this highly capitalized and dynamic industry to life, giving the reader an understanding of the decisions that have led to the current state of aircraft production and airlines that fly them. The book begins by giving the reader a historical perspective of the aircraft landscape, providing case studies that help with an understanding of the significance of decisions based on which aircraft were once built and aircraft were once bought.

Aircraft Finance highlights the financial sensitivities that contribute to the volatility that is inherent in the business today and details the challenges and dynamics currently facing this ever-changing industry. The reader will be intrigued by the trade-offs airlines and aircraft manufacturers make and the impact these trade-offs have on the valuation of the aircraft asset and airlines' fleets and route decisions. The book also provides insights into financing alternatives, as well as the structural ramifications of those decisions.

As the chapters guide you from a historical to modern-day perspective on the dynamics between manufacturers, airlines, and financing vehicles, you will be left wondering how the future of the industry will be affected given the current pace of change. Today, the industry is at a significant juncture in aviation as the advancement in aircraft technology and materials, together with the increasing costs of operating aircraft, are altering the aviation landscape. Globalization, technology, and consolidation continue to play critical roles in what the fleets and route networks of the future will look like. This guide helps explain why the pace of change is so rapid, the need to change so important, and why those who don't will be as obsolete as the aircraft that sit in the desert today.

—Zane Rowe
Executive Vice President and Chief Financial Officer of UAL

Aircraft Finance provides an accessible, highly readable, and fact-filled guide to the ins and outs of aircraft financing. The complexities are introduced by chapters that begin with an outline of the issues and discussions that lie ahead. Facts and concepts can be read all at once or easily gleaned for specific ideas. Brick by brick, the authors provide both a firm foundation for the student and, at the same time, a reference tool for the airline executive or investor.

This book introduces the reader to the evolving global aircraft industry and its structure, detailing the industry's origins, progressing through its struggles and reorganizations, to today's market of aircraft choices. The intricacies of the major manufacturers' fleets of offerings are explored. The reader is shown how to examine the general, physical, and operational characteristics of an array of the most important aircraft. This, in turn, leads into an exploration of comparative analyses among different fleet offerings.

The authors' emphasis on context is an important element of their approach. Examples of specific evaluation techniques for some of the industry's most important aircraft are provided in a clear and concise, step-by-step manner. Techniques include the important sensitivity analysis of critical valuation factors. The global nature of aviation is brought home with a chapter on aircraft export credit finance, export credit agencies, UNIDROIT, and the Cape Town Convention. *Aircraft Finance* also provides an excellent guide through the evolving intricacies of the New Aircraft Sector Understanding. This is especially important in view of the recent WTO rulings in the US-EU Airbus dispute.

This valuable guide is an ideal vehicle to introduce the student to a subject that lies at the heart of the commercial aviation industry. At the same time, it is an up-to-date reference tool for the airline executive. For student and expert alike, it provides a context-rich and informative excursion into the complexities of aircraft financing.

—Paul Mifsud, J.D.
Former Vice President of Government and Legal Affairs, KLM Royal Dutch Airlines
Co-Chairman, American Bar Association International Law Committee on Aviation

AIRCRAFT FINANCE

Strategies for Managing Capital Costs in a Turbulent Industry

Bijan Vasigh

Reza Taleghani

Darryl Jenkins

Copyright © 2012 J. Ross Publishing

ISBN-13: 978-1-60427-071-6

Printed and bound in the U.S.A. Printed on acid-free paper.

10 9 8 7 6 5 4 3 2 1

Library of Congress Cataloging-in-Publication Data

Vasigh, Bijan.
  Aircraft finance: strategies for managing capital costs in a turbulent industry /
by Bijan Vasigh, Reza Taleghani, and Darryl Jenkins.
    p. cm.
  Includes bibliographical references and index.
  ISBN 978-1-60427-071-6 (alk. paper)
  1. Aeronautics, Commercial—Finance. I. Taleghani, Reza, 1972- II.
Jenkins, Darryl. III. Title.
  HE9782.V368 2012
  387.7'30681—dc23

                              2012012382

Direct all inquiries to J. Ross Publishing, Inc., 5765 N. Andrews Way, Fort Lauderdale, FL 33309.

Phone: (954) 727-9333
Fax: (561) 892-0700
Web: www.jrosspub.com

This book is dedicated to the memory of my sister, Jaleh Vasigh. She was beloved and respected by all who knew her.

—Bijan Vasigh

Table of Contents

About the Authors

Bijan Vasigh is Professor of Economics and Finance in the College of Business at Embry-Riddle Aeronautical University, Daytona Beach, Florida. He received a Ph.D. in Economics from the State University of New York and has published many articles concerning the aviation industry. The articles were published in numerous academic journals, including the *Journal of Economics and Finance, Journal of Transportation Management, National Aeronautics and Space Administration (NASA) Scientific and Technical Aerospace Reports, Transportation Quarterly, Airport Business, Journal of Business and Economics*, and *Journal of Travel Research*. He has been quoted in major newspapers and magazines around the world. In 2006, his paper "A Total Factor Productivity Based for Tactical Cluster Assessment: Empirical Investigation in the Airline Industry" was awarded the Dr. Frank E. Sorenson Award for outstanding achievement of excellence in aviation research scholarship. Bijan is the author of *An Introduction to Air Transport Economics: From Theory to Application* and *The Foundations of Airline Finance: Methodology and Practice*.

Reza Taleghani is Managing Director with J.P. Morgan Securities in New York, where he has spent the majority of his career as an investment banker to the air transport sector. He received BA degrees in History and in Organizational Behavior and Management from Brown University, and an MBA and JD from Villanova University. He has a deep understanding of the operational aspects of the industry, having served as President and CEO of Sterling Airlines, a leading Scandinavian low-cost carrier. His expertise in aircraft finance arises from originating and structuring financings of transportation assets in J.P. Morgan's Securitized Products Group, as well as operating a fleet of jet aircraft at Sterling. During his time at J.P. Morgan, he also worked on mergers and acquisitions advisory; initial public offerings; secured, unsecured and ECA-backed financing in the syndicated finance and capital markets; leveraged finance; and restructuring advisory and risk management for airline and lessor clients in Europe, the United States, and Latin America.

Darryl Jenkins has aviation experience that covers more than thirty years, including extensive merger and acquisition experience at United Airlines and Delta Air Lines. Previously, he was at GWU, served as Director of the Aviation Institute, and was Director of the Graduate Certificate Program in Aviation Management from 2001 to 2003. He was visiting faculty at Embry-Riddle Aeronautical University in 2004. As a consultant, he has worked for most of the world's top airlines. He is a regular commentator for network media (ABC, NBC, CBS, Fox, CNN, MSNBC, and CNBC) on aviation issues and is regularly quoted in the print media as well. He is a regular speaker at conferences and is the author of several books.

Acknowledgments

The development and writing of any book is a long and trying experience. As authors, we received a lot of assistance and encouragement from a number of individuals. Acknowledgment is due to Christina Fredrick and Richard Heist at Embry-Riddle Aeronautical University.

Many Embry-Riddle Aeronautical University graduate students also helped in the preparation of this manuscript. We owe a special debt to graduate assistants Pascal Lawrence, Matthew Dixon, Krislen Keri, Vladislav Borodulin, Alexandru Milut, Lance Brabham, and Halnettige Perera.

Several people made written contributions that brought this book to life. We are particularly grateful to Zane Rowe, Paul Mifsud, Ken Dufour, Kelly Ison, Johan Visser, Peter Morrell, and Graham Deitz.

We also thank many friends and supporters in the airline and aviation industry: Fariba Alamdari, Sam Fanasheh and Don Ryther (the Boeing Company), Hossein Amir-Aslani, Chris Tarry, Vedapuri Raghavan, Habib Eslami, Chris Vogel, Robert Milton, G. Rod Erfani, Shahin Vassigh, Bert Zarb, Vitaly Guzhva, Gueric Dechavanne, Blair LaCorte, Javad Gorjidooz, John Thomas, Bill Franke, Michael Bell, Stephen Johnson, Victor Vial, Houman Motaharian, Thorsteinn Gudmundsson, Jose Ofilio Gurdian, Duncan Dee, Andrew Lobbenberg, Ron Wainshal, Norman Liu, Diego Simonian, Alvin Khoo, Michael Clare, Bob Genise, Steve Hazy, Tony Fernandes, Trevor Ricards, Pam Hendry, Dave Walton, Dave Siegel, Fritz Otti, Dominique Patry, Sydney Isaacs, John McEvoy, Calin Rovinescu, Marc Allinson, Michael T. Hansen, Aaron Moser, Vikram Rupani, Mark Streeter, Jamie Baker, Chris Avery, Patrick Ryan, Jeffrey Tenen, Gus Kelly, Scott Scherer, Elihu Robertson, Benoit Debains, Jeppe Gregersen, Tom McCormick, Ole Falholt,

Allan Eimert, David Arendt, and the entire team at Sterling Airlines—especially the flight and cabin crews!

We particularly acknowledge our families who supported us in this endeavor. For their patience and love as this book came together, we are grateful to: Behnoosh and Majid Vasigh, and Demetra, Nika, Dino, Babak, and Manijeh Taleghani.

We also thank Tim Pletscher and Stephen Buda at J. Ross Publishing, who encouraged us and helped to deliver a quality manuscript.

Any mistakes in the book are attributed to the authors, and we will be grateful for reader feedback.

Foreword

In recent years, author Bijan Vasigh has invited me to speak to his economics classes about current airline issues. Those class discussions spawned engaging conversations about how particular elements of economics and finance affect management decisions within the airlines. Relating basic academic concepts to real-world situations certainly enlivens what can sometimes be dull information. Discussion also brings the information to life in a way that provides both the logic and perspective of its application. That is the approach that Dr. Vasigh and the co-authors take in this book. The text applies basic economic and financial concepts in various calculations that result in a valuation framework for an airline's aircraft assets and the financing options available to fund their acquisition.

When Dr. Vasigh approached me regarding a book on aircraft valuation and finance, one question came to mind: How could the book increase the value of knowing how much an airplane is worth? As the book developed, the answer became clear: building an aircraft valuation framework requires a set of economic and financial assessments, which may change from one year to the next or from one airline to another. Understanding these building blocks of valuation gives the reader a basis for understanding the companies themselves. *Aircraft Finance* provides insights into:

- The basics of airline finance
- Corporate capital structure
- Leasing concepts and their associated advantages and disadvantages
- Management decisions that affect value creation
- Components of aircraft value, and how changes in components are reflected in the values
- Why an aircraft's value may differ from one airline to another

In short, the reader will learn the language of airline management. I am not aware of any book that brings together these topics in the same way or that shows the relationships between topics so clearly. Students will benefit from having this textbook, and seasoned airline professionals will want to keep it as a reference.

Kelly Ison, MSc, SPHR, ATP
Consultant, formerly Chairman—Negotiating Committee, US Airways

Preface

After World War II, four prominent players emerged in the business of building commercial aircraft in the United States—Boeing, McDonnell, Douglas, and Lockheed. These companies leveraged their experience in military aircraft production to address commercial aviation needs in the post-World War II years. The Boeing Airplane Company was established in 1916 in Seattle, WA, subsequently reorganized, and changed its name to the Boeing Company in 1961. McDonnell and Douglas would eventually merge in 1967, and the combined entity would remain a long-standing competitor to Boeing in North America until its ultimate merger with Boeing in 1997. Lockheed had a commercial aircraft focus with several products through the years, but ultimately chose to exit the commercial aviation business to focus exclusively on military and defense applications.

In Europe, Fokker, a Dutch aircraft manufacturer, became the world's largest aircraft manufacturer by the late 1920s, but went into bankruptcy and ceased operations in 1996. To counter the American dominance of commercial aircraft manufacturing, in 1967 ministers from the French, British, and German governments came together to develop a joint aviation technology group that would bring together the aviation expertise of each country. On December 18, 1970, Airbus Industrie was formally established as an Economic Interest Group. Through the years Airbus grew to become a force in aircraft production, so that today the two dominant manufacturers of commercial aircraft are Boeing and Airbus for larger aircraft, with newer companies such as Embraer of Brazil and Bombardier of Canada focusing on the regional side of the market.

While aircraft manufacturers have remained marginally profitable, airlines continued to suffer substantial losses since airline deregulation in the United

States in 1978. The airline industry has grown accustomed to routinely obliterating shareholder value as consumers benefit from fierce competition and continued downward pressure on fares. During this evolution in the industry, valuing commercial aircraft prices was not explored in depth by academic researchers.

Nonetheless, setting a value on an income-producing asset such as an aircraft has been a challenging, stimulating, and intellectually rewarding task. The problems posed by airlines, fleet managers, and capital budgeting officers who need help in making investment decisions are frequently complex and significant. Decisions regarding valuation affect the development of the organization as a whole. There are many rigorous skills that must be acquired to ensure careful judgment. The standards of analysis and performance imposed on decision makers are raised continually, as the demands of judgment problems increase and the significance of the decisions on which valuation assessments are based expands.

Airline executives view the acquisition of a commercial aircraft as an investment opportunity for increased productivity as well as a way to gain a competitive advantage. The value of an aircraft depends on internal factors that are directly related to the aircraft's specifications and documentation. The price of an aircraft is a function of its age, size, seat capacity, payload, fuel efficiency, degree of customization, and technical status. Fuel efficiency was not a major design driver until the 1980s, but today, fuel efficiency is a major design driver for aircraft and engine development. On December 1, 2010, Airbus announced a fuel-efficient engine option for the A319, A320, and A321—the A320neo, which will significantly boost overall cost-efficiency of those jetliners.

Another reason for varying aircraft prices is the value of buyer-furnished equipment such as in-flight entertainment, seats, and engines. In addition, aircraft prices depend on external factors such as macroeconomic indicators, market demand and its elasticity, fuel cost, and environmental regulations. External factors are extremely important because they indicate the point in the aviation industry cycle at which the aircraft analysis is being made, and this, in turn, has the greatest impact on aircraft value. New aircraft are 70% more fuel-efficient than 40 years ago. For used aircraft, high and unpredictable energy prices are a factor behind decisions to replace them with newer, more fuel-efficient aircraft and retire them early.

New aircraft are much more expensive than used aircraft, but the differences are offset by their lower operating costs. Hence, the theoretical value is highly correlated to assumptions underlying the variation of these factors. Therefore, since the air transport industry is highly dynamic, the theoretical value of an aircraft will fluctuate as the underlying assumptions change—such as economic growth. For example, China may need about 2,600 new planes in the next 20 years, at a cost of more than USD$210 billion. Another growing market is India, where, according to an Airbus forecast, up to 1,100 passenger and freighter aircraft over two decades valued around USD$105 billion might be ordered.

Aircraft transactions are relatively infrequent compared to the purchase and sale of other physical assets, and prices are not available to the general public. Many mega carriers and leasing companies order in bulk, and their bargaining position affords them significant discounts.

This book is directed toward academia, professionals, consultants, managers, and students of aircraft finance, with or without experience in the aircraft field, who have little or no background in asset valuation and finance. This book presents aircraft finance's basic principles and techniques. It introduces the income capitalization process as a fundamental, but extremely powerful, tool of analysis. It assumes an understanding and working knowledge of some fundamental principles of finance and the structure and operations of aviation markets. It expects the reader to be able to work comfortably with quantitative analysis and graphs.

Starting from a base of working knowledge and experience, this book provides the means to develop and sharpen the analytical tools and skills required in aircraft finance. It reviews the current thinking of valuation theorists and the cumulative experience of leading appraisal practitioners. The reader is given the benefit of this knowledge and experience to develop a strong foundation of his/her own. Subsequent knowledge and experience can be built on that foundation and combined to ultimately create the professional judgment needed in completing an aircraft valuation.

One skill, sensitivity analysis, is presented by using @Risk simulation software to explore the sensitivity of aircraft valuation under diverse market conditions. Once the analysis of the choice and valuation of the asset has been completed, a basic framework for the various alternatives open to the reader in financing the purchase of the aircraft is presented: through leasing, commercial lending, capital markets transactions, or use of export credit-supported finance.

Airlines regularly need to make decisions on the purchase of aircraft and flight equipment. The absence of financial capital to purchase new aircraft and financial and operational flexibilities are two major reasons for recent growth in the world aircraft leasing industry. Leasing has become a common technique to acquire an aircraft, since aircraft have become expensive and subject to economic volatility and types of risk. Aircraft leasing is an attractive option to purchasing, which may provide advantages to some airlines. Many aircraft leasing companies, including International Lease Finance Corporation (ILFC), GE Commercial Aviation Service, AerCap, Air Castle, CIT Aerospace, RBS Aviation Capital, and Babcock & Brown Aircraft Management LLC have dominated the aircraft market.

In this book, a process is given for determining whether leasing an aircraft is cheaper and more advantageous than purchasing. The worldwide commercial aircraft leasing market currently constitutes 6,864 aircraft and had a market value of USD$233B in 2011. Many of the ideas and some of the terminology used in this book are relatively new to valuation literature. They represent carefully considered efforts to improve, expand, or clarify communication and understanding in the field of aircraft valuation.

Much of the material in this book is presented in a framework that is innovative, treating valuation analysis as a systematic effort in problem solving directed at rational financial decision making. It incorporates a completely modern approach to financial investment decision making. The essential tools of flexibility, adaptability, and commonality of aircraft financial analyses can be applied to an almost infinite set of valuation problem situations. Once these links of analyses have been introduced, the reader will understand the underlying concepts of aircraft valuation processes and techniques and the subsequent financing alternatives available to fund the use of the aircraft asset.

Bijan Vasigh
Reza Taleghani
Darryl Jenkins

Prologue

The whole subject of appraisal of property: it's not an art and it's not a science; in my opinion, it's a mystery.

—The Honorable Carlisle B. Roberts, 1974

Attempts at aircraft valuation began shortly after the Wright Brothers' first flight, yet very little has been written or published regarding its theory, concepts, or practice. For many years, a lack of uniformity existed in terms of procedures; standardized appraisal techniques for aircraft had not been developed. Each appraiser had their own methods and concepts regarding how aircraft should be valued, and each was often reluctant to pass "hands on" knowledge to those entering the field. For the sharing of knowledge and information, it was a difficult time.

The valuation of aircraft was practiced in many ways, usually following the direction or backing of groups of appraisers whose interest was guided by the purpose of their valuation or by a company in the aerospace industry. Still, today, there is little agreement among appraisers, valuation users, and regulators regarding aircraft valuations. The recent global financial and economic crisis has only served to exacerbate the situation.

This book details the critical and complex aspects of modern-day valuation and appraisals. Students of finance as well as airline, business aircraft, and general aviation professionals should use this guide to master the valuation profession.

—Kenneth M. Dufour
Chairman Student Life Committee, Board of Trustees,
Embry-Riddle Aeronautical University

Web
Added
Value™

At J. Ross Publishing we are committed to providing today's professional with
practical, hands-on tools that enhance the learning experience and give readers an
opportunity to apply what they have learned. That is why we offer free ancillary
materials available for download on this book and all participating Web Added
Value™ publications. These online resources may include interactive versions of
material that appears in the book or supplemental templates, worksheets, models,
plans, case studies, proposals, spreadsheets and assessment tools, among other
things. Whenever you see the WAV™ symbol in any of our publications, it means
bonus materials accompany the book and are available from the Web Added Value
Download Resource Center at www.jrosspub.com.

Downloads for *Aircraft Finance* include spreadsheets on major airline cost
structure, aircraft operating cost structure, historical aircraft production, and
aircraft value.

The Globalization and Evolution of the Commercial Aircraft Industry

With a short dash down the runway, the machine lifted into the air and was flying. It was only a flight of twelve seconds, and it was an uncertain, wavy, creeping sort of flight at best; but it was a real flight at last and not a glide.

—Orville Wright, on the first flight of a heavier-than-air aircraft

In the aircraft business, as in a Trollope novel, things are often not what they seem. In the 1980s, Boeing still reigned supreme. Its airplanes covered the market. Its product support was exemplary. Boeing was universally judged one of America's best and most admired companies, partly because its sales of large commercial airplanes were the country's biggest export, and partly because it had learned to build those airplanes better, faster, and cheaper than anyone else had done... Today, things have turned around. Boeing and Airbus are the sole suppliers of big airliners, but over many of the past twenty years, the two companies were moving in opposite directions. Boeing's multiple troubles, most of them self-inflicted, signaled an end to its dominance and pointed up Airbus' methodical rise.

—John Newhouse, Writer and Correspondent

Aircraft manufacturing is a vital industry that greatly influences the entire economy of a nation. The industry receives significant attention from policymakers and industry analysts. Nowadays, the commercial aircraft industry is dominated by two companies, primarily due to high barriers to entry and high degrees of operating and financial leverage.

Those two companies are Airbus and Boeing. In 2010, Airbus delivered 510 aircraft and received net orders for 574 new planes.[1] During the same period, Boeing delivered 460 aircraft and received net orders for 530 jets.[2] In 2011, Boeing deliveries rose 3% to 477 from 462 the year before.[3] Total orders for Boeing commercial aircraft surged 52% to 805 in 2011, after 116 cancellations.

Development of new commercial aircraft requires massive initial investment in labor, capital, equipment, and technologies. Historically, this has led to the formation of large, consolidated firms with financing from public and government sources. For example, the A380 development cost was more than $14 billion, with one-third of the cost financed by European members of the Airbus consortium. France, Britain, Germany, and Spain have each invested heavily in the A380 program. The Boeing 777 cost approximately $5.5 billion to develop, of which $3 billion was used toward overcoming production delays.[4] While there were several aircraft manufacturers, including Ford in North America and Junkers in Europe, from the early 1900s through the late 1980s that made significant contributions, the industry has undergone considerable consolidation in the past two decades, resulting in the emergence of a relatively stable duopoly for narrow- and wide-body commercial airliners: Boeing Company in North America and Airbus S.A.S. in Europe.

This chapter presents a brief history and overview of the product offerings of major commercial aircraft manufacturers, as follows:

Early Contributions to Commercial Aircraft Manufacturing

- Ford Tri-Motor
- Junkers German Transport

Commercial Aircraft Manufacturing

- North America
- Western Europe
- Russia and Eastern Europe
- Asia
- Regional Jet Markets

At the end of the chapter is a Summary for chapter review and a Bibliography for further study.

---

[1] *The New York Times*, March 9, 2011.
[2] *Air Transport World (ATW)*, July 2011.
[3] The Associated Press, January 5, 2012.
[4] Oxford Analytical (November 1, 2006). Airbus must compete in mid-sized market. *Forbes International*.

Early Contributions to Commercial Aircraft Manufacturing

The commercial aircraft industry requires a large investment to develop and manufacture aircraft, avionics, and engines. Economic problems may significantly impact profitability. Many aircraft manufacturing companies have gone out of business or merged with peers. The industry is littered with the reminiscences of unsuccessful commercial aircraft endeavors. The three-engine Ford Tri-Motor aircraft series produced during the 1920s and 1930s were classic planes of that era. In Europe, Junkers was a major German aircraft manufacturer, manufacturing some of the best-known aircraft over the course of its 50-plus years in business. The Lockheed L-1011 was a wide-body aircraft that entered into commercial operations following the launch of the Boeing 747 and the McDonnell Douglas DC-10. However, Lockheed withdrew from the commercial aircraft business due to poor sales.[5] Subsequently, in 1997, McDonnell Douglas faced a financial crisis and merged with its rival, Boeing.[6]

Ford Tri-Motor

In the early 1920s, Henry Ford and his son Edsel, along with a group of 19 others, invested in the Stout Metal Airplane Company. The first Ford/Van Auken airplane, powered by a Model-T engine, arrived in 1909, only six years after the Wright Brothers' first flight. It would not be until 1927, however, that Ford would enter the commercial aviation arena with the first of the 4-AT series Ford Tri-Motor, referred to as the *Tin Goose*. Previous Ford-manufactured aircraft, like the model 2-AT *Air Transport,* had been used by Ford to ship auto parts, mail, and personnel between Denver, Detroit, and Cleveland.

The Ford Tri-Motor was the first plane primarily designed to carry passengers instead of mail. The aircraft could carry 14 or 15 people, possessed a cabin high enough for passengers to walk without stooping, and had room for a flight attendant.[7] The Tin Goose's three engines made it possible to fly as high as three miles at a speed of about 130 miles per hour. Its sturdy appearance and Ford name had a reassuring effect on the public's perception of flying (Ingells, 1968). The Tri-Motor had a range of approximately 500 miles and was not capable of crossing continents without refueling. Ford, unlike his cars, did not manufacture the engines for these airplanes.

---

[5]Greenwald, J., Hannifin, J., & J. Kane. "Catch a falling TriStar." *Time.* December 21, 1981.
[6]Boeing Company, Boeing Chronology, 1997-2001.
[7]Donald, D. (Ed.). (1997). *The complete encyclopedia of world aircraft.* New York: Barnes & Noble, Inc.

From 1926 through 1933, there were 199 Ford Tri-Motors built.[8] The Tri-Motor sales dropped from a peak of 86 per year in 1929 to only two sales in 1932.[9] The Ford Motor Company ceased manufacturing this aircraft in 1932 (Larkins, 2007). The end of Ford's contribution to commercial aircraft manufacturing was likely due to a combination of various issues at the time: the tightened market and economy of the Depression era, the overall loss incurred in the production of the airplanes, the diminished need for a three-engine aircraft, an increased need for a faster and more economical design for airline use, and Henry Ford's diminishing interest caused by the deaths of three test pilots in crashes.

Junkers German Transport

"Junkers" is a name that quickly became associated with important aerodynamic and structural advances in aircraft in post-World War I Germany. The company was founded by Hugo Junkers. In 1919, Junkers began designing aircraft that would become the world's first all-metal airliner and also the forerunner of all commercial transport aircraft. The single-engine, low-wing, cabin monoplane was of particularly small dimensions since it was necessary to work within the onerous restrictions forced upon Germany. It was in production for 13 years and in commercial use for about 20 years (Kay & Couper, 2004).

Junkers produced the F13 commercially, and the aircraft was made entirely of Duralumin. It was designed to be dismantled into sections for easy shipment to export markets.[10] The F13 first flew on June 25, 1919, and the first order for an F13 came from an American businessman named John Larsen, who planned to sell it as a JL6 in North America. A total of 322 F13s were produced, mainly between 1923 and 1925; most went into service in Germany and Russia (Kay & Couper, 2004).

Commercial Aircraft Manufacturing

As historical data on the commercial aircraft industry shows, the entire industry was influenced by a few major companies. Today, the industry enjoys a tight duopolistic, or oligopolistic, market structure due to significant barriers to entry. Since the merger of Boeing and McDonnell Douglas in 1997, the industry is dominated by two major players: Boeing in North American and Airbus in Europe.

---

[8]Herrick, Greg A. The Amazing Story of America's Oldest Flying Airliner, 2004.
[9]Russ Banham. The Ford Motor Company and the innovations that shaped the world.
[10]The J13 is an alternative designation for the F13.

North America

Worldwide aircraft manufacturing was, and to a large measure continues to be, dominated by North American manufacturers. After World War II, four prominent players emerged in the business of building commercial jets: Boeing, McDonnell, Douglas, and Lockheed. McDonnell and Douglas merged in 1967, and the combined entity remained a long-standing competitor to Boeing until its ultimate merger with Boeing in 1997.

Lockheed merged with Martin Marietta in 1995, and the combined entity later refined its focus to primarily military aircraft manufacturing (Sandler & Hartley, 2007). Both Boeing and Lockheed Martin competed for American defense contracts, and it has been claimed that Boeing used its defense division to cross-subsidize its commercial airline development.

Boeing and Lockheed dominated the North American aircraft manufacturing landscape both in terms of civilian and military aircraft. Together with McDonnell Douglas, Boeing was a world leader in commercial aircraft manufacturing into the 1980s, when Airbus Industrie evolved into a major competitor that would eventually surpass Boeing in market share. Figure 1.1 chronicles the mergers of commercial aircraft manufacturers in the U.S. over the last century, with omission of military aircraft manufacturer mergers for the sake of clarity.

Boeing Aircraft Company

Boeing has been a dominant player in the commercial aircraft market for the greater part of the last century. Recent loss of market share to Airbus does not diminish the fact that Boeing is a strong company and a leader in commercial aviation. While this section will focus on commercial aircraft history, it is important to note that Boeing's start and its success came from the sale of military aircraft. In 1916, William Boeing (founder and namesake) built his first seaplane, which he sold to the New Zealand government. The following year, Boeing sold 50 seaplanes to the U.S. Navy and continued to receive military and defense contracts from the U.S. government, including a $35 billion contract to build a new generation of refueling tankers for the Air Force.[11] The financial success of military aircraft projects allowed the company to enter into high-risk commercial aircraft projects that may not have been profitable. Having the financial ability to undertake high-risk commercial aircraft projects is one of the reasons that Boeing is at the forefront of aircraft development.

Boeing began to learn the aircraft manufacturing trade by first building and modifying existing designs from other manufacturers. In 1918, founder Boeing

[11]Bowman, Tom. (February 24, 2011). Air Force picks Boeing for major military contract. *NPR*.

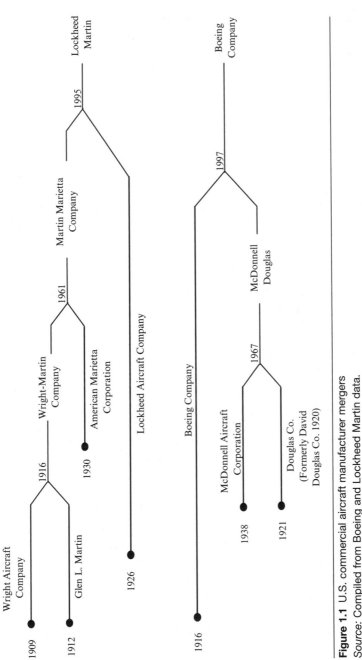

Figure 1.1 U.S. commercial aircraft manufacturer mergers
Source: Compiled from Boeing and Lockheed Martin data.

was contracted to build the Curtiss-designed HS-2L, a military patrol plane. Later, in 1919, he modified the de Havilland DH-4 (Heritage of innovation, 2009). These modifications allowed Boeing to take apart and rebuild aircraft in order to relocate the fuel tank. As most engineers know, being able to take apart and re-assemble a manufactured product such as an airplane allows one to see how the item is constructed and how it works, providing insights into how to make the item. The process of designing something through the deconstruction and reconstruction of a similar item is called *reverse engineering*. The use of reverse engineering helped Boeing to develop its own planes, including its first commercial aircraft, the B-1 mail plane, which was launched in 1919, beginning a 90-year history of building commercial airplanes.[12]

Boeing's real start into the commercial aviation business came through the U.S. mail network. The U.S. Postal Service awarded Boeing a contract to transport mail by air between San Francisco and Chicago in 1927. Boeing founded the airline Boeing Air Transport to fly this route, and used its own mail plane that Boeing had developed, the Model 40A. The Model 40A was unique in that it had a nose made from steel, combined with a wood and fabric fuselage (Heritage of innovation, 2009). Boeing built 25 mail planes for the Boeing Air Transport fleet. The Model 40A could hold two passengers, making it the first real passenger aircraft. Boeing continued to design passenger aircraft through the late 1920s and early 1930s, progressively building aircraft that could hold more passengers as well as mail. The 1932 Model 247 presented the best combination of speed and capacity, carrying 10 passengers and 400 pounds of mail at speeds of up to 200 miles per hour. Together with the Douglas DC-2, the Model 247 heralded the modern era of air transportation (Comprehensive index of historical products, 2009).

The 1930s were a slow time for Boeing, especially on the commercial aviation front, due to the Great Depression. During this time, Boeing mainly focused on military aircraft such as the B-17. Boeing could never have known how big the B-17 Bomber project would be. Nicknamed "The Flying Fortress," the B-17 would prove crucial in World War II for Allied forces in defeating the German and Japanese military (Heritage of innovation, 2009). Despite the tough economy and the B-17 being the only major success for Boeing at the time, Boeing was laying the groundwork for future successes. In 1936, Boeing bought the 28 acres that constitute the modern-day Boeing Field in Seattle (Heritage of innovation, 2009). In addition to buying the site, Boeing invested $250,000 to build a facility to manufacture airplanes on site. Boeing decided to develop two new commercial aircraft despite the ailing economy of the late 1930s. It developed the Model 307 Stratoliner and Model 314 Clipper, and the gamble of developing new aircraft

---

[12]United States Centennial of Flight Commission, *The Early Years of Boeing.*

during tough economic times paid off. Both models were bought by Pan American Airways and were wildly popular. The Pan Am Clipper became an icon of modern air transportation, opening up the Americas, Europe, and Africa to the world. However, all was not successful on the Model 307 project; the prototype crashed during a test flight, killing all 10 people on board (Heritage of innovation, 2009). The crash of the Model 307, along with the crash of a B-29 during test flights, led to the creation of improved pre-flight testing protocols for new aircraft, including the design of wind tunnels for performance testing.

World War II brought a renewed focus on military aircraft for Boeing as the defense business was lucrative at the time. It was not until 1952 that a major development in the commercial aviation industry would come from Boeing as it began to build a prototype of the 707, named the Model 367-80, or "Dash 80" for short. The Dash 80 would become Boeing's first commercial jetliner and one of the first jetliners in the world with military and government applications as well. The Dash 80, currently on display at the Smithsonian Museum in Washington, D.C., was the basis for the KC-135 military fuel tanker and the first Air Force One (Heritage of innovation, 2009). Used for mid-air refueling of other aircraft, Boeing would produce 820 of the KC-135 tankers by the time its production ended in 1965.

On the commercial side, the Dash 80 prototype would undergo a few years of testing before the first 707-120 was produced and delivered to Pan Am in 1958.[13] Before introducing the 707, Douglas and Lockheed aircraft were preferred by U.S. airlines. That changed after the 707 became the first U.S.-manufactured jetliner and Boeing became the premier aircraft manufacturer for U.S. airlines and airlines around the world. In all, 916 Boeing 707s were delivered to customers from 1958 to 1982 (Eden, 2008). The 707's success spurred the development of a line of narrow-body aircraft from the 1950s all the way through the 1980s. In addition to variants of the 707 itself, the fuselage cross-section of the 707 would be used as the basis for designs of the 727, 737, and 757. The first of these aircraft to be produced was the 727 in 1962.

The 727 was the only commercial tri-engine jet that Boeing would design and produce, as well as the only T-tail jet.[14] The three-engine design allowed for a compromise between airlines that wanted the efficiency of a twin-engine aircraft and airlines that wanted the performance of a four-engine aircraft. This mix of efficiency and performance led the 727 to be a popular aircraft for medium-haul routes.[15] The 727 became a mainstay of U.S. airlines like American, Delta, and

---

[13]The aircraft made its maiden flight on December 20, 1957.

[14] After McDonnell Douglas and Boeing merged in 1997, the 100-seater McDonnell Douglas T-tail MD-95 was renamed the Boeing 717.

[15]The 727 was the first airplane to have a triple-slotted flap system for superior take-off and landing performance.

United until the year 2000. The success of the 727 led Boeing during the 1970s to develop a stretch version of the airplane that would seat about 180 passengers. In part due to the oil crisis of the 1970s, Boeing eventually decided to scrap the idea of a stretched version of the 727 and developed a conventional two-engine replacement. This aircraft, the 757, provided a narrow-body aircraft that could be used on short-, medium-, and long-haul routes while still offering the superior performance that airlines had come to expect from the 727. The 757 could be found on diverse missions at short-field, noise-restricted airports (such as Orange County, CA) and transatlantic flights. Due to its versatility and performance, many 757s are still in service despite the fact that their service dates back to 1983 (757 Program, 2009).

The success of Boeing's 757 pales in comparison to the leader in the commercial aircraft market, the 737. The cargo version of the 757-200 was launched in 1985, and deliveries began in 1987 to United Parcel Service (UPS). Since taking flight in 1967, over 6,600 units of the Boeing 737 have been built and delivered.[16] Originally envisioned in 1964 and designed to compete with Douglas' 100-passenger twin-jet, the DC-9, the 737 was the first Boeing jetliner to feature a two-man cockpit crew instead of a three-man crew.[17] Since the introduction of the 737-100, Boeing has continued to develop new versions of the jet and today makes the 737NG.[18] The Boeing 737 Classic is the name given to the 300/400/500 series of the Boeing 737 after the introduction of the 600/700/800/900 series. The 737NG series offers four differently sized aircraft to meet the varying capacity needs of airlines while keeping a maximum amount of commonality. Why is the 737 so successful for Boeing? In large part, the success of the 737 has been due to its popularity with low-cost carriers, such as Southwest Airlines, Ryanair, WestJet, and Virgin Blue. Southwest operated 548 Boeing 737 jets, representing nearly 10% of all 737s produced, as of 2010. Ironically, the challenge of the success of the 737 program for Boeing is what to do for a replacement. As fuel prices and economic conditions continue to remain volatile, airlines want the next generation of narrow-body aircraft to have even greater gains in fuel efficiency and reductions in maintenance costs. Boeing and Airbus were under pressure from low-cost airlines to develop a narrow-body replacement for the 737 and A320, respectively. The new composite twin-aisle 737 replacement could give an airline a boost in its daily utilization and have cost advantages at above 200 seats.[19]

While the start of the 737 program led to huge success, Boeing was planning something even bigger (literally). In 1966, a new plant was built in Everett, WA,

---

[16]Orders and Deliveries. *Boeing.* December 31, 2010.
[17]Flight International, Reed Business Information, April 22, 2009.
[18]Next Generation includes the 600/700/800/900 series.
[19]Centre for Asia Pacific Aviation, March 18, 2011.

to manufacture another commercial aircraft, the 747. Boeing's 747 would be the largest commercial aircraft built at that time and would usher in a new category of airliners, the "jumbo jet." Two years later, the 490-passenger jumbo jet would roll out of the new plant and be placed into service with Pan Am in 1970.[20] Boeing developed the 747SP in the mid-1970s as a longer range, shortened 747, trading passenger seating for extra range. The 747SP was 48 feet, 4 inches shorter than the 747-100.[21] After a dormant period, the 747 program was revived by Boeing through the design of the 747-8. Sensing the need to compete with the Airbus A380, Boeing modernized the 747. Originally launched as a freighter with orders from Cargolux, the 747-8 met demand for both high-capacity passenger and cargo aircraft (The Boeing 747-8 family, 2009). While the 747 is the largest of Boeing's wide-bodies, Boeing also has three other twin-engine wide-body aircraft in production.

Next, the 767 was developed alongside the 757, and it would largely function as a replacement for the 707. Like the 707, the 767 is a medium- to long-haul aircraft, but with a slightly higher capacity. A military version of the 767, the KC-767 tanker, was also developed to replace the KC-135. The development of the 767 benefitted from significant economies of scope by being developed alongside the 757 during the 1970s. A single flight deck design, used on both aircraft, allowed the FAA to issue a single type rating for both airplanes. This offered significant economies in terms of training and standardization to airlines wanting to incorporate both aircraft into their fleet (Heritage of innovation, 2009).

Subsequently, Boeing developed the 777, or "Triple-Seven," which provided airlines with a twin-engine wide-body aircraft to bridge the gap between the 747 and 767. In 1992, Boeing founded Boeing Integrated Systems Laboratory to test the design of the 777. The Integrated Systems Lab enabled Boeing to integrate new systems before installing them in a production airplane (Heritage of innovation, 2009). With the help of the Lab, Boeing was able to produce and deliver the first 777 to launch customer United Airlines in May 1995. The 777 was the first aircraft to receive Extended-Range Twin-Engine Operations (ETOPS) approval before the aircraft ever entered into service, due to extensive flight testing by Boeing before delivery and advancements in engine technology.[22] ETOPS allowed twin-engine aircraft to fly over water for extended periods of time based on an ability to operate safely on one engine should one of the engines fail in-flight (Gunston, 1988). The 777 is a popular aircraft due to its excellent trade-off between high capacity and operating

---

[20]*Aviation Week and Space Technology*, September 4, 2006.

[21]The idea came from a joint request between Pan American World Airways and Iran Air which were looking for a high-capacity airliner with enough range to cover North America and Asia.

[22]*ETOPS* is the term introduced by the International Civil Aviation Organization (ICAO), which describes the operation of twin-engine aircraft on a route that contains a point further than one hour flying time from a diversion airport.

efficiency. While United Airlines was the launch customer and operated a fleet of 52 Boeing 777s, Emirates had the largest fleet in operation with 79 Boeing 777 variants (Fleet and order status, 2011). There have been a total of 949 Boeing 777s delivered as of July 2011 (Orders and delivers, 2011).

A subsequent Boeing aircraft to enter development and production was the 787, also known as the Boeing Dreamliner.[23] The Dreamliner features new technology such as an increased use of composite materials and presents significant improvements in fuel economy and automation. Boeing's first 787 test jet took its maiden flight in December 2009, after more than three years of delays.[24] However, since 2003, production delays pushed back flight testing and entry into service. The first deliveries of 787s were delayed until the second half of 2011.[25] Airlines with orders for the 787 were concerned about the delays and demanded compensation per the order contracts. Similar delays occurred during the production of the 777, when the process faced significant design and labor challenges. In order to maintain the 777's production schedule, Boeing spent an additional $3 billion over projected costs. The investment paid off in the case of the 777; however, in 2011, with a decline in air travel, airline revenues, and airline spending power that defines the current aviation market, it might be difficult to justify the same financing in the case of the 787. Boeing planned to produce three unique versions of the Dreamliner to optimize different passenger loads and distances.

Any discussion of the history of Boeing's commercial division should also mention that Boeing merged with McDonnell Douglas in 1997, taking over the production of McDonnell Douglas' commercial aircraft. Boeing acquired McDonnell Douglas for $13.3 billion, creating the world's largest aerospace company.[26] Boeing committed to finish all outstanding orders before phasing out all McDonnell Douglas aircraft, except the MD-95, which Boeing transformed into the 717. The 717 captured the 100-seat market after the collapse of Fokker, which had dominated the market with the Fokker 100 (Norris & Wagner, 1998). In addition, Airbus was rumored to be developing its A318 at the time to compete in the same 100-seat market segment. The 717 program lasted from 1998 until 2006, when Boeing made the final delivery to the original launch customer of the aircraft, AirTran Airways.

Boeing decided to end production of the 717 due to slow sales and the fact that Boeing's own 737-600 competed in nearly the same market. Despite discontinuing all McDonnell Douglas commercial aircraft, Boeing continued to build upon McDonnell Douglas' strong background of military aircraft, including the

---

[23]*Washington Business*, January/February 2004.
[24]U.S. Department of Energy, Office of Energy Efficiency and Renewable Energy, January 11, 2010.
[25]Boeing Company Chief Executive Officer, Jim McNerney, February 10, 2011.
[26]*The Baltimore Sun*, December 16, 1996.

F-15 and F-18 Hornet (Heritage of innovation, 2009). In recent years, Boeing continued to perform well financially despite instability in the airline industry. From 2005 to 2010, Boeing increased sales of its products from $44 billion to $64 billion (Orders and delivers, 2011). Figures 1.2 and 1.3 and Tables 1.1 and 1.2 show Boeing's in- and out-of-production aircraft from the mid-1950s.

McDonnell Douglas

McDonnell Douglas came into existence with the merger of McDonnell Aircraft and the Douglas Company in 1967.[27] Like Boeing, much of Douglas' early entry into aircraft manufacturing was on the military side of the market. The Douglas Company was incorporated in 1921 in California with the first flight of its DT-1 Bomber (Heritage of innovation, 2009). Douglas built other military planes, including the DT-2 and C-1, before developing its first commercial plane, a mail transport, in 1925. A Douglas mail plane, the M-2, flew Western Air Express' first two passengers on the mail route between Salt Lake City and Los Angeles for a fare of $90 (Heritage of innovation, 2009), which would be equivalent to $1,107.27 in today's dollars. To illustrate the effect of competition in the airline industry, in 2009 passengers could fly on this same route for just $79 (Southwest.com, 2009).

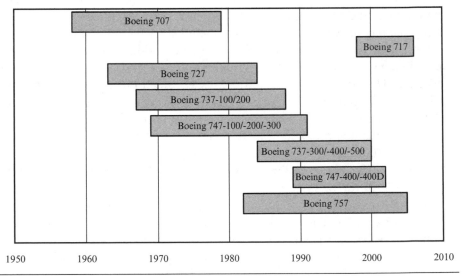

Figure 1.2 Boeing out-of-production aircraft
Source: Compiled from Boeing aircraft data.

---

[27]*Los Angeles Times,* October 9, 2004.

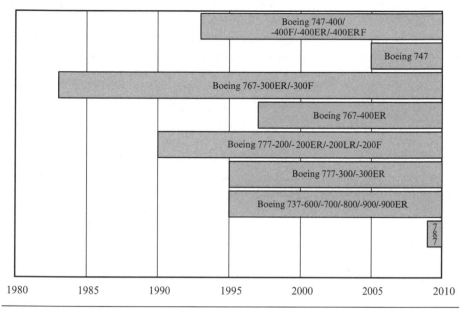

Figure 1.3 Boeing in-production aircraft
Source: Compiled from Boeing aircraft data.

Table 1.1 Boeing out-of-production aircraft

Aircraft model	Launch customer	Produced
Boeing 707	Pan Am	1,010
Boeing 717	AirTran	155
Boeing 727	Eastern Airlines	1,831
Boeing 737-100/-200/-300/-400/-500	Lufthansa	3,113
Boeing 747-100/-200/-300	Pan Am	1,369
Boeing 757	Eastern Airlines	1,050

Source: Compiled from Boeing aircraft data.

Table 1.2 Boeing in-production aircraft

Aircraft model	Launch customer	Produced
Boeing 737-600/-700/-800/-900/-900ER	SAS	3,716
Boeing 747-8	Lufthansa	In production
Boeing 767	American Airlines	1,005
Boeing 777	United Airlines	949
Boeing 787	Air Nippon	In production

Source: Compiled from Boeing aircraft data.

When the company merged with Boeing, over 40,000 aircraft had been built in various plants, some of which are still flying.

In 1928, the Douglas Company reorganized as the Douglas Aircraft Company and moved in 1929 to a new manufacturing plant in Santa Monica, CA. By 1932, Douglas fully entered into the air transport industry by agreeing to a contract with Trans World Airlines (TWA) to build Douglas' first airliner, the DC-1. The DC-1 became a prototype for the larger DC-2 airliner, which held 14 passengers and up to 3,600 pounds of cargo (Heritage of innovation, 2009). The production of the DC-2 began 64 years of aircraft production for Douglas. Out of the DC-2 design came a larger airliner, the popular DC-3. Accommodating 14-28 passengers, 455 DC-3s were sold to several airlines in the U.S., including American and United, and more than 16,079 DC-3s were sold globally.[28] However, the real popularity of the DC-3 became apparent on the military front, with the DC-3's conversion into the C-47. This aircraft was extensively utilized during World War II, and over 10,000 of these transports were produced.

Douglas' work on commercial aircraft that could also be used as military aircraft continued to pay dividends after World War II. Douglas developed the DC-6 for commercial transport and later developed military versions of the aircraft named the C-118A Liftmaster (DC-6/C-118 Liftmaster Transport, 2009). The original version of the DC-6 could carry 52 passengers and was one of the first commercial aircraft to feature a pressurized cabin; later versions featured a stretched fuselage with seating for up to 102 passengers. The first two DC-6s were delivered to American and United Airlines at a dual ceremony in 1947; in total, more than 700 DC-6s were produced from 1946 to 1958 (DC-6/C-118 Liftmaster Transport, 2009). Pan Am inaugurated its first transatlantic tourist class flights in 1952 by flying a DC-6B. The Douglas DC-6 was one of the first airplanes to fly a regularly scheduled around-the-world route.[29]

Douglas continued to work on military cargo transports during the late 1940s and the 1950s, developing the C-124 and C-133 transport planes. In 1953, Douglas developed the last of its propeller-driven passenger aircraft, the DC-7, which delivered quite amazing speed and range for its time. The DC-7 could carry up to 110 passengers and had a range of over 5,000 miles at speeds of up to 400 mph (DC-7 Commercial Transport, 2009).

At this time, the jet age began, and Douglas entered it with the production of the DC-8 in 1958. Produced about one year after the Boeing 707, the DC-8 was built to compete with that main rival with similar size and speed. Douglas offered new improvements to the DC-8 from the original Series 10 through Series 60. The

---

[28]Gradidge, J. (2006). *The Douglas DC-1/DC-2/DC-3: The First Seventy Years*, 1 and 2. Tunbridge Wells, Kent, UK: Air-Britain (Historians), Ltd.

[29]U.S. Centennial of Flight Commission, 2010.

Series 60 offered increased range and a stretched fuselage capable of seating up to 260 passengers (DC-8 Commercial Transport, 2009). An interesting note on the DC-8 is that United Airlines was, just as for the DC-6, one of the launch customers for the aircraft. United Airlines used to be part of Boeing before a government breakup, so in some sense the strength of the Douglas airplanes was reflected by the fact that United chose Douglas over Boeing aircraft.

The next major event for Douglas commercial transport was the introduction of the DC-9 in 1965. The DC-9 was essentially the catalyst for the 100+ passenger twin-jet, single-aisle jetliners that included the 737 family, A320 family, and MD-80/90/95. The DC-9, and its successor MD-80, proved to be reliable aircraft with many in service more than 40 years later. Delta Air Lines had a sizeable fleet of 53 DC-9s in service as of 2010.[30] The early success of the DC-8 and DC-9 in the 1950s and 1960s allowed Douglas to become an attractive target for a merger. In 1967, Douglas merged with aerospace and defense manufacturer McDonnell to form the McDonnell Douglas Corp. (Heritage of innovation, 2009). The combined company continued to be a force in both the commercial aviation and defense aircraft sectors. The C-9A Nightingale was a perfect example of the tradition of using aircraft designs for both commercial and military purposes. The C-9A was a version of the DC-9, which the military used as a transport for sick and wounded soldiers during the Vietnam War (Heritage of innovation, 2009). McDonnell Douglas continued this tradition with the DC-10.

The DC-10 was McDonnell Douglas' first attempt to enter into the jumbo jet segment of commercial aircraft. Entering into service in 1971 with United and American Airlines, the DC-10's entry was not without problems. As with any large object with hundreds of movable parts that need to work in order for the object to function properly, mechanical failures were a part of the DC-10's early years. In 1972, a cargo door blew off an American Airlines DC-10 after takeoff from Detroit (ASN Aviation Safety Database, 2009). Luckily, there were no fatalities in the incident; however, modifications to the design of the cargo door were needed. Other incidents with the DC-10 would not prove so fortunate.

In two other instances, engines—or parts thereof—were ripped from the wings of DC-10s: a National Airlines DC-10 successfully made an emergency landing in Albuquerque, NM, in 1973, and an American Airlines DC-10 crashed in Chicago in 1979, killing 273 people. These events led to the grounding of the aircraft by the FAA (ASN Aviation Safety Database, 2009). While the ultimate causes of the crashes were determined to be faulty procedures by airline maintenance personnel, the incidents demonstrated the DC-10's vulnerability to hydraulic failure. Hydraulic lines on the DC-10 were placed close to the engines. The hydraulic lines control the flight surfaces of the wing (slats, flaps, and ailerons). In these incidents, the separation

---

[30]Delta Air Lines Inc., 2010.

of the engines from the wing destroyed hydraulic lines and caused the aircraft to involuntarily retract the left slats (ASN Aviation Safety Database, 2009). McDonnell Douglas made design changes to the slats system to prevent this type of accident from reoccurring, and the aircraft was ultimately allowed back into service by the FAA. Despite its early failures, the DC-10 was still selected by the Air Force as an advanced aerial tanker and cargo transport aircraft (Heritage of innovation, 2009). The U.S. Air Force purchased 60 of these aircraft for its fleet, and both the DC-10 and KC-10 were produced up until the last aircraft was delivered in 1990.

In 1982, McDonnell Douglas decided that new aircraft models would have the designation MD, instead of the previous designator DC. The first model with the new designator was the MD-80, previously known during development and early deliveries as the DC-9 Series 80. The MD-80 featured a longer fuselage than its predecessor, but retained many of the same features, such as the 2 × 3 (or 3 × 2) seating. The 2 × 3 seating was preferred by many passengers to the 3 × 3 seating of its competitors, the 737 and A320, because there was only one middle seat per row. The popularity of the MD-80 led to nearly 1200 MD-80s being delivered during the aircraft's 19-year production run (MD-80 and MD-90 Commercial Transports, 2009). In 1995, McDonnell Douglas modernized the MD-80 with new versions, the MD-90 and MD-95. The MD-90 series featured a modernized cockpit, which included electronic flight instruments and LED lights to show crucial systems data on the aircraft's engines (MD-80 and MD-90 Commercial Transports, 2009). The MD-90 was designed to capture the same market as the MD-80, seating 140-150 passengers. The MD-95, which later became the Boeing 717, was designed to replace the DC-9-30 series, which held 100-115 passengers (MD-80 and MD-90 Commercial Transports, 2009). After Boeing's acquisition of McDonnell Douglas in 1997, production of the MD-80 and MD-90 eventually ceased when outstanding customer orders were fulfilled.

McDonnell Douglas produced one other commercial aircraft in the 1990s before being acquired by Boeing. The MD-11 went into production in 1990 in three different versions (passenger, combi, and freighter) as a replacement for the DC-10.[31] The first MD-11 was delivered to Finnair on December 7, 1990. The MD-11 had a longer fuselage for extra capacity and included new features, such as winglets, that would help to increase range and reduce fuel consumption (MD-11 Commercial Transport, 2009). The winglets were a compromise between airlines and McDonnell Douglas, between the inefficiencies of the current wing of the DC-10 and the cost to McDonnell Douglas to design an entirely new wing (Badrocke & Guston, 1999). The aircraft was a wide-body airliner, with two engines mounted on under-wing pylons and a third engine at the base of the vertical stabilizer.[32] While the aircraft was never popular (only 200 sold during a

---

[31]Airways online, September/October 1997.
[32]Steffen, A. (January 2002). McDonnell Douglas MD-11: A Long Beach swansong. Midland.

Table 1.3 McDonnell Douglas commercial aircraft data

Aircraft model	Launch customer	Produced
DC-2	TWA	156
DC-3	U.S. Army	16,079
DC-6	U.S. Army	700
DC-8	Delta	556
DC-9	Delta	976
DC-10	American Airlines	386
MD-11	Finnair	200
MD-80	Swissair	1,191
MD-90	Delta	116

Source: Compiled from McDonnell Douglas aircraft production data.

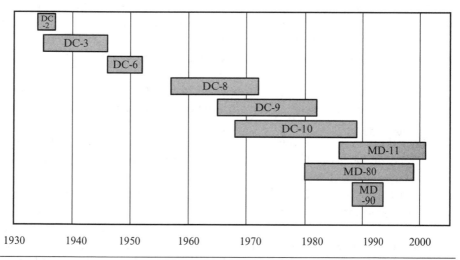

Figure 1.4 McDonnell Douglas commercial aircraft
Source: Compiled from Boeing aircraft production data.

10-year production run), it was popular with some cargo operators as a freighter. FedEx, UPS, and Lufthansa Cargo were the largest operators of MD-11s (MD-11 Commercial Transport, 2009). The last MD-11 built in 2001 marked the end of McDonnell Douglas commercial aircraft production[33] (see Table 1.3 and Figure 1.4). Despite shutting down the McDonnell Douglas commercial division, Boeing

---

[33]Boeing Announces Phase-Out of MD-11 Jetliner Program. Seattle, June 3, 1998.

continued to produce many of its military aircraft, including the F/A-18 Hornet and Super Hornet and C-17 transport planes (Heritage of innovation, 2009).

Lockheed

The Lockheed Aircraft Corporation, later named Lockheed Martin Corporation, began in 1912 with two brothers who wanted to fly. In a sense, the story of Allan and Malcolm Loughead (their name later changed to Lockheed) paralleled the stories of the Wright Brothers and William Boeing. Enamored with flying, the Lockheeds began their foray into aviation by building a two-seat flying boat and selling rides during the Panama-Pacific International Exposition in 1910 (Civil aircraft today, 2004). In the late 1910s and early 1920s, unable to get customers for their single-seat biplane, the brothers went their separate ways and closed their business, Lockheed Aircraft, in 1921.[34] Eventually, Allan Lockheed teamed up with aviation businessman Jack Northrop to form the Lockheed Aircraft Corporation and returned to building aircraft with the introduction of the Lockheed Vega.

Despite the fame of the Vega—it was used by aviators like Amelia Earhart on her two record-breaking flights across the Atlantic in 1932 and Wiley Post for his high-altitude record-breaker at 50,000 feet in 1934—the Vega's notoriety was not enough to keep the company afloat; Lockheed Aircraft went into bankruptcy a few years later. The company was sold to investor Robert Gross, but Allan Lockheed would keep an informal relationship with the company for many years (Civil aircraft today, 2004).

After the company was purchased by Gross, Lockheed began development of the 10-passenger Electra. The Electra featured a unique twin fin and rudder design that was the result of wind tunnel testing of the prototype (Model 10 Electra, 2009). Lockheed produced two different versions of the aircraft. One was a single-tail four-engine turboprop, powered by Allison. The military used a version of that airplane called the P3 Orion as a submarine hunter. There were 148 Electras built between 1934 and 1941, including five military versions (Model 10 Electra, 2009). The Electra became most famous for being the aircraft that Amelia Earhart attempted to pilot around the world before (presumably) crashing somewhere in the Pacific Ocean.

The company's next commercial aircraft foray was requested by famous aviator and TWA majority owner Howard Hughes. Hughes wanted an airplane with superior speed and range for transcontinental flights, comparable to Boeing 307 Stratoliners.[35] Lockheed kept the project secret until World War II, when the military version of the plane, the C-69, was pressed into service (Civil aircraft today,

---

[34]World War II-Lockheed Burbank Aircraft Plant Camouflage. *Amazing Posts.* August 16, 2008.
[35]The Boeing Model 307 Stratoliner was the world's first high-altitude commercial transport and four-engine airliner in scheduled domestic service.

2004). After World War II, the passenger version of the plane, the Constellation, entered passenger service with TWA in 1945. The Constellation and a longer range version, the Super Constellation, were incredibly advanced for their time, reaching top speeds of 340 miles per hour and, thanks to a pressurized cabin, an altitude ceiling of 35,000 feet (Civil aircraft today, 2004).

A "perfect storm" for Lockheed. Lockheed's success was short-lived. The TriStar had problems after the first of the 300-passenger jets rolled off the Palmdale, CA assembly line. Production was temporarily stopped in February 1971, when Britain's Rolls-Royce, the prime engine supplier, went bankrupt. The British government took over Rolls-Royce's aero-engine division, demanding proof that Lockheed was financially sound before providing the engines. Lockheed was in trouble, but Congress approved a controversial $250 million loan guarantee for the company. The first TriStar went to Eastern Airlines in April 1972, about six months later than scheduled. The delays and uncertainties caused by the Rolls-Royce bankruptcy gave Boeing and McDonnell Douglas a competitive lead in the wide-bodied market, and Lockheed was never able to make up its disadvantage, even though airlines found the TriStar plane reliable and efficient. The largest TriStar customer was Delta Air Lines, which operated 35 of them, buying three of the remaining 24 on firm order (Greenwald, Hannifin, & Kane, 1981).

Lockheed stayed out of the commercial jet revolution for a while. In fact, Lockheed had no plans to build a commercial jet aircraft until American Airlines approached manufacturers with a request for a high-capacity, medium-range jet (Civil aircraft today, 2004). It was evident from the very beginning that Douglas and Lockheed would be in competition with each other, as they were both developing essentially the same aircraft.[36] Like the DC-10, the Lockheed L-1011 was a tri-jet capable of carrying up to 300 passengers. Similar to the DC-10, the L-1011 ran into engine trouble—Rolls-Royce developed an entirely new engine for the L-1011, and it suffered from reliability problems during testing (Karlsson, 1998). Receiving federal loan guarantees from their respective governments, Lockheed and Rolls-Royce[37] continued work on the L-1011, and a suitable engine, the RB211-22B, was developed.[38] However, it was too late; American Airlines had already chosen the DC-10 due to its earlier date of service entry (Civil aircraft today, 2004). Although the L-1011 received early orders from Eastern and Delta, the DC-10 proved to be more popular than the L-1011. Even with its problems, the DC-10's popularity was due to range and timing (Sedaei, 2006). Douglas had a

---

[36]*Beyond the Horizons: The Lockheed Story.* St. Martin's Press, New York, 1998.
[37]Rolls-Royce went bankrupt while developing the engines for Lockheed's L-1011; Lockheed officials persuaded the British government to take over Rolls-Royce and continue the engine production.
[38]*The Washington Post,* July 7, 1987.

long-range version of the DC-10 (the DC-10-30) almost immediately after introducing the basic model. Lockheed waited until 1978, eight years after the L-1011 went into service, before developing a long-range version that could compete directly with the DC-10-30 (Karlsson, 1998).[39]

In some sense, the L-1011's production doomed Lockheed's future. The project ran into problems from the outset because the L-1011 was conceived as a twin-engine design and had to be redesigned into a three-engine model (Eden, 2008). Further, the project ran into cost overruns associated with the Galaxy C-5 government contract. The development of the C-5 was undergoing innovation problems like critical wing weakness and production slippage. Additionally, the bankruptcy and nationalization of Rolls-Royce in 1971 led to more production delays, and by the time the L-1011 was eventually delivered, most of the 144 orders that were to drive the program into profitability had been lost to the DC-10. Once the choice of aircraft was made, the switching costs for most airlines in terms of fleet planning were too high, and the L-1011 found itself at a distinct disadvantage. Further, the original L-1011 had a substandard performance in hot and high-elevation environments and a significantly truncated range, compared to the DC-10. By the time Lockheed designed a long-range version of the L-1011 (the L-1011-500), the DC-10 was well-established among airlines that were reluctant to switch. Add to this the softening of the economy in the 1970s, and Lockheed found itself in dire financial straits. The L-1011 program eventually collapsed.[40] Lockheed needed to sell 500 planes to break even, but in 1981 announced production would end with only 250 aircraft delivered by 1984.[41]

The collapse of the L-1011 program led to Lockheed's exit from commercial aircraft manufacturing (see Table 1.4 and Figure 1.5), at which point Lockheed decided to focus exclusively on military aircraft, an area in which it had a comparative advantage. Lockheed continued to refine and progress in the development of the C-5, a cornerstone of the U.S. military to this day. Through a series of strategic acquisitions and internal development, Lockheed created an impressive product portfolio, including the F-16, more than 4,300 of which were produced and used by governments throughout the world; the F-22 Raptor; and the C-130 Hercules.

We would be remiss in this discussion of Lockheed to ignore one of the greatest aviation accomplishments of the twentieth century: The SR-71 Blackbird was not only a revolutionary technology for the U.S. Air Force, but it shattered all existing speed records. The SR-71 first flew in 1964 and was the first aircraft able to sustain speeds above Mach 3 (SR-71 Blackbird, 2009). In addition, the SR-71 flew at altitudes of over 85,000 feet, unheard of at the time it entered service. From its

---

[39]An unusual aircraft, it had a center landing gear in addition to the tricycle gear.
[40]*Sumter Daily Item*. December 8, 1981.
[41]Saddened Lockheed workers still view L-1011 with pride. *Los Angeles Times*. December 8, 1981.

Table 1.4 Lockheed commercial aircraft data

Aircraft model	Launch customer	Produced
Model 10 Electra	Pan Am	149
Model 14 Super Electra	Northwest	112
Martin M-130	Pan Am	3
Model 049 Constellation	Pan Am	79
Model 188 Electra	American Airlines	170
L-1011 TriStar	American Airlines	250

Source: Compiled from Lockheed commercial aircraft production data.

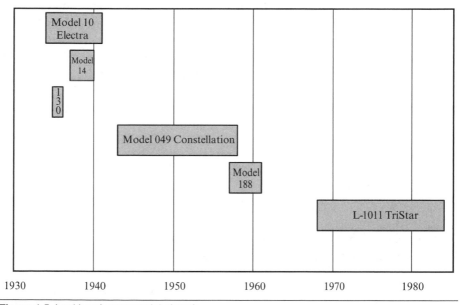

Figure 1.5 Lockheed commercial aircraft
Source: Compiled from Lockheed aircraft data.

first operations in 1966, the SR-71 was a valuable tool in military reconnaissance until its retirement 25 years later. Today, civilians can view the SR-71 on display at the Udvar-Hazy Center near Washington Dulles International Airport (SR-71 Blackbird, 2009).

The Lockheed Martin Corporation grew into a leading defense company in the United States. With many government contracts, Lockheed Martin should be able to withstand fluctuations in the aviation industry and the general economy, performing well financially in 2010. Net sales for 2010 were nearly $46 billion, an increase of over $1.8 billion from the previous year and $4.4 billion from 2008. In addition, net profit was over $2.9 billion in 2010. Lockheed Martin is well-positioned for future development as it had a low debt-asset ratio of about 14%.[42]

Western Europe Aircraft Companies: Evolution and Constellation

Airbus and Boeing have been in continuous competition to become the world's leading commercial aircraft manufacturer. In 2003, Airbus became the market share leader, delivering 52% of all commercial airplanes that year. Airbus' success in surpassing Boeing showed how far the company has come in 40 years. It should be noted that Airbus had the luxury of learning from the mistakes of the more well-established Boeing. Airbus' dramatic growth is attributable to the introduction of advanced materials and technology in its aircraft, including automating the flight engineer role common to Boeing aircraft. As in North America, the aircraft manufacturing industry in Western Europe has been characterized by several small manufacturers that consolidated or went of business over the past 60 years. Airbus S.A.S. emerged as the single largest aircraft manufacturer, while other commercial aircraft companies (e.g., Fokker) had their commercial aircraft business go bankrupt or turned their focus to military contracts.

Airbus Societé par Actions Simplifiée (S.A.S.)

Airbus is a relatively new company.[43] In 1967, ministers from the French, British, and German governments came together to develop a joint aviation technology company to unite the aviation expertise of each country. The British and French had worked together on the Concorde program, a supersonic passenger jet. The three founding nations, and later the Dutch and Spanish governments, each would be assigned different components of the proposed twin-engine passenger jet to manufacture. By having each country be responsible for a different portion of the aircraft, the idea was that each country could focus on its respective engineering and manufacturing comparative advantages and collaboratively develop the "best" possible airplane.

However, the project was not without setbacks. The first problem of the proposed wide-bodied twin-engine passenger jet was the lack of a suitable engine. Airbus believed it had an agreement with Rolls-Royce to develop an engine, the RB207, for the plane known as the Airbus A300. However, Rolls-Royce found itself stretched for resources and focused its effort on the RB211 for the U.S.

---

[42]Lockheed Martin Annual Report, 2010.
[43]Airbus Industrie started as a consortium supported by the British, French, German, and Spanish governments.

market, eventually signing an exclusivity deal with Lockheed for the RB211's use of the L-1011. Airbus had to find a replacement engine. Airbus decided to buy the engine "off the shelf" and in the process made the development costs of the A300 more manageable. Additionally, Airbus modified the size of the aircraft after demand forecasts for air travel in Europe were reduced. The capacity of the aircraft was reduced from the original design of 300 passengers down to 250 passengers. Finally, in 1969, Airbus had an aircraft design and engine partner to officially launch the aircraft. The aircraft was named the A300B, used the GE CF6-50A engine, seated 250 passengers, and had a range of 1,200 nautical miles (The Airbus story, 2008).

Despite gathering information and input from potential customers prior to the launch of the A300B, Airbus was still without an order for it in 1970. The company seemed doomed to fail. Without an order, Airbus had to go back to the drawing board and modify the aircraft. Air France worked with Airbus to develop an airplane that would meet Air France's specifications. The plane would be stretched to seat 270 passengers and was ordered by Air France in September of 1970. Later in 1970, Airbus S.A.S. was officially recognized as a consortium with equal controlling shares by French and German companies. Two years later, in October 1972, Airbus made its first flight of the new version of the aircraft, which was called the A300B2. The aircraft went into service with Air France in May 1974.

Airbus added the A300B4 to the A300 family line; the B4 added range at the urging of airlines due to the relatively short range of the original model. Despite making these modifications, the A300 was on the verge of failure because of economic factors in conjunction with a nascent company that was just beginning to emerge with a viable product portfolio. Over a period of 18 months during the 1970s oil crisis, the A300 failed to receive a single order. If Airbus was to survive as a commercial airplane manufacturer, something drastic had to happen.

That drastic occurrence was an unusual lease agreement that Airbus offered to Eastern Airlines, a major U.S. carrier. Airbus allowed Eastern to lease four A300s over a six-month period at no charge; if Eastern did not like the aircraft at the end of six months, it could return them to Airbus. This innovative program essentially gambled the company on a six-month trial period with one major customer, and it paid off. Eastern was so impressed by the performance of the aircraft that at the end of the trial period in 1978, it ordered 23 of the longer range A300B4s. The enthusiastic response from Eastern Airlines to the A300 helped Airbus to grow from a struggling business to a company that would later surpass Boeing as the commercial aircraft market share leader.

Despite initial struggles to sell just one model of aircraft, Airbus executives knew that Airbus' success hinged on offering a family with modifications according to customer needs. By having various models and sizes of aircraft, Airbus could transfer technology between models and take advantage of the lower learning curve associated with developing multiple products based on existing technology and processes. Airbus took the lessons learned from the A300 to develop a derivative model, the A310. The A310 was a shortened, longer range version of the A300; it incorporated all of the high-performance features of the A300 while adding new technology such a composite tail fin that reduced the weight of the aircraft by nearly 250 pounds and enhanced performance. Due to the performance of the A300B4 model, the A300 and A310 became the first family of twin-engine aircraft to become ETOPS certified.[44]

Technological advances continued to guide Airbus' rise in the commercial aviation market. The first Airbus entered into the narrow-body market was equipped with fly-by-wire (FBW) technology.[45] The main feature of the Airbus FBW system is a computer that aids the flight control services by responding to pilot inputs on a side stick and replaces the traditional control column. The side-stick technology debuted on commercial aircraft when the A320 rolled out in 1987 to the excitement of many in the aviation community. Since then, the A320 family of aircraft, which includes the A318 through A321, has grown to over 3,100 aircraft worldwide and is regarded as one of the most popular families of aircraft ever produced.

As the A320 was making its first flight, Airbus worked on new wide-body aircraft. To capture the expanding demand for air travel and to replace older aircraft, Airbus created the twin-engine A330 and four-engine A340. These two wide-bodies featured a newly designed wing that was thicker and had a greater aspect ratio, allowing for reduced drag and increased aerodynamic efficiency (Gunston, 1988). Another major feature of the A330 and A340 was the degree of cross-commonality among the two wide-bodies and the A320. Cross-commonality allowed pilots who were type rated in one of the three Airbus models to earn the type-rating for the other models with little additional training. Cross-commonality allowed greater flexibility for airlines in scheduling airplanes and pilots.[46]

Additional derivatives of the A320 and A340 families in the 1990s expanded the Airbus family from 100 to 380 seats. Consequently, the number 380 inspired the next Airbus project, the A380 "super-jumbo" aircraft. In 1996, Airbus began plans to develop its own large airliner, designated as A380, a double-decker passenger aircraft that holds approximately 600 people. It was designed to compete in long-haul, highly trafficked intercontinental routes,[47] in a class above the Boeing 747.

---

[44]U.S. Department of Transportation Federal Aviation Administration, Advisory Circular, AC:120-42B, June 13, 2008.

[45]Brière, D., Favre, C., & Traverse, P. (2001). Electrical flight controls, from Airbus A320/330/340 to future military transport aircraft: A family of fault-tolerant systems. In *Avionics Handbook*. Spitzer, C. (Ed.). CRC Press.

[46]The Airbus-Boeing subsidy row. *The Economist*, March 23, 2005.

[47]Airbus will reveal plan for super-jumbo. *The Independent*, June 4, 1994.

Airbus would have to overcome many challenges and obstacles in the design and performance of an aircraft as large as the A380. One design challenge was to develop an aircraft that would be acceptable to airports around the world. The aircraft would weigh over 380 tons, so Airbus had to develop a landing gear configuration to support that weight without crushing the runway (Aris, 2004). Another issue in the design was the method of emergency evacuation of the aircraft; Airbus developed an escape mechanism to allow passengers to safely exit from the A380's 27-foot-high second deck (Aris, 2004). After four years in the design and planning stages working through many issues, the A380 was launched in December 2000. The break-even for the A380 was initially at 270 units, but due to technical problems, delays, and the falling exchange rate of the U.S. dollar, it increased to 420 units.[48]

The challenge to Airbus after launching the A380 was to convince airlines to buy the aircraft. Airbus needed to communicate that despite the increase in weight over the 747, the A380's cost per available seat mile was lower due to the aircraft's greater capacity (Aris, 2004). In addition to selling the aircraft's cost advantages, Airbus used the capacity of the A380 to offer other selling points. The large interior of the A380 was marketed as a space that could install anything from sleeping quarters to saunas in the airplane, making the travel experience more like a cruise ship than a plane (Aris, 2004). Airbus' marketing team convinced Maurice Flanagan, a founder of Emirates Airlines, to purchase the aircraft; he stated, "We decided fairly quickly that the A380 was the aircraft that we wanted. Not because we wanted to put gymnasia or saunas in there. It's not there for that: it's there for people" (Aris, 2004).

The year 2000 saw the launch of the A380 and a new owner for Airbus. Airbus was now controlled by the European Aeronautic Defense and Space Company (EADS), and the name of the company was subsequently changed to Airbus Societé par Actions Simplifiée (S.A.S.).[49] EADS was formed in July 2000 as a merger between the French company Aérospatiale-Matra and the German company Daimler Chrysler Aerospace AG (DASA), which had also merged with Construcciones Aeronáuticas, S.A. (CASA) of Spain. The idea behind EADS was to set up a company to rival Boeing in both the defense and commercial aircraft industries as the premier aerospace manufacturer (Aris, 2004). By achieving the greatest market share of any commercial airplane manufacturer, EADS could lay claim to being the premier manufacturer on the commercial side. However, it remained to be seen whether EADS would become the premier company on the defense side of the aerospace industry.[50]

---

[48]Global Investor Forum, Andreas Sperl, Airbus Chief Financial Officer, October 19-20, 2006.
[49]BAE was still a 20% shareholder at this time and sold its stake in Airbus to EADS in October 2006.
[50]Hoover's Company Information, 2010.

In 2004, Airbus reorganized its manufacturing process to coincide with the production of the A380 (see Table 1.5 and Figure 1.6). Airbus set up *centers of excellence* near its manufacturing sites to help improve production quality and efficiency. In the same year, Airbus opened the A380 final assembly line in Toulouse, France; this assembly line rolled out the first A380 for unveiling to the aviation community and general public. On January 18, 2005, the A380 was displayed at the Toulouse factory for national leaders from Spain, Germany, France, and Great Britain as well more than 5,000 guests and reporters. The first aircraft delivered was handed over to Singapore Airlines and entered into service on October 25, 2007, with an inaugural flight between Singapore and Sydney.[51] The A380 has since taken to the skies and serves with airlines such as Singapore and Emirates.[52] Airbus continued to develop new aircraft, including the A350, a new wide-body designed to compete with Boeing's 787. Airbus subsequently focused on developments to the narrow-body segment by re-engineering the A320 family to create the A320neo, which is expected to offer a 15% fuel savings with respect to comparable aircraft.

Today, Boeing and Airbus have monopoly-like power in the global market for commercial jets comprising narrow-body aircraft, wide-body aircraft, and jumbo jets. Between 2000 and 2010, Boeing received 5,927 orders, and Airbus received 6,173 orders. In 2010, Airbus scored a surprise victory by selling 644 planes worth over $84 billion, compared with Boeing's 530 planes, giving Airbus a market share of 52% (see Figure 1.7).

Table 1.5 Airbus commercial aircraft production data

Aircraft model	Launch customer	Produced
A300	Air France	561
A310	Swissair	255
A318	Air France	74
A319	Swissair	1,305
A320	Air Inter	2,722
A321	Finnair	659
A330	Air Inter	802
A340	Lufthansa	375
A380	Singapore Airlines	54

Source: Compiled from Airbus production data.

---

[51]Wallace, James. Airbus all in on need for jumbo—but Boeing still doubtful. *Seattle P. I.*, October 24, 2007.

[52]Sixty-three A380s were delivered to airlines as of March 19, 2011.

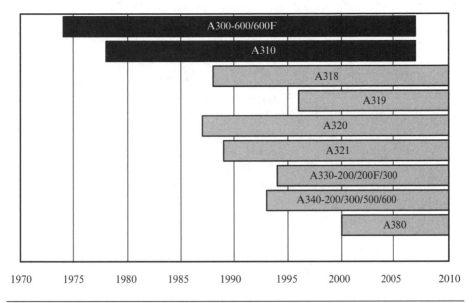

Figure 1.6 Airbus commercial aircraft
Source: Compiled from Airbus production data.

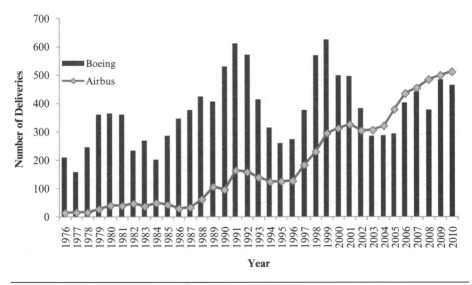

Figure 1.7 Airbus and Boeing market share
Source: Compiled from Airbus and Boeing delivery data.

Fokker

Fokker officially originated in Amsterdam in 1919, when Anthony H. G. Fokker established the Netherlands Aircraft Factory Fokker (The Fokker heritage, 2009). That year, the Fokker F2, an airplane capable of carrying four passengers, was constructed and cruised at 100 miles per hour. The F2 was the predecessor to the F7 Trimotor that was extremely popular with airlines and with prominent aviators such as Charles Lindbergh. KLM Airlines used the Trimotor for the longest aircraft route at that time, between the Netherlands and the East Indies (The Fokker heritage, 2009). By 1934, Fokker began to concentrate on military aircraft production, including the T9 bomber, the first Fokker plane built entirely of metal. Anthony Fokker died in 1939, but his company lived on.

During World War II, the Fokker aircraft factory in Amsterdam was destroyed and production halted. In 1951, the Fokker Company was back on its feet through the construction of a new factory next to Schiphol Airport in Amsterdam (The Fokker heritage, 2009). During the 1950s, Fokker concentrated on a return to the commercial airliner market, and in 1958, the company developed the F27 Friendship turboprop. The F27 became the world's best-selling turboprop with 768 produced and sold to airlines throughout the world (The Fokker heritage, 2009). The F28 was spacious compared to contemporary aircraft of the same size and was considered one of the first regional jets. With seating for 60-70 passengers, the F28 was ideal for routes where turboprops were too small and 100-seat jets were too large.

In the 1980s, Fokker modernized its commercial aircraft fleet and offered replacements for the F27 and F28 with the Fokker 50 turboprop and the Fokker 100 jet, respectively. The Fokker 100, a larger jet than the F28, tried to tap into the 100-seat market that the DC-9 and 737 were so successful at capturing. Prominent airlines bought the Fokker 100, including American, US Airways, and Piedmont.[53] Piedmont operated the F28-1000 and -4000 (configured to 65 and 85 seats, respectively), and US Airways operated the F100. It was not until the 1990s that Fokker made a true 70-seat replacement for the F28 (the Fokker 70). However, the market domination of Boeing and Airbus, coupled with the airline crisis of the 1990s, negatively affected Fokker 70 sales (see Table 1.6 and Figure 1.8). In 1996, the commercial aircraft division of Fokker Aviation went bankrupt, and the company was divided into five parts: Fokker Elmo, Fokker Aerostructures, Fokker Services, Fokker Special Products, and Fokker Defense Marketing (The Fokker heritage, 2009). The five divisions were bought by Stork Aerospace Group and all of these divisions exist today except for the Fokker Defense Marketing division. Presently, the Fokker Services division assists current Fokker commercial aircraft operators

---

[53]Piedmont Airlines (1948-1989) was absorbed by US Airways in 1989.

Table 1.6 Fokker commercial aircraft data

Aircraft model	Launch customer	Produced
F7 Trimotor	Sabena	230
F27 Friendship	Aer Lingus	768
F28	Braathens	241
Fokker 50	DLT	213
Fokker 100	Swissair	283
Fokker 70	Ford Motor Company	47

Source: Compiled from available aircraft production data.

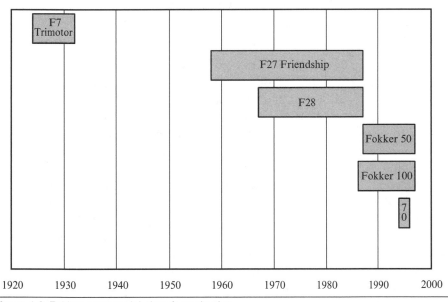

Figure 1.8 Fokker commercial aircraft production
Source: Compiled from Fokker aircraft production data.

in the day-to-day operations of their fleet and with remarketing and selling used Fokker 50 and Fokker 100 aircraft (The Fokker heritage, 2009).

Fokker Services' parent company, Stork, went through some turmoil through the 2000s until 2008, when the Dutch company was taken over by a private equity consortium (Investor relations, 2009). In 2007, speculation about the company's future may have led to a net income decrease to 67 million Euros from 150 million in the previous year. In addition, Stork finished the year with a negative cash position (Stork Technical Services annual report, 2007). Despite new ownership, Stork continues on as before with all of the four Fokker-related divisions, although future viability is tenuous.

Russia and Eastern Europe

Before World War I, the development of aviation in the Russian Empire was mostly driven by military needs. More than 307 different aircraft models were designed by the end of the war, but only one of them could have been characterized as a passenger aircraft. The world's first four-engine bomber, created by Igor Sikorsky, performed the first charter flight with passengers onboard in July 1914. A month later Russia went to war, and then faced a communist coup and civil war. Consequently, regular air services were not resumed until 1921, when three converted Sikorsky "Ilya Muromets" began flying between Moscow and Nizhniy Novgorod. However, the first experiments were not successful, and after 43 flights, the first airline in Russia ceased operations. In 2010, seven aircraft were delivered, including two Tu-204s, one Tu-214 and four An-148s.[54]

The Early Years

The first sustainable air service was established by the Soviet-German airline Deruluft in November 1921. From then until the mid-1930s, there were several independent airlines in the Union of Soviet Socialist Republics (USSR). German Junkers F13, Dornier Merkurs, and Junkers Ju-52/3m were the main types of aircraft in the early years of commercial air services for domestic and international routes. Gradually, Soviet models replaced foreign-made models. The most common aircraft at the time were Tupolev ANT-9 (PS-9), Kalinin K-5, Stal 2/3 and KhAI-1, which had four to nine seats. Slightly fewer than 600 of these aircraft were produced prior to World War II. Only one larger capacity airplane was utilized by Aeroflot on transport routes in the late 1930s, the Tupolev PS-124, which had 64 passenger seats. Besides the mass production aircraft, some experimental or converted military bombers were flying passengers and cargo.

In 1932, the Soviet government decided to centralize the independent airlines and establish a single national carrier named Aeroflot. To ensure its operations, a license to manufacture the Douglas DC-3 was purchased in the United States in 1935. Under the local designations of the PS-84 in 1939 and the military variant Lisunov Li-2 in 1942, this model was in production until 1952. The total number of these aircraft produced in the USSR was 4,853; most of them were transferred to the Soviet Air Force in order to run supply lines during World War II.

After the unification of air carriers under Aeroflot, the Soviet airline industry acquired the shape that it retained for the next 60 years. The sole national carrier was responsible for all types of air operations, from crop-dusting to intercontinental passenger service. In addition, the Ministry of Civil Aviation, which controlled

---

[54]Annual Report. (2010). Joint Stock Company United Aircraft Corporation.

Aeroflot, was responsible for managing aircraft repairs, pilot and engineer training, and construction and operation of airports.

However, the production side of the industry was not centralized. Different design bureaus engaged in multiple projects—from creating a light biplane to designing heavy bombers or transport aircraft. However, the economic environment did not involve open competition. The customer (the government) remained the same, and new orders were not based on market perception of the aircraft. The design bureau's success depended on the art of delicate maneuvering among different interest groups in the Soviet government decision-making process. The development situation was even worse for civil aviation projects because military assignments had absolute priority for the design bureaus.

Moreover, until the 1960s, every aircraft designed in the Soviet Union had to be tested by the Soviet Air Force before entering service in civil aviation. At that time, the easiest route to serial production was presenting newly designed aircraft as military models and converting them into civilian versions afterward. However, if the Soviet Air Force generals were concerned that the development of a new civil aircraft might jeopardize work on a military aircraft, the order could be handed over to a competing firm.

Features of Soviet Aircraft Manufacturing

Features of Soviet design were used in one of the most successful Soviet aircraft—the Antonov An-2. When the An-2 was developed, nobody was interested in the project. The Soviet Air Force believed that there was no need for a slow piston-driven biplane in the upcoming jet era. Aeroflot proclaimed that it was too small for Aeroflot's main lines and too large for Aeroflot's feeder routes. Yakovlev Design Bureau, which employed Oleg Antonov, also did not demonstrate enthusiasm regarding the aircraft because of its old-fashioned style. In order to push the An-2 into the air, Antonov turned for support to Communist Party leaders to obtain permission to build an experimental aircraft. However, serial production of the An-2 was in question because every assembly line in the Soviet Union was overloaded with the manufacturing of military aircraft. Again, Antonov used his contacts with top members of the Communist Party. This time, Nikita Khrushchev, who in a few years would succeed Stalin, helped him. If Khrushchev had not supported the project, the most long-lived and most-produced Soviet-era aircraft would have never seen the light of day. However, after 60 years of production in the USSR, Poland, and China, more than 18,000 An-2s were produced before production ended in 1991.[55]

---

[55]Gordon, Y., & Komissarov, D. (2004). Antonov An-2. Midland. Hinkley.

As in the rest of the world, the early postwar decade in the Soviet Union saw the production of the first jet engines in the aviation industry. At the same time, the last piston-driven aircraft entered commercial service in the 1950s. Two Ilyushin[56] piston twins were the last mainline piston aircraft in serial production. The aircraft made its maiden flight on August 15, 1945, and about 660 Ilyushin Il-12s were produced from 1945 to 1948.[57] The Ilyushin Il-14, which first took off in 1950, was more successful and was used for mainline operations until the mid-1960s. After that, this 30-seat aircraft was used in polar and Far East operations until the 1980s. The Il-14 was manufactured in the Soviet Union, East Germany, Czechoslovakia, and China, and the total number produced reached 3,500 units.

The transfer of Il-14 production to countries with communist governments was an effective way to support Soviet-friendly regimes. For East Germany, the production of the Il-14 was an important sign of recovery of lapsed industrial greatness, and authorities used it as a piece of propaganda. While capitalists in West Germany were able to make only primitive three-wheeled BMWs, socialists were producing aircraft. Similarly, the Il-14 was the plane of influence in Czechoslovakia—a country that had lost in the war one of the most high-tech economies of that time. Subsequently, technology transfer would be used more frequently for Eastern European allies that were producing military and regional aircraft and flying into space onboard Soviet spacecraft. In the 1970s, this was a priceless accomplishment.

After phasing out the last generation of piston-driven commercial aircraft, the Soviet Union joined a race with the leader in civil aviation at the time—the United Kingdom. The UK was the only country in the world that had a commercial jet aircraft. Using British engines and the work of German engineers, the Soviets designed their own engine that was powerful enough to propel large aircraft. A bomber, the Tupolev Tu-16 that first took off in 1952, was transformed over two years into the Tupolev Tu-104, the first passenger jet in the USSR and the second passenger jet in the world. The Soviets called it *the world's first passenger jet aircraft* in sustainable operations (due to a series of crashes, the British Comet 1 was grounded for several years). Production of the Tu-104 was brief. In less than five years, about 200 aircraft were produced in several variants that ranged from 60 to 100 seats. The first Soviet experience with the commercial jet aircraft was also controversial. Even though the aircraft remained in the fleet of Aeroflot through the 1970s, the Tu-104 had a terrible safety record, low reliability, and high operating costs. Over one-third of the Tu-104s produced were lost in accidents, and the only foreign carrier that used it was a Czech airline, CSA.

---

[56]The company was founded by Sergey Vladimirovich Ilyushin in the Soviet Union and its operations began on January 13, 1933.

[57]Ilyushin Aviation Complex. Dates of Maiden Flights.

The experiences with the Tu-104 operations led to a delay in the Soviet development of new commercial jets. Turboprops were the predominant aircraft type during the 1950s in the Soviet Union. In fact, one of the most successful attempts to create a turboprop was the design of the Ilyushin Il-18. This four-engine airplane originally was intended to be used on medium-haul routes, but shortly became the backbone of the entire Aeroflot network. The later versions of the Il-18 had ranges of up to 4,000 miles and capacities of up to 120 people. The Il-18 was phased out of mainline operations in the late 1970s, and since then, many Il-18s have been converted to freighters. Some of them still fly routes in Africa and the Far East.

Another four-engine turboprop was created at the same time. The Antonov An-10 was similar to the Il-18 in size, but had a completely different design and proposed area of operations. It was designed for short-haul routes with the idea of combining in one body the strength of a cargo aircraft and the luxury of a first-class rail car. However, neither plush seats nor ceiling fans helped to keep this aircraft in the fleet of Aeroflot. After a series of crashes caused by structural weakness, the An-10 was retired.

A different approach to the design of regional turboprops was demonstrated by Antonov a few years later. In 1959, the 50-seat An-24 made its maiden flight. The An-24 quickly became a workhorse of regional airlines of Aeroflot and former Soviet Union allies. More than 1,300 copies of the An-24 were produced, and a cargo version, the An-26/32, added 1,100 more units to this number. In China, a significantly modernized version of this aircraft, the MA60, is still in production.

Another Antonov aircraft, although less successful compared to the An-24, was the An-14, a piston-driven 14-seater for local routes. The An-14 was in far less demand than the An-24. Conceived as a replacement for the An-2, the An-14 was unable to compete with its cheaper and simpler predecessor. The An-14 with piston engines was in production until 1972. More modern versions of the An-14 with turboprop engines were still in production as the An-38 in Russia and as the M-28 *Skytruck* in Poland. After more than 40 years of production, only about 500 airframes have been released.

Another passenger turboprop designed by Tupolev became the most famous Russian turboprop ever. The 220-seat Tu-114 was equipped with four powerful turboprop engines and was the first Soviet intercontinental airliner. Such an aircraft could appear only in a country that had no competition in its air transport industry but had a lot of strategic bombers. The Tu-114 was the Tu-95 *Bear* strategic bomber with a larger fuselage. Although only 33 were built, the Tu-114 was utilized until the mid-1970s on both domestic and international routes of Aeroflot. It was especially useful for flights from Moscow to Havana.

Soviet models created in the 1950s defined the face of commercial aviation in the USSR and, in many ways, the entire Eastern bloc for more than a decade and a half. In the West, propeller-driven commercial aircraft were phased out quickly and retained only on regional routes. In the USSR, however, turboprops played a crucial role in aviation until the mid-1970s.

Despite the fact that the development of jet aircraft was driven by the latest achievements in science and technology, Soviet engineering was very conservative. Soviet designers were aware of their limited technological capabilities and typically preferred to follow the rule "if it works, don't fix it." Tupolev's Tu-124, the first Soviet airplane created in the 1960s, was a classic representative of this philosophy. Envisioned as an aircraft for low-density routes, the Tu-124 was a scaled-down version of the Tu-104. Similar to its prototype, the new Soviet aircraft did not have any outstanding features, but had inherited the former problems of the bomber. Engine installation in the wing made engine maintenance and replacements expensive and almost impossible. The lack of air conditioning and small cabin made the plane uncomfortable for passengers. However, there were no other regional jets for Aeroflot, and the national carrier had to accept the Tu-124. By 1965, 165 units of the Tu-124 were produced and sold to Aeroflot, East German Interflug, CSA, and the Iraqi Air Force.[58] Despite its limited commercial success, the Tu-124 made a mark on the history of jet aviation. In August 1963, due to problems with the fuel system, an Aeroflot Tu-124 plane performed an emergency landing in the Neva River in the heart of the city of Saint Petersburg. All passengers safely escaped through the only rescue hatch on the roof of the aircraft.

While the Tu-124 ceased operations in 1980, other Soviet commercial aircraft designed in the 1960s remain in the fleets of airlines of former USSR-allied countries. All this time, disputes have raged about how original the Soviet-designed airplanes were and to what extent the credit for every Soviet airliner design belongs to ubiquitous KGB spies.

For example, was the Il-12/Il-14 just a copy of the Convair 240? What about the similarity of the Il-18 and the Britannia? If the VC-10 and the BAC-111 were designed differently, how would the Il-62 and the Tu-134 have looked? If Dutch designers had built the Fokker F27 as a low-wing airplane, would the An-24 still have a high-wing airframe? If the Boeing 727 had four engines rather than three, how many engines would the Tu-154 have had? The main question, of course, is should the Soviet supersonic passenger aircraft have been called the Tu-144 or should it have been called the Concordski? There are no simple answers to these questions. The Soviets admitted that their first strategic bomber, the Tupolev Tu-4, was a full copy of Boeing's B-29 (except for the engines). However, the KGB played no role in obtaining information about the Superfortress, although several B-29s were delivered to the USSR by American pilots who were forced to land in Soviet territory after raids on Germany and Japan during World War II.

---

[58]Duffy & Kandalov. (1996), *The Man and His Aircraft*. p. 224.

The 1960s

It seems, in retrospect, that industrial espionage was an integral part of Soviet intelligence. It is difficult to assess now to what extent Soviet aircraft designs were copied or to what extent they were original. However, the general rule for Soviet engineers was that the airplane design that had an equivalent in the West would have preference over other designs. There were two reasons for that. First, it would save time and resources in designing an aircraft, and second, the Soviet industry would receive the benefits of market-based competitive selection procedures without spending money on development and without questioning the ideological foundations of the regime. Soviet commercial aircraft designed in the 1960s illustrated those reasons. The Ilyushin Il-62, which first took off in 1963, apparently resembled the British VC-10. Designed to replace the monstrous passenger bomber Tu-114, the 200-seat aircraft would satisfy the needs of the USSR and its allies in long-haul transport for almost a quarter of a century. In more than 30 years of production, 292 units of the Il-62 were produced. That was the second Soviet aircraft that could be seen in capitalist livery. Additionally, Japan's JAL and Aeroflot jointly operated the Paris-Moscow-Tokyo route using the Tu-114. In the 1970s, with the introduction of the Il-62, transcontinental routes became very popular. Aeroflot received Sixth Freedom rights for flights between Japan and London (with British Airways), Copenhagen (with S.A.S.), Rome (with Alitalia), and Frankfurt (with Lufthansa). In addition, the Il-62 was used by Air India for flights between Delhi and London.

Modernization of the failed TU-124. The design of a new short-haul commercial jet, which became known as the Tu-134, was originally an attempt to modernize the failed Tu-124. However, shortly after the beginning of the Tu-134 project, the decision was made to create a clean-slate design. The Tu-134 was born at about the same time as a similar breed of Western aircraft. The BAC-111 took off one month after the first flight of the Tu-134, while the DC-9 and the Fokker F28 first flew two and four years later, respectively. The 70- to 90-seat Tu-134 aircraft was a success, with more than 1,000 units ultimately built. Most of these aircraft still fly within the former Soviet Union.

Another Tupolev model—the medium-haul Tu-154—was popular among Eastern European air carriers. This airplane became the core of the fleets of airlines within the Soviet bloc for more than 30 years. In the mid-1980s, the Tu-154 received new, more efficient engines that helped it continue in production until 2006, with about 1,000 airplanes produced overall.

Building on the wave of success of the Tu-134 and Tu-154, Tupolev's design bureau attempted to create a supersonic passenger plane. The Tu-144 was a little ahead of its only rival, the French-British Concorde. The Tu-144 took off in December 1968, only two months earlier than the Concorde. Also, the Tu-144 first started commercial operations flying cargo from Moscow to Alma Ata in December 1975.

The only area in which the Tu-144 did not succeed was efficiency. Obviously, there was no need to transport mail over a distance of 2,500 miles with supersonic speed. These flights were promotional efforts to rehabilitate the aircraft reputation after a crash at the Paris Air Show in the summer of 1973. A few months of passenger service was enough to disappoint Aeroflot with the lack of economic efficiency and technical characteristics of the Tu-144. The aircraft's fuel consumption was too high even by generous Soviet standards, and the airplane's reliability was low. Eventually, all 20 Tu-144s went to rest. Some of them went to museum displays, others were used to train pilots for the Soviet space shuttle "Buran" program, and one aircraft was used as a test for NASA's SST-2 program.

The only aircraft of the 1960s that was entirely free from suspicion of copying Western designs was the Yakovlev Yak-40. This 32-seater became the world's first commercial jet aircraft for short-haul routes. It seems that the Soviet Union, as early as the mid-1960s, developed a regional jet concept that led to the success of Brazil's Embraer and Canada's Bombardier. However, the conservatism and lack of similar aircraft in the West played a negative role in this case. Throughout its life, the Yak-40 was produced virtually with no modifications—with 28 or 32 seats, fuel-guzzling engines, and Soviet avionics sets. Only a few airplanes out of more than 1,000 manufactured were exported to Italy and Germany. Virtually all Yak-40s remained in the USSR and with its allies.

Two more aircraft that performed maiden flights in the 1960s were turboprops for feeder lines. The Czech-built Let L-410 was commissioned by Aeroflot and was the main airplane for its feeder routes for many years. More than 1,100 units of the L-410 were produced. Slightly bigger than the 19-seat L-410, the An-28/38 was a vast modernization of the obsolete An-14. While still in limited production in Russia and Poland (as the M-28 "Skytruck"), this airplane has not been successful.

In the first five years after World War II, passenger traffic in the Soviet Union increased four-fold. In 1940, the year before the USSR entered the war, 400,000 passengers were transported by air. In 1950, this number grew to 1,600,000. Over the next 10 years, passenger traffic grew by a factor of 10—in 1960, Aeroflot transported more than 16 million people. By 1970, passenger traffic on domestic and international routes grew to 68 million. At that time, the USSR was the second-ranked country in the world in terms of commercial air traffic. Only in the U.S. did airlines carry more commercial air traffic—about 170 million people.

The 1970s

The results of passenger aviation in the 1970s were much more modest. In 1980, only 90 million passengers were transported in the USSR. The exponential growth of previous decades was followed by only 30% cumulative growth over the next 10 years. The Soviet aviation industry witnessed lack of enthusiasm and lost its momentum. In terms of the development of new commercial aircraft, the 1970s was one of the worst decades in the history of the USSR, whereas the most successful decade for the Soviet aircraft industry was the 1960s. Eight brand new designs took off during the 1960s, and most of them are still in operation. The 1950s were also good for the Soviet aviation industry, with seven new aircraft from this time period making it into mass production. However, from 1970 to 1980, only two new commercial aircraft were designed in the Soviet Union—a short-haul regional jet known as the Yakovlev Yak-42 and the short- to medium-haul wide-body known as the Ilyushin Il-86. Thus, the 1970s were a lost decade for the Soviet aviation industry.

The 1980s

The Yak-42, a regional jet with 120 seats, filled a niche between the Tu-134 (80 seats) and the Tu-154 (160 seats). The Yak-42 had three turbofan engines and was designed to operate on short routes—up to 1,500 miles. Even though the Yak-42 was economically efficient by Soviet standards, the aircraft's narrow specialization led to limited success. With the capacity and comfort of a mainline jet, the Yak-42 could fly from short runways and had a built-in ladder. Its minimum wing sweep angle resulted in excellent takeoff and landing characteristics, but significantly reduced the cruise speed. Because of its range, the Yak-42 could operate only in the European part of the Soviet Union, where the passenger demand could not justify the use of the larger Tu-154. But in the eastern part of the county, with its great distances between cities, the Yak-42 was not suitable due to its short range and low speed. The Yak-42 was the second failed attempt to create a commercial airplane for a very narrow market niche. The An-10, built in the 1960s, tried to combine the comfort of a mainline plane with the ability to take off and land on unpaved airstrips. As a result, only a small number of these two aircraft types were ultimately produced—188 of the Yak-42 and 108 of the An-10.

The Ilyushin Il-86 made its first flight in 1976. This 350-seat wide-body commercial jet was also designed for a very narrow niche determined by the geography of the Soviet Union. The majority of the country's population lived within 2,000 miles from Moscow. Therefore, the main passenger traffic in the Soviet Union was condensed in the European side of the country and flowed primarily from north to south, and vice versa. Latitudinal traffic flow from west to east was relatively light and could be handled with the smaller and longer range Il-62.[59]

---

[59]For example, the SIP-PKC route (Simferopol-Petropavlovsk-Kamchatskiy), with a distance of about 5000 nm, was the world's longest domestic flight and the longest transcontinental route ever.

Accordingly, Aeroflot needed a large-capacity, medium-range airplane to satisfy passenger demand. The viability of this concept was confirmed by the designs of the European Airbus A300, which had slightly smaller capacity and about the same range, and the U.S.-built Lockheed L-1011 and McDonnell Douglas DC-10, which had similar capacity and slightly greater range.

Evidence of how badly Aeroflot needed such an airplane could be found in the fact that the Soviet government did not use industrial espionage to expedite the development of this type of aircraft, but decided to officially acquire a production license instead. In the mid-1970s, the Vietnam War was over, and the USSR and the United States were considering a number of joint projects, including the Apollo-Soyuz space program and the transfer of technology to produce a wide-body commercial jet. In the middle of 1973, top-ranked Soviet officials arrived in the United States to buy several wide-body aircraft for Aeroflot and to purchase a license to produce these aircraft at an assembly line in the city of Ulyanovsk. The Soviet delegation visited the three American commercial aircraft manufacturers at that time—Boeing, McDonnell Douglas, and Lockheed Martin. The Soviet officials divided themselves into two groups. The industrial part of the delegation supported the L-1011 as a base model for a new Soviet aircraft, but Aeroflot managers backed the Boeing 747. After two years of discussions, the project was taken off the table, and instead of buying a ready-to-fly production model, the Soviets decided to design their own wide-body aircraft. Over the following five years, they built the Ilyushin Il-86 with the exact same number of seats as the L-1011.

The 1990s to the Present

Introduced into commercial operation in 1980, the Il-86 generally delivered what was expected; only 112 were ever built. The only other country that utilized the Il-86 was China, where, as in the USSR, there were several medium- and short-haul high-density routes linking the country's major industrial and political centers. Other Soviet allies had no interest in the Il-86. For Eastern European countries the aircraft was too large for domestic service, but had insufficient range for intercontinental flights.

The Soviet commercial aircraft industry came back to life in the mid-1980s. The fleet of commercial aircraft had to be replaced with more efficient and modern machines. The three oldest models—the regional turboprop Antonov An-24, the medium-range Tu-154, and the long-haul Il-62—were the first candidates for replacement. Since the planned Soviet economy could not afford to spread money around and organize design competitions, the decision was made to use the same engine for both the Tu-154 and the Il-62. In the early 1980s, nobody anticipated the economic and political crisis the country would go through in the next few years, and all of the new aircraft were designed to be larger than their predecessors to accommodate the continuous growth of demand for air transportation. Between 1980 and 1990, passenger traffic in the Soviet Union increased by almost one-and-a-half times and reached 140 million enplanements. Therefore, the Il-114 that was intended to replace the An-24 was designed with a 25% increase in size, reaching a capacity of 60 passengers. The Tu-204 was also designed with a 25% larger capacity of 200-220 passengers than the model it would replace, the Tu-154. The Il-96, intended to replace the Il-62, had a 300-seat capacity, more than 50% greater than the Il-62. It was unclear what aircraft would fill the gaps among these three airplane sizes.

Being close in size to the Boeing 777-200 and Airbus 340-200, the Il-96 had four newly designed PS-90 engines. While the engine was a substantial achievement of Soviet technology, it remained inefficient and unreliable by Western standards. However, the real problem of the Il-96 was not in its engine, but a dramatic change in the economic environment by the time the airplane was ready for mass production. In the early 1990s, the Soviet Union ceased to exist, and its 15 newly formed states fell into a deep economic crisis that led to a sharp decline in passenger traffic. In 1990, a year before the Soviet Union's collapse, the number of passengers carried by Aeroflot in Russia reached an historic high of 91 million people, compared to 1999 when fewer than 22 million people flew on domestic and international routes.[60] In the new states, larger airplanes were no longer needed. The Ilyushin design bureau's attempts to market the Il-96 with Pratt & Whitney engines and Rockwell-Collins avionics were also unsuccessful.

The commercial success of larger aircraft in the Soviet Union had been negatively affected by the traditional inflexibility of the system. In an economy with no competition among manufacturers, the process of negotiation between buyers and sellers was distorted. In rare cases, buyers could get what they wanted. More often, though, manufacturers were pushing customers to buy what they could develop. Under pressure from the Russian government, the flag carrier Aeroflot agreed to buy 12 Il-96s. However, only six planes were delivered, and the remaining six were rejected by Aeroflot even though they were modified into freighters. As of 2008, only 22 Il-96s had been built. Some of them are used as VIP transports for Russian, Venezuelan, and Cuban leaders, while others are utilized for charters.

It has been asserted that the core expertise required for Soviet aircraft manufacturing was political connections and influence, and not effective design and/or manufacturing capabilities. Labor and fuel were cheap, so efficiency was not highly valuable. Consequently, it was not the most effective or efficient products that made it to the market. It was probably not a problem until those products and industries had to compete with leading manufacturers.

---

[60]Before the Soviet Union's collapse, Russian traffic represented about 75% of all traffic in the Soviet Union.

Designed similarly to the Boeing 757, the Tu-204 was not as successful as the Tu-154. However, the Tupolev design bureau was better prepared than the Ilyushin firm to work in the new, post-Soviet environment, and the Tu-204 had more sales. A few derivatives were developed—the Tu-204-200, with increased maximum takeoff weight and range of up to 4,000 miles; the Tu-204C, for cargo; and the Tu-204-300, aimed at a specific niche of long-haul, low-demand routes. The Tu-204-300 has a capacity of 160 seats and a range of 6,000 miles. Another variant of the Tu-204 is still in development. The Tu-204SM will be a direct replacement of the outdated Tu-154 and will have a lighter structural design, reduced maximum takeoff weight, and smaller passenger capacity. It is anticipated that this aircraft will become an intermediate model between the original Tu-204 and a new generation of narrow-body aircraft, the MS-21. According to Tupolev, the Tu-204SM should enter the market in 2012 before Boeing and Airbus release their replacements for the 737 and the A320.

The last commercial airplane made in the USSR was the Ilyushin Il-114 regional turboprop. Traditionally, for Soviet aircraft development, the confirmation of the chosen design was based on Western influences. British BAe ATRs had similar features—low wing design and maximum capacity of 60 passengers. Similar to the ATR, the Il-114 was not a commercial success. Despite the manufacturer's attempts to improve the turboprop by installing Western engines and avionics, only a few aircraft were delivered to customers in Russia and Uzbekistan. It seems that for domestic markets, the aircraft was too large and expensive, while internationally, the Il-114 could not compete with large families of regional turboprops from ATR and Bombardier.

Despite the failure of the Il-114, manufacturers from CIS countries continued attempts at commercial success in the niche encompassing the market under Boeing's and Airbus' production lines. CIS manufacturers assumed that the huge market for regional air transportation in ex-Soviet countries would recover and that a simple and rugged replacement for the old An-24 would be needed. Beginning in 2000, the demand for air travel in the former USSR had started to grow. However, the demand structure had undergone radical changes. During more than a decade of economic crisis, the national airport network had deteriorated, with small regional airports being affected the most. There were once 1,300 airports in Soviet Russia, but by the year 2000, this number had decreased to 300, with only about 100 of them in operational condition.

In addition, the passenger-flow directions had changed dramatically. In the USSR, the vast majority of passengers flew on domestic routes. In 2008, the proportion of domestic and international flights was about fifty-fifty, with 90% of all connecting passengers flying through Moscow's three airports. These factors led to the stagnation of the key markets for new small turboprops. From 2000 to 2008, the total annual passenger traffic in Russia more than doubled, from 23 million to 51.4 million, while the regional traffic remained almost unchanged, staying around 1 million passengers per year (in the Soviet Union, this figure was 10 million passengers per year).[61]

The first post-Soviet plane was the Ukrainian-built An-140 turboprop. With its 50-seat capacity and simple design, this model targeted regional routes in former Soviet countries. Even though the An-140 is currently being produced in Ukraine, Russia, and Iran, it has not yet achieved any significant commercial success.

More attempts to avoid direct competition with Boeing and Airbus have resulted in the development of two regional jets in former Soviet counties—the Ukrainian-built An-148 and Russian-built Sukhoi SuperJet (SSJ) 100. These two aircraft, however, have a number of important differences in market positioning and design. The An-148 is positioned to capture regional markets in the former USSR and Iran. This 70-seat aircraft was designed with minimal use of Western equipment. On the other hand, the key market for the SSJ 100 is outside the former Soviet Union, and it is designed to compete against the Embraer E-Jets and the Bombardier CRJ programs.[62]

According to Sukhoi, out of a planned production of 800 units, only about 200 aircraft are intended for the Russian market. At the beginning of its development in early 2000, the SSJ 100 was envisioned as a line of aircraft with capacities from 60 to 100 passengers. However, the Sukhoi design bureau admitted that in the high fuel price environment, there was no economically justifiable way to create a family of aircraft with such a wide range of capacities—the base model with 80 seats, the shortened version with 60 seats, and the stretched derivative with 100 seats. Therefore, Sukhoi's plans to create a 60-seater were dropped. The 100-seat derivative became the basic model, and the 130-seat version was under consideration.

The first flight of the Sukhoi SuperJet 100 took place in May 2008.[63] At the 2009 Paris Air Show, Hungarian national carrier Malev Airlines signed a statement of intent to purchase 30 SuperJet 100s. In another transaction, the Mexican low-cost carrier Interjet signed a firm order to purchase 15 SuperJet 100 regional jets plus five options, which opens that market of the Russian-built aircraft to Western customers. As of April 18, 2011, there were confirmed orders for 170 SuperJets.[64]

This capacity range satisfies Aeroflot, which is the launch customer of the SSJ 100.[65] Aeroflot urgently needs to replace its outdated fleet of regional Tu-134 aircraft with a plane that has a smaller capacity than the Tu-154. To compete internationally, Sukhoi invited some Western companies to participate in the SSJ 100

---

[61]See http://www.gks.ru.

[62]International. export driven: The Sukhoi SuperJet, *Flight*, web site, January 17, 2010.

[63]Aerospace-technology, web site, January 14, 2010.

[64]*Airline News Europe*, April 18, 2011.

[65]Flight Global, May 5, 2008.

project. Alenia Aeronautica of Italy became a 51% shareholder in the SSJ and is in charge of marketing, sales, customization, and delivery of the SSJ 100 in Europe, the Americas, Oceania, Africa, and Japan. This Italian firm was also in charge of worldwide after-sale support. Boeing was involved as a consultant, and some component manufacturers (Snecma) were risk-sharing partners. The first SSJ 100 was delivered to launch customer Armenian airline Armavia on April 12, 2011, with Aeroflot taking delivery shortly thereafter as the second operator in June of 2011 (see Table 1.7 and Figure 1.9).

Asia

The playing field may change dramatically in the near future as China enters the market for the manufacturing of commercial airliners. China's aeronautics industry was established in the 1950s and has been trying to become a viable commercial aircraft manufacturer in the world. In 2008, China announced that it had formed the China Commercial Aircraft Company, with an initial investment of $2.7 billion. China plans to build a 150-seat aircraft by 2020 to compete with Boeing and Airbus. Since the aircraft manufacturing industry is strategically important for national security and the balance of payments, most governments support firms either by direct support or indirect subsidization through defense contracts.

Commercial aircraft manufacturing in Asia is still at an embryonic stage. Since the region is comprised mostly of developing economies, it had lacked the technology and the capital to undertake aircraft manufacturing. Most Chinese aircraft

Table 1.7 Russia and Eastern European bloc commercial aircraft data

Aircraft model	Launch customer	Produced
An-24	Aeroflot	1,367
An-140	Aeroflot	28
An-148	Aerosvit Airlines	6
Tu-104	Aeroflot	200
Tu-124	Aeroflot	164
Tu-134	Aeroflot	852
Tu-144	Aeroflot	16
Tu-154	Aeroflot	1,015
Tu-204	Aeroflot	65
Il-114	Aeroflot	14
Il-96	Aeroflot	24
Il-62	Aeroflot	292
SSJ 100	Armavia/Aeroflot	4

Source: Compiled from Antonov, Ilyushin, Sukhoi, and Tupolev data.

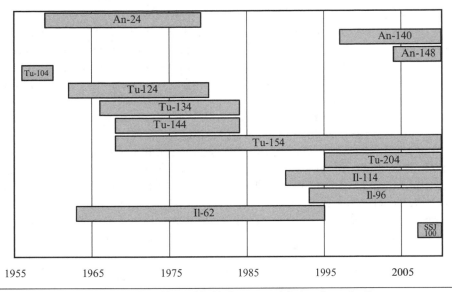

Figure 1.9 Antonov, Tupolev, Ilyushin and Sukhoi commercial aircraft production
Source: Compiled from aircraft production data.

manufacturing was driven by the military. Established during the Korean War in 1951, the aviation industry in China went through twelve reforms, and the last reform in 1999 resulted in splitting China Aviation Industry Corporation (AVIC) into two arms, AVIC I and AVIC II. AVIC I specialized in large military aircraft while AVIC II focused on smaller civilian airliners, transports, and helicopters. The companies that constituted AVIC II are Harbin Manufacturing Corporation, Hongdu Aviation Industry Corporation, Shaanxi Aircraft Company, Changhe Aircraft Industries Corporation, and Shijiahuang Aircraft Manufacturing Company.

Harbin Manufacturing was the only civilian aircraft producer in the consortium. The main offering of Harbin was the Y-11[66] and Y-12, which entered production in 1975 in response to the Chinese government's requisition for a light utility aircraft. The Y-11 was a twin-engine turboprop airliner with short takeoff and landing (STOL) characteristics, which was superseded by the Y-12. Some airlines in China, the South Pacific and Japan still operate the Y-12. In 2003, Embraer entered into a partnership with Harbin Manufacturing to produce the ERJ 145 in China for the Chinese market. The other companies produce supersonic military aircraft, transports, helicopters, and avionics test beds.

---

[66]Twin-engine STOL utility transport aircraft.

The Commercial Aircraft Corporation of China (COMAC) is set to fabricate large domestic passenger jets by using world-class manufacturing techniques in the production of the homegrown C919 airplane. China plans to build an assembly line for its homegrown C919 jetliners in Shanghai for narrow-body commercial airliners with 168-190 seats.[67] The C919 is due to make its maiden flight by 2014 and to begin deliveries by 2016.[68] The aircraft is expected to compete against the Boeing 737NG and Airbus A320 family.

The development of a commercial aircraft manufacturing center in China is a logical progression of its forecasted traffic increase and rapid economic growth. China is expected to handle approximately 260 million passengers, up 13% from 2009. Even amid the global economic downturn, growth of Chinese air traffic has continued unabated (Reuters, January 13, 2010). In the long term, China has had a relatively low passenger-to-population ratio (0.13 per thousand population) compared to developing economies in Asia (ICAO traffic data, 2010). Coupled with a robust population growth projection, the demand for airline transportation and, consequently, for aircraft in China is likely to be extremely high. Therefore, the Chinese government has an active interest in developing a local manufacturing solution to aircraft manufacturing.

Japan had manufactured a successful commercial jetliner during the 1950s through the Nihon Aircraft Manufacturing Corporation, a consortium of Japanese heavy industry companies. Japan had manufactured numerous aircraft during World War II, but could not engage in aircraft manufacturing in accordance with the post-war terms of its surrender to Western Allies. However, during the 1950s, these restrictions were gradually lifted to allow Japan to manufacture the civilian turboprop YS-11. This was designed as a replacement to the DC-3. However, further expansion was infeasible due to the extensive capital requirements associated with developing or purchasing jet aircraft engines, and the company was dissolved in 1983.

Regional Jet Markets

In discussing Boeing, McDonnell Douglas, and Lockheed Martin, attention was primarily paid to the history of wide-body or narrow-body airliners with seating capacity of 120 or more passengers. There is a secondary yet vital market for commercial aircraft that pertains to regional jets. Regional jets are roughly classified as aircraft that seat between 37 and 122 people and have a short- to medium-haul range (Schedule tapes, 2009). The market for regional jets is similarly dominated by two players: Embraer from Brazil and Bombardier from Canada. The rest of the

---

[67]Dimensions of the C919 are similar to the Airbus A320 to allow for a common pallet to be transferred.

[68]*Tulsa World*. Nov. 20, 2009.

aircraft manufacturers ultimately grew to have an exclusively military focus such as Lockheed Martin and Northrop or were eventually absorbed into the major players.

One can split this segment into the jets below 70 seats and those between 70 to 120 seats. These are used mainly by commuter, feeder, or air taxi operations to serve markets too thin to justify the costs of operating a full-size jet. Primarily, commuter operations are usually part of a major airline, either via code-sharing, shared branding, or regional partnerships. United Express, a network of commuter airlines operating as feeders for United Airlines, and Delta Connection for Delta Air Lines, are examples of commuter airline operations. They serve to fill in the network structure of a mainline hub-and-spoke model by linking low-traffic origins and destinations to the primary hub-and-spoke network. Generally, these airlines have a mixed fleet of turboprops and regional jets.

Another type of commuter airline aims to provide specialized, point-to-point service to select, thin markets. Cape Air and Colgan Air are examples of this latter type of commuter airline. The recent global economic crisis and an increase in fuel costs make small regional jets unaffordable for airlines because of the high cost per available passenger seat mile.

The two major players in the regional jet manufacturing industry have been the Brazilian Embraer and the Canadian Bombardier. In addition, the Japanese heavy machinery and automobile manufacturer Mitsubishi is expected to enter the market with six different versions of its regional jet, seating 70-96 passengers, with plans to make delivery of the first MRJ90 during the first quarter of 2014.[69]

Embraer

Empresa Brasileira de Aeronáutica, S.A. (Embraer) was established by the Brazilian government in 1969. Embraer had a mixed capital structure and was controlled by the government. Embraer was the world's third-largest commercial plane maker and the world's largest producer of regional jets as of 2011.[70] The first aircraft produced by Embraer was a twin-engine turboprop, the IPD-6504, known as the Bandeirante. The Bandeirante was intended to be a light-transport aircraft for military and civilian use by the Brazilian Aeronautics Ministry, and the aircraft's popularity soared because of its combination of efficiency, speed, and capacity. The Bandeirante underwent 11 incarnations, with Embraer embarking on variants and improvements almost immediately after the first Bandeirantes were delivered. In addition to the basic 12-seat transport (EMB 110), there was the aerial photography version, the initial airline version with 15 seats (EMB 110C), the 18-seat enlargement (EMB 110P), the convertible passenger/freight model

[69]Mitsubishi to Delay MRJ First Flight, Aerospace Industry, *Aircraft*, September 9, 2009.
[70]Reuters, July 29, 2011.

(EMB 110P1), and several other models that were the result of customization or improvements. As of 2011, 83 Bandeirantes remained in service, in use primarily by North, Central, and South American commuter airlines and air taxi services (Kaminshi-Morrow & Fafard, 2011). The Bandeirante ceased production in 1990.

The next major commercial aircraft produced by Embraer was the EMB 120, the Brasilia, developed in 1980, with its maiden flight in 1983. The Brasilia could seat 30 passengers and was developed expressly for the regional jet market. It was a twin-engine, T-tail turboprop that found a burgeoning market in the regional airlines of the United States, which were just beginning to come to the fore (Eden, 2008). Like the Bandeirante, the Brasilia went through several variants, each offering better takeoff and landing performance, extended ranges, aerofoil improvements, and passenger/freighter modifications. Besides finding a solid market among regional airlines, the Brasilia was the prototype upon which the Embraer ERJs would be developed. Many of the components of the famous ERJ 145/135 were initially used in the EMB 120, and the EMB 120 formed the perfect "bridge" aircraft for Embraer to enter the jet playing field in 1989. The biggest operator of the Brasilia was the U.S. commuter airline SkyWest, which had a fleet of 43 aircraft as of July 2011 (Kaminshi-Morrow & Fafard, 2011).

In 1986, in partnership with Argentina, Embraer embarked on the CBA 123 Vector, a 19-seater developed in conjunction with Argentina's Fabrica Militar de Aviones (FMA). The CBA 123 Vector incorporated cutting-edge technologies, such as the pusher propeller with the 1,300 shp TPF 351-20 engine developed by the Garrett Engine Division of the Allied Signal Aerospace Company. The CBA 123 Vector was also the first turboprop to incorporate Full Authority Digital Engine Control (FADEC) to yield increased power plant efficiencies (Reuland, 1991). The aircraft was designed to cruise at a maximum altitude of FL41 with a speed of 360 ktas. However, production costs and rising fuel prices in the early 1990s led Embraer to price this aircraft at $6 million, in a market dominated by the Beech 1900 and the Fairchild-Swearingen Metroliner, each priced at around $2 million. In light of the fuel crisis and the wake of the Gulf War, there was no way that regional commuter airlines could justify paying such a premium price for a 19-seat aircraft, and the project met with poor demand.

The early 1990s saw Embraer take on a huge amount of debt, both to finance the CBA 123 Vector and the upcoming regional jet project. In 1989, Embraer issued $85 million in convertible debt and hoped to raise $100 million more through a conversion of commercial bank-held foreign debt (from previous aircraft sales) into non-voting equity. The Brazilian government blocked this particular plan at the last minute and refused to release funds from the already-authorized debt conversion. This, coupled with rising development costs and weak demand, drove Embraer into a deep financial crisis. In October 1990, Embraer laid off 32% of its workforce and posted a loss of $265 million. Further aircraft development slowed to a trickle, and after prolonged upheaval, Embraer was eventually privatized in 1994.

Embraer began the ERJ 145 project in 1989, nine years after the launch of the Brasilia, and this was a much larger project than any project the 20-year-old company had undertaken to date. Total development costs were projected at $300 million, primarily because of the requirement of a swept wing and engine redesigns (Eden, 2008). After the 1990s crisis, the ERJ 145 project took a back seat to internal reorganization at Embraer for a period of time. The prototype of the 50-seat ERJ 145 was assembled in October 1994, and the aircraft began regular revenue flights with Continental Express in 1997. This was quite a success, and over the next several years, variants were developed with increased range and capacity. The ERJ 145 found a receptive market with U.S. and European commuter airlines, such as Continental Express and Switzerland's Crossair.

A smaller version of the ERJ 145, the ERJ 135, was developed close on the heels of the ERJ 145 and found similar success in a reviving commuter airline market.[71] Subsequently, Embraer decided to take a different tack and develop the EMBRAER 170 (78-86 passengers), the 175 (98-106 passengers), the 190 (98-106 passengers), and the 195 (118 passengers). The E-190/195 family is a larger stretch of the E-170/175 family fitted with a new, larger wing, larger horizontal stabilizer, and a new engine. This placed Embraer jets in direct competition with the narrow-bodied aircraft of Boeing and Airbus, the industrial giants (see Table 1.8 and Figure 1.10). Embraer's major rival, Bombardier, was expanding in the same direction. The outcome of such competition was uncertain, but both Embraer and Bombardier were primarily looking to capture the fleet-modernization market. Both Embraer and Bombardier jets may be replacement candidates for older 100-seat aircraft, such as Fokker 70/100s, DC-9s, and MD-80s, as well as early Boeing 737s, thousands of which were still in service and needed to be replaced. The EMB 190 and 195 at 100+ seats are being operated by US Airways mainline, Flybe, JetBlue, Lufthansa CityLine, Augsburg Airways (on behalf of Lufthansa), and other airlines globally. Boeing and Airbus may not respond until they can leapfrog the current aircraft technologies.

Of course, a main reason for the 50-seat (and below) jets was due to scope provisions in pilot contracts. Otherwise, the economics did not necessarily fully justify the aircraft's existence. Embraer also entered into a joint venture with Harbin Manufacturing in China to produce the ERJ 145 for the Chinese market. After entering this agreement, Embraer delivered a total of 246 jets in 2010 and had a firm order backlog of 261 aircraft worth $15.8 billion as of June 30, 2011.[72]

---

[71]ERJ 135 has 37 passengers, ERJ 140 has 44 passengers, and ERJ 145 has 50-passenger configuration capacities.
[72]Embraer (2011) *Embraer Order and Deliveries data.*

Table 1.8 Embraer commercial aircraft production data

Aircraft model	Launch customer	Produced
EMB 120	ASA	352
CBA 123	—	2 prototypes
ERJ 135	Continental Express	108
ERJ 140	American Eagle	74
ERJ 145	Continental Express	708
EMBRAER 170	LOT Polish Airlines	182
EMBRAER 175	Air Canada	136
EMBRAER 190	JetBlue	349
EMBRAER 195	Flybe	75

Source: Compiled from Embraer aircraft production data.

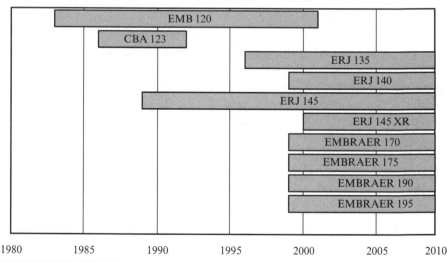

Figure 1.10 Embraer commercial aircraft production
Source: Compiled from Embraer aircraft data.

The major operators of the ERJ 195 were Flybe, Lufthansa, Air Europa Royal Jordanian, LOT Polish Airlines, and Azul.

Bombardier Aerospace

One of the few aircraft manufacturers that did not start out with an airplane, Bombardier was established by Joseph Armand Bombardier in 1942 as a result of his commercial success in building a snowmobile that could handle the inhospitable winters of rural Quebec (Bombardier, 2009). Bombardier's company, originally known as L'Auto-Neige Bombardier Limitée, manufactured his snow-mobiles and launched the iconic Ski-Doo in 1959. After the death of its founder in 1964, Bombardier went on to acquire mass transit technologies and won the contract to build the Montreal subway system. In 1986, Bombardier expanded into Europe by acquiring a stake in the Belgian manufacturer BN Constructions Ferroviaires et Métalliques, S.A. That same year, Bombardier expanded into the aerospace industry by acquiring Canadair, a leading aircraft manufacturer known for producing the popular Challenger wide-body business jets (About us, 2009). Bombardier's most popular aircraft were its Dash 8, CRJ100/200/440, and CRJ700/900/1000 lines of regional airliners.

Most of Bombardier's growth and diversification since its inception was derived from mergers and acquisitions. Bombardier's strategy differed markedly from other North American aircraft manufacturers in that Bombardier had little engineering or original design-oriented growth. Rather, Bombardier specialized in acquiring strategic business interests from other manufacturers and incorporating them into innovative business models or continuing previously started initiatives. In 1986, Bombardier purchased Canadair, which had been the developer of the Challenger Business Jet and the twin-engine T-tail design that would become the basis for the Bombardier CRJ.[73] With funding by Bombardier, the 50-seat regional jet rolled out in 1991. The 50-seat Canadair Regional Jet (CRJ), known as the CRJ100 program, beat Embraer to market because the Brazilian company was embroiled in a financial crisis that was not resolved until the mid-1990s.

In the meantime, the Bombardier CRJ dominated the skies, enjoying first-mover advantage in a market that was previously deemed impractical for anything except turboprops (Eden, 2008). However, due to design innovations in turbo-fan engines, jets were slowly becoming economical, especially in aircraft with a 40- to 50-passenger capacity. Due to a strong consumer preference for jets over propellers, once a regional airline had successfully introduced jets in its service, the others would have to follow its lead (Eden, 2008). Therefore, once jets were introduced into the regional jet market, subsequent market growth was inevitable. To help with the certification and construction of the CRJ, Bombardier bought Short Brothers, an Irish firm that became the chief provider of sub-assemblies for the CRJ. Lufthansa was the launch customer, and the first CRJ100 was delivered in 1992. Comair, a U.S. commuter airline, was the U.S. launch customer.

The CRJ proved to be highly popular, and several versions (with extended range and fuselage elongation) were produced. When the Embraer ERJ 145 came into the market in the mid-1990s, it found itself in competition with the Bombardier CRJ, which was dominating the 50-seat market. Embraer, however, addressed itself to the 70- to 110-seat market, which was precisely between the

---

[73]Bombardier Launches C Series Jet. *New York Times*, July 13, 2008.

smallest offering of Airbus and Boeing and the market served by Bombardier (ICMR, 2007). By concentrating on this underserved segment, Embraer was able to compete viably with Bombardier, especially since the economics of the regional airline market favored a gradual increase in capacity due to economies of scale (Eden, 2008). In 1999, Bombardier developed a stretched version of the CRJ100, the CRJ700, which could seat 70 passengers. This achieved a level of commercial success comparable to that of the CRJ100, and both went on to become mainstays of regional airlines like United Express, Delta Connection, and Lufthansa CityLine.

Following its strategy of acquisition-led growth, Bombardier acquired Learjet in 1990 and used Learjet's assets to launch the innovative Flexjet program in 1995. Following the example of NetJets (1986), Bombardier entered the field of fractional jet ownership, through a mixture of owned Learjet business aircraft and subcontracted assets. Fundamentally, this differed from the charter business in that customers purchased a fraction of the aircraft and were not charged for repositioning legs. This program was extremely popular, and has been the basis for competitors like Raytheon Travel Air in 1997, renamed Flight Options. Currently, the Flexjet program offers Learjet 40 XR, Learjet 45 XR, Learjet 60 XR, and Challenger aircraft. In 1999, Flexjet started European operations, and in 2000, they acquired Skyjet, a pioneer in online charter reservations and scheduling. In 2001, Flexjet entered the Asia market.

Additionally, in 1992, Bombardier acquired the de Havilland Aircraft Company, then a subsidiary of Boeing, specializing in bush and STOL aircraft.[74] In the 1980s, de Havilland had begun to develop a 36-seat, twin-engine turboprop airplane, the Dash 8, to fill the market gap between its popular bush Twin Otter (20 seats) and the Dash 7 (50 seats). The Dash 8 had two initial versions, the Dash 8-100 and -200 (offering better performance and cruising speed over the -100), both of which met with success among regional airlines like the Austrian-based Tyrolean and the Dutch-based Schreiner. A stretched version, the -300, was later conceived, and the resulting increase in passenger capacity (and corresponding fall in cost per available seat mile) made the Dash 8 even more attractive. The -400 series was introduced shortly thereafter in 1987.

Under Bombardier's leadership, the production of all four versions of the Dash 8 was reinstated with significant improvements, including a noise and vibrations suppression system, which resulted in significant decreases in noise production. While the Dash 8 series' success was undermined to an extent by a new wave of regional jets from Embraer and Bombardier's own product line, the Dash 8 series continued to find a niche market among operators that flew relatively short-haul routes and required the excellent economies offered by this aircraft family (Eden, 2008). Once again, Bombardier's growth strategy was to acquire de Havilland at a

---

[74]Reed Business Information, UK, June 16-June 22, 2009.

strategically crucial point in Bombardier's development cycle, reinvent and remarket the purchased product, and expand its own product portfolio in the process.

In recent years, Bombardier has remained competitive in the regional jet market. Bombardier introduced the CRJ1000 NextGen, which featured flight deck improvements and an increased use of composite materials to compete in the market for large regional jets, on December 15, 2010 with inaugural delivery to Air France affiliate Brit Air. Furthermore, Bombardier has been aggressively expanding into the business jet sector. For example, in 2002, Bombardier launched the Global Business 5000, a super-large business jet and followed it up a few years later with the Global Express XRS, which offered improvements in speed and cabin size for transatlantic travel (Bombardier Aerospace, 2009). See Table 1.9 and Figure 1.11 for detailed production data.

Mitsubishi Aircraft Corporation

The Mitsubishi Regional Jet (MRJ), the first entrance of a Japanese manufacturer into the regional jet market, was a family of 70- to 90-seat next generation regional jets.[76] Total development costs were expected to be $67 million with seating for 70-90 passengers. The first mock-up was introduced at the Paris Air Show in 2007, and the product was launched in 2008. Japan's All Nippon Airways placed an order for 15 MRJs with an option for 10 more in 2008 (*Aerospace Technology*, January 2009). Mitsubishi Aircraft was a joint venture of MHI and Toyota Motor, with numerous contractors such as JAMCO, Rockwell Collins, and Spirit AeroSystems to design various parts of the jet. The other major partners included Pratt &

Table 1.9 Bombardier commercial aircraft production data

Aircraft model	Launch customer	Produced
CRJ100	Lufthansa	226
CRJ200	Northwest	709
CRJ700	Brit Air/Air France	328
CRJ900	Mesa Airlines	252
Q100	NorOntair	299
Q200	BPX Colombia	105
Q300	Time Air	267
Q400	All Nippon Airways	368
CRJ1000	Air Nostrum/Brit Air[75]	13

Source: Compiled from Bombardier aircraft production data.

---

[75]The Associated Press, June 15, 2009.
[76]Mitsubishi Aircraft News, No. 1, 2, January 13, 2010.

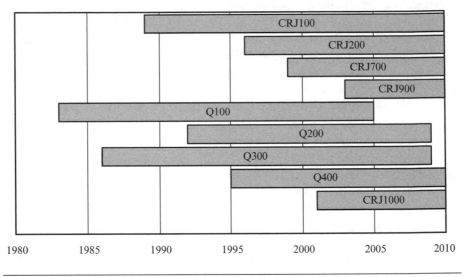

Figure 1.11 Bombardier commercial aircraft production
Source: Compiled from Bombardier aircraft production data.

Whitney, which supplied the geared turbofan engines; Parker Aerospace, which supplied the aircraft's hydraulic system; and Hamilton Sundstrand, which provided electrical power.[77]

Mitsubishi was developing six variants of the MRJ—MRJ90STD, MRJ90ER, MRJ90LR belonging to the MRJ90 class, and MRJ70STD, MRJ70ER, MRJ70LR belonging to the MRJ70 class (Mitsubishi regional jet, 2009). Once the jet was developed, it would be a direct competitor to the Embraer and Bombardier regional jets, with a strong presence in Asian and Pacific markets. Trans States Airlines was the first international customer, with an order of 100 jets, and All Nippon Airways[78] was the first domestic customer, with an order for 15 MRJ90s and an option for 10 more.[79] The MRJ was scheduled to make its first flight in 2011, but the date was delayed to 2012, with initial deliveries scheduled for 2013.[80]

Summary

The global commercial aircraft manufacturing industry has been dominated by two major manufacturers: Boeing and Airbus. In the 1960s, U.S. commercial

[77]Mitsubishi Aircraft News, No. 2, January 13, 2010.
[78]ANA Selects Mitsubishi Regional Jet, Company News.
[79]First Foreign Order for Mitsubishi Jet, 100 Planes to America.
[80]Mitsubishi Aircraft News, No. 3, September 4, 2008.

aircraft manufacturers had more than a 90% market share. Recently, Airbus has had more than a 50% market share. The industry is characterized by massive capital requirements and massive research and development costs, in the tens of billions of dollars. Therefore, the industry is distinguished by a tendency toward natural monopolies, with smaller manufacturers consolidating into larger entities in an effort to gain greater economies of scale, scope, and density.

Historically, most large commercial aircraft manufacturing is cross-subsidized by regional governments, either through direct subsidies or investments or through defense contracts that are executed by the same company. Typically, aircraft manufacturing is not as exposed to the volatilities in consumer demand as airlines or airports are. Aircraft manufacturers have highly inelastic supply schedules, since an expansion in production involves extensive capital and human resource investment. Generally, manufacturers maintain a backlog of orders that grows shorter if demand is slack and lengthens if demand is high. Therefore, production and sales are maintained at a relatively constant level.

The two main commercial aircraft manufactures at present are Boeing and Airbus for airliners with greater than 90 seats and Embraer and Bombardier for the regional jet market. Recent developments have included the emergence of the ERJ 170 and 190 series, which emerged as direct competition to the Boeing 737s, and the planned entrance of China into large commercial aircraft manufacturing. In addition, Russian commercial aircraft will gain worldwide acceptance with Western countries, and Western manufacturers will continue to expand their presence in Russia on a sub-assembly level. However, given highly inflexible cost structures, and the existence of a stable duopoly in aircraft manufacturing, neither the development of large regional jets nor the entrance of China is likely to alter the dynamics of the industry profoundly in the short term. Aircraft manufacturing will always remain a technological and capital-intensive undertaking, and the high switching costs associated with aircraft purchases can imply that most airlines will continue to face a monopoly supplier.

References

757 Program. (2009). Commercial airlines. *The Boeing Company*. Retrieved from http://www.boeing.com/commercial/757family/index.html.

About us. (2009). *Bombardier Aerospace*. Retrieved from http://www.bombardier .com/en/aerospace/about-aerospace?docID=0901260d8000daa7.

The Airbus story. (2008). History. *Airbus S.A.S.* Retrieved from http://www.airbus .com/en/corporate/people/company_evolution/history.

Aircraft data. (2011). *Airliners.net*. Retrieved from http://www.airliners.net/ aircraft-data/.

Aris, S. (2004). *Close to the sun: How Airbus challenged America's domination of the skies*. Chicago: Agate.

ASN Aviation Safety Database. (2009). *Aviation Safety Network*. Retrieved from http://aviation-safety.net/database/dblist.php?Type=352.

Badrocke, M., & Guston, B. (1999). *From Cloudster to Boeing: The illustrated history of McDonnell Douglas aircraft*. Osprey Publishing Limited.

The Boeing 747-8 family: A proud tradition of value continues. (2009). Commercial airlines: 747 family. *The Boeing Company*. Retrieved from http://www.boeing .com/commercial/747family/747-8_background.html.

Bombardier Aerospace. (2009). Retrieved from http://www.bombardier.com/en/ aerospace.

Civil aircraft today: The world's most successful commerical aircraft: 1903-2003. (2004). *Erudition*. Retrieved from http://www.eruditiononline.com/06.04/ aviation_lockheed_bros.

Comprehensive index of historical products. (2009). *The Boeing Company*. Retrieved from http://www.boeing.com/history/master_index.html.

DC-6/C-118 Liftmaster Transport. (2009). *The Boeing Company*. Retrieved from http://www.boeing.com/history/mdc/dc-6.htm.

DC-7 Commercial Transport. (2009). *The Boeing Company*. Retrieved from http://www.boeing.com/history/mdc/dc-7.htm.

DC-8 Commercial Transport. (2009). History: Products. *The Boeing Company*. Retrieved from http://www.boeing.com/history/mdc/dc-8.htm.

Eden, P. E. (2008). *Civil aircraft today: The world's most successful commercial aircraft*. London, UK: Amber Books.

Fleet and order status. (2011). Fact files. *The Emirates Group*. http://www.thee miratesgroup.com/english/media-kit/fact-files.aspx.

The Fokker heritage 1911-2009. (2009). *Fokker history*. Retrieved from http:// www.fokker.com/frp-History.

Gunston, B. (1988). *Airbus*. Osceola, WI: Osprey.

Greenwald, J., Hannifin, J. & Kane, J. (December 21,1981). Catch a Falling Tristar. *Time*.

Heritage of innovation. (2009). History. *The Boeing Company*. Retrieved from http://www.boeing.com/history/narrative/n001intro.html.

ICAO traffic data. (2010). *International Civil Aviation Organization*. Retrieved from http://icaodata.com/.

Ingells, D. J. (1968). *Tin Goose: The fabulous Ford Tri-Motor*. Fallbrook, CA: Aero Publishers.

International Civil Aviation Organization (ICMR). (2007). Embraer: The Brazilian aircraft manufacturer's turnaround and growth. *Collection of Case Studies.* 31.

Investor relations. (2009). *Stork N.V. Investor Relations.* Retrieved from http://www.stork.com/page.html?ch=DEF&id=1242.

Kaminshi-Morrow, D., & Fafard, A. (2011). World airliner census. *Flightglobal,* 27. Retrieved from http://www.flightglobal.com/features/census-2011/.

Karlsson, M. (1998). History—L-1011. Retrieved from http://home4.swipnet .se/~w-48037/l1011history.htm.

Kay, A. L., & Couper, P. (2004). *Junkers aircraft and engines, 1913-1945.* London: Putnam Aeronautical Books.

Larkins, W. T. (2007). *The Ford Tri-Motor, 1926-1992.* West Chester, PA: Schiffer Publishing.

MD-11 Commercial Transport. (2009). History: Products. *The Boeing Company.* Retrieved from http://www.boeing.com/history/mdc/md-11.htm%22.

MD-80 and MD-90 Commercial Transports. (2009). History: Products. *The Boeing Company.* Retrieved from http://www.boeing.com/history/mdc/md-80md-90 .htm.

Mitsubishi regional jet. (2009). *aerospace-technology.com.* Retrieved from http://www.aerospace-technology.com/projects/mitsubishi-jet/.

Model 10 Electra. (2009). History. *The Lockheed Martin Corporation.* Retrieved from http://www.lockheedmartin.com/aboutus/history/Model10Electra. html.

Norris, G., & Wagner, M. (1998). *Boeing.* Osceola, WI: MBI Publishing.

Orders and delivers. (2011). *The Boeing Company Commercial Airplanes.* Retrieved from http://active.boeing.com/commercial/orders/index.cfm? content=displaystandardreport.cfm&pageid=m25065&RequestTimeout= 20000.

Reuland, R. S., Inc., A.S.A. (1991). Pusher turboprop installation technology for the Embraer CBA-123 Vector. Paper presented at the General, Corporate and Regional Aviation Meeting and Exposition, Wichita, KS.

Sandler, T., & Hartley, K. (2007). *Handbook of defense economics: Defense in a globalized world, 2.* North Holland.

Schedule tapes for June 2009. (2009). Official airline guide (OAG) BACKOffice schedules. *Official Airline Guide (OAG).*

Sedaei, S. (2006). Commercial aircraft industry. *Lux Esto Law Review, 2*(1), 7.

Southwest.com. (2009). Retreived from http://www.southwest.com/.

SR-71 Blackbird. (2009). *The Lockheed Martin history.* Retrieved from http://www
.lockheedmartin.com/aboutus/history/SR71Blackbird.html.

Stork Technical Services annual report. (2007). Retrieved from http://www.stork
.nl/d/STCf/Stork JV2007 ENG.pdf.

2

Aircraft Variants and Manufacturing Specifications

We built a [727] jet airplane to get in and out of a 5,000-ft field. No one believed it could be done...

It wasn't until the jet engine came into being and that engine was coupled with special airplane designs—such as the swept wing—that airplanes finally achieved a high enough work capability, efficiency and comfort level to allow air transportation to really take off.

—Joseph F. Sutter, Boeing Commercial Airplanes

Choosing the correct aircraft is crucial to ensuring reliable and profitable operations. Airlines have developed a comprehensive range of models that allows them to assess the financial impact of using different aircraft. Several attributes of an aircraft, including the aircraft price; operating cost and revenue estimates; aircraft operational specifications such as range, payload, speed, and fuel efficiency; and the potential revenue from ticket sales and non-ticket revenue, are used to assess the value of an aircraft to a particular airline. Additionally, macroeconomic factors such as economic and population growth, the future air transport demand, as well as other exogenous factors such as air transport liberalization, privatization, passenger bills-of-rights, regulations and deregulations, legal restrictions, and labor restrictions are critical to aircraft selection and valuation.

The financial and physical specifications of the commercial jetliners currently in service differ for each manufacturer and for each narrow-body and wide-body aircraft. Airlines utilize this, as well as other data, in order to determine the type of aircraft they are going to acquire.

This chapter presents the general, physical, and operating metrics for a variety of airline models in order to provide a roadmap for valuation. The chapter is organized as follows:

Boeing Commercial Aircraft

- Boeing Existing Fleet
- Boeing Retired Fleet
- Comparative Analysis of the Boeing Aircraft Family

Airbus Commercial Aircraft

- General Characteristics of the Fleet
- Physical Characteristics of the Fleet
- Operational Characteristics of the Fleet
- Comparative Analysis of the Airbus Aircraft Family

McDonnell Douglas Commercial Aircraft

- General Characteristics of the Fleet
- Physical Characteristics of the Fleet
- Operational Characteristics of the Fleet
- Comparative Analysis of the McDonnell Douglas Aircraft Family

Lockheed

- Commercial Aircraft Characteristics

Regional Jets

- Embraer
- Bombardier

At the end of the chapter is a Summary for chapter review and References for further study.

Boeing Commercial Aircraft

Airlines develop a comprehensive range of models that allows for thorough assessment of the financial effects of different aircraft. This is the heart of airline fleet planning—a detailed model, incorporating the aircraft price, operating cost estimates, and aircraft operational specifications such as range, payload, speed, and potential revenue. Fuel and labor costs are, by a significant margin, the largest single cost of operating an aircraft. Nonetheless, macroeconomic factors such as economic and population growth, and future air transport demand, are critical to aircraft selection and pricing.

The recent fuel crisis and the global recession prompted a dramatic drop in load factors, beginning in the middle of 2008. In response, airlines took aircraft out of service and rethought plans to order replacements for existing planes. Airlines have taken at least 2,000 aircraft out of their fleets since October 2009, while aircraft manufacturers have only produced 1,000 new aircraft during the same period.[1] Commercial aircraft prices dropped by an average of 20% and older aircraft dropped by as much as 35%.[2]

Since its entry into the large jet market in 1954, Boeing produced both narrow- and wide-body jets, each with several variants and specifications. Choosing the appropriately sized aircraft is an extremely important and complicated process for every airline. The majority of low-cost airlines' business models are based on a single passenger class on a single type of aircraft. Ryanair, for example, operates only the narrow-body Boeing 737 aircraft on over 850 routes across Europe and North Africa.[3] The airline's fleet reached 272 aircraft for the first time in June 2011.[4] Commonly used aircraft for low-cost carriers like Ryanair include members of the Airbus A320 or Boeing 737 families, which reduces training, inventory, and servicing costs. Narrow-body aircraft are also more suitable for short-haul markets and enable faster enplanement and deplanement than wide-body aircraft.

Boeing Existing Fleet

Nearly 4,500 out-of-production aircraft are still in service throughout the world, either as passenger airliners or freighters, with an active secondary market for used aircraft. Only the Boeing 737 Next Generation (NG)—the 747, 767, 777, and 787s—are in production. The newest, the 787, is a twin-engine jet airliner, with its inaugural delivery to Japan's ANA and entry into commercial operations in 2011. Boeing commercial aircraft range from 110 seats (in the Boeing 737NG models in mixed configuration) to 550 seats (Boeing 747, high-density configuration). The 787 seats between 210 and 290 passengers, using 20% less fuel than any other airplanes of its size, targeted at the market between narrow- and wide-body aircraft while providing extended range and greater fuel efficiency.[5]

---

[1] Woes of Aircraft Leasing Companies Could Mean Higher Ticket Price, *New York Times*, October 6, 2009.

[2] Ibid.

[3] http://www.ryanair.com/site/about/invest/docs/2010/q1_2010_doc.pdf.

[4] http://www.ryanair.com/doc/investor/2011/q4_2011_doc.pdf.

[5] Boeing Commercial Airplanes, 2011.

General Characteristics of the In-production Fleet

The general characteristics of Boeing's in-production commercial aircraft from the 737NG to the 787, which had its maiden flight in December of 2009, are outlined in Table 2.1. The development cycle of commercial aircraft typically begins with the creation of a base aircraft model from which variants with unique range, seating, power plant, capacity, and other characteristics are developed. Boeing has produced five narrow-body (not including MD-80/90 models) and four wide-body aircraft base models since its entry into commercial jet aircraft manufacturing. The base models are divided into variants with varying operational, physical, and technical specifications. For example, the Boeing 737 base model has several variants including the 737-100, -200, -300, -400, and -500 (Classic) and 737-600, -700, -800, and -900 (NG).

The Boeing 737NG continues to build on the base model's strength as the most popular (and only) Boeing narrow-body aircraft design in production for both orders and deliveries and number in service,[6] with the second being the Boeing 757. During 23 years of production, Boeing produced 1,049 757s, with 1,030 still in service. The newest 747 variant, the 747-8 Intercontinental, is more than 10% lighter per seat than the Airbus A380 and consumes 11% less fuel per passenger. The 747 family stands as Boeing's top-selling wide-body aircraft, with 1,369 deliveries as of July 2011. A close second in the wide-body category is the 767 family, with 1,005 aircraft delivered as of July 2011.

Physical Characteristics of the In-production Fleet

The main physical characteristics of the Boeing commercial aircraft in production are shown in Table 2.2. In-production Boeing aircraft operate with Pratt & Whitney, General Electric, CFM, and Rolls-Royce variants for the various aircraft types. Similar to the commonality benefits of operating the same aircraft model, a common engine type across aircraft models and variants provides maintenance, time, and cost savings benefits to airlines utilizing more than one aircraft model.

Boeing aircraft offer a significant variety of capacity types, catering to the needs of a wide range of commercial aircraft operators. The smallest member of the 737NG family, the 737-600, can carry 110 to 132 passengers. The largest of the 737NG family, the 737-900, can carry up to 180 passengers in a two-class layout, compared to the highest density capacity available of a 568-seat 747-400. The 737NG incorporates a new wing design that helps increase fuel capacity and efficiency, both of which increase range. The new wing area is also 25% greater, thereby providing 30% more fuel capacity.[7]

---

[6] As of July 2011, orders for the Boeing 737NG were 5,862, with 3,716 deliveries.
[7] Boeing 737NG Technical Specifications.

Table 2.1 Boeing in-production aircraft general characteristics

Model	Type	Variant	First flight	Major operators	Total ordered	Total delivered	Total in world air traffic fleet
737	Narrow-body	-600	22-Jan-98	SAS/WestJet/Tunis Air	69	69	69
		-700	9-Feb-97	Southwest/WestJet/AirTran	1,518	1,193	1,019
		-800	31-Jul-97	Southwest/WestJet/AirTran	3,908	2,303	1,915
		-900	3-Aug-00	Alaska/Continental/Lion Airlines	367	151	123
		-8	–	Lufthansa	36	–	–
747	Wide-body	-8F	8-Feb-10	Cargolux	78	–	
		-200ER	6-Mar-84	El Al	121	121	773
		-300ER/-300F	30-Jan-86	Japan/Delta/American	662	614	
767	Wide-body	-400ER	9-Oct-99	Continental	38	38	
		-200/-200ER/-200LR	12-Jun-94	United/American/Singapore	572	555	554
777	Wide-body	-300/-300ER	16-Oct-97	Cathay Pacific/Emirates	574	350	280
		F	14-Jul-08	Air France	96	44	23
787	Wide-body	-8	15-Dec-09	ANA	561	1	1
		-9	–	–	266	–	

Source: Boeing Commercial Products data.

Table 2.2 Boeing in-production aircraft physical characteristics

Model	Variant	Wingspan	Length	Capacity: mixed	Capacity: high density	Power plant manufacturer	# of engines
737	-600/-700/-800/-900 (NG)	112' 7"–117' 5"	102' 6"–138' 2"	110	215	CFM International	2
747	-400/-400F	211' 5"	231' 10"	416	568	Pratt & Whitney, General Electric, Rolls-Royce	4
	-8	224' 7"	250' 8"		467		4
767	-200/-200ER	156' 1"	159' 2"	181	255	Pratt & Whitney, General Electric	2
	-300/-300ER/-300F	156' 1"	180' 3"	218	350	Pratt & Whitney, General Electric	2
	-400ER	170' 4"	201' 4"	245	375	Pratt & Whitney, General Electric	2
777	-200/-200ER/-200LR/-200F	199' 11"–212' 7"	209' 1"	301	440	777-200 Pratt & Whitney, General Electric, Rolls-Royce; 777-200LR General Electric	2
	-300/-300ER	199' 11"–212' 7"	242' 4"	365	550	777-300 Pratt & Whitney, General Electric, Rolls-Royce; 777-300ER General Electric	2
787	-8	197'	186'	210	250	General Electric, Rolls-Royce	2
	-9	197'	206'	250	290		

The Boeing 757 was produced in two fuselage lengths: the 757-200 entered service in 1983 and the stretched 757-300 entered service in 1999, with each having a maximum range of 5,700 to 7,200 km. The 757-200 was designed to carry 200 passengers in a typical mixed-class configuration, putting it between the 737-900 and 757-300 in terms of capacity. The 757-200 and twin-aisle 767 were developed concurrently, accounting for significant similarities between the models. The aircraft are so similar that a common type rating exists for the 757 and 767; flight crews trained on either model are permitted to fly the other.

A key issue in early Boeing 767 operations was proving the aircraft's reliability for overseas operations. The 767 can be equipped with special features to enable it to fly extended-range operations in remote areas. Prior to the 767, the FAA restricted twin-engine aircraft to over-water flights of 90 minutes or less distance from diversion airports. The 767 was the main competitor of the Airbus A310. The first 767 accommodated seven-abreast seating in the economy class (2-3-2) compared to the eight-abreast interior of the A310. The aircraft was designed based on fly-by-wire controls, glass cockpit, flexible interior, and 10% better seat mile costs than the A330 and MD-11. The 767-400ER flight deck instrument panel has 82% fewer parts than other 767s, driving production time down from 180 hours to only 20 hours. The aircraft was the first Boeing aircraft to be stretched twice; the 767-400ER is 21 feet longer than the 767-300, which is 21 feet longer than the original 767-200. Size-wise, the 767 fits the gap between the 737NG and 777 aircraft as it is four feet wider than single-aisle jetliners, allowing five-, six-, seven- or eight-abreast seating. In a typical three-class seating of 181 to 245 passengers, there are five-abreast first class, six-abreast business class, and seven-abreast economy class seats.[8]

The Boeing 777 is a long-range aircraft that seats from 301 to 368 passengers, with a range from 9,695 to 17,370 km, produced in two fuselage lengths. The 777-200 variants are 209 feet compared to the 242-foot 777-300 variants. The 777 is the world's largest twin-jet and is powered by two PW4090 turbofans, Trent 892 GE90-92Bs, or PW4098s. Since its entry into service in June 1995, Boeing expanded the 777 family to five passenger models and a freighter version.

Other Boeing aircraft and variants purposefully and competitively fill in the gap between the highest capacity available and the lowest. For example, the Boeing 767-400ER has a 375-seat capacity, halfway between that offered by the 737NG and the 747-400. The newest member of the 747 family (747-8) fits the seat market between the 555-seat Airbus A380 and 365-seat Boeing 777-300.

Operational Characteristics of the In-production Fleet

Table 2.3 lists some of the major operational characteristics of Boeing aircraft. Since the time of the 737, the industry (and therefore the manufacturer's) focus has

---

[8] Boeing 767 Family Technical and Production Facts.

Table 2.3 Boeing in-production aircraft operational characteristics

Model	Variant	Max. takeoff weight (lbs)	Cruising speed (mph)	Fuel capacity (U.S. gallons)	Range (nm)	Max. altitude (Ft)	Total flying cost per block hour ($)	Total maintenance cost per block hour ($)	Total cost per block hour ($)	Average flight stage length (miles)
737	-600/-700/-800/-900 (NG)	145,500-187,700	514	6,875-7,837	2,700-5,510	41,000	2,242	400	3,075	1,051
747	-400/-400F	875,000-910,000	567	53,735-57,285	4,445-7,670	N/A	8,104	1,363	10,456	4,663
	-8	970,000	567	60,211	4,420-8,000	43,000	–	–	–	–
767	-200/-200ER	395,000	530	23,980	3,950-6,590	N/A	3,736	678	4,873	2,721
	-300ER/-300F	412,000	530	23,980	3,255-5,975	N/A	4,282	828	5,829	2,918
	-400ER	450,000	530	23,980	5,625	N/A	4,624	790	5,922	3,015
777	-200/-200ER/-200LR/-200F	545,000-766,000	615	31,000-45,220	5,235-9,380	43,100	5,677	1,492	8,074	4,180
	-300/-300ER	660,000-775,000	615	45,220	6,015-7,930	43,100	–	–	–	–
787	-8	502,500	561	33,528	7,650-8,200	43,000	–	–	–	–
	-9	545,000	561	36,641	8,000-8,500	43,000	–	–	–	–

Source: Boeing aircraft data.

been on producing more fuel-efficient aircraft rather than continuous increases in cruising speed or range. The Boeing 747 represented the first real speed/range increase over the out-of-production 707, albeit in a completely different market: the wide-body jetliner market.

Continuous improvements in the 747 program, with the emerging 747-8, promised even more efficiency as well as greater speeds and ranges—a capacity of over 60,000 gallons resulting in a range up to 8,000 nm.[9] The 747-8 also has seat-mile costs that are 13% lower than for the 747-400, with 2% lower trip costs. The 747-8 Intercontinental is also more than 10% lighter per seat than the Airbus A380 and consumes 11% less fuel per passenger. Similarly, the 777 was designed as the most advanced Boeing aircraft of its time, outperforming the Classic versions of the 747 in terms of efficiency and range, although smaller in capacity. Although the Boeing 767 appears to have the lowest operating and flying cost per block hour, it is considerably limited in range compared to the 777.

The Boeing 787 program continued a trend of producing fuel-efficient aircraft amid a global aircraft market that tended to favor efficiency over speed. The 787-8 with its 8,000- to 8,500-nm range has the ability to replace aging, less efficient aircraft on long-haul routes such as Los Angeles-Bangkok by carrying 210 to 250 passengers at a cruising speed of 0.85 Mach with 20% greater fuel efficiency and lower emission levels compared to other available aircraft. The next 787 model to be developed, dubbed the 787-9, is expected to seat between 250 and 290 passengers.[10]

Boeing Retired Fleet

Some of Boeing's most successful and pioneering commercial aircraft products, including the successful Boeing 737 Classic family, have gone out of production. Despite this, all Boeing aircraft models built since the 707 remain in service in various capacities around the world. The most recently retired commercial aircraft models are the 757-200 and -300 families. Boeing's decision to retire narrow-body aircraft models has historically been based on dwindling aircraft sales and orders.

General Characteristics of the Out-of-production Fleet

The general characteristics of Boeing's out-of-production aircraft from the 707 to the 757 are given in Table 2.4. Of the five Boeing narrow-body base models developed, four are out of production (with the exception of the Boeing 737 base model

---

[9] *nm* is the abbreviation for nautical mile. By international agreement, it is set at exactly 1,852 meters.

[10] Boeing 787 Technical Information.

Table 2.4 Boeing out-of-production aircraft general characteristics

Model	Type	Variant	In/Out of production	First flight	Major operators	Total ordered	Total delivered	Total in world air traffic fleet
707	Narrow-body		Out of production	20-Dec-57	Pan American Airways	1,010	1,010	121
717	Narrow-body		Out of production	2-Sep-98	AirTran	155	155	155
727	Narrow-body	-100/-100C	Out of production	9-Feb-63	United Airlines	571	571	117
		-200/-200F	Out of production	27-Jul-67	Delta Air Lines	1,260	1,260	526
737	Narrow-body	-100/-200/-200C/-300/-400/-500 (Classic)	Out of production	24-Feb-84	Lufthansa/United Airlines/Southwest Airlines/Malaysia Airlines/Continental Airlines	3,113	3,113	2,520
		-600/-700/-800/-900 (NG)	In production	9-Feb-97	SAS/Southwest Airlines/Korean Air/Lion Air	5,225	3,149	2,628
757	Narrow-body	-200/-200M/-200PF	Out of production	19-Feb-82	American Airlines/Nepal Air/UPS	994	994	1,021
		-300		2-Aug-98	Northwest Airlines	55	55	

Source: Boeing Commercial Products data.

from which the Boeing 737NG was developed). It can be noted from Table 2.4 that each out-of-production aircraft family sold at least 1,000 individual units, except for the Boeing 717. The Boeing 717 was originally part of the McDonnell Douglas family, designated as the MD-95, prior to the 1997 merger. However, despite weak Boeing 717 sales, all 155 aircraft produced remain in service worldwide.

Physical Characteristics of the Out-of-production Fleet

The physical characteristics of Boeing's out-of-production aircraft are outlined in Table 2.5, showing evidence of Boeing (and the industry's) move toward creating more efficient aircraft with lower operating costs. The first commercial Boeing 707 carried 189 passengers with four engines. In comparison, the 727-200 had the same capacity, but reduced the number of engines to three. When further compared to the later 757 models, which supported 100 more passengers with two engines, it can be inferred that Boeing aircraft and engines became more efficient and powerful.

Operational Characteristics of the Out-of-production Fleet

The first point of interest in Table 2.6 is that no current out-of-production Boeing aircraft had achieved any significant increase in speed since the Boeing 707. The oldest Boeing commercial jetliner, the 707, had a range of 3,735-5,000 nm with a fuel capacity of 23,000 gallons. In comparison, the Boeing 757 family would achieve a range of 3,395-3,900 nm with a capacity of 11,466-11,489 gallons.

Table 2.5 Boeing out-of-production aircraft physical characteristics

Model	Variant	Wingspan	Length	Capacity: mixed	Capacity: high density	Power plant manufacturer	Number of engines
707		145' 9"	152' 11"	141	189	Pratt & Whitney	4
717		93' 3"	124'	106	117	Rolls-Royce	2
727	-100/ -100C	108'	133' 2"	94	131	Pratt & Whitney	3
	-200	108"	153' 2"	148	189	Pratt & Whitney	3
737	-300/ -400/ -500 (Classic)	94' 9"- 102' 5"	101' 9"- 119' 7"	128-108	138-149	CFM International	2
757	-200	124' 10"	155' 3"	200	228	Pratt & Whitney Rolls-Royce	2
	-300	124' 10"	178' 7"	243	280	Pratt & Whitney Rolls-Royce	2

Table 2.6 Boeing out-of-production aircraft operational characteristics

Model	Variant	Max. takeoff weight (lbs)	Cruising speed (mph)	Fuel capacity (U.S. gallons)	Range (nm)	Max. altitude (ft)	Total flying cost per block hour ($)	Total maintenance cost per block hour ($)	Total cost per block hour ($)	Average flight stage length (miles)
707		336,000	607	23,000	3,735-5,000	36,000				
717		110,000-121,000	504	3,673	1,430-2,060	N/A	1,888	466	2,930	569
727	-100/-100C	170,000	570	7,680	3,110	36,100	1,288	617	1,938	680
	-200/-200 Adv	191,000-210,000	570-605	10,570	1,500-2,500	40,000	4,290	1,046	5,615	1,115
737	-300/-400/-500 (Classic)	116,000-150,500	485	5,331-6,295	2,270-2,402	37,000	2,113	708	3,283	617
757	-200	255,000	500	11,489	3,900	42,000	2,867	946	4,335	1,398
	-300	272,500	500	11,466	3,395	42,000	3,145	902	4,604	1,477

Therefore, while the aircraft do not appear to have gotten much faster in absolute terms, they did become massively more efficient.

Comparative Analysis of the Boeing Aircraft Family

The 707 was the first narrow-body jet to be produced in 1953. It is currently out of production. It was the fastest aircraft as well as the longest range aircraft in the narrow-body market until the advent of the 737s, and even then, it was only out-performed in efficiency. It would not be until the 737NGs entered production that the 707 would be outperformed entirely.

The Boeing 717 was originally a McDonnell Douglas designed aircraft and competed in the 100-seat market. The 717 was designed to replace older DC-9s and competed against the Fokker 100, Airbus A319, and smaller versions of Boeing's own 737. The 727 was designed to compete against the similar de Havilland Trident and replace propeller-driven aircraft on short- and medium-haul routes. Boeing developed two versions of the 727, the original -100 and a stretched version, the -200. In addition to being popular with passenger airlines, the 727 became popular with cargo airlines as a freighter and was used by carriers such as FedEx and UPS.

The 727 was a tremendous success for Boeing. It was the world's best-selling jetliner until surpassed by 737 sales, and it went out of production in 1984 with 1,832 units delivered (Eden, 2006). Out of these, 643 were still in service as of December 2009.

The Boeing 737 nearly never happened, as the company contemplated pulling the twin-engine jetliner before production began, when Eastern decided to order the DC-9 instead (Eden, 2006). Boeing, however, moved forward with the project and developed the 737 to compete in the 100-seat short-haul passenger aircraft market; the early versions of the 737 (-100, -200) began to take flight in 1967.

The 737 then became the best-selling commercial aircraft in history with over 7,000 orders. The 737NG replaced the 737 Classic series, which included the 737-300, -400 and -500, with longer range and improved performance. Over 5,000 orders were placed for the 737NG since its introduction in 1997 (Boeing Company, 2009j).

The 737NGs represented the first leap in fuel efficiency, since they achieved nearly two-thirds of the range of the 707 with a quarter as much fuel capacity. After the Pratt & Whitney JT8D-powered -100 and -200 series, later 737s were powered by two CFM International engines. The twin-engine narrow-body design, combined with innovations in propulsion and aircraft design, gave the 737s unique advantages in the low-cost market. The advent of the 737 also marked the beginning of viable low-cost carriers such as Southwest Airlines.

The 757 was developed alongside the 767 during the late 1970s and early 1980s. After originally designing another stretch version of the 727 design, Boeing decided on a twin-engine, instead of a tri-engine, aircraft in order to improve fuel efficiency. The fuselage remained the same width as the 727 and 737 and featured cockpit commonality with the 767 (Eden, 2006). This cockpit commonality allowed pilots to fly both the 757 and 767 under one type certificate—a large advantage for airlines in achieving labor cost savings. The last 757 was produced in 2004, although most of the 1,021 sold remain in service today (Airline Monitor, 2008).

The Boeing 747 was developed in the mid-1960s, following a failure to obtain a U.S. military contract for a large jet transport—a contract that eventually went to Lockheed's C-5 Galaxy. However, the research and development that was conducted as part of a military transport aircraft was reapplied toward a high-capacity, four-engine civilian jetliner that was capable of servicing high-traffic routes both domestically and internationally. The 747-100's first flight occurred on February 9, 1969, and it entered commercial use in 1970. This aircraft altered the economics of long-haul commercial air transportation. Boeing delivered 250 of the 747-100s, the last in 1986. Subsequent variants included the Boeing 747-200 with a stretched upper deck, the immensely popular extended-range Boeing 747-400, and the 747SP, which is a shortened version of the 747 with a longer range. The 747 represented a significant improvement in range, speeds, and fuel efficiency; it was two and a half times the size of the Boeing 707 and achieved longer ranges with greater fuel efficiency than its predecessor. It presented a viable long-range, high-capacity commercial airline to service transatlantic and intercontinental American routes.

After the 747 became established as the market standard for wide-body, long-range aircraft, Boeing recognized the need for a medium-haul wide-body. Airbus was targeting that particular market with its A300, and in response, Boeing developed the twin-engine 767 wide-body. The extended-range (ER) versions of the 767 would provide greater range than the A310, an advantage that many airlines appreciated.

The Boeing 777 was designed in the early 1990s as the most technologically-advanced aircraft in Boeing's portfolio. New features in the 777 included a large-scale use of composites, fly-by-wire technology, and a five-screen integrated glass flight deck. New design variants are constantly being developed, such as the 777LR, which will have a range of 16,417 km. The 777 is a popular aircraft which fills the wide-body space between the Boeing 767 and the 747. Since the introduction of this aircraft, 949 aircraft were delivered and a total of 1,242 orders placed as of July 2011.[11]

Boeing's 787 represented a new technological and manufacturing frontier in aircraft manufacturing. The maiden flight took place on December 15, 2009. By then, the order backlog was 851 aircraft, making it the fastest selling aircraft

---

[11] Boeing, Orders and Deliveries, August, 2011.

in history. The Boeing 787 features an all-composite construction with a 210- to 300-passenger seating capacity. It is also the first aircraft to be built primarily by outsourcing and assembly; the parts were outsourced to independent contractors and later assembled at the Boeing plant in Everett, WA. This resulted in leaner manufacturing techniques and lower costs.[12] One of the main benefits offered by the 787 to airliners is in fuel efficiency; the materials, structure, design, and power plant improvements will serve to make it about 20% more efficient than the 767, according to Boeing estimates.[13] In April 2004, All Nippon Airways (ANA) became the launch customer for the 787 Dreamliner by ordering 50 aircraft with an option for 50 more. By August 2011, 827 Boeing 787s had been ordered by 59 airlines. Boeing had originally planned for a first flight by the end of August 2007 and to enter service in May 2008. The project encountered many delays and was more than three years behind schedule. The FAA on August 26, 2011 approved certification of the 787 and ANA took delivery of the first unit later that year.

Airbus Commercial Aircraft

Airbus commercial jetliners include the A300, A310, A320 family, A330, A340, A380, and the proposed A350XWB. Airbus planes span about the same range of size and capabilities as Boeing jetliners, making competition for an airline's business intense. In the late 1990s, Airbus overtook Boeing in market share, and the two companies have competed evenly since then. Figure 2.1 outlines the market share in terms of orders between Boeing and Airbus during 1989-2010. Figure 2.2 exhibits the market share in terms of deliveries.

The two companies tend to move in lockstep with each other, generally trading places in terms of market share every few years. This is expected to continue as Boeing and Airbus generate similar products for the future. The Airbus A320neo improves upon the best-selling A319, A320, and A321, providing two newer jet engine choices: CFM International's LEAP-X and the PW1100G PurePower from Pratt & Whitney. The newer engines generate a 15% reduction in fuel consumption while adding 500 nm of range, which equates to 16% less fuel burn per seat compared to the Boeing winglet-equipped 737-800. Entry into service for the Airbus A320neo is scheduled to start in October 2015, followed by the A319neo and then the A321neo.[14] The A320neo has won more than 1,000 orders and commitments since its launch in December 2010.

Boeing's latest aircraft redesign, the Boeing MAX family, builds upon the best-selling 737NG family, replacing it with more fuel-efficient CFM International LEAP-1B engines. The Boeing MAX 7, MAX 8, and MAX 9 are based on the

---

[12] Boeing's Big Dream. *Fortune Magazine*, May 5, 2008, p. 182.
[13] Norris, Guy. (September 1, 2009). Boeing rules out 787 window change. *Aviation Week*.
[14] Airbus. (2011). A320neo Aircraft Information.

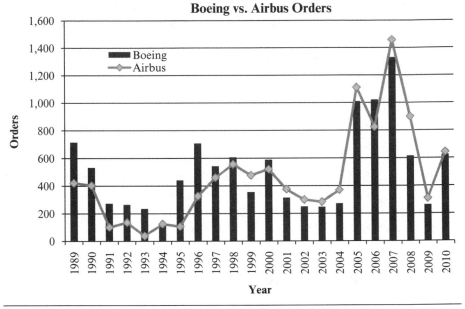

Figure 2.1 Market share in terms of orders between Boeing and Airbus
Source: Compiled from Airbus and Boeing order data.

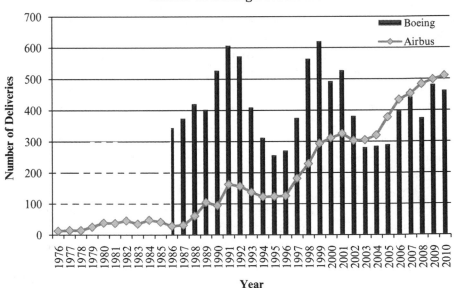

Figure 2.2 Market share in terms of deliveries between Boeing and Airbus
Source: Compiled from Boeing and Airbus delivery data.

737-700, 737-800, and 737-900, respectively. The Boeing MAX is stated to give a 7% greater fuel reduction than the A320neo, with deliveries expected in 2017, two years after the Airbus A320neo.[15]

General Characteristics of the Fleet

Some of the general characteristics of Airbus commercial aircraft are outlined in Table 2.7. Airbus has produced only one narrow-body family, the strong-selling A320 family. The rest of Airbus families of aircraft have been wide-bodied aircraft. The first Airbus wide-body model, the A300, was later developed into the A310 and is the only Airbus aircraft model out of production. More than 600 A300s and A310s were still in service as of February 2010 (Airbus S.A.S., 2012). The next wide-body family that Airbus developed was the A330 and A340, with over 1,000 of those two models still in service. Airbus' newest models are the twin-deck A380 and the in-development A350.

Physical Characteristics of the Fleet

Table 2.8 shows a comparison of the major physical characteristics of Airbus commercial aircraft. The out-of-production aircraft, like the A300 and A310, used solely General Electric and Pratt & Whitney engines while later models, such as the A320 and A340, utilized primarily CFM International and Rolls-Royce engines. The Airbus A320 family is significantly shorter in terms of length and wingspan than the other Airbus aircraft models available, accentuating the variety offered by Airbus. The shortest member of the family, the A318, is approximately 90 feet shorter in both length and wingspan than the next available family of aircraft, the A330 family. The cornerstone of the A320 family, the A320, accommodates 150 passengers in a typical two-class arrangement and up to 180 passengers with high-density seating. The stretched-fuselage A321 version seats 185 passengers in the two-class layout and up to 220 passengers for a high-density cabin.

The A330 base models and their variants cover a significant portion of the commercial aircraft market. The A330-300 carries 300 passengers on routes of up to 6,000 nm while the shorter A330-200 accommodates 250 passengers on routes of up to 7,230 nm. True to an Airbus commitment to commonality in aircraft design, the A330-200 and A330-300 are nearly identical, except for length and the A330-300's activated center tank and extended fin and rudder.[16] The A340 comes in four versions with four fuselage lengths; this range of lengths makes the seating capacity of this family of aircraft vary between 240 to 349 passengers, in two-class cabin configurations, with a range of 9,000 nm.[17]

---

[15] Boeing. (August 30, 2011). Press release: Boeing introduces 737 MAX with launch of new aircraft family.

[16] Airbus A330 Technical Specifications.

[17] Airbus A340 Technical Specifications.

Table 2.7 Airbus aircraft general characteristics

Model	Type	Variant	In/out of production	First flight	Major operators	Total ordered	Total delivered	Total in world air traffic fleet
A300	Wide-body	-B2/-B4/-600/ -600F/-600ST	Out	28-Oct-72	Asiana Airlines	561	561	385
A310		-200/-200F/-300	Out	3-Apr-82	FedEx/Air Transat/Air India/	255	255	205
A320	Narrow-body	-318/-319/-319CJ/ -320/-321	In	22-Feb-87	US Airways/EasyJet/ United/Air France	7,692	4,760	4,671
A330		-200/-200F/-300	In	2-Nov-92	Delta/Cathay Pacific/ Qatar/Emirates	1,155	802	797
A340	Wide-body	-200/-300/-500/-600	In	25-Oct-91	Lufthansa/Iberia/Virgin Atlantic/South African	379	375	367
A350		-800/-900/-1000	Development	2012 (est.)	N/A	567	–	–
A380	Double-deck, wide-body	-700/-800-800F/-900	In	27-Apr-05	Emirates/Singapore/ Qantas	236	53	53

Source: Compiled from Airbus production data.

Table 2.8 Airbus aircraft physical characteristics

Model	Variant	Wingspan	Length	Capacity: mixed	Capacity: high density	Power plant manufacturer	Number of engines
A300	-B2/-B4	147' 1"	175' 11"	250	336	General Electric, Pratt & Whitney	2
A300	-600/-600F	147' 1"	177' 5"	266	298	General Electric, Pratt & Whitney	2
A310	-200/-300	144'	153' 1"	212	280	General Electric, Pratt & Whitney	2
A32X	A318	111' 10"	103' 2"	107	117	Pratt & Whitney, CFM International	2
A32X	A319/-319CJ	111' 3"	111'	124/39	142	CFM International, International Aero Engines (IAE)	
A32X	A320	111' 10"	123' 3"	150	179		
A32X	A321	111' 10"	146'	186	220		
A330	-200/-200F	197' 10"	193' 7"	256	293	General Electric, Pratt & Whitney, Rolls-Royce	2
A330	-300	197' 10"	210'	295	335		
A340	-200	197'	194' 10"	263	303	CFM International	4
A340	-300	197'	209'	303	335	CFM International	
A340	-500	208' 11"	222' 5"	316	359	Rolls-Royce	
A340	-600	208' 11"	247'	372	419	Rolls-Royce	
A350	-800	212' 5"	198' 8"	270	N/A	Rolls-Royce	2
A350	-900	212' 5"	214' 1"	314	N/A		
A350	-1000	212' 5"	242' 5"	350	N/A		
A380	-700	N/A	N/A	480	N/A	Rolls-Royce, Engine Alliance	4
A380	-800/-800F	261' 10"	238' 8"	555	840		
A380	-900	N/A	N/A	656	N/A		

Source: Compiled from Airbus aircraft data.

The Airbus families of aircraft provide significant variety in terms of capacity. The narrow-body A318, with its high capacity of 117 seats, caters to one end of the airline spectrum, while the wide-body A380 seats 840 in high capacity. The typical layout for the A380, however, is a three-class configuration, which seats 525 passengers for an 8,300-nm range. Other available aircraft fill in gaps between the wide-body and narrow-body market.

Operational Characteristics of the Fleet

One of the biggest operating hindrances to early Airbus aircraft was limited range. The early model A300s had a range of between 1,850 and 3,400 nm. The A330 improved upon the range for Airbus wide-bodies, reaching a range of up to 6,750 nm. The four-engine A340 improved range by increasing it up to 8,500 nm. The A340 also allowed Airbus to gain faster cruising speeds, up to 632 miles per hour (Mach 0.83), compared to the 534 miles per hour (Mach 0.70) offered by the A330 (Airliners.net, 2010b) (see Table 2.9).

Comparative Analysis of the Airbus Aircraft Family

The out-of-production A300 was the first aircraft produced by Airbus. The A300 was a twin-engine wide-body aircraft that seated between 250 and 336 passengers. It first flew in April, 1974 (Airliners.net, 2010a). While as successful as Airbus' first product, the A310 was hampered by limited range, especially compared to the competitive Boeing 767ER. Airbus' answer to the 767 was the introduction of the A330, a twin-engine wide-body with similar range and capacity. With over 1,000 orders and nearly 400 backorders, the A330 remains a very popular intercontinental aircraft for airlines today (Airbus S.A.S., 2012).

The A320 narrow-body family includes the A318, A319, A320, and A321. The A320 family is the only narrow-body family in the Airbus aircraft lineup. The A320 was the first of these aircraft to be flown in 1987. The A320 was followed by production of the stretched version, the A321, and then two shortened versions, the A319 and A318. These aircraft competed directly with Boeing's 737NG series by offering similar seating capacities and ranges. There have been 6,321 orders for the A320 family since its inception, with over 3,700 of the planes delivered. With 3,104 aircraft on backorder as of September 30, 2011, it is clear that the A320 family is popular among the world's airlines.[18] Indeed, the A320 family may become only the second commercial jetliner to reach the 7,000-order mark, a mark previously set by the rival 737.

The A340 first flew in 1991 and gave airlines a viable option to replace older DC-10s and L-1011s. The four-engine wide-body offers seating for 260 to 400

---

[18] Airbus Order and Delivery Summary, September 30, 2011.

Table 2.9 Airbus aircraft operational characteristics

Model	Variant	Max. takeoff weight (lbs)	Cruising speed (mph)	Fuel capacity (U.S. gallons)	Range (nm)	Max. altitude (ft)	Total flying cost per block hour ($)	Total maintenance cost per block hour ($)	Total cost per block hour ($)	Average flight stage length (miles)
A300	-B2/-B4	313,055-363,760	526	N/A	1,850-3,400	N/A	4,501	2,129	7,853	1,239
	-600/-600F	365,745-378,535	544	18,000	2,650-4,070	N/A	N/A	N/A	N/A	N/A
A310	-200	313,055	528	16,130-19,940	3,670	N/A	N/A	N/A	N/A	N/A
	-300	330,695-361,560			4,310-5,170	N/A	N/A	N/A	N/A	N/A
A32X	A318	130,100-149,900	624 (Max)	6,400	1,500-3,100	N/A	1,921	384	2,634	842
	A319/ -A319CJ	141,095-166,450	522	6,300-7,885	1,831-3,697/6,300	N/A	2,039	471	3,041	962
	A320	162,040-169,755	522	6,300-7,885	2,615-3,055	37,000	2,222	596	3,322	1,132
	A321	183,000-205,000	515	6,260-6,850	2,300-2,650	N/A	2,609	594	3,872	1,268
A330	-200/-200F	500,400-513,700	534	25,770-36,750	3,200-6,750	N/A	N/A	N/A	N/A	N/A
	-300	272,500	534	25,670	4,500-5,500	N/A	4,776	622	6,170	3,727
A340	-200	573,200	547	40,960	7,450	N/A	N/A	N/A	N/A	N/A
	-300	573,200-606,275	547	37,150-39,060	6,700	N/A	N/A	N/A	N/A	N/A
	-500	804,675	632	56,750-58,646	8,500	N/A	N/A	N/A	N/A	N/A
	-600	804,675	632	51,746-54,023	7,500	N/A	N/A	N/A	N/A	N/A
A350	-800	546,700	647	34,082	8,300	43,100	N/A	N/A	N/A	N/A
	-900	590,800	647	36,460	8,100	43,100	N/A	N/A	N/A	N/A
	-1000	657,000	647	41,215	8,000	41,450	N/A	N/A	N/A	N/A
A380	-800/-800F	1,234,600-1,300,700	647	84,535	5,600-8,000	43,000	N/A	N/A	N/A	N/A

Source: Airbus commercial aircraft data.

passengers (Airliners.net, 2010b). The A340 has competed with the Boeing 777 since the 777 entered the market in the mid-1990s. The 777 has been a greater success than the A340 was for Airbus because the four-engine design of the A340 is less efficient with higher fuel prices than a twin-engine wide-body. Still, with 379 orders as of September 2011, the A340 is more of a success as a DC-10 replacement than McDonnell Douglas' own DC-10 replacement, the MD-11 (Airbus S.A.S, 2012).

As Airbus' newest product offering, and the world's largest airliner, the A380 holds promise for continued success for the company. The double-decker wide-body A340 offers a direct operating cost per passenger that is 15% lower than its direct competitor, the Boeing 747-400 (Airbus S.A.S, 2012). Airbus, as of October 2011, had 237 firm orders for the A380, with 59 aircraft already delivered and in operation around the world.[19]

McDonnell Douglas Commercial Aircraft

McDonnell Douglas and Boeing were the top two commercial aircraft manufacturers for many years before the rise of Airbus. McDonnell Douglas products competed directly for orders with many Boeing products: the DC-8 against the 707, the DC-9 and later the MD-80 against the 737, the DC-10 against the 747, and the MD-11 against the 777. The popularity of McDonnell Douglas products eventually faded, and the company was merged with Boeing in 1997. McDonnell Douglas airplanes continued to be delivered by Boeing until the last 717s (formerly known as MD-95s) were delivered in May 2006 to AirTran Airways and Midwest Airlines (Boeing Company, 2010).

While no longer in production, McDonnell Douglas aircraft are still flown around the world by a variety of operators. Largely known for their reliability, McDonnell Douglas airplanes, such as the DC-9, are 40 years old or older and still found in the fleets of major airlines, including Delta.

General Characteristics of the Fleet

General characteristics of the currently out-of-production McDonnell Douglas aircraft are given in Table 2.10. The McDonnell Douglas aircraft family includes the narrow-body DC-8, DC-9, MD-80, and MD-90 and the wide-body DC-10 and MD-11. All McDonnell Douglas aircraft were developed from three basic base models: the DC-8, DC-9, and DC-10. The DC-8 had many variants within the DC-8 family, while the DC-9 and DC-10 were the basis for the MD-80/MD-90 and MD-11, respectively.

---

[19] Airbus, News and Events. China Southern Airlines receives its first *Pearl of the Sky* A380 jetliner. October 21, 2011.

Table 2.10 McDonnell Douglas aircraft general characteristics

Model	Type	Variant	In/Out of production	First flight	Major operators	Total ordered	Total ordered	Total delivered	Total in world air traffic fleet
DC-8	Narrow-body	10/-20/-30/-40/-50/-50CF/-50AF	Out of production	30-May-58	DHL/UPS	294	556	294	25
		-60/-70		14-Mar-66		262		262	178
DC-9	Narrow-body	-10/-15/-20/-30/-30CF/-30F/C-9	Out of production	25-Feb-65	Delta	809	976	809	474
		-40/-50		28-Nov-67		167		167	99
DC-10	Wide-body	-10/-15/-30/-30CF/-30ER/-30AF/-40/-MD-10	Out of production	29-Aug-70	FedEx/OmniAir/World Airways/Arrow Air	386	446	386	180
		KC-10A/KDC-10				60		60	–
MD-11	Wide-body	MD-11/-F/-C/-CF/-ER	Out of production	10-Jan-90	FedEx/Lufthansa Cargo	200	200	200	–
MD-80	Narrow-body	-81/-82/-83/-88	Out of production	18-Oct-79	Allegiant/American/Delta/People's Republic of China	1,116	1,191	1,116	–
		-87		4-Dec-86		75		75	–
MD-90	Narrow-body	-30/-30ER/-30T	Out of production	22-Feb-93	Delta/Saudi Arabian Airlines	116	116	116	–

The MD-80 was McDonnell Douglas' most successful product, by the time production ended, with 1,191 aircraft deliveries. Another acclaimed commercial aircraft success for McDonnell Douglas was the DC-9, with 976 units ordered and delivered, of which 573 remain active in aircraft fleets worldwide.

Physical Characteristics of the Fleet

Most of the McDonnell Douglas aircraft came with Pratt & Whitney jet engines as the sole engine choice. This close relationship between McDonnell Douglas and Pratt & Whitney spanned from the DC-8 to the MD-80. The MD-90 was the only passenger jet aircraft built by McDonnell Douglas not to have Pratt & Whitney engines as an option.

Early DC-8 versions had approximately the same 170-seat capacity and 150-foot length as the MD-80 and MD-90, McDonnell Douglas' smallest models at the time that the company merged with Boeing (see Table 2.11). The physical difference between the models was in the length, where the DC-8 had a nearly 40-foot wider wingspan than the MD-80 and MD-90 in order to accommodate two extra engines.

Operational Characteristics of the Fleet

Table 2.12 lists the operating characteristics for McDonnell Douglas aircraft and shows that the total cost per block hour is actually lower for the DC-9 than the MD-80. The low operating costs may explain why Northwest Airlines (now Delta) kept so many of its aging DC-9s. The MD-90 also has lower operating costs than the DC-9 or MD-80 on similar stage lengths due to lower maintenance costs. In order to replace older planes (including the DC-9 and MD-80), Delta was buying 11 additional MD-90s to add to its fleet (Yamanouchi, 2010).

Comparative Analysis of the McDonnell Douglas Aircraft Family

McDonnell Douglas aircraft only came in three basic families: the DC-8, DC-9, and DC-10. The three later models, the MD-11 and MD-80/90, were derivatives of the DC-10 and DC-9, respectively. This strategy of continuously modifying existing designs rather than introducing new designs generated mixed success for McDonnell Douglas.

The MD-11 was not as successful as its predecessor, the DC-10. Only 200 MD-11s were ordered, significantly less than the MD-11's competitors (the Boeing 777 and A330/340). The older, three-engine design of the MD-11 could not compete with the efficiencies of newer, twin-engine designs of the 777 and A330.

The DC-9 can be described as somewhat of a predecessor to the regional jet phenomenon. Early DC-9 versions held between 80 and 90 passengers and were

Table 2.11 McDonnell Douglas aircraft physical characteristics

Model	Variant	Wingspan	Length	Capacity: mixed	Capacity: high density	Power plant manufacturer	Number of engines
DC-8	10/-20/-30/-40/-50/-50CF/-50AF	142' 5"	150' 6"	132	179	Pratt & Whitney	4
	-60/-70	142' 5"–148' 5"	157' 5"–187' 5"	180–220	259	CFM International, Pratt & Whitney	
DC-9	-10/-15/-20	89' 5"–93' 5"	104' 5"	80	90	Pratt & Whitney	2
	-30/-30CF/-30F/C-9	93' 5"	119' 4"	105	115		
	-40	93' 5"	125' 7"	110	125		
	-50	93' 5"	133' 7"	125	139		
DC-10	-10/-15/-30/-30CF/-30ER/-30AF	165' 5"	182' 1"	250–270	380	General Electric	3
	-40	165' 5"	182' 1"	250–270	380	Pratt & Whitney	
MD-11	MD-11/-F/-C/-CF/-ER	169' 6"	200' 10"	298	410	General Electric, Pratt & Whitney	2
MD-80	-81/-82/-83/-88	107' 10"	147' 10"	142	172	Pratt & Whitney	2
	-87	107' 10"	130' 5"	109	139		
MD-90	-30/-30ER/-30T	107' 10"	152' 7"	153	172	IAE	2

Source: Boeing commercial aircraft data.

Table 2.12 McDonnell Douglas aircraft operational characteristics

Model	Variant	Max takeoff weight (lbs)	Cruising speed (mph)	Fuel capacity (U.S. gallons)	Range (nm)	Max altitude (ft)	Total flying cost per block hour ($)	Total maintenance cost per block hour ($)	Total cost per block hour ($)	Average flight stage length (miles)
DC-8	10/-20/-30/-40/-50/-50CF/-50AF	325,000	580	23,393	4,970-6,078	–	–	–	–	–
	-60/-70	325,000-355,000	528	23,393-24,275	3,256-5,210	–	–	–	–	–
DC-9	-10/-15/-20	90,700-98,000	557-561	3,679-3,693	570					
	-30/-40	110,000-114,000	561-570	3,679	1,555-1,670	–	–	–	–	–
	-50	121,000	558	4,259	1.795	–	2,370	349	2,817	414
DC-10	-10/-15	430,000-455,000	600	21,700-26,647	3,300-3,785	–	7,001	2,681	10,818	2,458
	-30/-40	555,000-572,000	600	36,650	4,000-6,505	–				
MD-11	-11	602,555-630,500	544-587	38,615	6,821	–	–	–	–	–
	-11F	602,555-630,501	544-587	41,615	3,910	–	–	–	–	–
	-11ER	630,500	544-588	41,615	7,240	–				
MD-80	-81	140,000	504	5,840	1,565	35,000	2,610	537	3,501	803
	-82/-88	149,500	504	5,840	2,052	35,000				
	-83	160,000	504	7,000	2,504	35,000				
	-87	140,000-149,000	504	5,840-7,000	2,374	35,000				
MD-90	-30/-30ER/-30T	156,000-166,000	504	5,840-6,405	2,085-2,389	35,000	2,218	237	2,736	768

Source: Boeing commercial products data.

used on many of the same short-haul routes that regional jets fly today. DC-9s were popular with airlines and passengers due to their five-abreast (2 x 3) seating compared to the six-abreast seating of other narrow-bodied aircraft. The MD-80 was even more popular than the DC-9, with nearly 1,200 airplanes ordered. The reliability of the DC-9 and the fuel efficiency of the MD-80 compared to the Boeing 737 Classics helped to contribute to the MD-80's popularity.

Lockheed

Lockheed produced only one commercial jetliner, the L-1011. Competing against the DC-10, A300, and 747 in the wide-body market, the L-1011 never could secure enough orders to make the production of the aircraft profitable. While sales of the other three wide-body aircraft of the time were good, Lockheed sold only 250 of the airplane before production ended in 1983. The L-1011 was not more popular even though it featured advanced technology and Lockheed boasted that it was quieter than a 747 or DC-10 (Eden, 2006). The major flaw of the L-1011 was its range; early versions of the L-1011 lacked the range sufficient for long-haul operations that the rival DC-10 was being used on. The shortened L-1011-500 finally corrected the range deficiencies; however, by the time the airplane was built, the market for such aircraft had already been filled. The aircraft was first delivered to British Airways in 1979 and the next year to Pan American Airways. Characteristics of Lockheed commercial aircraft are given in Table 2.13.

Regional Jets

Like the wide-body and narrow-body commercial aircraft market that is currently dominated by Airbus and Boeing, Bombardier and Embraer have emerged as the key players in the regional jet market. Both companies have produced several products that provide a 37- to 122-seat range on short- to medium-haul routes. The Embraer family of aircraft offers a variety from the 30-seat twin turboprop EMB 120 to its largest aircraft, the 122-seat Embraer 195. Embraer's direct competitor, Bombardier, offers similar variety with its 50-seat CRJ100/200 and up to the 70- to 100-seat CRJ700/900 series.

Embraer

Embraer (Empresa Brasileira de Aeronáutica, SA) is one of the world's main aircraft manufacturers, headquartered in São José dos Campos, Brazil. Embraer has had U.S. operations for more than 30 years and has about 800 U.S. employees. The company delivered 246 aircraft in 2010. Embraer prides itself on being a leader in the industry, with innovative regional and commercial jet product lines.

Table 2.13 Lockheed commercial aircraft characteristics

Model	Variant	First flight	Wingspan	Length	Max. takeoff weight (lbs)	Cruising speed	Range	Max. altitude	Engines	Capacity
L-1011	-1/-100/-200	16-Nov-70	155' 4"	177' 8"	430,000-466,000	556	3,110-4,918	42,000	3	256-400
	-500	16-Oct-78	164' 4"	164' 2"	510,000	556	6,100	42,000	3	246-330

Source: Lockheed commercial data.

Table 2.14 Embraer aircraft general characteristics

Model	First flight	Major operators	Total ordered	Total delivered	Total in world air traffic fleet
EMB 120	29-Jul-83	SkyWest, OceanAir, Swiftair	352	330	208
ERJ 135	1998	ExpressJet, American Eagle	108	108	108
ERJ 140	27-Jun-00	ExpressJet, American Eagle, Chatauqua Airlines	74	74	74
ERJ 145	1995		708	708	701
EMBRAER 170	19-Feb-02	Shuttle America, Compass Airlines, Republic Airlines	190	182	180
EMBRAER 175	Jun-03		189	136	130
EMBRAER 190	Mar-04	JetBlue Airways, Tianjin, Air Canada	519	349	301
EMBRAER 195	7-Dec-04	Flybe, Azul Linhas	105	75	60

Source: Compiled from Embraer 2011 order book and Airline Monitor data.

With nearly complete (up to 95%) commonality among the ERJ 135, 140, and 145 families of aircraft, Embraer has found success ulilizing one base model of aircraft, stretching and shortening the fuselage accordingly, to create tremendous versatility for airlines seeking to tailor capacity to market size.

General Characteristics of the Fleet

Table 2.14 outlines the general characteristics of Embraer's fleet of regional jets. Embraer's most successful regional jet in terms of orders and deliveries, by a wide margin, is the ERJ 145. With 708 orders as of October 2010, the ERJ 145 remains a strong selling point for Embraer and the entire family of ERJ aircraft by offering the versatility necessary for building a successful regional network. The ERJ family of aircraft as a whole is the most successful product line for Embraer, with over 1,100 deliveries. This family of aircraft shares 98% parts, systems, and training commonality. With the same fuselage, wing and tail structure, engine hardware, crew type rating, and common equipment, the ERJ family of aircraft offers tremendous benefits to airlines seeking to capitalize on reduced operating costs.[20]

The EMB 120, despite having serial production stopped in 2001, is available for one-off orders since it shares much of the same production equipment with other Embraer aircraft. The 208 EMB 120s are being operated commercially around the world; for example, SkyWest Airlines operates 50 EMB 120s on its feeder routes.

Embraer's 170, 175, 190, and 195 aircraft models, with seating capacities ranging from 70 to 120, are commonly referred to as E-Jets. Within these four models, the E-190 has had the most success, with 301 aircraft in use as a narrowbody medium-range jet. There is 95% systems commonality between the E-170 and E-175, as well as between the E-190 and E-195; an 89% commonality exists between the two families.[21]

Physical Characteristics of the Fleet

The ERJ family of aircraft offers a variety of lengths and seat capacities on a base model, as outlined in Table 2.15. The ERJ 140, for example, is essentially a shortened version of the ERJ 145, offering six fewer seats and 96% commonality. The largest member of the family, the ERJ 145, is 12 feet longer than the smallest ERJ 135 and seats 13 more passengers, while maintaining the same wingspan and engine type. The ERJ family employs strictly Rolls-Royce engines while the E-Jets utilize General Electric power plants.

Similarly, the Embraer 195 is a stretched version of the Embraer 190, which, in turn, is a stretched version of the Embraer 175 and 170. Accordingly, the Embraer

---

[20] Embraer ERJ 145 Technical Information.
[21] Embraer E-Jets Specifications.

Table 2.15 Embraer aircraft physical characteristics

Model	Wingspan	Length	Capacity	Power plant manufacturer	Number of engines
EMB 120	64' 11"	65' 7"	30	Pratt & Whitney	2
ERJ 135	65' 9"	86' 5"	37	Rolls-Royce	2
ERJ 140	65' 9"	93' 5"	44	Rolls-Royce	2
ERJ 145	65' 9"	98' 0"	50	Rolls-Royce	2
EMBRAER 170	85' 4"	98' 1"	70-80	General Electric	2
EMBRAER 175	85' 4"	103' 11"	78-88	General Electric	2
EMBRAER 190	94' 3"	118' 11"	94-114	General Electric	2
EMBRAER 195	94' 3"	126' 10"	106-122	General Electric	2

Source: Compiled from Embraer aircraft data.

195 is roughly 28 feet longer than the Embraer 170 and at high capacity can accommodate 40 more passengers.

Operational Characteristics of the Fleet

The operating characteristics of Embraer's aircraft are shown in Table 2.16. It is interesting to note that within the E-Jets and ERJ families, cruising speeds, fuel capacity, and range are nearly identical for all models, with the ERJ 145 as an exception. The E-Jets family has normal cruising speeds of 870 km/h, fuel capacities of 2,466 gallons, and a range that differs by less than 500 nm. The ERJ 135 and 140 have identical cruising speeds, fuel capacities, and ranges that differ by 50 nm; the exception to this is the highly successful ERJ 145 that carries 300 more gallons of fuel, which translates into 200-1,000 extra nautical miles of range.

Comparative Analysis of the Embraer Aircraft Family

The complete Embraer family of aircraft offers a high degree of commonality, which allows airlines to cut down on training and operation costs, thereby increasing their flexibility and strengthening profitability. This philosophy of commonality began with the EMB 120 and the subsequent ERJ family.

The EMB120 with its 30-seat capacity achieved a speed of roughly 500 km/hr and enjoyed relative success until the 1980s. In response to the demand of the global market of the 1980s, Embraer developed a jetliner, the ERJ 145, which could seat 20 more passengers than the twin-turboprop EMB 120. The EMB 145, in its design, kept the EMB 120's three-abreast (2 + 1) seating configuration, but replaced the turboprops with Rolls-Royce engines, achieving a more than doubled range of 1,500 to 2,300 nm.

Table 2.16 Embraer aircraft operational characteristics

Model	Max. takeoff weight (lbs)	Cruising speed (km/h)	Fuel capacity (U.S. gallons)	Range (nm)	Max. altitude (ft)
EMB 120	26,433	584	687	800	32,000
ERJ 135	42,990	828	1,525	1,300	37,000
ERJ 140	45,415	828	1,525	1,650	37,000
ERJ 145	50,816	828	1,828	1,550	37,000
EMBRAER 170	79,344	870	2,466	1,950-2,300	41,000
EMBRAER 175	82,673	870	2,466	2,100	41,000
EMBRAER 190	105,359	870	2,466	1,950-2,650	41,000
EMBRAER 195	107,564	870	2,466	1,650-2,400	41,000

Source: Compiled from Embraer aircraft and Airline Monitor data.

The EMB 140 was the next aircraft developed by Embraer and was based on the EMB 145, with 96% parts commonality and the same crew type rating. The only difference between the models is the shortened fuselage with fewer seats, and the slightly increased range of the EMB 140 compared to the EMB 145 to accommodate the needs of the regional jet market.

Optimized for the 70- to 120-seat-capacity segment is the new-generation E-Jets aircraft. The E-Jets family is composed of two base model aircraft (the E-170 and E-175) and their stretched versions, the E-190 and E-195. The E-170 and E-175 have 95% commonality, as do the E-190 and E-195. Between the two families there is 89% commonality, with identical fuselages, cross sections, and avionics.

Bombardier

As the world's third largest civil aircraft manufacturer, Bombardier is Embraer's direct competitor in the regional jet market.[22] Bombardier's commercial products are part of three main families: the CRJ series, the Q-Series, and the in-development C-Series. The CRJ family of products remains one of the world's most successful regional jet programs and the Q-Series remains the workhorse of many fleets. Bombardier's NextGen family of aircraft builds upon previous success by improving operating costs and increasing the use of composite materials.

General Characteristics of the Fleet

The CRJ200 is Bombardier's most successful aircraft in terms of sales and deliveries; 709 have already been delivered and are part of the global aircraft fleet. With

---

[22] *Wall Street Journal*, July 29, 2011.

over 650 Q-Series aircraft in service worldwide, operating in a variety of capacities, the Q-Series also remains one of Bombardier's greatest successes despite production having ended on the Q100, 200, and 300 versions of the series. Table 2.17 shows some of the general characteristics of Bombardier's fleet.

Physical Characteristics of the Fleet

Table 2.18 outlines some of the physical characteristics of the aircraft Bombardier manufactures and differences between various aircraft in the series. The airframe of the original Q100 with its 37- to 39-seat capacity was the same airframe used on the Q200. The difference between the models lies in the power plant used, in that, although both were Pratt & Whitney models, the Q200 offered more powerful engines, which improved performance.

The CRJ700 and CRJ900 have the same engine type, which allows for greater commonality and lower maintenance costs. The largest member of the family, the CRJ900, seats a maximum of 90 passengers and is approximately 20 feet longer than the original CRJ100 and 200, which sat 39 and 50 passengers, respectively.

Operational Characteristics of the Fleet

Bombardier offers aircraft with a variety of operating characteristics. These characteristics are outlined in Table 2.19 for the Q-Series and CRJ Series. Table 2.19

Table 2.17 Bombardier aircraft general characteristics

Model	First flight	Major operators	Total ordered	Total delivered	Total in world air traffic fleet
Q100	20-Jun-83	US Air Express, Northwest, Horizon Air	299	299	217
Q200	19-Apr-95	US Air Express, Horizon Air, Wideroe	105	105	76
Q300	15-May-87	Air New Zealand, Air Nostrum	267	267	227
Q400	31-Jan-98	Flybe, Horizon Air, Qantas	408	368	238
CRJ100	10-May-91	Comair, Lufthansa CityLine, Brit Air	226	226	226
CRJ200	1-Dec-95	Delta Connection, SkyWest, Independence Air	709	709	709
CRJ700	May-99	American Eagle, SkyWest	340	328	299
CRJ900	21-Feb-01	Delta Connection, Mesa	265	252	226

Source: Compiled from Bombardier aircraft and Airline Monitor data.

Table 2.18 Bombardier aircraft physical characteristics

Model	Wingspan	Length	Capacity	Power plant manufacturer	Number of engines
Q100	85'	73'	37-38	Pratt & Whitney	2
Q200	85'	73'	37-39	Pratt & Whitney	2
Q300	90'	84' 3"	50-56	Pratt & Whitney	2
Q400	93' 3"	107' 9"	68-78	Pratt & Whitney	2
CRJ100	69' 7"	87' 10"	37-39	Pratt & Whitney	2
CRJ200	69' 7"	87' 10"	50	General Electric	2
CRJ700	76' 3"	106' 8"	78 (max.)	General Electric	2
CRJ900	81' 6"	119' 4"	90 (max.)	General Electric	2

Source: Compiled from Bombardier aircraft and Airline Monitor data.

Table 2.19 Bombardier aircraft operational characteristics

Model	Max. takeoff weight (lbs)	Cruising speed (km/h)	Fuel capacity (U.S. gallons)	Range (nm)	Max. altitude (ft)
Q100	36,300	500	N/A	1,020	25,000
Q200	36,300	537	835	925	25,000
Q300	43,000	528	835	1,098	25,000
Q400	64,500	667	1,724	1,362	25,000
CRJ100	51,000	785	N/A	2,003	41,000
CRJ200	51,000	786	1,714	2,491	41,000
CRJ700	72,750	829	2,331	2,655	41,000
CRJ900	80,500	850	2,331	2,956	41,000

Source: Compiled from Bombardier aircraft and Airline Monitor data.

shows that, for consecutive models of aircraft, a complementary incremental increase in cruising speed occurred, from 500 km/h for the Q100 and up to 850 km/h for the CRJ900.

With the exception of the Q200, which had a shorter range than its predecessor, Bombardier aircraft have progressively become more fuel efficient. In the CRJ family for example, the CRJ700 and CRJ900 have the same fuel capacity and engines, but the CRJ900 has an increased range of 2,956 nm, which is 300 nm further than the CRJ700.

Comparative Analysis of the Bombardier Aircraft Family

Over 850 Q-Series aircraft are in service in a multitude of roles and operating in three sizes: the 37-seat Q100/200, the 50-seat Q300, and the 70-seat Q400. The original Q100 did so well in developing regional airline routes that its operators soon required an aircraft with more power and more seats. The answer was the Q300, which was 11 feet longer than the Q100/200 and had the capacity to seat 56 passengers, although most versions are configured to hold 50 seats. The Q200 is a more powerful version of the Q100 airframe, with a larger payload and more powerful Pratt & Whitney PW123 engines (the same engines used on the Q300).

The Q400 is a stretched and improved 70- to 78-seat turboprop that entered service in 2000. Its cruise speed is 140 km/h higher than its predecessors. By having an increase in cruise speed, the Q400's 667-km/h cruise speed approaches jet speeds and presents an advantage to short-haul airlines that can usually replace a regional jet with a Q400 without having to change their gate-to-gate schedules.

Over 1,300 Bombardier CRJ aircraft currently fly all over the world, making the CRJ program one of the most successful regional aircraft programs in the world. The smaller aircraft capacity of the CRJ, compared to mainline narrow-bodies, allows the use of secondary airports to fly to key destinations, thus avoiding traditional hubs.

The CRJ200 was designed to provide superior performance and operating efficiencies in the regional airline industry. When compared to its nearest competition, it flies faster and further, while burning less fuel and having lower operating costs. The Bombardier CRJ200 was designed to carry 50 passengers in a four-abreast configuration and boasts an outstanding maximum speed of 860 km/h.

The CRJ700 was developed as an evolution of the CRJ200, keeping the cockpit commonality while incorporating new structure and systems. With an increased passenger seat capacity of 70-78 passengers and an increased maximum cruising speed of 875 km/h, the CRJ700 improved upon the performance of the CRJ200 and the range by up to 150 nm. The all-new wing was also designed to incorporate full span leading-edge slats, which allow excellent airfield performance with only a small increase in wingspan from the CRJ200. Designed to hold 86-90 passengers in the same four-abreast configuration as other members of the CRJ family, the CRJ900 further improves upon the features and design of the CRJ700.

Summary

Different companies have pursued different types of production processes on a variety of aircraft with varying product characteristics. Some of the physical and operating specifications that aircraft operators have to take into consideration, when determining which available products to purchase from various aircraft manufacturers, can be grouped together. From an aircraft design perspective, it is important to look at an aircraft's capacity, fuel efficiency, and range.

For example, generally, a regional airliner is designed to fly up to 100 passengers on short-haul flights. The ERJ195's maximum passenger capacity is slightly less than that of the 737-600; however, it seems to be slightly faster. The E-195 has less range capability than the -600, but it is much lighter and therefore more fuel efficient. With the introduction of longer range regional aircraft, these aircraft increasingly found their niche feeding newer, longer range markets. Consequently, Sukhoi developed the SuperJet 100 as a new regional aircraft to compete with Embraer and Bombardier.

The specifications for a particular aircraft can be compared to a competing model from a different manufacturer or to a variant or different model from the same manufacturer. Comparing specifications allows an accurate determination of the aircraft most suited for the operations. These specifications also provide the roadmap to aircraft valuation.

References

Airbus S.A.S. (2012). Aircraft families. Retrieved from http://www.airbus.com/en/aircraftfamilies/.

Airliners.net. (2009). Aircraft data: The Fokker F-28 fellowship. Retrieved from http://www.airliners.net/aircraft-data/stats.main?id;eq219.

Airliners.net. (2010a). Aircraft data: Airbus A300B2/B4. Retrieved from http://www.airliners.net/aircraft-data/stats.main?id;eq17.

Airliners.net. (2010b). Aircraft data: Airbus A340-500/600. Retrieved from http://www.airliners.net/aircraft-data/stats.main?id;eq28.

Aris, S. (2002). *Close to the sun: How Airbus challenged America's domination of the skies.* London, UK: Aurum Press Ltd.

Aviation Safety Network (ASN). (2009). ASN Aviation safety database. Retrieved from http://aviation-safety.net/database/dblist.php?Type;eq352.

Badrocke, M., & Gunston, B. (1999). *The illustrated history of McDonnell Douglas aircraft.* Botley, Oxford: Osprey Publishing Limited.

Boeing Company. (June 14, 2002). The secret behind high profits at low-fare airlines: A majority fly the Boeing 737 exclusively. Retrieved from http://www.boeing.com/commercial/news.

Boeing Company. (2009a). History: Heritage of innovation. Retrieved from http://www.boeing.com/history/index.html.

Boeing Company. (2009b). History: Products. Retrieved from http://www.boeing.com/history/index.html.

Boeing Company. (2009c). Commercial airplanes: 757 program. Retrieved from http://www.boeing.com/commercial/757family/index.html.

Boeing Company (2009d). The Boeing 747-8 family: A proud tradition of value continues. Retrieved from http://www.boeing.com/commercial/747family.

Boeing Company. (2009e). DC-6/C-118A Liftmaster transport. Retrieved from http://www.boeing.com/history/mdc/dc-6.htm.

Boeing Company. (2009f). DC-7 commercial transport. Retrieved from http://www.boeing.com/history/mdc/dc-7.htm.

Boeing Company. (2009g). DC-8 commercial transport. Retrieved from http://www.boeing.com/history/mdc/dc-8.htm.

Boeing Company. (2009h). MD-80 and MD-90 commercial transports. Retrieved from http://www.boeing.com/history/mdc/md-80md-90.htm.

Boeing Company. (2009i). MD-11 commercial transport. Retrieved from http://www.boeing.com/history/mdc/md-11.htm.

Boeing Company. (2009j). 737 milestones. Retrieved from http://www.boeing.com/commercial/737family/pf/pf_ng_milestones.html.

Boeing Company. (2009k). 767 family. Retrieved from http://www.boeing.com/commercial/767family/back/index.html.

Boeing Company. (2009l). 787 Dreamliner. Retrieved from http://www.boeing.com/commercial/787family/programfacts.html.

Boeing Company. (2010). The Boeing 717. Retrieved from http://www.boeing.com/commercial/717/index.html.

Boeing Company. (2012). The Boeing Company 2007 annual report. Chicago, IL.

Eden, P. E. (2006). *Civil aircraft today: The world's most successful commercial aircraft*. London, UK: Summertime Publishing, Ltd.

Erudition Online. (June 2004). The history of commercial aviation: 1903-2003. Retrieved from http://www.eruditiononline.com/06.04.

European Aeronautic Defense and Space Company. (November 14, 2008). Financials and guidance. Retrieved from http://www.eads.net/1024/en/investor/Financials_and_Guidance/Keyfigures.html.

Fokker Services. (2009). Fokker history. Retrieved from http://www.fokkerservices.com/page.html?id;eq5401.

Gunston, B. (1988). *Airbus*. London, UK: Osprey Publishing Limited.

IATA. (December 2008). Financial forecast. Retrieved from http://www.iata.org/economics.

Karlsson, M. (1998). History—L-1011. Retrieved from http://home4.swipnet.se/~w-48037/l1011history.htm.

Lockheed Martin. (February 28, 2008). Lockheed Martin 2007 annual report. Bethesda, MD.

Lockheed Martin. (2009a). Model 10 Electra. Retrieved from http://www .lockheedmartin.com/aboutus/history/Model10Electra.html.

Lockheed Martin. (2009b). SR-71 Blackbird. Retrieved from http://www .lockheedmartin.com/aboutus/history/SR71Blackbird.html.

McDonnell Douglas. (2009). MD-11 statistics. Retrieved from http://www .planespotters.net/Production_List/McDonnell-Douglas/MD-11/statistics. html.

Norris, G. (1998). *Boeing.* Osceola, WI: MBI Publishing Company.

Norris, G., Thomas, G., Wagner, M., & Forbes Smith, C. (2005). *Boeing 787 Dreamliner—Flying redefined.* Aerospace Technical Publications International.

Northwest Airlines Corporation. (2008). 2008, 3rd quarter SEC filing. Minneapolis, MN.

Pritchard, D. (2005). *Globalization of commercial aircraft manufacturing.* University of Buffalo.

Ray, S. (December 4, 2008). Boeing reviews Dreamliner schedule for more delays. *Bloomberg.* Retrieved from http://www.bloomberg.com.

Southwest Airlines. (2008). 2008, 3rd quarter SEC filing. Retrieved from http:// www.southwest.com/investor_relations/fs_sec_filings.html.

Stork B. V. (2008). Annual report 2007. Retrieved from http://www.stork.com/ page.html?id;eq1245.

Stork B. V. (2009). Investor relations information. Retrieved from http://www .stork.com/page.html?ch;eqDEF&id;eq1242.

Yamanouchi, K. (January 20, 2010). Delta to buy used MD-90 jets. *Atlanta Business News.*

3

Aircraft Efficiency: Operating and Financial Metrics

The Wright Brothers created the single greatest cultural force since the invention of writing. The airplane became the first World Wide Web, bringing people, languages, ideas, and values together.

—Bill Gates, CEO, Microsoft Corporation

Like any other asset, aircraft values depend on two factors: technical efficiency and allocative efficiency. *Technical efficiency* in this context refers to the operating efficiency of the aircraft itself and operating metrics such as gross takeoff weight, convertibility, fuel burn, maintenance expenses per block hour, consumable parts expense, aircraft wear and tear, cruising speed, and landing distance. Aircraft efficiency can be measured by single factor or multifactor measures. Single factor measures are based on a single input and output including fuel burn, crew costs per block hour and average seats per aircraft. Single factor ratios can be broken down into three types: technical, operational, and financial.

In this chapter, several single factor ratios are outlined to benchmark aircraft financial and operational performance for both narrow- and wide-body aircraft. Four narrow-body and four wide-body aircraft were selected—the Boeing 737-700 and 757-200 and Airbus A319 and A320 in the narrow-body category; and the Boeing 767-200, 767-400, 777, and Airbus A330 in the wide-body category. Efficiency ratios are demonstrated that can be used to compare and benchmark commercial aircraft, laying the foundation for use of these metrics as determinants of aircraft value in subsequent chapters. The chapter is organized as follows:

Airline Fleet Composition

Single Factor Ratios

- Aircraft Technical Performance Ratios
- Operating Ratios

Financial and Operational Performance

Comparative Analysis of Efficiency

- Narrow-body: Boeing 737NG vs. Airbus A320
- Wide-body: Boeing 777-200 vs. Airbus A330-300
- Regional Jets: CRJ100/200 vs. ERJ 145

At the end of the chapter is a Summary for chapter review and References for further study.

Airline Fleet Composition

Technical metrics are aircraft characteristics that are considered fixed in the short term. Examples include average seats per airplane, cargo capacity, airspeed, and range. These are characteristics that influence an aircraft operator when purchasing the aircraft, but once determined are considered outside of airline operations. Operational characteristics impact aircraft value and are determined by the aircraft operators. Many factors further influence operational characteristics, of which aircraft utilization is considered the most important. Other factors include scheduled stage length and fuel efficiency.

Some operating procedures can affect fuel efficiency, but basic aircraft fuel characteristics are much more a determinant of overall efficiency than the airline's patterns of use of the aircraft itself. The financial characteristics of an aircraft include crew costs, maintenance, depreciation, and other operating costs. In the 1960s, the three U.S. commercial aircraft manufacturers—Boeing, Lockheed, and McDonnell Douglas—had over 90% market share. Surprisingly, today Airbus has over 50% market share. Until 1980, the U.S. commercial aircraft industry enjoyed a monopolistic position in the world market, despite the European-based Airbus Industrie being founded in 1970. The entry of Airbus was one of the major factors leading to the demise of McDonnell Douglas. McDonnell Douglas had two families of aircraft, the DC-9, targeting the short-haul market with a low seating capacity, and the DC-10, a medium- to long-haul aircraft with a medium seating capacity.[1]

---

[1] These aircraft were extended and updated with the MD-80 and MD-90 as derivatives of the DC-9, and the MD-11 as a derivative of the DC-10.

A summary of aircraft types in the United States is presented in Table 3.1. Boeing dominates the market, constituting over 50% of the U.S. commercial aircraft fleet. In contrast, Airbus Industrie has a market position that been growing steadily over the past decade. Another interesting feature is a 4.4% fleet reduction in 2008, primarily due to the economic recession. In order to counteract some of the severe losses experienced by North American carriers, massive fleet reductions were initiated. Fleet reduction continued into 2010 before returning to 1.5-2% growth per year. Due to the emergence of low-cost carriers and continuing competition in the airline industry, it is reasonable to surmise that the Boeing 737NG and Airbus A320 family of aircraft will continue to dominate the U.S. markets for the near future.

Next, general ratios for numerous wide-body and narrow-body aircraft are presented, including detailed financial ratio analysis for four narrow-body and four wide-body aircraft—the Boeing 737-700 and 757-200 and the Airbus A319 and A320 in the narrow-body category; and the Boeing 767-200, 767-400, 777, and Airbus A330 in the wide-body category.[2] Efficiency ratios can be used to compare and benchmark commercial aircraft, and these same metrics can be used to determine aircraft value.

Single Factor Ratios

Ratios show a mathematical relationship between one variable over another variable. Suppose you have 100 aircraft and 500 pilots; the ratio of pilots to aircraft is 500/100 or 5:1. Single factor ratios can be extremely useful for comparing and benchmarking aircraft efficiency across aircraft types. However, they are limited to the consideration of one or two operational aspects at any given time and are unsuitable for comprehensive aircraft efficiency comparisons. For example, an aircraft with superior fuel efficiency and maintenance costs per block hour may be unsuitable for short-haul markets, if the depreciation per block hour is too high and hurts profitability. Multifactor productivity comparisons attempt to address this shortcoming by integrating several input and output measures into a single productivity measure.

This section essentially concerns the calculation of relationships between outputs and inputs to provide necessary information to management about the operations and financial performance of an aircraft. There are three *operational indicators* to use in evaluations: fuel efficiency or average fuel burn (per block hour), average aircraft utilization (in block hours), and average stage length.

---

[2] On August 30, 2011, the Boeing Company announced that it would build the 737 MAX. The new family of aircraft—737 MAX 7, 737 MAX 8, and 737 MAX 9—built on the strengths of the Next Generation 737.

Table 3.1 Boeing and Airbus fleets in the United States

United States Fleet Data—Boeing Aircraft

	Actual year end fleet					Projected year end fleet				
	2007	**2008**	**2009**	**2010**	**2011**	**2012**	**2013**	**2014**	**2015**	**2016**
737-600	69	69	69	69	69	69	69	69	69	69
737-700	904	966	1,019	1,046	1,136	1,236	1,326	1,406	1,476	1,526
737-800	1,312	1,503	1,789	2,113	2,378	2,663	2,983	3,313	3,633	3,908
737-900	60	90	118	133	158	193	228	268	308	358
747-400	669	682	690	690	690	690	690	690	685	672
747-8	–	–	–	–	1	30	55	80	100	120
757-200/300	1,027	1,021	1,007	1,004	999	991	979	962	944	921
767-200/400	920	926	928	932	942	955	944	928	917	897
777-200/300	686	746	834	908	978	1,063	1,158	1,253	1,328	1,378
787-8/-9	–	–	–	–	1	90	190	320	460	605
Total Boeing	5,647	6,003	6,454	6,895	7,352	7,980	8,622	9,289	9,920	10,454

United States Fleet Data—Airbus Aircraft

	Actual year end fleet					Projected year end fleet				
	2007	**2008**	**2009**	**2010**	**2011**	**2012**	**2013**	**2014**	**2015**	**2016**
A300	412	402	387	381	374	366	358	349	345	340
A318	53	66	72	74	79	84	84	84	84	84
A319	1,034	1,132	1,220	1,271	1,336	1,406	1,466	1,516	1,556	1,596
A320	1,795	1,991	2,194	2,491	2,806	3,146	3,496	3,845	4,157	4,380
A321	421	487	574	625	665	705	755	805	855	905
A330-200/300	512	584	659	746	841	956	1,056	1,131	1,206	1,281
A380	1	13	23	41	66	96	131	166	201	236
Total Airbus	4,228	4,675	5,129	5,629	6,167	6,759	7,346	7,896	8,404	8,822

United States Fleet Data—Regional Aircraft

	Actual year end fleet					Projected year end fleet				
	2007	**2008**	**2009**	**2010**	**2011**	**2012**	**2013**	**2014**	**2015**	**2016**
Bombardier	1,405	1,460	1,514	1,549	1,594	1,634	1,699	1,764	1,849	1,939
Embraer	1,200	1,362	1,482	1,582	1,687	1,757	1,827	1,897	1,987	2,077
Total Other	2,605	2,822	2,996	3,131	3,281	3,391	3,526	3,661	3,836	4,016

Source: Compiled from Airline Monitor data.

The level and historical trends of those indicators can be used to make inferences about an aircraft's operational performance and its attractiveness as an investment. Likewise, there are four *financial indicators*: crew cost per block hour; depreciation per block hour, fuel cost, and maintenance cost per block hour.

Aircraft Technical Performance Ratios

Technical ratios are aircraft characteristics that influence the costs and profitability of the aircraft to the airline. While the airline can determine technical efficiency factors while acquiring aircraft, once the acquisition is complete, the airline has relatively little control over these factors. Technical ratios to examine are: average seats per aircraft, cargo capacity, fuel capacity, range, and maximum takeoff weight (MTOW).

The aircraft that will be discussed come from industry giants Boeing and Airbus. Both manufacturers have two main aircraft types, narrow-body and wide-body aircraft, within which exist sub-categories differentiated by seat capacity, aircraft range, and configuration. The Airbus A320 family is demanded by many carriers for their domestic and short-haul markets. Competing with the Airbus A320 family is the Boeing 737 family that has comparable characteristics. Technical specifications of Boeing narrow- and wide-body aircraft and comparable Airbus models are shown in Tables 3.2 and 3.3, respectively.

Average Seats per Aircraft

The key measurements of aircraft productivity are *seat density* and *aircraft utilization*. When making decisions on aircraft acquisition and fleet planning, airlines consider the seating capacity and its compatibility with operations. Narrow-body aircraft have lower seat capacity and fewer aisles than wide-body aircraft, making

Table 3.2 Narrow-body aircraft technical specifications

	737-700	737-800	737-900	757-200	A319	A320	A321
Seats (2-class configuration)	126	162	180	200	124	150	185
Cargo volume (cubic ft)	966	1,555	1,585	1,670	975	1,320	1,508
MTOW (lbs)	133,000	155,500	187,700	220,000	142,000	162,900	196,200
Fuel Ccapacity (U.S. gal)	6,875	6,875	7,837	11,726	6,300	6,300	6,350
Range (nm)	3,440	3,115	3,265	2,430	2,000	2,900	3,200

Source: Compiled from Airbus family data and Boeing Reference Guide.

Table 3.3 Wide-body aircraft technical specifications

	A330-200	A340-300	A380	747-400	767-400	777-300
Seats (3-class configuration)	253	295	523	416	245	368
Cargo volume (cubic ft)	4,800	5,761	6,554	5,332	4,905	7,120
MTOW (lbs)	507,000	606,000	1,235,000	875,000	400,000	660,000
Fuel capacity (U.S. gal)	36,750	37,150	84,600	57,285	23,980	45,220
Range (nm)	7,250	7,400	8,300	7,260	4,375	6,005

Source: Compiled from Airbus family data and Boeing Reference Guide.

them inherently ideal for thinner markers and short-haul segments. For a given seat capacity, the airline then decides on the aircraft seat configuration.

Seat configuration is a characteristic of an aircraft that is limited to the original decision; usually, there are three specifications in which seats are allocated:

- One-class configuration where all the seats are economy seats has become the mainstay of low-cost carriers (LCCs) such as Ryanair, Air Asia, JetBlue, EasyJet, Wizz Air, and Southwest Airlines. Interestingly, Etihad Airways introduced its first "all economy" class aircraft to its fleet in October of 2010. Etihad is the only non-LCC in the Middle East operating with such a configuration.
- A two-class configuration is used by many domestic network carriers and some LCCs. US Airways' first class flatbed seats in its Airbus A330-300s have a seat pitch of 94 inches. A number of Asian airlines, including Air India, Jet Airways, Kingfisher Airlines, Mahan Air, Oman Air, Royal Jordanian, and Saudi Arabian Airlines, operate some economy services, as well as business and first class. AirAsia X has become the first LCC to offer flatbed seats on its long-haul route, which combines the comfort of premium travel with the affordability of no-frills flying.[3]
- The three-class configuration is in low use by North American carriers, but remains a popular choice for international hub-to-hub routes in Europe and Asia. For example, in the Swiss International Air Lines fleet of 88 planes, there are 10 A330-300s that each have a total seating capacity of 236 passengers in three-class layouts (8 seats in first class, 45 seats in business class, and 183 seats in economy).[4]

---

[3] Osman-Rani, AirAsia X CEO, Air Transport Aviation Society, 15th Annual Conference, Sydney, Australia, July 2, 2011.
[4] Swiss International Air Lines Aircraft Fleet Figures, Summer 2011.

Seat pitch of a low-cost airline is usually 28 inches, compared to a traditional conventional economy class pitch with 32 inches.[5] Lower seat pitch can mean more rows of seats and higher productivity, resulting in much lower cost per available seat mile (CASM). In Tables 3.2 and 3.3, all seat capacities are estimates based on a two-class (business and economy) configuration.

It should be stressed that seat capacity is a major indicator of the revenue capabilities of a particular aircraft. The Boeing 737-700 in a two-class configuration holds 126 passengers per aircraft, while its competitor, the Airbus A319, holds slightly less at 124 passengers per aircraft.[6] As the number of seats per aircraft increases, the cost per seat for the airline is lowered. The higher the number of seats, however, the less the level of comfort that will be experienced by passengers, and subsequently the higher the possibility of revenue loss.[7] Increasing the number of seats may potentially lower the price premium that can be charged because while cost per seat may decline, it may be offset by decreased yields per seat. Furthermore, certain seat configurations may require higher power plant requirements to counteract increased airplane weight, increasing seat costs in the process. Given its operating cost profile and product placement, an airline chooses an optimal seat configuration. Once this is determined, it remains invariant under normal operations.

Cargo Capacity

Cargo capacity is another important technical efficiency factor, not only to freighters, but also to passenger aircraft, which have to be able to carry passenger baggage and capitalize on cargo space as a good source of ancillary revenue. The aircraft identified in Tables 3.2 and 3.3 have two cargo spaces forward and aft in the belly of the aircraft. After filling the cargo spaces with passenger baggage, the remaining available space is used by carriers for commercial cargo. Most wide-bodies and the A320 family allow containerized cargo pallets called Unit Load Devices (ULDs). These devices allow an efficient turnaround time for an aircraft, increasing its cargo carrying capacity and, therefore, its value. The average revenue yield for cargo operations is six-fold that of passenger yield; air carriers place a high importance on cargo capacity as an important technical metric. Tables 3.2 and 3.3 show the cargo volumes that are available for Boeing and Airbus narrow- and wide-body aircraft products. From these tables, it can be seen that the A380 offers the most cubic feet of cargo at 8,300 ft³.

---

[5] Measuring the distance between rows of seats (one behind the other).
[6] Seat capacity is taken from Airbus and Boeing aircraft technical specifications and dimensions data.
[7] The biggest single cost advantage enjoyed by the LCC is seating density.

Range Capability

The range of an aircraft model is a balance between the MTOW and airspeed. With the expansion of international trade and the progress in trade liberalization, the aircraft with the longest range is preferred, since this gives the airline flexibility in fleet assignments. An aircraft with a 4,000-mile range can be used in short-, medium-, or long-haul markets, whereas an aircraft with a 2,000-mile range is restricted to the short-haul market. However, longer range implies higher operating costs, since these aircraft require larger engines, consume more fuel, and have cost profiles that are efficient only if the range capability is fully utilized. Range often determines an aircraft's deployment within the airline network. The narrow-body, short-range aircraft are suited for short-haul markets and are preferred by LCCs and domestic network carriers. Wide-body aircraft are suited for the long-haul market and are widely used by legacy carriers on international and long haul domestic routes.

Maximum Takeoff Weight

MTOW is literally the maximum amount of weight that the aircraft can carry and become safely airborne on a standard length runway. MTOW is highly regulated by national aviation authorities and explicitly stated by aircraft manufacturers. Regulatory agencies, including the Federal Aviation Administration (FAA) and Joint Aviation Authorities (JAA), specify rigorous structural and performance requirements, including various engine-out performance capabilities, structural integrity requirements in turbulent air and crosswind restrictions, all of which use MTOW as a key input. The MTOW restricts operations for certain aircraft, the number of passengers, and cargo that airlines can safely carry.[8] This becomes an especially important consideration for freighters. The MTOW is influenced by these factors:

- Airfield altitude
- Air temperature
- Condition of runway
- Length of runway
- Obstacles and terrain beyond the end of the runway
- Runway wind direction and velocity

Operating Ratios

Operating ratios are factors that an airline can influence by changing some aspect of its operations. These are variable in the short run and consist of metrics such

---

[8] Bowers, 1989, pp. 516-517.

as aircraft utilization, fuel efficiency, and average stage length, although the latter is an indirect function of aircraft range. In a sense, operating ratios present a mixed indication of efficiency since they are determined by the operating airline. However, operating ratios are an important determinant of aircraft value and have roots in technical and financial aircraft characteristics. Three ratios—fuel efficiency, aircraft utilization and average stage length—are discussed in detail.

Fuel Efficiency

Fuel efficiency is determined largely by the fuel burn of the aircraft, the average speed, and other technical design factors. However, it can also be controlled by airlines by the flying techniques employed, the distance flown, and other variables. Fuel efficiency is an important part of air carrier operations. Fuel cost is a top expense, accounting for more than 50% of operating costs for most airlines; reducing and optimizing fuel consumption may be central to the financial survival of the airline. Fuel efficiency is calculated by dividing the gallons consumed per block hour by the average number of seats and average stage length for each aircraft category. For passenger aircraft, the cabin layout and the seating density are important factors in determining fuel costs. A high-density, one-class seat configuration used by LCC operators will have lower average fuel consumption than a legacy carrier with a three-class configuration. Another factor is the average stage length of the aircraft.

An aircraft has maximum fuel burn during takeoff and climbing to cruising altitude, as well during the descent and landing phase. Therefore, an aircraft with a high stage length would increase its efficiency, since it has lower landing and takeoff cycles. Aircraft with longer ranges are likely to have higher stage lengths, and thus are likely to be more fuel efficient. A longer range is often accompanied with higher airspeeds. Higher airspeeds that tend to increase fuel consumption, and thus decrease efficiency, are indicated in Table 3.4.

Figures 3.1, 3.2, and 3.3 depict the fuel efficiency of various regional jets, narrow-body aircraft, and wide-body aircraft in terms of gallons of fuel burned per seat mile. Table 3.4 also shows fuel efficiency by displaying the fuel consumption per block hour across the regional, narrow-body, and wide-body market. As the number of aircraft seats and the average stage length increase, the average fuel consumption ($CASM_{fuel}$) decreases. Another trend that is visible is that efficiency has increased with newer models, which is attributable to aircraft manufacturers' incorporation of aerodynamic and power plant efficiency with new technological innovations.

Aircraft Utilization

Aircraft utilization is the number of hours an aircraft is used in a given day. This metric is looked at in conjunction with the average stage length. Airlines have a

Table 3.4 Fuel efficiency by aircraft type

		CRJ 100/200	CRJ 700	CRJ 900	EMB 145	EMB 190		
Regional jet	GF per BH	331	395	467	338	586		
	GF per BH per seat	6.61	5.80	5.87	6.76	5.87		
	GF per BH per seat per mile	0.01576	0.00987	0.01032	0.01293	0.00953		
		MD-80	**717-200**	**737-700**	**737-800**	**757-200**	**A319**	**A320**
Narrow-body	GF per BH	922	671	695	784	1,037	723	777
	GF per BH per seat	6.56	5.99	5.14	5.06	5.75	5.66	5.20
	GF per BH per seat per mile	0.00828	0.01094	0.00675	0.00398	0.00399	0.00589	0.00456
		767-200	**767-300**	**767-400**	**777-200**	**747-400**	**A330-200**	
Wide-body	GF per BH	1,429	1,550	1,710	2,130	3,319	1,847	
	GF per BH per seat	7.93	6.94	6.88	8.12	8.99	6.56	
	GF per BH per seat per mile	0.00270	0.00231	0.00199	0.00180	0.00191	0.00177	

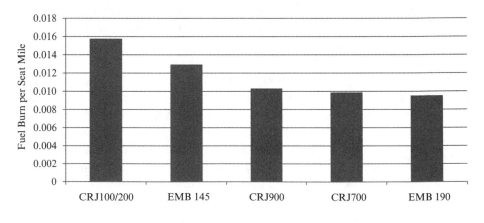

Figure 3.1 Fuel efficiency (regional aircraft)
Source: Compiled from Airline Monitor data.

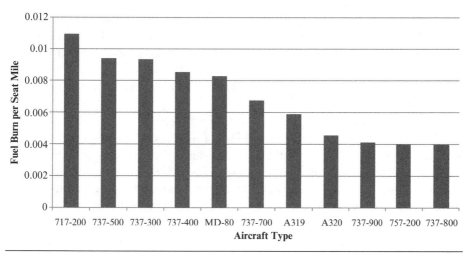

Figure 3.2 Fuel efficiency (narrow-body)
Source: Compiled from Airline Monitor data.

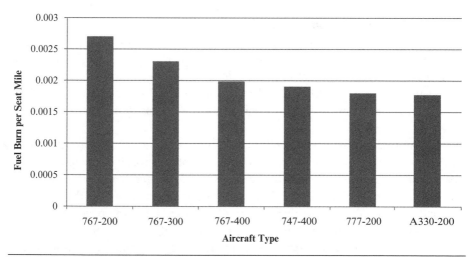

Figure 3.3 Fuel efficiency (wide-body)
Source: Compiled from Airline Monitor data.

better chance of making a profit with higher aircraft utilization, since the fixed costs are spread out over a greater number of revenue hours. Efficient fleet utilization is one of the key factors in an airline's efficiency, productivity, and profitability. While this is clearly a function of airline operations, the costs associated with high aircraft utilization can often become a factor in determining the optimal utilization rate for the airline.

Aircraft utilization is a measure of productivity. To get an average number of block hours per day, divide the number of block hours flown per year by the service days per year. Aircraft utilization is determined by each carrier, as well as the costs and times associated with maintenance and other events. Aircraft utilization is an indicator of operational efficiency. Southwest Airlines uses its aircraft on many short hops per day, which leads to a high aircraft utilization. This creates a quick turnaround time, with little idle time being spent on the ground. Figures 3.4, 3.5, and 3.6 depict aircraft utilization by average stage length. If you were taking a flight from Narita, Japan (NRT) to Shanghai Pudong International (PVG) with two stops along the way, then that flight would have three stage lengths. Note that, on average, higher stage length implies higher aircraft utilization because the longer the stage length, the longer the flight time for a given aircraft.

However, a significant anomaly exists in the utilization pattern of the Boeing 737-700 (Figure 3.5). This aircraft has a significantly higher utilization time compared to a short stage length due to the "Southwest Effect."[9] The Southwest business model is based on short stage length flights with low turnaround time, and efficient scheduling is the reason the Boeing 737-700 exhibits an above normal utilization given the relatively short stage length. Southwest's average flight length of 643 miles is less than United (1,165), Delta (1,208), and AirTran (747). This means, with more than 10 hours of utilization, Southwest aircraft get more cycles each day.[10]

In the case of the Boeing 767-300, a below average utilization given stage length is shown, while the Boeing 767-400 has above average utilization. Delta operates the majority of 767-300s and -400s in the United States, and this effect may be partly attributable to the designated routes being served by these aircraft. International routes that involve an overnight stop at a foreign destination are likely to have lower aircraft utilization (due to the idle time experienced by the aircraft when the airport is inactive) compared with routes that do not involve overnighting.

---

[9] The Southwest Effect is generally referred to as the downward pressure on fares when Southwest enters a market.

[10] Boyd Group International, May 31, 2011.

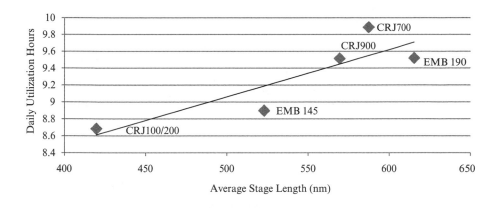

Figure 3.4 Aircraft utilization by stage length (regional jets)
Source: Compiled from Airline Monitor data.

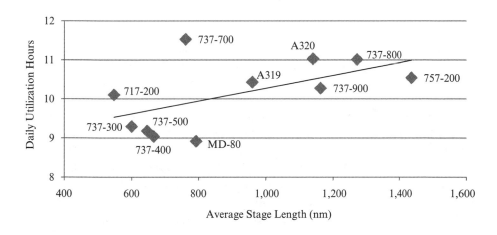

Figure 3.5 Aircraft utilization by stage length (narrow-body)
Source: Compiled from Airline Monitor data.

Average Stage Length

Average stage length is determined by the airline's flight schedule, and generally the longer the stage length, the greater the number of available seat miles (ASM) and the lower the total operating cost per seat mile. The average stage length is largely determined by the aircraft's range.

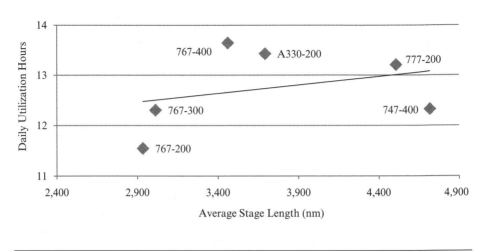

Figure 3.6 Aircraft utilization by stage length (wide-body)
Source: Compiled from Airline Monitor data.

Figures 3.7, 3.8, and 3.9 calculate the fuel efficiency and its correlation with the average stage length. Fuel efficiency was calculated by gallons consumed per block hour per seat per mile. Stage length is the number of miles an aircraft travels between a takeoff and landing. The average is a ratio between total distance travelled and the number of takeoffs (or landings). The graphs illustrate data for regional jets, narrow-body, and wide-body aircraft. The regional jet aircraft category has the least fuel efficiency due to the ratio of number of seats to stage length. The average seat capacity of a regional jet is between 50 and 100, and the stage length is approximately 500 nm. Regional jets are typically used as feeders and an important element of a hub-and-spoke network. Therefore, the additional costs are often guaranteed and subsidized by the legacy carriers and/or through higher fares.

The 737-800 and A320 have very similar operating characteristics as far as average stage length. Both aircraft burned about the same amount of fuel per block hour. The narrow-body aircraft depicted in Figure 3.8 have a better fuel efficiency profile than the regional aircraft, but lag behind wide-body aircraft on an ASM basis. This is because, on average, wide-body aircraft have a much higher ASM per block hour. Even with LCCs such as Southwest operating narrow-bodies, their ASM is likely to be lower than that of a legacy carrier operating wide-bodies over long transatlantic and transpacific routes.

One development in the operations of the 737-800 has been the increase in the average flight stage length in recent years. This increase in stage length may be due

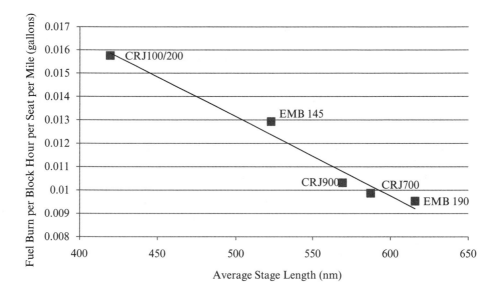

Figure 3.7 Fuel efficiency by stage length (regional jets)
Source: Compiled from Airline Monitor data.

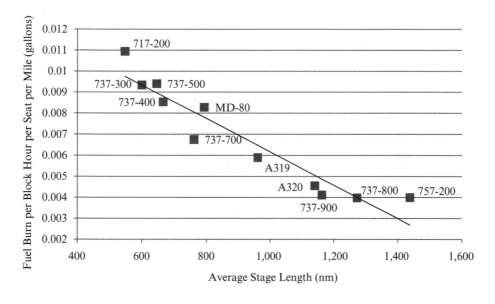

Figure 3.8 Fuel efficiency by stage length (narrow-body)
Source: Compiled from Airline Monitor data.

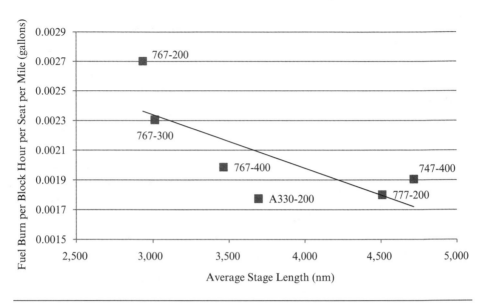

Figure 3.9 Fuel efficiency by stage length (wide-body)
Source: Compiled from Airline Monitor data.

to the increasing use of the 737-800 for Extended-Range Twin-Engine Operations (ETOPS) performance standards.[11] ETOPS operations require certification from the FAA, including the use of additional safety equipment, such as life rafts and/or vests, onboard the aircraft. Both American Trans Air (before its demise) and Alaska Airlines have used the 737-800 for flights from the West Coast to Hawaii.[12]

Finally, wide-body aircraft retain the most fuel-efficient position with a higher capacity of seating and longer stage lengths. For example, the Boeing 747-400 consumes 3,320 gallons of fuel per block hour and carries an average of 370 seats with an average stage length of 4,700 nm.

Figures 3.10, 3.11, and 3.12 show the fuel efficiency of the aircraft against airspeed per block hour. First, it is important to note that since a block hour starts at chocks-off time and ends with chocks-on, this calculation is influenced by taxiing time. The average speed shown in these figures is lower than the cruising speed of the aircraft and is a clear illustration of the economies of greater airspeed trading off with the increased fuel consumption associated with high airspeeds. The

---

[11] U.S. Dept. of Transportation, Federal Aviation Administration, Advisory Circular, AC No. 120-42B.

[12] U.S. Dept. of Transportation, Federal Aviation Administration, Information for Operators. InFO 07004, January 26, 2007.

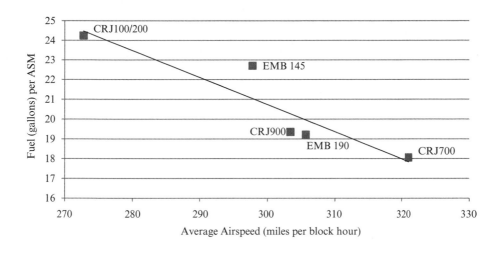

Figure 3.10 Fuel consumption per ASM vs. airspeed (regional jets)
Source: Compiled from Airline Monitor data.

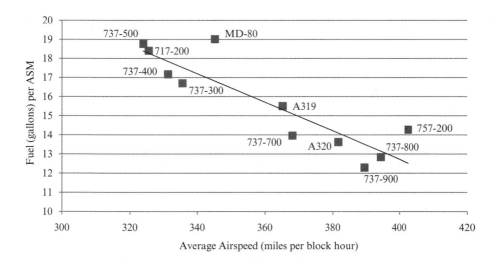

Figure 3.11 Fuel consumption per ASM vs. airspeed (narrow-body)
Source: Compiled from Airline Monitor data.

aircraft spends a great deal of its flight time below cruise speed for reasons other than fuel consideration. Takeoff and climb to cruise altitude are done at less than cruise. All times below 10,000 feet are restricted to 250 kts.

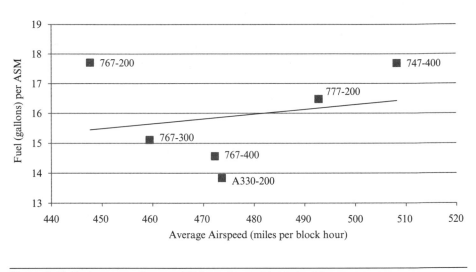

Figure 3.12 Fuel consumption per ASM vs. airspeed (wide-body)
Source: Compiled from Airline Monitor data.

Air traffic control frequently slows aircraft for spacing or sequencing, particularly in congested airspace such as the East Coast. High airspeeds lead to greater ASMs, which lowers the cost of fuel consumed per ASM. However, high airspeeds often consume more fuel, which could cause a decrease in fuel efficiency. The 737-800s and -900s present a good trade-off in this case—they have the lowest fuel burn for a given airspeed. Generally, Boeing aircraft outperform Airbus in terms of fuel efficiency, and Boeing claims the 747-8I is over 10% lighter per seat and consumes 11% less fuel per passenger for a trip cost reduction of 21% and a seat mile cost reduction of more than 6%, when compared to the A380.

Financial and Operational Performance

The performance of different narrow-body aircraft models can be compared and measured to illustrate the financial metrics and variability that exist. An important aspect of analyzing any aircraft is the cost to operate the aircraft. Operating costs can vary significantly from one aircraft type to another. For example, crew and other operating costs vary by airline, so analyzing existing CASM data may be more a function of which airline is operating the aircraft rather than inherent characteristics of the aircraft itself. However, fuel prices are relatively the same across most airlines (unless hedging strategies differ), so analyzing the fuel cost for competing aircraft should reveal which aircraft is more fuel efficient. In addition, other factors to look at are seats per aircraft, stage length, and aircraft utilization. Comparisons will be made on aircraft which are currently in production that compete in the same segment. Furthermore, the comparisons will be broken down into an operating comparison and a financial comparison.

A comprehensive analysis of operating and financial performance of commercial aircraft is provided in this section. Financial performance evaluation has become increasingly important to airline managers due to recent global financial problems. Aircraft financial and operational performance allows the managers to plan for capital investment as efficiently as possible. Productivity measurements may be used as comparisons and guidelines in strategic planning, in the internal analysis of operational efficiency, and the competitive position of an aircraft in the air transportation market.

Aircraft Financial Performance through Financial Ratios Analysis

Financial ratios are used to analyze aircraft efficiency. Financial ratios are an important tool for airline managers to measure the progress for achieving targeted goals. If an airline buys an aircraft from Boeing, the airline can compare the financial performance of other aircraft produced by Airbus or other manufacturers. For example, the 787 is billed as the most advanced and efficient aircraft in its class, carrying 200 to 300 passengers, providing airlines with savings in fuel and operating costs.[13] The FAA's Form 41 requires airlines to report aircraft operating costs in significant detail, providing an in-depth analysis of aircraft operating costs for airlines in the United States. Some of the important cost components and financial metrics that an airline would like to analyze prior to aircraft procurement are: crew costs, depreciation and leases, maintenance costs, and soft costs.

Crew Costs

Crew cost is defined as the costs attributed to pilots, flight attendants, test pilots, reserve pilots, trainee pilots, and instructors for that aircraft type. One of the most important developments in aircraft technology was the use of a two-man flight deck. This feature, coupled with advanced glass displays,[14] made the third member of the crew, the flight engineer, redundant, and provided cost advantages.

---

[13] Jane's World Defense Industry, November 18, 2010.
[14] The third crew member was made redundant prior to the introduction of advanced glass displays.

Crew costs do not include maintenance or flight dispatch personnel, since these are allocated to the maintenance costs and administrative costs categories. A two-person cockpit crew reduced crew costs, and the aircraft's common pilot type rating has ensured greater crew scheduling flexibility and efficiency to carriers that had operated multiple aircraft types.

The Airbus commonality of flight deck controls is why many airlines prefer Airbus aircraft over Boeing. Boeing adopted this technology with the 757 and 767. Cockpit commonality makes it easier for pilots to move across a full family of aircraft, saving time and money in training. In addition, a larger savings comes from eliminating the need for a completely separate group of reserve crews. Commercial airlines are particularly pleased with the use of fly-by-wire technologies and the common cockpit systems in use throughout the Airbus aircraft. An analysis of crew costs and the relevant methodologies for calculating them is provided in Chapter 6.

Depreciation and Leases

Two of the most important financial estimates that airline management teams must make are the aircraft depreciation rate and aircraft residual value assumptions. Airlines review periodically whether the residual value attributed to their aircraft has been appropriately done. The tax system will generally stipulate the useful life of an aircraft and depreciation rate rather than leaving it to the imagination of management for tax purposes. *Depreciation and leases* represent the capital cost of aircraft ownership. A large part of an airline's cost structure is aircraft depreciation. That amount will ultimately depend on what period of time the cost is spread over. Depreciation and leases proxy the financing and usage costs of aircraft ownership. Lease payments also represent significant expenditures, which can affect an airline's free cash flow.

Airline financing is quite complicated, since companies have high financial and operational leverages. Since the Airline Deregulation Act of 1978, many major airlines have declared bankruptcy and have either ceased operation or reorganized under bankruptcy protection.[15] The volatile demand, combined with increased fuel costs, and cost of capital and bankruptcies, led to anemic profit for the entire industry.[16] While other industries generally have a significant advantage to ownership over leasing due to the tax shield offered by depreciation, the airline industry

---

[15] U.S. Airline Bankruptcies and Service Cessations, Air Transport Association (ATA), 2011.

[16] Air Transport Association of America (ATA), Statement on the State of the Airline Industry, Statement for the Record of the Sub-committee on Aviation, Transportation and Infrastructure Committee, U.S. House of Representatives, June 2004.

has typically experienced an extremely low corporate tax rate due to accumulated net operating losses (NOLs). NOLs can be utilized for up to 20 years after they are incurred, and, on average, the airline industry enjoys an effective tax rate of around 11.94%, whereas the corporate tax rate for similar-sized corporations is 35%.[17]

Depreciation policy varies from one airline to another. Airlines prefer to depreciate aircraft using different salvage value and depreciation lives because of their respective financial policies regarding the appropriate depreciation expense. For example, Thai Airways reduced its new aircraft depreciation rate from 20 years to 15 years.[18]

Maintenance Costs

Maintenance costs are defined as the costs of materials and labor that constitute routine and non-routine aircraft repair. Maintenance costs are measured, not maintenance expense, since maintenance costs contain accrued costs for periodic aircraft checks that will be expensed as a check is conducted. In general, there are two categories of aircraft maintenance costs. First, *direct maintenance cost* is the cost of materials, equipment, and workers directly related to maintenance as a whole. Second, *indirect maintenance cost* is the cost related more to the organization of an airline than to the design of the aircraft. In this section, maintenance cost is divided into the following general classes:

- Labor cost, usually one of the larger components of airframe maintenance cost, is comprised of inspection checks, removal, installation, and operational checks.
- Materials and parts, which include all consumable and non-consumable materials, component usage, and other material used in the aircraft maintenance process.

In 2009, the average direct maintenance cost per flight hour was $893, and the average direct maintenance cost per cycle was $2,091.[19] The direct maintenance cost per flight hour varied according to the aircraft category, from an average of $682 per flight hour for narrow-body aircraft to $1,430 per flight hour for wide-body aircraft equipped with three or more engines and $1,204 per flight hour for wide-body aircraft equipped with two engines.

---

[17] United States Department of the Treasury, Internal Revenue Service, 2011.

[18] Thai Airways Company Report, 2008.

[19] An exclusive benchmark analysis (FY2009 data) by IATA's Maintenance Cost Task Force, 2010.

Soft Costs

Soft cost metrics capture airline management's opportunity to select the right aircraft at the right time to support business objectives. Soft costs are defined as a catch all category. Soft costs capture aircraft insurance, navigation costs, and other miscellaneous operating costs:

$$\text{Soft costs} = \text{Total operating costs} - (\text{Fuel} + \text{Maintenance} + \text{Crew} + \text{Depreciation and leases})$$

To demonstrate the applicability of financial metrics, narrow-body aircraft from Boeing and Airbus are compared in Table 3.5 and Figure 3.13, which also present the variability that exists between aircraft products.

Figure 3.13 shows a five-way comparison of aircraft operating costs across four different narrow-body aircraft. The smaller the cost envelope, the more operationally efficient the aircraft. In other words, airlines prefer to utilize the aircraft

Table 3.5 Narrow-body aircraft analysis

	A319	A320-200	737-700LR	757-200
Crew cost/Block hour	436.68	412.35	533.35	636.69
Depreciation and leases/Block hour	116.99	167.17	230.61	271.89
Maintenance costs/Block hour	512.78	585.84	315.84	1,052.46
Soft cost/Block hour	526.40	403.85	216.22	388.30
Fuel cost/Block hour	2,236.17	2,244.93	1,758.05	3,296.17

Source: Compiled from Airline Monitor data.

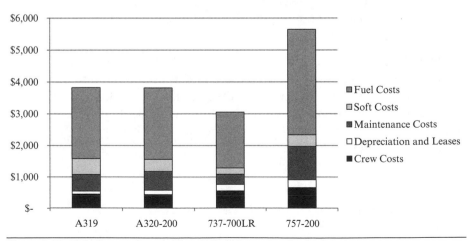

Figure 3.13 Aircraft operating cost breakdown for narrow-body aircraft
Source: Compiled from Airline Monitor data.

with the smallest cost envelope. The disadvantages of the 757-200 are immediately apparent when compared to the 737-700LR and the Airbus A319 and A320. The 757-200 has the largest cost envelope of these narrow-body aircraft. In terms of fuel consumption, the 757-200 has the highest consumption by far, with $3,296.17 per block hour. The 737-700LR has half the cost of the 757-200 at $1,758.03 per block hour and the lowest among the four narrow-bodies, while also outperforming in terms of fuel efficiency on a block hour and ASM basis. The 757-200 underperforms in every category except soft costs. Its maintenance costs and crew costs are also significantly higher than the other narrow-body aircraft. However, the soft costs are lower than those of the A319 and A320, and the depreciation and leases costs are comparable. The trade-off for these lower costs of owning the 757-200 is the higher costs of operation. The cost envelope is higher overall than the other narrow-bodies, indicating that the 757-200 is more expensive to operate overall.

In contrast, the Boeing 737-700 presents the best cost profile. It is the most fuel-efficient aircraft among the four narrow-bodies shown, as well as the most inexpensive to maintain and lease. It is interesting to note that while Boeing aircraft appear to be more expensive to crew than Airbus aircraft, they are less expensive to insure (lower soft costs). This may be a function of Airbus' higher degree of automation—crew training might be lower, but insurance costs and other soft costs are higher due to the greater degree of automated technology. In terms of total costs, the Boeing 737-700 dominates the profiles of the four aircraft shown.

The Airbus A320 and A319 present similar operating profiles to each other. The A319 is a shortened version of the A320. The A320 has seven more rows of seats than the A319. With the same fuel capacity and fewer passengers, the range with 124 passengers in a two-class configuration extends to 1,810 nm with sharklets.[20] They are both less expensive in terms of crewing, but more expensive in terms of soft costs. They also present a higher maintenance cost profile, indicating that equipment upkeep is more expensive than the Boeing 737-800. This also could be a function of greater automation and the necessity for more extensive and expensive checks to ensure normal operation. The Airbus A320 and A319 are also less fuel efficient than the Boeing 737-700, since they have a higher fuel cost per block hour.

To build on the discussion of fuel efficiency as an operating ratio, additional analysis is warranted. Interestingly, all four aircraft have very similar depreciation and leasing expenses, indicating that they are all approximately in the same price range. Their vastly different operating cost profiles, however, point to significant differences in aircraft value. Fuel costs account for nearly 60% of the operating costs of an aircraft. Therefore, Table 3.6 presents a more detailed fuel efficiency analysis for each of the four narrow-body aircraft.

---

[20] Meeting Demands, *Flight International*, August 30, 1995.

Table 3.6 Fuel efficiency analysis

	A319	A320-200	737-700LR	757-200
Fuel cost per ASM (cents per ASM)	4.95	4.27	3.53	4.77
Fuel cost per block hour	2,236.17	2,244.93	1,758.05	3,296.17
Fuel efficiency	63.02	73.23	72.34	66.87
Total ASM (millions of miles)	50,932.41	86,083.13	90,681.83	136,853.77
Average number of seats per aircraft	128	149	135	172
Average airspeed	354	352	368	402
Block hours	1,127,251	1,636,310	1,821,438	1,979,490

The Boeing 737-700 is over 70 cents per ASM less expensive than the Airbus A320, which is the closest aircraft in terms of efficiency. In an industry with wafer-thin profit margins per route, this cost difference represents significant savings to the major operating cost driver. This could be attributed to the inherent technical efficiency of the aircraft, but also to significant economies of scale and the fact that 737s are extensively used by LCCs in the United States.

Another comparison emerges between the A319 and the 757-200. While the 757-200 is more expensive on a block hour basis, fuel costs per ASM indicate that the Airbus A319 is the more expensive of the two, nearly 20 cents per ASM more than the Boeing 757. This can be accounted for by the fact that the 757-200 has a higher airspeed, as well as a much larger number of seats per aircraft than the A319, or even the 737-700. This allows it to offer a much higher ASM per block hour, simply because there are, on average, nearly 50 more passengers transported per flight than the Airbus A319. While the block hours are low, the ASMs are extremely high, allowing the 757-200 to remain efficient even with relatively higher fuel costs. In contrast, the A319 is appealing from a block hour cost standpoint, but the low passenger capacity makes it inefficient on an ASM basis. Coupled with lower soft costs, the Boeing 757-200 may be an efficient airplane in a low-cost, high-passenger-density configuration when compared to the Airbus A319 or A320.

Comparative Analysis of Efficiency

Ladies and gentlemen, welcome to Glasgow; we hope you enjoyed your flight and thank you for flying EasyJet. If you didn't enjoy your flight, thank you for flying Ryanair.

—EasyJet flight attendant announcement, 2005

The financial and operational performance of the two different types (narrow-body and wide-body) of aircraft by Boeing and Airbus can be compared. The narrow-body Boeing 737NG and Airbus 320 start the discussion.

Narrow-body: Boeing 737NG vs. Airbus A320

The 737 series is the best-selling jet airliner in the history of the airline industry.[21] There are on average 1,250 737 aircraft flying at any given time, with 24 departing or landing somewhere every minute, as of 2009. The Boeing 737-700, 737-800, and 737-900 compete directly with the Airbus A319, A320, and A321 in the narrow-body, short- to medium-haul commercial aircraft market. As of June 2011, a total of about 4,700 Airbus A320 family aircraft were delivered, of which 4,607 were in active service. These two families of aircraft are widely popular with LCCs. Southwest, Virgin Blue, and Ryanair use the 737NG while JetBlue, Virgin America, and AirAsia use the A320 family; EasyJet uses both. United, Delta, and American Airlines are legacy carriers that use the 737NG family. Of these, United and Delta also operate members of the A320 family. US Airways is the only U.S. legacy carrier that currently uses A320 aircraft but not any 737NG aircraft. Other users of the A320 family are Frontier and Spirit Airlines, both with over 25 A319s in their fleet.

In order to complete a comparative analysis of the 737NG vs. the A320 family, a competing model from each manufacturer, the Boeing 737-700 and the Airbus A319, was selected. Block hour costs of these models for legacy carriers and LCCs individually are compared and then further analyzed for the aircraft's costs and associated benefits and savings that they offer. To set the proper framework for analysis, two products from the operational standpoint of legacy carriers are evaluated, as shown in Figure 3.14. In the operational characteristics, numerous

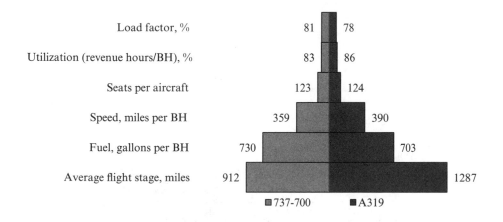

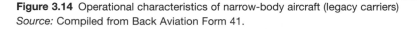

Figure 3.14 Operational characteristics of narrow-body aircraft (legacy carriers)
Source: Compiled from Back Aviation Form 41.

---

[21] Kingsley-Jones, M. 6,000 and counting for Boeing's popular little Twinjet. *Flight International,* Reed Business Information, April 22, 2009.

similarities are shown in 737-700 and A319 operations with few significant differences. Both aircraft, with similar seat numbers and utilization per day, have significantly different average flight stage lengths. Legacy carriers that use the 737-700 compared to the A319 use it on a stage length that is 375 miles longer.

When examining these two aircraft from an operational and financial standpoint, it is important to realize that costs are dependent on the airline. Some costs are relatively invariant to airline operations; fuel burn, for instance, is invariant although it is indirectly affected by stage length and flight procedures. However, other costs, including crew costs, depreciation and leases, and soft costs, are all highly dependent on an individual airline's operating characteristics.

Figure 3.15 highlights the advantages that the Boeing 737-700 offers to legacy carriers in comparison to its competitor, the Airbus A319. The 737-700 presents cost savings on all of the measured metrics. One of the most significant cost differences is in the flight crew costs of each aircraft. The 737-700 flight crew costs a significant $160.98 less per block hour than the A319. In terms of the biggest cost factor to airlines, fuel, the 737-700 also has the upper hand for legacy carriers by costing approximately $65 less per block hour. This number quickly translates into real savings when the fleet sizes and numbers of hours legacy carriers fly are taken into account.

The effect of airlines' operational characteristics must be taken into account when interpreting this data. For example, if Southwest Airlines' financial data was included in Figure 3.15, the fuel cost per block hour for the 737-700 would decrease from $2,241 to $1,758. In other words, the highly efficient operating characteristics of Southwest Airlines lower the overall fuel costs for the 737-700, but other carriers actually experience a much higher fuel cost.

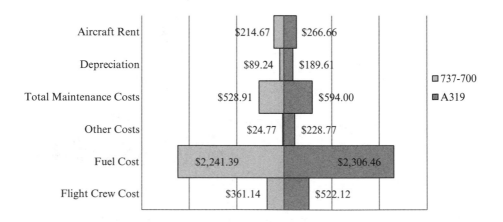

Figure 3.15 Block hour cost comparison (legacy carriers)
Source: Compiled from Back Aviation Form 41 data.

Figure 3.16 shows that CASM is significantly less for legacy carriers that operate the 737-700. With greater fuel efficiency and longer average stage lengths, the 737-700 has a CASM of 8.18 cents per seat mile while the A319 has a CASM of 9.39 cents per seat mile. After factoring out fuel costs, it still holds that the 737-700 has a cost advantage over the A319. CASM, after excluding fuel costs per average seat mile, is 3.55 and 4.21 for the 737-700 and A319, respectively.

The opposite trend in operating characteristics for LCCs is shown in Figure 3.17. The 737-700 is flown on significantly shorter stage lengths and the average is 491 miles less than the A319. Airlines using the A319 use the aircraft on longer stage lengths in order to compensate for the high fuel burns. The Boeing 737-700 is utilized for 11.7 block hours per day while the A319 is utilized for 11.9. Frontier, Spirit and United operate their aircraft for over 11 hours per day, while Delta and US Airways had an aircraft utilization of less than 10 hours per day.

Aircraft do not make money sitting on the ground; US Airways and Delta would likely need to increase aircraft utilization of the A319 in order to become more profitable. Load factors are 9% less on the 737-700, which on average has three fewer seats than the A319 when utilized by LCCs. By increasing daily utilization, airlines certainly enjoy the lower CASM produced by these aircraft.[22] By serving smaller, uncongested airports and by focusing on point-to-point flights, airlines can maximize the number of daily block hours and, thus, aircraft utilization. A word of caution: This also may have an adverse effect on profitability if the managers deploy these aircraft on routes to sparsely populated local airports with

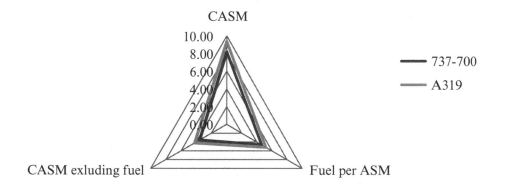

Figure 3.16 CASM (in cents) for narrow-body aircraft (legacy carriers)
Source: Compiled from Back Aviation Form 41 data.

---

[22] *Aircraft daily utilization* is the ratio of aircraft hours flown divided by aircraft days available.

a very competitive yield. To add ASMs into current markets (lowering yields as a result), or to deploy incremental ASMs into markets where the yields are already lower or there is insufficient traffic to support the increased capacity, would reduce profits. Other operational characteristics displayed in Figure 3.17 include the fact that the A319 flies faster at 381 miles per block hour over an average stage length of 1234 miles compared to the 737-700 flying at 359 miles per block hour over a 743-mile average stage length. Fuel consumption is also 22 gallons less per block hour for the 737-700 at 694 gallons, compared to the 703 gallons of the A319.

The operating characteristics shown in Figure 3.17 translate into the cost comparisons shown in Figure 3.18. The Boeing 737-700 costs significantly more when it comes to crew costs, $172 more than the A319 per block hour. This can be attributed to Southwest's higher crew compensation when compared to other LCCs (and, as we will see later on, legacy carriers as well). LCC crew compensation amounts are therefore dominated by the relatively high-paid crew of Southwest Airlines.

With a longer average stage length, one would expect CASM to be lower for the A319 if the fuel efficiency of each aircraft were equal. The data shows that despite a longer average stage length for the A319, fuel usage during 2007 was about the same per block hour. CASM on the A319 is higher than the 737-700 at 7.19 cents per seat mile, compared to 5.98 cents per seat mile on the 737-700. Some of the CASM differences are due to the fact that 737-700 operators paid less on average for fuel than A319 operators in 2007 ($3.45 per gallon compared to $4.23 per gallon). The lower fuel price for the 737-700 was due in part to the successful fuel hedging of Southwest Airlines, which operated a fleet of more than 300 737-700s. If factoring out the fuel costs per ASM, the 737-700 still has a lower

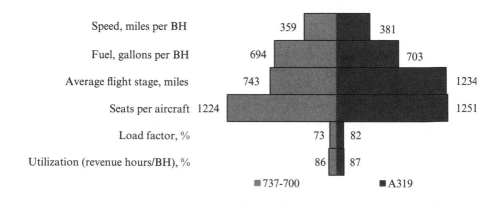

Figure 3.17 Operational characteristics of narrow-body aircraft (LCCs)
Source: Compiled from Back Aviation Form 41 data.

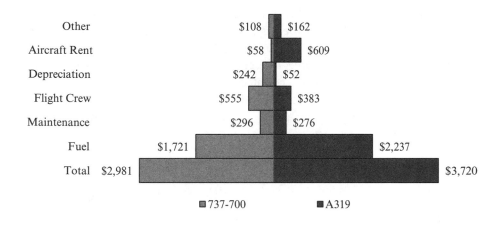

	737-700	A319
Other	$108	$162
Aircraft Rent	$58	$609
Depreciation	$242	$52
Flight Crew	$555	$383
Maintenance	$296	$276
Fuel	$1,721	$2,237
Total	$2,981	$3,720

■ 737-700   ■ A319

Figure 3.18 Block hour cost comparison of narrow-body aircraft (LCCs)
Source: Compiled from Back Aviation Form 41 data

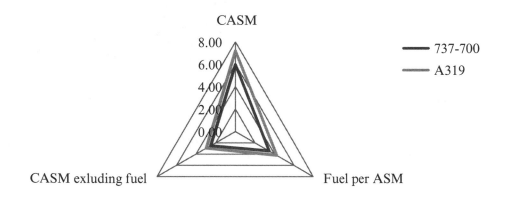

CASM

—— 737-700
—— A319

CASM exluding fuel

Fuel per ASM

Figure 3.19 CASM (in cents) for LCCs
Source: Compiled from Back Aviation Form 41 data.

CASM than the A319 at 2.52 cents per seat mile compared to 2.97 cents per seat mile. This data shows that the 737-700 holds a cost advantage over the A319, most likely due to lower maintenance costs or other costs of operation (see Figure 3.19).

On most fronts, the costs experienced by LCCs are lower than those of legacy carriers on a block hour basis. These cost advantages enable LCCs to compete on the basis of price in a highly commoditized market, giving them a significant competitive advantage. In part due to Southwest's successful fuel hedging, LCC fuel costs are $1,721 compared to $2,242 for legacy carriers. Another way of interpreting cost comparisons, shown in Figure 3.20, is to identify the cost structure in terms of percentages for the legacy carriers and LCCs. This is represented in Figure 3.21 as a breakdown of the Boeing 737-700 cost structure. There are similar cost structures, but notable differences. For both legacy airlines and LCCs, the biggest cost was fuel, which accounted for 57 and 58% of costs, respectively. Legacy carriers had 14% of total costs attributable to maintenance costs, while LCCs only had 10% of costs for the same factor. However, LCCs had a higher percentage of flight crew costs partially due to the relatively highly compensated

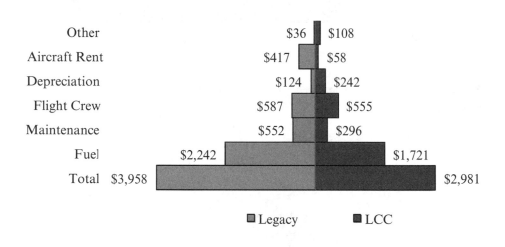

Figure 3.20 Boeing 737-700 block hour cost comparison (legacy vs. LCC)
Source: Compiled from Back Aviation Form 41 data.

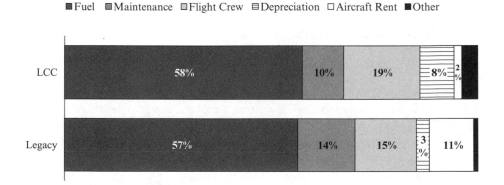

Figure 3.21 Boeing 737-700 cost structure (legacy vs. LCC)
Source: Compiled from Back Aviation Form 41 data.

Southwest Airlines flight crews. A higher percentage of costs (8% compared to 3%) for LCCs in terms of aircraft depreciation was also determined. Legacy carriers faced a significantly higher percentage of aircraft rent costs. This differential reflected the lease vs. buy decision, which was made by carriers that chose to work with operating lessors to rent aircraft vs. owning, and subsequently depreciating, their planes.

Fuel hedging certainly contributed to the lower CASM of LCC operators of the 737-700. Southwest paid a lower price per gallon of fuel ($1.70 compared to over $2 for the other three carriers), achieving lower fuel costs per ASM and a lower total CASM. AirTran, now a part of Southwest Airlines, was able to achieve a low CASM of 5.2 cents, due in part to its low crew costs of 0.65 cents per ASM. However, even after removing the effects of fuel costs, the CASM experienced by LCCs is 2.52 cents compared to 3.55 cents for legacy carriers (see Figure 3.22).

Figure 3.23 compares the block hour cost of the legacy carriers and LCCs that operate the A319. Overall, legacy carriers pay more per block hour when using the A319 compared to LCCs. However, legacy carriers paid, on average, $44 less on fuel per block hour and $83 less on depreciation costs. The costs reduction for LCCs was significant; on average legacy carriers paid $564 more per block hour when operating the A319 compared to LCCs.

Looking at the normalized costs (in terms of their respective percentages), there are similarities as well as differences between legacy carriers and LCCs (see Figure 3.24). The majority of the costs for both types of operators were for fuel, as expected, and similar percentages of costs were attributable to flight crew costs. However, a larger percentage of legacy carrier costs was attributable to

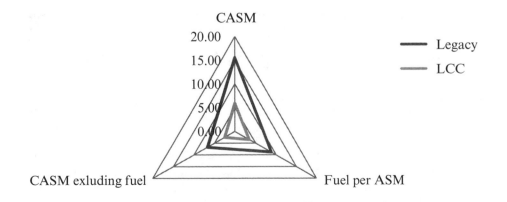

Figure 3.22 Boeing 737-700 CASM (in cents) comparison (legacy vs. LCC)
Source: Compiled from Back Aviation Form 41 data.

Airbus A319 block hour cost comparison

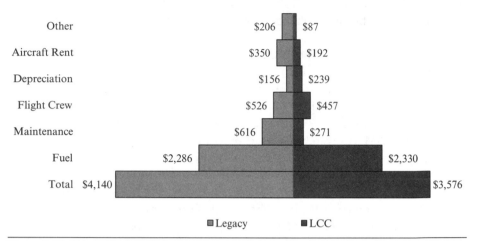

	Legacy	LCC
Other	$206	$87
Aircraft Rent	$350	$192
Depreciation	$156	$239
Flight Crew	$526	$457
Maintenance	$616	$271
Fuel	$2,286	$2,330
Total	$4,140	$3,576

■ Legacy   ■ LCC

Figure 3.23 Airbus A319 block hour cost comparison (legacy vs. LCC)
Source: Compiled from Back Aviation Form 41 data.

Airbus A319 Cost Structure (Legacy vs. LCC)

■ Fuel   ■ Maintenance   ▨ Flight Crew   ▤ Depreciation   ☐ Aircraft Rent   ■ Other

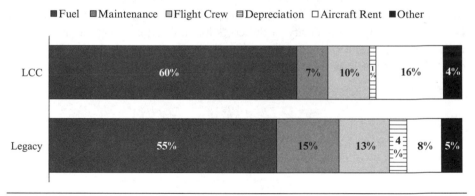

LCC: 60% | 7% | 10% | 1% | 16% | 4%

Legacy: 55% | 15% | 13% | 4% | 8% | 5%

Figure 3.24 Airbus A319 cost structure (legacy vs. LCC)
Source: Compiled from Back Aviation Form 41 data.

maintenance costs, at 15%. Maintenance for LCC operators was less than half that of the legacy carriers, at 7%. Higher cost percentages were also present for depreciation cost to the legacy carriers. Many network airlines such Delta, Northwest, United, Continental, and several others filed for bankruptcy in the past. Chapter 11 protection allowed those airlines to pursue cuts in wages and make changes to pension and health benefits for workers and retirees. CASM numbers for the Airbus A319 showed a similar pattern to that of the Boeing 737-700 despite a smaller cost differential between legacy airlines and LCCs (see Figure 3.25). The CASM for legacy carriers was 9.39 cents compared to 7.19 cents for LCCs. Even after removing the effects of fuel, the CASM was still 1.24 cents lower for LCCs.

Looking at individual operators, some interesting facts appear. Since the merger with America West Airlines in 2005, US Airways claimed to be an LCC; however, it had the highest A319 CASM in 2007 (US Airways, 2009). If US Airways planned to become a profitable airline, and successfully transition into an LCC, then lowering the A319's CASM to be more in line with other airlines was a critical component. Another note on CASM is that Spirit Airlines was supposed to be an ultra-low-cost carrier (ULCC), yet Northwest Airlines (now Delta) had a nearly identical CASM to Spirit in 2007. If Delta were able to keep CASM in line with Spirit, it meant that the legacy carrier was able to compete with low-cost competition.

Wide-body: Boeing 777-200 vs. Airbus A330-300

The 777-200 and A330-300 compete in the long-haul commercial aircraft market. Both aircraft are twin-engine and heavily used by airlines on high-demand transatlantic routes. Notable 777-200 operators include United Airlines, American Airlines, and British Airways; notable A330-300 operators include Cathay Pacific, Air Canada, and US Airways. Delta Air Lines operates both aircraft since its merger with Northwest Airlines. The A330-300 burned less fuel per block hour than the 777-200; lower fuel burn provides a huge advantage to airlines that operate the A330 when fuel prices are high. The A330-300 also holds, on average, 18

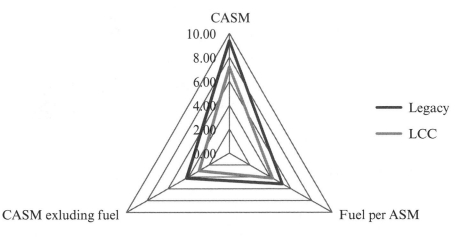

Figure 3.25 Airbus A319 CASM (in cents) comparison (legacy vs. LCC)
Source: Compiled from Back Aviation Form 41 data.

more passengers than the 777-200 (280 seats vs. 262 seats); however, this may be more a function of airline seating layouts rather than the actual potential seating capacity of the two aircraft, as Boeing lists a higher seating capacity for the 777-200 (Thomas et al., 2008). Both aircraft have a high aircraft utilization rate of over 13 hours per day, which is due to the fact that they are operated on longer stage lengths than narrow-body aircraft.

The A330, from most indications, is more economical to operate than the 777-200, specifically on fuel, maintenance, flight crew and depreciation costs. Maintenance costs for the A330 are less than half that of the 777; the A330's average total maintenance costs were $672 compared to $1,431 for the 777-200. The lower fuel costs for the A330 can be traced in part to the lower fuel burn per hour, compared to the 777. The A330's fuel cost per block hour is $6,380 while the 777 costs $331 more per block hour (see Figures 3.26 and 3.27).

Due to the lower fuel burn, the A330 has a much lower CASM than the 777 (4.65 cents compared to 6.30 cents) as shown in Figure 3.28. In addition, the A330 also holds a significant advantage in non-fuel cost per ASM (1.75 cents compared to 2.77 cents). This indicates that the A330 is less expensive to operate when it comes to other costs and maintenance. Further, compare the A330 and 777 by looking at the individual operators of the two aircraft types. Using the Back Aviation database to analyze U.S. operators of the two aircraft types can achieve a better idea of the economics of the two aircraft. Delta and Continental had the lowest CASMs, with 5.53 and 6.14 cents respectively, of U.S. 777 operators in

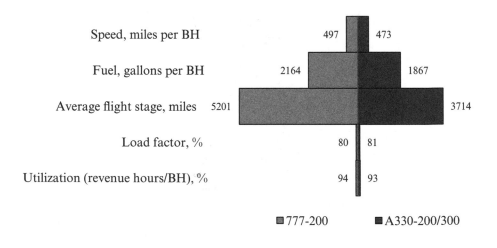

Figure 3.26 Operational characteristics of wide-body aircraft
Source: Compiled from Back Aviation Form 41 data.

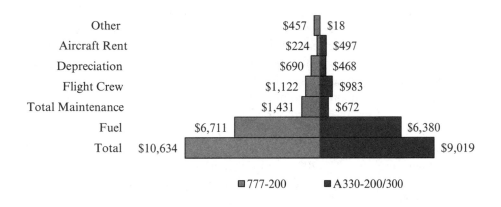

Other		$457	$18
Aircraft Rent		$224	$497
Depreciation		$690	$468
Flight Crew		$1,122	$983
Total Maintenance		$1,431	$672
Fuel	$6,711		$6,380
Total	$10,634		$9,019

■ 777-200   ■ A330-200/300

Figure 3.27 Block hour cost of wide-body aircraft
Source: Compiled from Back Aviation Form 41 data.

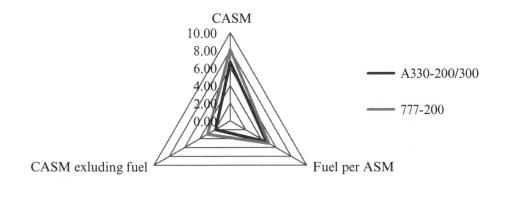

Figure 3.28 CASM comparison (in cents) of wide-body jets (777-200 vs. A330-200/300)
Source: Compiled from Back Aviation Form 41 data.

2007. This may go back to the aircraft utilization statistic; an aircraft that is being utilized more is spreading its costs out over a larger number of available seat miles.

One interesting point to note is how few A330-300s are in service with U.S. airlines. Despite having been in service for fifteen years around the world, there are only three operators of that aircraft type: Northwest Airlines (now Delta), US Airways, and Hawaiian Airlines. Delta operates 21 A330-300s and 11 A330-200s, while US Airways operates a meager 9; Hawaiian started operations of the type as a result of its refleeting program, replacing its Boeing 767-300ERs.

Another interesting note is the relationship between the aircraft's average speed and fuel burn. Northwest Airlines steadily decreased the average speed of the A330 over the first five years of its operation (2003-2007), in order to achieve a lower fuel burn. Many airlines are implementing similar procedures to reduce the speed of aircraft while in flight in order to conserve fuel.[23] Boeing uses a cost index in the flight computer to compute the best cruise speed for each flight given flight conditions, fuel, and block hour costs. The 777, on the other hand, has been popular with U.S. carriers since its introduction into service with United Airlines in 1995 (Eden, 2006). U.S. operators include American, Delta, and United, with United having the most 777-200s of all U.S. carriers.

The advantage of wide-body aircraft over narrow-body aircraft is in the CASM numbers. The A330 in particular has a very low CASM; the Northwest Airlines CASM was 4.49 cents in 2007, while the US Airways CASM was 5.15 cents for the aircraft type. This means that wide-body aircraft like the A330 and 777 aircraft compensate for a higher fuel burn by flying more people over longer distances, thereby reducing their CASM.

Regional Jets: CRJ100/200 vs. ERJ 145

Bombardier and Embraer compete head to head for the regional jet market, offering tremendously similar aircraft with similar capacities, ranges, and other operating and financial specifications. To complete a regional jet analysis, competing models from each manufacturer were selected.

The CRJ program was launched in 1989, and with it, Bombardier became the pioneer of the 50-seat jet class aircraft. The CRJ100/200 family competes directly with the ERJ 145 for the niche 50-seat segment with unit costs of $24-$39 million. The CRJ200 provides 70 seats, the CRJ700 up to 78 seats, and the CRJ1000 more than 100 seats. As of July 2011, a total of 1,647 CRJ's were delivered to the airlines.[24] The major operators of the CRJ100/200 include Comair, SkyWest Airlines, MexicanaLink,[25] Pinnacle Airlines, and Atlantic Southeast Airlines.

The ERJ 135/145 family of commercial airplanes is composed of three variants with seating capacity varying from 37 to 50 seats. The ERJ 135 has 37 seats, the ERJ 140 has 44 seats, and the ERJ 145 has 50 seats. The Embraer ERJ 145 is a single-aisle, cabin-pressurized, twin-engine, regional jetliner with a price tag of $10-12 million. Operators of the ERJ 145 include ExpressJet,[26] American Eagle, and Chautauqua[27] Airlines. The

---

[23] According to Airbus, the reduction from max. cruise to long-range cruise is 7%, which is the widest possible range.

[24] Bombardier, 2011.

[25] MexicanaLink was a subsidiary of Mexicana Airlines and ceased operations on August 28, 2010.

[26] ExpressJet Airlines is an American regional airline based in the Greenspoint area of Houston, TX.

[27] Chautauqua is a subsidiary of Republic Airways Holdings based in Indianapolis, IN.

.competing CRJ100/200 family is similarly heavily utilized by ASA, SkyWest, Pinnacle, and Comair. The largest operators of these two products, ExpressJet and SkyWest, respectively operate 244 ERJ 145s and 148 CRJ100/200s.

Comparing the operational characteristics shown in Figure 3.29, the CRJ 100/200 and ERJ 145 families have nearly identical operating characteristics, with the primary differences traceable to their utilization by individual airlines. Both aircraft families offer the same fuel burn. CRJ100/200s are, on average, flown on longer flight segments and utilized 9.25 block hours per day, compared to 8.65 for ERJ 145s. The CRJ100/200 is flown on an average stage length of 516 miles at 296 miles per block hour, while the ERJ 145 covers 118 fewer miles per flight at a speed of 265 miles per block hour.

In further analyzing these two regional jet offerings, a much smaller range of differences is apparent than in the narrow-body and wide-body jet market (see Figure 3.30). After incorporating all the block hour costs, there is a $262 difference between the CRJ100/200 and the ERJ 145. The ERJ 145's cost savings comes from a lower fuel and aircraft rent cost. The ERJ 145 costs $349 per block hour for maintenance compared to $332 for the CRJ100/200. The flight crew costs for both families are comparable, despite the ERJ 145 costing on average $5 more per block hour. Aircraft rent costs for the CRJ100/200 are threefold that of the ERJ 145 ($380 and $124, respectively).[28]

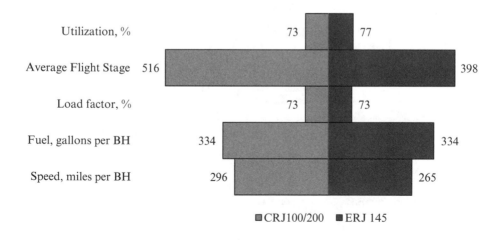

Figure 3.29 Operational characteristics comparison (regional jets)
Source: Compiled from Back Aviation Form 41 data.

---

[28] Driven by the lower sales prices of Embraer vs. Bombardier.

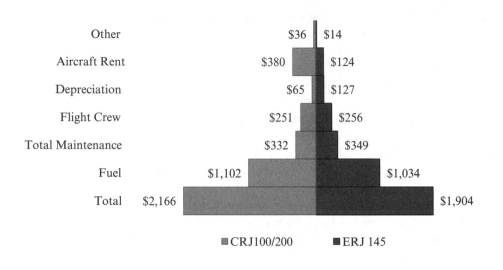

Figure 3.30 Regional jet block hour cost comparison
Source: Compiled from Back Aviation Form 41 data.

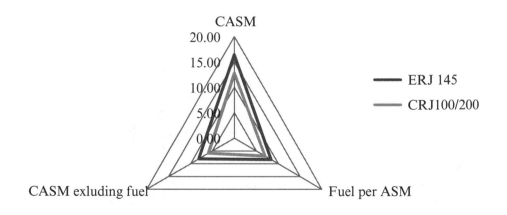

Figure 3.31 CASM comparison (ERJ 145 vs. CRJ100/200)
Source: Compiled from Back Aviation Form 41 data.

The CRJ100/200 has a longer average stage length and identical fuel efficiency as the ERJ 145, so a lower CASM for the CRJ100/200 can be expected. Figure 3.31 corroborates this expectation; the CRJ100/200 has a lower CASM, and thus holds a cost advantage over the ERJ 145 for regional jet operators. After correlating this with the cost metrics shown in Figure 3.30, it is likely that the advantage is due to the lower maintenance costs and other operational efficiencies utilized by operators of the CRJ100/200. The CRJ100/200 has a CASM of 12.42 cents, while the ERJ 145 has a CASM of 16.46 cents. After excluding the effects of fuel costs, the CRJ100/200 still has a lower CASM of 5.87 cents compared to 8.11 cents for the ERJ 145.

Summary

Aircraft efficiency can be examined from numerous perspectives: technical, operating, and financial. Technical efficiency is derived directly from an aircraft's physical characteristics, over which the airline has relatively little control. This includes average airspeed, fuel burn, and available seats. Operating characteristics are those that an airline can influence during the course of normal operations. The most prominent among these are aircraft utilization and average stage length. Financial characteristics are the financial implications to an airline of an aircraft's technical and operational characteristics, often expressed as fuel cost per block hour and fuel cost per available seat mile. Maintenance and depreciation characteristics are determined by the aircraft model and expressed in the form of maintenance and depreciation costs. To illustrate these characteristics and efficiencies, competing narrow-body, wide-body, and regional jet aircraft models from major manufacturers can be analyzed by using the various operating, financial, and technical metrics.

References

Alaska Airlines. (August 28, 2008). Alaska Airlines completes transition to all-Boeing fleet. Retrieved from http://www.alaskasworld.com/Newsroom/ASNews/ASstories/AS_20080828_140339.asp.

Alaska Airlines. (2009). Route map. Retrieved from http://www.alaskaair.com/as/alaska/images/asqxroutemap.pdf .

American Airlines. (2008a). AMR Corporation reports second quarter 2008 loss of $284 million excluding special items, as record fuel prices drove $838 million in higher costs compared to a year ago. Retrieved from http://www.americanairlines.jp/content/jp/aboutUs_en/pr20080724.jhtml.

American Airlines. (2008b). 2008, 3rd quarter SEC filing. Retrieved from http://phx.corporate-ir.net/phoenix.zhtml?c=117098&p=irol-IRHome.

Bowers, P. (1989). *Boeing aircraft since 1916*. London: Putnam Aeronautical Books.

CH Aviation. (2009). Fleet lists. Retrieved from http://www.ch-aviation.ch/air-craft.php.

Delta Air Lines. (January 27, 2009). Delta Air Lines 2008 annual financial reports.

Eden, P. E. (2006). *Civil aircraft today: The world's most successful commercial aircraft*. London: Summertime Publishing, Ltd.

Snyder, B. (February 4, 2009). JetBlue pilots vote down union. Retrieved from http://www.cbsnews.com/8301-505123_162-43640408/jetblue-pilots-vote-down-union/.

Thomas, G., et al. (2008). *Plane simple truth: Clearing the air on aviation's environmental impact*. Perth, Australia: Aerospace Technical Publications International.

US Airways. (2009). US Airways chronology. Retrieved from http://www.usair-ways.com/awa/content/aboutus/pressroom/history/chronology.aspx.

4

A Methodology
for Aircraft Valuation

There are a lot of parallels between what we're doing and an expensive watch. It's very complex, has a lot of parts and it only has value when it's predictable and reliable.

—Gordon Bethune, Chairman and CEO, Continental Airlines, 1997

An aircraft's valuation and the projection of its future price is an intricate process. This and the following chapter provide a comprehensive review of aircraft valuation and present a methodology that accurately measures return on investment, improves the efficiency of managing operating costs, and effectively determines yield analysis.

The *value* of an aircraft depends on internal factors that are directly related to the aircraft's specifications and documentation. Some examples of these factors are the aircraft's age, size, seating capacity, fuel efficiency, and technical status. In addition, the aircraft *price* depends on external factors such as market demand and elasticity, fuel cost, and environmental regulations. The external factors are extremely important because they indicate where in the aviation industry cycle the aircraft is, and this, in turn, has the greatest impact on aircraft value. Consequently, the theoretical value of a commercial aircraft is highly responsive to the assumptions underlying the specification of the valuation model. By examining the relationship between an aircraft's physical and operational characteristics such as fuel efficiency, revenue, and costs of aircraft systems, the key parameters in an aircraft pricing model can be developed. This chapter will cover the following topics on aircraft valuation:

Intricacy and Resourcefulness

Current Market Practices

Aircraft and Data Selection

• Boeing Aircraft
• Airbus Aircraft

Potential Sources of Revenue

• Passenger Revenue
• Cargo Revenue
• Ancillary Revenue

Aircraft Total Cost Structure

• Total Operating Costs
• Direct Operating Costs
• Indirect Operating Costs
• Non-operating Costs

Aircraft Valuation Methodology

• Weighted Average Cost of Capital
• Discounted Cash Flow Model

At the end of the chapter is a Summary for chapter review and References for further study.

Intricacy and Resourcefulness

Aircraft valuation is a complicated process, but nonetheless critical for nearly every airline, leasing companies, and lending institutions. With the continued deregulation of the airline industry in the U.S. and privatization abroad, commercial airlines have adjusted to a volatile industry with some degree of success.

One of the major assets of airlines is the aircraft itself. Therefore, it is considerably important to develop a methodology for estimating an aircraft's value as well as its efficient utilization to ensure an acceptable rate of return on the asset. However, estimating an aircraft's value is a complex process. Factors determining an aircraft's value not only include the physical characteristics of the aircraft such as size, age, seating capacity, fuel efficiency, and physical condition, but also items such as maintenance status and maintenance documentation, operating expenses, and revenue. Exogenous factors such as demand and its elasticity, inflation rates and interest rates, fuel cost, safety issues and regulation, and, finally, environmental regulations will influence prices.

During this analysis, it should become evident that many internal characteristics of the aircraft contributed toward value disparities between Airbus and Boeing. Although there are numerous factors involved, the seating capacity, class configuration, containerized cargo space, cargo capacity, fuel consumption, and capital cost rates all drive cash flows. For example, having containerized cargo space could automate cargo handling, an otherwise labor- and time-intensive work process. The consequential reduction in on-ground time and labor cost would then contribute to a lower operating cost.

Exogenous factors such as a fuel crisis, terrorism,[1] financial crisis, and predatory practices can significantly alter the demand for aircraft and therefore change the estimated value.[2] For instance, there is an increase in demand for older wide-body aircraft when there is a capacity shortage or significant diminution in fuel costs. On the other hand, technological progress that reduces the operating costs of new aircraft, environmental regulations that restrict older aircraft, or higher fuel prices would have a dampening effect on values of older wide-body aircraft.[3] In addition, since the value of an aircraft depends on its operating costs, older aircraft are retired when the break-even load factor is too high to generate enough revenue to cover operating costs. These operating costs are mainly determined by fuel efficiency, range, seat capacity, maintenance expenditures, and airport fees.

In general, higher operating costs result in lower aircraft value. In particular, airlines pay higher prices for new aircraft if the aircraft lowers operating costs by allowing for more fuel-efficient operations. An airline's evaluation is based on this trade-off between one-time capital investment and lifetime operating expenses, including depreciation and fuel costs.

Recent decades, however, have seen a marked lowering of operating costs through several factors that contributed to an increase in energy efficiency; among these are aerodynamic improvements and enhancements in engine thrust. The wear and tear of an aircraft is appraised on the basis of flight hours and the number of cycles. This can vary significantly from one operator to another, since the same type of aircraft can be operated on different routes with different distances and a varying number of landings per hour. Macroeconomic factors are also extremely important because they indicate the aviation industry cycle, which can

---

[1] In the period immediately after 2001, values of the 737-300 fell to record lows, with some being scrapped. *Aircraft Value News*, April 20, 2008.

[2] Aloha Airlines filed for Chapter 11 bankruptcy protection on March 12, 2008. The airline said that it was unable to generate sufficient revenue due to what it called "predatory pricing" by Mesa Air Group Inc.'s go! Airline.

[3] Values of older wide-bodied aircraft continue to face weakness as the effects of higher maintenance and operating costs take precedence over lack of newer products. *Aircraft Value News*, 2008.

have the greatest impact on aircraft values. All of these factors make aircraft valuation complex and dynamic.

The question of valuing commercial aircraft has not been explored in any great depth by researchers in academia. Gibson and Morrell (2005) explored the actual practice regarding aircraft financial evaluation. They proposed the net present value (NPV) approach (with close attention to the choice of discount rates to flesh out investment/financing interactions), the use of Monte Carlo analysis to quantify risk up front, and real options analysis to better understand the value of flexibility to aircraft operators. They suggest that a better approach to value uncertainty is to use a moderate cost of capital, either using market measures or utilizing broad, long-term regional benchmarks. They then surveyed the use of sophisticated asset valuation strategies by airlines to evaluate the benefits of their risky investments in aircraft. An advanced method of risk-adjusted return was utilized and substantial interaction considered. This included cash-based, rather than accounting-based, returns.

A cash-based method adjusts returns for the time value of money and demonstrates the increase in value for the investors and interest payments for the lender. This research provided a significant contribution to aircraft financial evaluation, particularly in the areas of risk and cost of shareholder equity estimation. Substantial interactions were identified between the investment analysis and the way the projects were financed. It can be concluded that while substantial use of the more sophisticated techniques in aircraft financial evaluation existed, airlines did not appear to consistently use the most advanced techniques available in the market. In addition, they claim that, among cash-based measures, the use of NPV to estimate the value of an aircraft is about the same as the internal rate of return. This method has probably come about by advances in the knowledge of the techniques to estimate the cost of capital.

In another look at an asset valuation model, an options-based analysis of the large aircraft market was surveyed by Clarke, Miller, and Protz (2003). They argue that in order to determine the strategic value of infrastructure, it is necessary to calculate the value of the options that it brings. The methodology described here combines financial and real options theory and uses a Monte Carlo simulation in a system dynamics framework to determine value. This methodology overcomes some of the weaknesses associated with standard real options analysis, such as the selection of the underlying asset and the inclusion of market dynamics. It can be used to evaluate a wide array of investments under uncertainty. Some examples are expenditures in research and development for a new aircraft model by an aircraft manufacturer and improvements in the air traffic control infrastructure for the National Airspace System (NAS).

In another asset-intensive field, Breidenbach, Mueller, and Schulte (2006), compare property and market betas for both private real estate (using the NCREIF

Index) and public real estate (using the NAREIT Index), so that investors can have a more accurate risk premium beta or benchmark for their decisions. Their goal was to develop a model based on the capital asset pricing model (CAPM) that would allow investors to derive their required rate of return for individual property types in specific markets. The required rate of return is an important component in achieving risk-adjusted returns. Specifically, their research concentrated on the development of meaningful beta proxies for application to the CAPM, examining current approaches used in the industry to calculate market risk premiums and suggesting improvements.

In another survey, an exact Bayes test of asset pricing models with application to international markets was researched by Avramov and Chao (2006). Their paper developed and implemented an exact finite-sample test of asset pricing models with time-varying risk premiums by using posterior probabilities. This procedure was applied to international equity markets by testing and comparing the international capital asset pricing model (ICAPM) and conditional ICAPM versions of Fama and French (1998). Specifically, this approach allowed simultaneous comparison of the performance of multiple asset pricing specifications, both nested and non-nested, and optimally combined those models into one general weighted model that could be useful for making investment decisions under uncertainty. Conclusions about asset valuation articles are difficult to draw since the researchers have used various pricing models to test subject matter in diverse areas.

Vasigh and Erfani (2004) identified internal factors, such as the aircraft specification and age, and external factors, such as the state of the economy and inflation rate, that affect the theoretical value of an aircraft. Operating costs and revenues have a major impact on the theoretical value. They argued that the expected theoretical value of revenue depends on the load factor, revenue per revenue miles, and other factors. The value of an aircraft is, to a great extent, dependent on the expected net cash flows that can be generated from the use of the aircraft. Future generation of net cash flow depends on factors affecting revenue and costs and how those factors are expected to change. However, the value of an aircraft is also determined by the relationship between supply and demand. Although there is one single market, similar aircraft may be traded at significantly different prices.

Often, company valuations are calculated using the dividend discount model. Expected future net cash flows in the form of dividends are discounted to estimate the value of the company. Foerster and Sapp (2005) concluded that the dividend discount model explained the value of equity for a large, mature dividend-paying company. This model can be extended to aircraft valuation. The profits generated by an aircraft over time can be considered as net cash flows, which can be discounted to estimate the theoretical value of an aircraft.

Current Market Practices

Several independent companies and sources provide appraisal and consulting services for a wide variety of aircraft types with special emphasis on commercial aircraft:

- AVITAS
- Morten Beyer & Agnew
- Ascend
- *Aircraft Value Reference*
- *Aircraft Bluebook Price Digest*

These companies and sources provide reference prices for many aircraft types and provide aircraft valuation services. Reports are used by aircraft brokers and a number of financial institutions to have a third-party view on aircraft values. Most major jet aircraft data by carrier is included for passenger and cargo operations. Some even provide reference prices for turboprop aircraft.

Other reports provide cost and performance components for each aircraft type. For example, The *Aircraft Block Hour Operating Costs and Operations Guide* from AVITAS is designed to assist airline managers in formulating fleet and route analyses and monitoring specific maintenance productivity capital budgeting decisions and performance against industry standards. The guide provides direct operating costs for flying operations, maintenance reserves, and maintenance burden and provides average aircraft utilization per day for various operational indices such as departures, available seat miles (ASM), and seat mile operating costs.

The accuracy of reports depends on the technical abilities of the person completing the aircraft datasheet and the use of proper financial models. Many reports utilize certain rudimentary assumptions that limit the veracity of the values. The valuation is simply based on the physical inspection of the aircraft and/or auditing the maintenance records and status without financial analysis of the potential earning ability of the aircraft during its lifetime.

The aircraft value model in this book depends on factors such as an aircraft's overall condition, maintenance quality, the time to the next major check, fuel and seating capacity, *and* on general economic conditions, which significantly improve estimation of the intrinsic price of an aircraft.

Aircraft and Data Selection

The aircraft and data selection model explained here is a comprehensive aircraft valuation technique and provides a multidimensional model for aircraft appraisal and valuation. It presents a methodology that will more accurately measure return on investment, improve the efficiency of managing operating costs, and effectively determine yield analysis. As such, it should provide the basis for an improved negotiating position for the purchase or lease of new or used aircraft.

Additionally, the methodology provides quantitative evidence to determine when an aircraft should be retired and replaced. In the following model, two popular narrow-body and wide-body aircraft produced by Boeing and Airbus were selected and a modified discounted cash flow model was applied. The theory assumes that the value of an investment can be estimated from the future cash flows that are expected to be generated. This discounted cash flow model provides the best estimate of aircraft value. However, since many factors are considered in the discounted cash flow model, small variations in these factors can significantly affect the theoretical value of any aircraft.

Relevant expense and revenue data for the four aircraft were collected for the time period starting with the first quarter of 2005 through the fourth quarter of 2010. Data sets were obtained for the A320-200, the 737-700, the A330, and the 767-400. Both Boeing and Airbus only produce aircraft that they have sold, received deposits for, and subsequently were then paid in full upon delivery.

It should be noted that the equations in this methodology have a number of terms that cancel out when the equations are multiplied out. The reason for this cancellation is the fact that the revenue and expense data were disaggregated as much as possible. Disaggregation allowed for separate specific components of the data, so that we could calculate the sensitivity of the overall theoretical value of the aircraft to changes in specific components of revenues and costs. The following main factors were defined: passenger and cargo revenues, direct expenses (e.g., personnel, fuel), maintenance, depreciation and amortization, general administrative costs and other transport-related expenses. Some figures had to be calculated, as they were either not directly available (total gallons consumed), not segregated by aircraft type (e.g., servicing, sales and general expenses), nor dependent on other figures (e.g., total block hours).

Boeing Aircraft

Boeing received the first order for a B-737-100 (the 737 program) in 1965. In 1991, Boeing started the 737 Next Generation (NG)[4] program on which the current versions of the 737-600/-700/-800/-900 series are based. According to *Air Transport Intelligence* (2010),[5] 73 airlines operate 737-700s, and 1,060 aircraft are in service. The three top airlines operating 737-700 aircraft are Southwest Airlines (370), WestJet (69), and AirTran (52). The Boeing 737-700 model was launched in 1993

---

[4] Next Generation program includes the 737-600, 737-700, 737-800, and 737-900 airplane models.
[5] All fleet information as obtained from www.rati.com, May 16, 2006.

and the 737-700ER on January 31, 2006.[6] More than 6,943 737 family of aircraft have been delivered and there are (2011) about 5,215 aircraft currently in service.

The wide-body 767 family from Boeing is in service with 100 airlines worldwide. According to *Air Transport Intelligence* (2010), the total of aircraft in service is 832. The Boeing 767 family includes four models: the 767-200ER, 767-300ER, 767-300F, and 767-400ER. In 1989, the FAA approved the 767 as the first jetliner for 180-minute extended operations (ETOPS). According to Boeing, 767s burn significantly less fuel and produce lower emissions per pound of fuel used than any comparably sized jetliner, including the A330-200. The two top operators of the 767-400ER are Delta with 21 aircraft and Continental with 16 aircraft. The aircraft selected for valuation is the 767-400ER, which was launched in 2000.

Airbus Aircraft

Airbus started with its A320 program in 1984 with the A320-100. A newer version, the A320-200, was introduced in 1988.[7] Based on information from *Air Transport Intelligence* (2010), 191 airlines operated a fleet of 2,547 Airbus A320-200 models. The three top airlines operating A320s are JetBlue (119), China Eastern Airline (107), and United (97). To compare the wide-body Boeing 767-400 with a model from Airbus, the A330-200 was selected. This aircraft is the only wide-body from Airbus that is operated by a U.S. airline. The A330-200 was launched in 1993. According to *Air Transport Intelligence*,[8] 65 airlines currently operate a total fleet of 405 Airbus A330-200 models. The three top global operators of the A330-200 are Emirates (27), Air China (22), and TAM Linhas Aéreas (20).

Table 4.1 summarizes some characteristics of the aircraft selected. The current operators of each aircraft model are given for the United States only because only financial data of U.S. carriers was obtainable through Back Aviation Solutions' Form 41 database.

Potential Sources of Revenue

Airlines are constantly in search of new revenue sources. Travelers have gotten used to paying for food on board. But it's going to be harder to adjust to fees for services that used to be free.

—Chris McGinni[9]

---

[6] Boeing Company, News Release, Seattle, January 31, 2006.
[7] The A320 family comprises four aircraft that share the same cockpit, have the same cabin cross-section and fly with the same operating procedures.
[8] *Air Transport Intelligence*, website, November, 2011.
[9] *The Ticket Editor*, a travel newsletter.

Table 4.1 Aircraft type specifications

	A320-200	737-700	A330-200	767-400
Launch	1988	1993	cert. 1998	2000
Normal seating	164	126	293	243
Range (miles)	2,167	5,179	7,674	4,315
Speed (Mach)	0.78	0.79	0.82	0.8
Fleet (world/U.S.)	2,547 / 415	1060 / 486	405 / 23	37 / 37
U.S. operators	JetBlue–119	Southwest–370	Delta–11	Delta–21
	United–97	AirTran–52	US Airways–7	Continental–16
	US Airways–72	Continental–33	Hawaiian–5	
	Delta–69	Alaska–17		
	Virgin America–32	Delta–10		

Passenger Revenue

The following is a practical application of the valuation technique offered in this book. This theoretical model allows the airline operators to disaggregate revenues and costs for various types of aircraft and then estimate the potential value of the aircraft over an expected useful life of the asset. An aircraft valuation model is necessary to stay in business, as every big or small airline needs to earn a profit. Financial theory indicates that the value of an investment is estimated from the future cash flow that such an investment is expected to generate, and a commonly used approach is the discounted cash flow model, which is discussed below. A generic model requires a present value calculation of projected future cash flows (e.g., dividends and earnings). In order to apply the discounted cash flow model, future cash flows have to be projected first. For aircraft valuation purposes, revenues (cash inflows) generated by passengers and cargo/freight transport are estimated.

Cash inflow estimates can be complex and require several assumptions. To calculate the revenue per aircraft type, the total revenue passenger miles is calculated and added to the revenue ton miles (multiplied by the cargo yield). For narrow-body aircraft, the yield is lower because the freight has to be hand loaded due to the fact that no containers can be loaded mechanically. The wide-body aircraft can be loaded with cargo containers using lifts to load them onto the aircraft. Therefore, the cost is lower, which results in a higher yield. Based on the cargo yield analysis per aircraft model, the average industry cargo yield was used for the narrow-body models. For wide-body aircraft models, the cargo yield was estimated by weighting the overall cargo yield for airlines that operate the respective aircraft model.

The next question is how best to measure aircraft cash inflows. To value an aircraft, we have to forecast the expected cash inflows over the aircraft life.

Table 4.2 Calculated factors

Factor	Calculation
Total block hours	Daily utilization × 365.25
Gallons consumed	Gallons per block hour × total block hours
Passenger revenue	RPM x overall passenger yield
Cargo revenue	RTM × overall cargo yield
Aircraft fuel	Gallons consumed x fuel cost (price per gallon)
Servicing, sales and general expense	Allocated based on ASM

Passenger revenue includes income from transportation of passengers by air from the origin to the destination. Generally, the largest percentage of a passenger airline's revenue is created through passenger revenue which amounts to about 90% of the total carrier's revenues. Legacy carriers traditionally have multiple-class cabin configurations, typically set as premium and economy class. The premium class cabins subsequently create higher margins of passenger revenue, but offer the carrier less seating volume due to the typically larger seat pitch.

Many low-cost carriers have a one-class cabin configuration and charge for amenities above the minimum provided. These extra amenity charges are part of ancillary revenue, which will be discussed later. A traditional airline relies upon passenger cash streams and freight revenue, while ancillary revenue is usually less than 10% of the carrier's total revenues. To compute the revenue for passenger operations, we have to take into account the revenue passenger miles (RPM), aircraft utilization block hours (BH), and revenue per revenue passenger miles (RRPM):

$$\text{Passenger Revenue per BH} = \left(\frac{\text{RPM}_{i,t}}{\beta_{i,t}} \times \text{RRPM} \right)$$

Cargo Revenue

Similar to passenger revenue, revenue generated from freight transportation is an important revenue stream for the airlines. Many passenger-oriented wide-body aircraft can accommodate substantial amounts of cargo in addition to passenger luggage. The amount of cargo revenue generated depends on the type of aircraft, its "belly space," destination, maximum takeoff weight, and other factors. Separate from fully fledged cargo airlines, passenger airlines tend to have a cargo department that handles commercial cargo accounts. The demand for air cargo transportation has been growing with the demand from logistic delivery optimization widely used in the commercial sector. The fee charged for checked passenger baggage is, however, not considered as cargo revenue, but rather as ancillary revenue.

To compute cargo revenue, revenue ton miles (RTM), aircraft block hours, and revenue per revenue ton miles (RRTM) are taken into consideration:

$$\text{Cargo Revenue per BH} = \left(\frac{\text{RTM}_{i,t}}{\beta_{i,t}} \times \text{RRTM}_{i,t} \right)$$

Ancillary Revenue

The ancillary revolution is happening in all geographies and all segments, if not evenly. Ultra-low-cost carriers like Ryanair and AirAsia are the most aggressive adopters, while the U.S. market is the most active overall.

—Airline Weekly, February 2010

The airline industry is experiencing an ancillary revenue revolution, leading to more profitable airline operations. Many airlines in Europe, North America, and other parts of the world are using this additional source of revenue to enhance ticket revenues. In fact, ancillary revenues are the foundation of the new airline business model and, therefore, critical to the future of airline operations.[10]

Ticket prices around the world have fallen sharply since the onset of the recession, further increasing the importance of ancillary revenue items for the airline industry. Furthermore, innovations in technology enabled handheld point-of-sale devices to make direct transactions in the cabin, facilitating ancillary revenue sales and improving management reporting.

The sources of ancillary revenue can be divided into many segments:

- Pre-flight items such as the sale of improved seat selection, increased checked baggage allowances, pre-boarding preferences, charges for overhead bin space, etc.
- Buy onboard food, beverages, in-flight entertainment, pillows, etc.
- Buy onboard duty-free sales such as alcohol, tobacco, jewelry, etc.
- Commissions from the sale of:
    a. Hotel accommodations
    b. Car rentals
    c. Travel insurance at airline websites
- Virtual merchandise (theater tickets, credit cards and even theme park entry)

Ancillary revenue includes the extra fees being charged for baggage, food, pillows, drinks, and improved seating. In 2008, airline ancillary revenues rose 346% to USD$11.25 billion. Many airlines in the United States and around the world turned to the ancillary revenue generated by charging passengers for different

---

[10] Bejar, Raphael. Looking back at the recession's impact and looking forward: The changing face of the airline industry and ancillary revenues in 2010, an industry briefing. *Airsaving.*

services to improve their financial positions. Over the past few years, ancillary revenue has become an important component of airlines' income. Airlines such as Allegiant, EasyJet, Jet2.com, and Ryanair are targeting a higher percentage of their income to come from non-ticket sources. Qantas emerged as one of the world's top five airlines for ancillary revenues. Recently, Delta Air Lines and Continental Airlines raised their fees for first and second checked bags to $25 and $35, respectively, while offering discounts to travelers who checked in online. In percentage of revenue from ancillary revenue, U.S. low-cost carriers Allegiant Air and Spirit Airlines ranked first and second, at 29.2% and 23.9%, respectively, and Ryanair, EasyJet, and Tiger Airways rounded out the top five, followed by Jet2.com, Aer Lingus, Alaska Airlines, Flybe, and AirAsia.[11]

Given ancillary revenue factors, the total revenue (cash inflows) became the sum of revenue generated from passengers, revenue generated from cargo, and any additional ancillary revenue.

TR = Revenue from passengers + Revenue from cargo + Ancillary revenue

$$TR_{i,t} = \beta_{i,t} \times \left[\left(\frac{RPM_{i,t}}{\beta_{i,t}} \times RRPM \right) + \left(\frac{RTM_{i,t}}{\beta_{i,t}} \times RRTM_{i,t} \right) \right] + AR$$

where:

TR = total revenue

β = aircraft block hours[12]

RPM = revenue passenger mile[13]

RTM = revenue ton mile[14]

RRPM = revenue per revenue passenger mile (passenger yield)[15]

RRTM = revenue per revenue ton mile (cargo yield)[16]

AR = ancillary revenue

i = individual aircraft

t = time

---

[11] *Airline Weekly*, July 26, 2010.
[12] Typically includes taxi time plus airborne time.
[13] One fare-paying passenger carried one mile.
[14] One ton carried one mile.
[15] A measure of unit revenue, calculated as the gross revenue generated per RPM.
[16] RRTM is a measurement of revenue earned on the movement of a ton of freight over one mile.

Aircraft Total Cost Structure

In addition to cash inflows, cash outflows must also be estimated. These include operating expenses as well as non-cash expenses (e.g., frequent flyer miles, amortization, and depreciation). Generally, there are three main kinds of costs related to the operation of an aircraft. These include the airborne operating costs, the ground costs, and the variable costs.

The challenging economic environment and high fixed cost bases force airlines to minimize costs by optimizing their operations. Direct operating expenses for an aircraft include the cost of fuel, flight crew expenses, maintenance costs, and indirect costs such as flight equipment capital costs, as well as expenses for marketing, sales, and general administration. There are numerous characteristics that can be used to classify airline cost structure (drivers). In the following analysis we will discuss the different cost components of a commercial aircraft and compute the ownership and operating costs. Generally, the cost structure of an airline refers to the collection of operating costs and non-operating costs. Non-operating costs can be divided into true variable costs and step variable costs. The operating cost categories include: pilot crew, cabin crew, fuel, landing fees, enroute air traffic control charges, airframe maintenance, maintenance, the ownership costs of the aircraft, and airport charges.

- Direct operating costs:
  a. Fuel and oil
  b. Maintenance
  c. Landing fees
  d. Enroute and navigation fees
  e. Handling fees
  f. Crew expenses
  g. Traffic-related direct operating costs
  h. Passenger and cargo commissions
  i. Airport load fees
  j. In-flight catering
  k. General passenger-related costs
- Indirect operating costs:
  a. Aircraft standing charges
  b. Flight crew pay
  c. Cabin crew pay
  d. Maintenance pay
  e. Handling costs
  f. Overheads
  g. Sales costs
- Administration:

Table 4.3 Forecasting factors for narrow-body aircraft

		Airbus A320-200			Boeing 737-700LR	
Factor	%	Year 2005	Year 2034	%	Year 2005	Year 2034
Daily utilization (hours)	0.1	11.63	11.97	0.1	11.65	11.99
Gallons per block hour	−0.05	793.49	782.07	−0.05	709.43	699.22
Fuel cost ($ per gallon)	2	1.67	2.97	2	1.31	2.32
RPM (millions)	0.05	204.71	207.7	0.05	159.76	162.1
Passenger yield (cents)	1.25	11.92	17.09	1.25	11.92	17.09
RTM (millions)	0.01	20.81	20.87	0.01	16.5	16.54
Cargo yield (cents)	1.25	70.18	100.61	1.25	70.18	100.61
Direct maint. ($)	3.75	1,677,664	4,879,329	7.1	734,221	5,357,781
All other factors (costs)	2			2		

Note: Base is the year 2005. For every year, the previous year's figure is increased by the percentage listed (compounding), for a total of thirty years (estimated asset lifetime).

Table 4.4 Forecasting factors for wide-body aircraft

		Airbus A330			Boeing 767-400ER	
Factors	%	Year 2005	Year 2034	%	Year 2005	Year 2034
Daily utilization (hours)	0.1	13.85	14.26	0.1	14.26	14.68
Gallons per block hour	−0.05	1,858.69	1,831.92	−0.05	1,651.91	1,628.12
Fuel cost ($ per gallon)	2	1.73	3.07	2	1.73	3.07
RPM (millions)	0.05	546.56	554.5	0.05	500.79	508.1
Passenger yield (cents)	1.25	11.99	17.19	1.25	11.99	17.19
RTM (millions)	0.01	71.5	71.71	0.01	64.35	64.54
Cargo yield (cents)	1.25	39.5	56.63	1.25	48	68.82
Direct maint. ($)	12.5	700,000	21,034,024	12.7	830,000	26,259,277
All other factors (costs)	2			2		

Note: Base is the year 2005. For every year, the previous year's figure is increased by the percentage listed (compounding), for a total of thirty years (estimated asset lifetime).

    a. General management
    b. Real estate costs, etc.

Tables 4.3 and 4.4 provide a unit metrics comparison between narrow- and wide-body aircraft.

It should be noted that airport costs may be out of an airline's control, and costs are rising at major international hubs. To estimate costs the following are applied: total operating costs, direct operating costs, variable direct operating costs, indirect operating costs, and non-operating costs.

Total Operating Costs

Total operating cost for an aircraft has two major components, direct cost and indirect cost. With the addition of non-operating we have the total cost incurred. These cost structures have been explained in detail above and are presented in the form of the following formula:

Total Operating Cost = Direct Cost + Indirect Cost + Non-operating Cost

Direct Operating Costs

Direct operating costs are those costs that can be easily and conveniently traced to a unit of product or other cost objective. Direct operating costs can be expressed in terms of dollars per hour, cents per mile, cents per seat mile, or, for cargo aircraft, cents per ton mile. The increase in fuel efficiency is mainly attributable to the progress in aircraft engine and aerodynamic technologies. As a result of these technological developments, and new managerial skill to enjoy higher load factors, airlines have been able to achieve higher aircraft fuel economy efficiency. Aircraft operating costs include:

- Crew cost
- Fuel cost
- Maintenance cost
- Ownership

Results show that the same aircraft can exhibit different fuel efficiency characteristics (consumption) under different operating conditions. For example, fuel burn per ASM for the B-737-800 improves with respect to the increase in the number of seats in the aircraft.

Variable Direct Operating Costs

- Fuel and oil costs = Cost per gallon × Number of gallons consumed
- Fuel and oil costs = $\theta \times \gamma$

- Total fuel cost = $\left[\dfrac{\theta \dfrac{\gamma}{\beta}}{\dfrac{ASM}{\beta}} \right] \times ASM$ (4.1)

- Flight operations
  - o Aircraft fuel and oil
  - o Insurance and uninsured losses
  - o Lease/rental of aircraft

- Flight crew salaries, expenses, and training $= \left[\dfrac{\dfrac{\lambda}{\beta}}{\dfrac{ASM}{\beta}}\right] \times ASM$ (4.2)

Given λ as crew cost, this includes both variable and direct cost. The availability of data is limited to analysts outside of an aircraft operator. In a more perfect scenario, airline analysts would have separate variable and fixed cost segments. For the ease of data extraction, the fixed and variable costs were combined in the resulting function:

- Direct engineering costs
- Airport and enroute charges
- Passenger service costs

- Fixed and variable maintenance cost $= \left[\dfrac{\dfrac{\mu}{\beta}}{\dfrac{ASM}{\beta}}\right] \times ASM$ (4.3)

μ is given as the combined elements of variable and fixed maintenance cost. As with the flight crew, maintenance cost elements may be categorized into fixed and variable components, given that sufficient data is available. These components include:

- Labor
- Maintenance and repairs:
  - o Avionics
  - o Basic structure including fuselage, tail and wing
  - o Engine
  - o Power plant
- Materials
- Fixed direct operating costs:
  - o Aircraft standing charges
  - o Annual flight and cabin crew costs
  - o Engineering overheads

An aircraft's fixed operating costs are those costs of operation that occur whether or not flights are operated. These costs include aircraft leases, terminal leases, and crew salaries. Variable direct operating costs are those costs that are incurred based on the level of activity (number of flights) an airline operates. Fuel, landing fees, passenger services, and maintenance are all considered variable operating costs since they vary depending on the number of flights taken over the course of a year. Some flight crew costs, such as overnight accommodations, could also be deemed variable operating costs.

Indirect Operating Costs

Indirect operating costs cannot be directly associated with the actual flight of the aircraft and are sometimes more difficult to identify. Indirect operating costs are those costs not directly related to the core function of the airline, such as some labor training costs, selling expenses and administration costs. These costs are necessary for an airline to operate; however, indirect costs cannot be directly linked to a specific flight since the expenses provide support to all operations. Since they do not directly impact an airline's operation, indirect costs represent the first area of concentration for a manager aiming to reduce total operating costs.

In Equations 4.1–4.3, the indirect cost is denoted as i/ASM to get unit metrics:

- Baggage and cargo handling
- General and administrative costs
- Passenger service costs:
  - o Staff
  - o Variable flight
  - o Indirect cabin crew
  - o Insurance expenses
- Reservations and sales
- Station and ground expenses
- Ticketing, sales and promotion related costs

Non-operating Costs

Airlines also incur costs that are not related to operations. Non-operating costs are expenses arising from activities not associated with the rendering of air transport services. Usually this category of cost is related to the financial structuring of the company. These are the strategic financial instruments used by an air carrier. Interest expense is the most common non-operating cost in the airline industry, a result of the sizeable debt loads airlines carry. While debt is necessary to fund the operations, interest expense is considered a non-operating cost because the cost is not directly related to an airline's operations. Other non-operating costs for an airline include any loss on the sale of aircraft and other assets and expenses in non-aviation activities. Airlines may receive income from investments or from non-core activities, such as hotel management, car rental, and other non-aviation operations.

Interest expense costs are another non-operating cost incurred in the airline industry, which must be incorporated in the model. The most common reason for mergers and acquisitions between airlines is the savings in non-operating costs they create.

Aircraft Valuation Methodology

Weighted Average Cost of Capital

Another factor to estimate is the rate at which the periodic net cash flows are discounted to derive the aircraft value today. This rate reflects the current market rate of return adjusted by the risk of the investment. An airline's overall cost of capital reflects the required rate of return on the airline's investment as a whole. The cost of capital depends on the risk, and hence primarily on the use of the funds and the potential return on this investment. Commonly, the required rate of return is estimated as a function of the firm's weighted average cost of capital (WACC) and reflects the costs of debt, equity, and preferred stock.[17] The WACC reflects both the current market rates of return as well as the risk specific to the company. The formula defining the WACC is:

$$WACC = w_d k_d (1 - T) + w_e k_e$$

where:

w_d = proportion (weight) of debt financing

k_d = cost of debt

k_e = cost of equity

w_e = proportion (weight) of equity financing

T = corporate tax rate

Applying the WACC method is effective in determining the necessary rate of return at which to discount the expected net cash flows (Lloyd and Davis, 2007). However, to obtain a valid NPV (and subsequently a correct theoretical asset value), the investment or asset discounted under the WACC method must have a risk similar to the average risk of the firm's existing investments. This is probably truer for the airline industry than most other industries because the principal existing investment is the aircraft fleet. Based on WACC factors, the estimated total costs or (cash outflows) may be defined as:

TC = Variable Direct Operating Costs + Direct Maintenance Costs + Indirect Costs + Non-operating Costs

$$TC = \sum_{t=0}^{n} ASM \left\{ \left[\frac{\theta \frac{\gamma}{\beta}}{\frac{ASM}{\beta}} \right] + \left[\frac{\frac{\lambda}{\beta}}{\frac{ASM}{\beta}} \right] + \left[\frac{\frac{\mu}{\beta}}{\frac{ASM}{\beta}} \right] + \left[\frac{\iota}{ASM} \right] + \left[\frac{W}{ASM} + \frac{OHC}{ASM} \right] \right\} \quad (4.4)$$

---

[17] WACC is calculated by multiplying the cost of each capital component by its proportional weighting and then summing.

where:

TC = Total costs

OHC = Overhead costs

ASM = Available seat miles[18]

β = Aircraft utilization block hours

θ = fuel cost per gallon

γ = gallons of fuel consumed

λ = flight crew costs

μ = maintenance costs (labor and materials)

ι = indirect costs

W = aircraft

t = year

n = expected aircraft life

In Equation 4.4, ASM/β signifies the efficiency of aircraft energy use in terms of work created per unit energy input. Many of these factors depend on how many seats are offered for travel in the aircraft (ASM) as well as on how long the aircraft is utilized on a daily basis (block hours).

The resulting *net cash flow* (inflows minus outflows) is the profit generated by an aircraft, at a specific airline, during a year. Lifetime net cash flows represent the net benefit to the airline for that specific aircraft in the fleet.

Discounted Cash Flow Model

A discounted cash flow (DCF) analysis can be performed on a number of physical assets such as aircraft, airport, real estate, and many others. Estimating the value of an aircraft is a complicated task, but nonetheless important for nearly every airline, aircraft manufacturer, aircraft leasing company, and credit agency. DCF analysis is widely used by management professionals in investment finance, real estate development, and corporate financial management. The DCF model is based on the theory that the current price of a physical or financial asset represents all the information about the future income generated by the asset discounted at a proper rate.

In this section, the DCF model is applied to estimate the value of aircraft under different physical and market conditions. The following series of equations can be used to discount the future cash flows in order to compute the present value of an investment. The sum of all the future cash inflows and outflows is the NPV.

---

[18] Number of seats available multiplied by the number of miles flown.

These computations can assist in the valuation of the aircraft, according to the perceived future cash inflows and outflows:

$$\text{NPV} = \frac{\text{CF}_1}{(1+k)^1} + \frac{\text{CF}_2}{(1+k)^2} + \cdots + \frac{\text{CF}_n}{(1+k)^n} + \frac{\text{RV}_n}{(1+k)^n}$$

$$\text{NPV} = \sum_{t=1}^{n} \frac{\text{CF}_t}{(1+k)^t} + \frac{\text{RV}_n}{(1+k)^n}$$

where:

$$\text{CF} = \text{cash flow}$$
$$k = \text{discount rate (WAAC)}$$
$$\text{RV} = \text{residual value}$$

Cash flows are the net of inflows and outflows. In the case of aircraft valuation, the operating costs are outflows and total revenues are inflows. However, a net cash flow received further in the future has less value to the buyer today. Therefore, the future net cash flow needs to be discounted in order to determine today's value of that specific cash flow. After calculating the operating cash flows of an airline, the value is divided by the difference between the discount rate and the growth rate to obtain the value of the aircraft. The sum of all discounted future net cash flows represents the value of the asset and the maximum amount the buyer should be willing to pay for it. This theoretical aircraft valuation model is defined in the following equations:

$$\text{Net cash flow} = \text{Total revenue} - \text{Total cost}$$

$$\text{Net cash flow} = \text{TR}_t - \text{TC}_t$$

$$\text{Value}_{\text{Aircraft}} = \sum_{t=0}^{n} \frac{\text{Net cash flow}_t}{(1+k)^t}$$

$$\text{Value}_{\text{Aircraft}} = \sum_{t=0}^{n} \frac{(\text{TR} - \text{TC})_t}{(1+k)^t}$$

The resulting *net cash flow* (inflows minus outflows) is the profit generated by an individual airline utilizing that specific aircraft for one year. Each *periodic* net cash flow represents value received by the buyer of the aircraft. Utilizing the DCF model, the theoretical aircraft valuation can be determined by the following equation:

$$V_{\text{aircraft}} = \sum_{t=0}^{n} \frac{\left\{ \left| \left\{ \beta \times \left[\left(\frac{\text{RPM}}{\beta} \times \text{RRPM} \right) + \left(\frac{\text{RTM}}{\beta} \times \text{RRTM} \right) \right] \right\} - \left| \text{ASM} \times \left\{ \left[\frac{\theta \times \frac{\gamma}{\beta}}{\frac{\text{ASM}}{\beta}} \right] + \left[\frac{\frac{\lambda}{\beta}}{\frac{\text{ASM}}{\beta}} \right] + \left[\frac{\frac{\mu}{\beta}}{\frac{\text{ASM}}{\beta}} \right] + \left[\frac{1}{\text{ASM}} \right] + \left[\frac{\varpi}{\frac{\text{ASM}}{\beta} \times \beta} \right] \right\} + \text{Admin} \right| \right| \right\}}{(1+k)^t}$$

$$\tag{4.5}$$

$$V = \text{total aircraft value}$$

From Equation 4.5, the impact that various factors have on aircraft value can be determined. An increase in fuel cost or gallons of fuel consumed, denoted in the equation as θ and γ respectively, leads to an increase in total costs and a subsequent decrease in aircraft value. This effect of increased fuel consumption by an aircraft partially explains the shift that airline manufacturers have undertaken to produce more fuel-efficient aircraft in order to increase the value of the aircraft and its attractiveness to operators.

Similar trends in aircraft design can also be explained by Equation 4.5. The minimization of cockpit crew through technology advances increases the value of the aircraft. Early entrants in the commercial aircraft world required as many as four cockpit crew members. Today, the standard has become two-man cockpit crews even for the largest aircraft on the market. Any decrease in flight crew costs, λ, decreases the total cost sector of the equation, thus increasing the value of an aircraft.

Summary

In this dynamic air transportation market, it is difficult to put a number on the value of special aircraft. All different external as well as internal factors should be examined to obtain an accurate value for a given type of aircraft. Value is almost derived from the market forces of supply and demand. Using a modified DCF model to forecast the net cash flows generated by an aircraft over time takes into consideration factors such as revenue per passenger mile, revenue per ton mile of cargo, ASM, block hours, fuel consumed, flight personnel labor rate, maintenance and material costs, expected economic life, indirect costs, and capital cost per aircraft day in order to accurately forecast net cash flows. These net cash flows are then discounted at an appropriate cost of capital to estimate the theoretical value of an aircraft. This value provided a benchmarking procedure that can be an acceptable first approximation to the value of the aircraft. Since the air transport industry is in a dynamic environment, it is likely that one or more of the base assumptions may change and, in turn, change the theoretical value of an aircraft. The model provides a comprehensive review of aircraft valuation. It presents a methodology that will accurately measure return on investment, improve the efficiency of managing operating costs, and effectively determine yield analysis.

References

Avramov, D., & Chao, J. (2006). An exact Bayes Test of asset pricing models with application to international markets. *Journal of Business, 79*(1), 293–323.

Breidenback, M., Mueller, G., & Schulte, K. (2006). Determining Real Estate Betas for Markets and Property Types to Set Better Investment Hurdle Rates. *Journal of Real Estate Portfolio Management* 12(1), 73-80.

Clarke, J. P., Miller, B., & Protz, J. (2003). *An options-based analysis of the large aircraft market.* American Institute of Aeronautics and Astronautics. Retrieved from http://www.aiaa.org/content.cfm?pageid=2.

Fama, E. & French, K. (1998). Value versus growth: the international evidence. *Journal of Finance* 53, 1975-1999.

Foerster, S. R., & Sapp, S. G. (2005). The dividend discount model in the long-run: A clinical study. *Journal of Applied Finance, 15,* 55–75.

Gibson, W. & Morrell, P. (2005). *Theory and Practice in Aircraft Financial Evaluation.* Retrieved from https://dspace.lib.cranfield.ac.uk.

Lloyd, J., & Davis, L. (2007). Building long-term value. *Journal of Accountancy, 204*(5), 56–61.

Vasigh, B., & Erfani, G. R. (2004). Aircraft value, global economy and volatility. *Aerlines Magazine*, December, pp. 28.

Vasigh, B., Owens, J., & Yoo, K. (2003). A price forecasting model for predicting value of commercial airports: a case of three Korean airports. *International Journal of Transport Management,* 1(4), 225–236.

5

Aircraft Valuation and Sensitivity Analysis

Continental now has a fleet plan that makes us competitive in every market well into the next century. This latest order will reduce our total cost while providing the latest in technology and comfort to our customers.

—Gordon Bethune, Continental Airlines CEO, from 1997

Determining the current value of physical assets can be challenging, as pointed out in Chapter 4. The theoretical value of a commercial aircraft depends on the expected future net cash flows (inflows minus outflows). The cyclicality of the airline industry, and the high level of volatility that fuel prices exhibit, inherently translate into a higher variation of aircraft prices and higher operating costs.[1] An aircraft's operating costs vary significantly over the typical life cycle. Calculating an aircraft's periodic future cash inflows and outflows requires certain assumptions and estimates to be made, which are further explained and detailed in this chapter. The forecasting of the periodic aircraft revenues and expenses also depends on external factors such as the state of the economy, currency exchange rates, inflation, and the age of the aircraft.

The developed aircraft valuation methodology integrates the aircraft costs, capacity, and performance, along with ticket, cargo, and ancillary revenues. Four competing aircraft models, two narrow-body and two wide-body products from Boeing and Airbus current product lines, were selected for analysis in this chapter. The same methodology could be applied to other makes and models.

---

[1] In 2007, Airbus reported a loss of over €1 billion due to the weakness of the U.S. dollar and was said to be under pressure to secure higher prices for new aircraft.

The selected aircraft are first analyzed and valued individually, utilizing the methods described in previous chapters. It is important to note that a major obstacle exists when attempting to properly calibrate this and other methodologies that involve aircraft prices; the world of aircraft prices is a highly confidential one and subject to the bargaining power of the purchaser and manufacturer. Therefore, obtaining transaction prices for both new and used aircraft is highly difficult. The chapter is organized as follows:

Value of Physical Assets

Theoretical Value of Airbus Aircraft

- Theoretical Aircraft Value vs. List Price
- Theoretical Aircraft Valuation Trends
- Aircraft Value Volatilities
- Impact on Theoretical Aircraft Valuation of Input Changes over Lifespan of Aircraft

Theoretical Value of Boeing Aircraft

- Theoretical Aircraft Value vs. List Price
- Aircraft Value Volatilities

Theoretical Aircraft Valuation Trend Comparison

Elasticity

At the end of the chapter is a Summary for chapter review and References for further study.

Value of Physical Assets

The price of everything rises and falls from time-to-time and place-to-place; and with every such change the purchasing power of money changes so far as that thing goes.

—Alfred Marshall

The impact of the economy on aircraft valuations, and other factors such as fuel consumption, fuel prices, economic booms and recessions, terrorism, and passenger spending habits, which affect the demand for aircraft by airlines, are the focus of this section. The valuation model, developed in Chapter 4, accounts for a variety of factors, including the cost of fuel, fuel consumption levels, technological advancement, and other endogenous factors. Sensitivity analysis is at the heart of this valuation, and this chapter covers the volatility of cost of capital, fuel prices, maintenance expenses, passenger yield, and block hours and their subsequent impact on aircraft values.

The aircraft valuation process is a part of the overall business model, and its performance is reflected in the company's financial forecast. *Net present value (NPV)* is one of the most commonly used metrics in the financial valuation of aircraft. In general, there are two ways that the results from the NPV calculation can be applied and evaluated. As was discussed in the previous chapter, the NPV is computed by summing discounted future cash flows. Under the NPV framework, the longer the period of time over which an annuity occurs, the greater the sensitivity of the present value of that annuity to uncertainty in the variation in revenue, cost, and interest rate. Uncertainty in cash flows and outflows is accounted for by using scenario analysis to evaluate their impacts on aircraft prices. Investments in commercial aircraft may provide investors with characteristics similar to those of real estate.

The actual price of an aircraft in the market can then be observed. Comparing how close the calculated theoretical value comes to this price, one may then sensitize the theoretical valuation of the asset to changes in the price of the input factors (revenues or costs). The major obstacle to these approaches is that the actual aircraft transaction prices are highly confidential and subject to a variety of complex metrics of stipulations and conditions that may make such comparisons impossible and erroneous. The theoretical aircraft valuation is defined by the following equation:

$$\text{Net cash flow}_t = \text{Total revenue}_t - \text{Total cost}$$

$$\text{NCF}_t = \text{TR}_t - \text{TC}_t + \frac{\text{RV}_n}{(1 + \text{WACC})^n}$$

$$\text{Value}_{\text{Aircraft}} = \sum_{t=0}^{t \to n} \frac{\text{NFC}_t}{(1 + \text{WACC})^t} + \frac{\text{RV}_n}{(1 + \text{WACC})^n}$$

$$\text{Value}_{\text{Aircraft}} = \sum_{t=0}^{t \to n} \frac{(\text{TR}_t - \text{TC}_t)}{(1 + \text{WACC})^t} + \frac{\text{RV}_n}{(1 + \text{WACC})^n}$$

where:

RV = residual value at the time of sale (n)

$\text{NCF} = \text{TR} - \text{TC}$

WACC = the weighted cost of capital[2]

$t = 0 - n$, time

n = the time of sale

Theoretical Value of Airbus Aircraft

The theoretical value at which a security should be traded is dependent on investor expectations and market conditions. Depending on how much revenue is generated, and cost incurred by utilizing an asset, the expected theoretical value of the asset would change accordingly. A theoretical value intended to show the volatility of the potential revenue is generated from the use of the asset and the cost of utilizing the asset during the life of the project. In the real world, the actual price of an asset usually differs from the theoretical price.

Theoretical Aircraft Value vs. List Price

The evaluation process of the business plan proposes the best aircraft for an airline based on its capacity, potential costs, and potential revenues (Benninga and Sarig, 1997). For the purposes of this discussion, the narrow-body Airbus A320-200 and the wide-body A330-200 were selected. As part of the Airbus design principle, these aircraft feature a high degree of commonality in airframes, onboard systems, cockpits, and handling characteristics, which subsequently increased their value to customers who sometimes enjoy reduced training and crew costs. Table 5.1 shows the high, low, and average prices as well as the calculated theoretical price of the A320 and A330.

It is important to note that aircraft prices occupy a wide scale based on various configurations and available options, including performance capability, interiors, avionics, and fuel capacity. Airbus and Boeing often sell planes at a discount to list price, and the final aircraft purchase price often is the result of negotiations, which are highly weighted on global economics, the buyer's position, and other environmental and financial factors. In 2005, Ryanair enjoyed a huge discount from Boeing for its big order for 737-800s. Each aircraft was priced at $29 million, with a retroactive pricing benefit to its previous order.[3] In 2011, Airbus offered 130 of the current-generation A320s and 130 of the more fuel-efficient A320neo to American Airlines at significantly lower than the $23 billion list price.[4] American Airlines signed letters of intent to purchase a total of 260 A320neo with 365 options and purchase rights for additional aircraft between 2013 and 2022. Airbus had never won a narrow-body order from American Airlines, just a small order for the A300 wide-body.[5]

---

[2] WACC is measured as the weighted average of the component sources of financing, where the weights are determined by the percentage obtained from each funding source.
[3] Commercial Aviation Report, February 15, 2006.

Table 5.1 Airbus aircraft prices ($ millions)

Aircraft type	High	Low	Average	Theoretical value	Difference between average and theoretical value
A320-200	85.3	77.4	81.4	68.4	16.0%
A330-200	198.6	186.5	192.6	155.8	19.1%

Source: Airbus 2011 data and Airline Monitor 2011 data.

From Table 5.1, it can be seen that the wide-body A330 costs approximately $100 million more across the range of list, maximum, and average price over the narrow-body's (A320) price. Table 5.2 shows the technical characteristics of these aircraft and illustrates the A330's capability of carrying 103 more passengers in a normal configuration and flying roughly twice as far as the A320. Despite surpassing the A320 in these performance metrics, the A320 is a vastly more popular aircraft with carriers worldwide, with over 2,500 in service (more than six times the number of A330s that are in service worldwide).

Table 5.1 also gives the theoretical NPV, which was calculated using the NPV formula established in Chapter 4. As the table shows, the discounted NPV approach produced values that were less than the minimum listed sale price for all of the aircraft. For the A320-200, the difference between the theoretical valuation and the average sales price is 16.0% while the difference for the A330-200 is 19%. Thus, the theoretical valuation may represent a cyclical decline in the financial condition of the aviation industry, or it may represent the increase in price (decrease in present value) for some of the inputs (in this case, most likely fuel). Taking the four aircraft models examined in this chapter, the average difference amounts to about 10%.

Table 5.2 Airbus aircraft type specifications

	A320-200	A330-200
Launch year	1988	1998
Normal seating	150	253
Range, miles (maximum payload)	3,300	7,250
Speed (Mach)	0.82	0.86
In service	2,516	405

Source: Airbus 2011 data.

---

[4] Reuters, July 11, 2011.
[5] National News, *National Public Radio (NPR)*, July 20, 2011.

Theoretical Aircraft Valuation Trends

The method outlined in the previous chapter is essentially a benchmarking procedure that provides an estimated theoretical value (under the assumptions of the model) to compare with a list price for the aircraft. This valuation, based on the assumed future revenues and costs characteristics, is also an application of the benchmarking potential of the technique. That is, if the assumptions are reasonably accurate, the method provides a base value for the aircraft for sale or a theoretical economic value of the asset for business decision making. By providing an economic value, this method can materially aid in managerial financial decisions that involve the sale or purchase of capital assets in a timely manner.

A secondary approach to aircraft valuation is more of a relative valuation that determines the most critical of the input assumptions. This relative valuation approach can also aid in managerial financial decisions by identifying those inputs that have the largest impact on the value of the asset. That is, it might give the financial decision maker a quantitative method to evaluate the impact of a specific decision such as the installation of winglets to increase fuel efficiency.

While the differences are subject to various assumptions, the theoretical values are close enough to the minimum list price to validate the present value approach as a reasonable first approximation to the valuation of an asset using this technique. In any event, the final sale or purchase price will always be a function of market equilibrium and the bargaining power of the buyer and the seller. However, the valuation methodology used to determine the values in Table 5.1 appears to give at least a reasonable "lower end" valuation for the capital asset. Commercial aircraft have an approximate lifespan of 30 years and market values can show noticeably different patterns during that time period, depending on the costs and revenue characteristics. Figure 5.1 and Figure 5.2 illustrate the theoretical aircraft valuation trend over the 30-year period for the Airbus A320 and A330 aircraft.

Tables 5.3 and 5.4 summarize the assumptions and estimates of changes in certain factors for the narrow-body A320 and the wide-body A330. The second column represents the cumulative overall growth rate for the 30-year period. For the Airbus A320, the daily utilization rate can be expected to grow about 0.10% for the 30-year period, and gallons per block hour can be expected to decrease by about 0.5% over the same time period. (Note: RPM is revenue passenger miles and RTM stands for revenue ton miles in these tables.) Next, the impact of these increases and decreases on various input factors is discussed.[6]

---

[6] These assumptions are based on historical trends and the previous five-year weighted average.

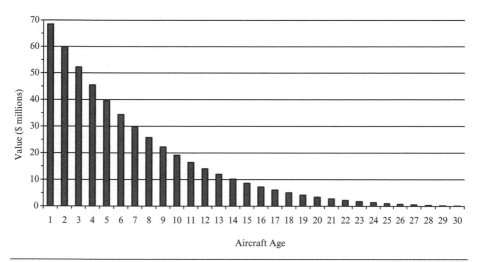

Figure 5.1 Theoretical aircraft valuation trend for Airbus A320-200

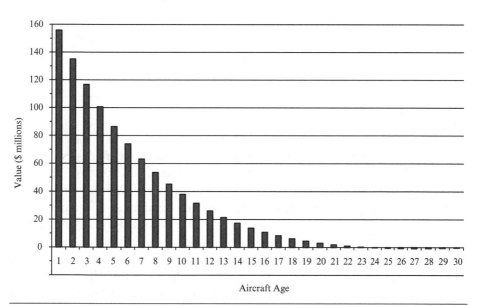

Figure 5.2 Theoretical aircraft valuation trend for Airbus A330-200

Table 5.3 Forecasting factors for Airbus A320-200

| Factor | % | Airbus A320-200 | |
		Year 2010	Year 2040
Daily utilization (hours)	0.10	11.16	11.50
Gallons per block hour	-0.5	790.22	778.45
Fuel cost ($ per gallon)	2.00	2.26	4.09
RPM (millions)	0.05	74,074.38	75,193.59
RTM (millions)	0.01	7,518.34	7,540.93

Source: OAG Form 41 data and Airline Monitor 2011 data.

Table 5.4 Forecasting factors for Airbus A330-200

| Factor | % | Airbus A330-200 | |
		Year 2010	Year 2040
Daily utilization (hours)	0.10	12.60	12.98
Gallons per block hour	-0.5	1,810.98	1,784.01
Fuel cost ($ per gallon)	2	2.29	4.15
RPM (millions)	0.05	12,888.56	13,083.30
RTM (millions)	0.01	1,721.83	1,727.00

Source: OAG Form 41 data and Airline Monitor 2011 data.

Aircraft Value Volatilities

A second way by which the model can be applied is to calculate the sensitivity of the value of the aircraft to changes to input prices. This model provides financial justification on the aircraft price changes due to variation in costs or revenues. Table 5.5 presents the results in the change in present value of the aircraft for a plus or minus 1% change for various input factors. The capabilities of the methodology and how sensitive an aircraft's theoretical value is to changes in these volatile factors can now be explored. The factors analyzed include fuel price, passenger yield, block hours, maintenance expense, and cost of capital. The model can be easily applied to changes in other factors. The sensitivity of the Airbus aircraft to each factor is first analyzed individually and then analyzed against a competing Boeing model.

As is clear from Table 5.5, changes in the passenger yield have the largest impact on the present value of the aircraft. This is clearly a result of the compounding value of increased revenue over the relatively long lifespan of an aircraft as a capital asset. On the other hand, a 1% increase in fuel cost has a bigger impact than the same 1% increase in maintenance costs, and so forth.

Table 5.5 Net aircraft value trend changes

	Discount rate +/– 1%	Fuel cost +/– 1%	Maintenance +/– 1%	Pax yield +/– 1%	Block hour +/– 0.1%
Narrow-body					
+	−5,403,298.86	−4,593,908.33	−1,771,205.98	17,973,530.99	1,940,246.46
A320-200					
−	6,166,950.61	4,019,127.94	1,490,405.89	−15,821,149.01	−1,941,625.81
+	−3,843,702.44	−3,223,495.48	−1,253,483.90	14,047,543.89	1,578,608.41
737-700					
−	4,386,930.35	2,820,178.34	1,076,016.99	−12,327,185.36	−1,558,857.94
Wide-body					
+	−12,994,586.12	−13,254,621.43	−2,850,478.44	48,316,100.60	4,643,621.30
A330-200					
−	14,831,102.01	11,596,230.38	2,410,338.72	−42,398,979.69	−4,585,520.25
+	−12,753,536.92	−12,140,706.04	−3,496,076.36	44,273,757.28	4,554,906.01
767-400ER					
−	14,555,985.49	10,621,685.80	2,954,927.68	−38,851,689.45	−4,497,914.97

Fuel Price Sensitivity

From the A320-200 theoretical value changes, the significant impact that fuel prices have on an aircraft's value become apparent. That is why airlines switching to more technologically advanced aircraft, with higher fuel efficiencies, has become a trend in the commercial aviation industry. For purposes of this analysis, fuel prices were derived from U.S. Department of Transportation figures, which reported an average fuel price per gallon for scheduled commercial aviation. A 5% increase in fuel price from $2.31 resulted in a consequential $3.04 million drop in the theoretical aircraft value of the Airbus A320-200. Figure 5.3 shows how highly

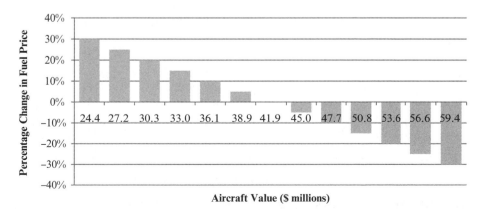

Figure 5.3 Sensitivity of theoretical A320-200 aircraft value to fuel prices

correlated the A320-200's value is to the rise and fall of fuel prices, which remains one of the most volatile factors impacting commercial aircraft values.

This extreme sensitivity to fuel prices is part of the reason for the re-engineering efforts of several Airbus products, including the A320. The A320neo, slated for delivery in 2015, is expected to increase fuel efficiency and help reduce the impact that changing fuel prices have on the way airline operators perceive an aircraft's value; increasing the aircraft's value to its operators effectively increases the price that future and current customers are willing to pay for the aircraft. The theoretical aircraft value of the wide-body Airbus A330 in Figure 5.4 exhibits a similar trend. As the fuel price decreases, the value of the aircraft increases significantly, and vice versa. For example, as shown in Figure 5.4, increasing fuel prices by 5% for the A330 decreases the aircraft value by 3.7%, or approximately $10.6 million.

Cost of Capital Sensitivity

A less sensitive response is generated by changes in the cost of capital utilized, as increasing the cost of capital decreases the aircraft's value. For the A320, an increase of 10% in the cost of capital decreases the aircraft value by $980,640

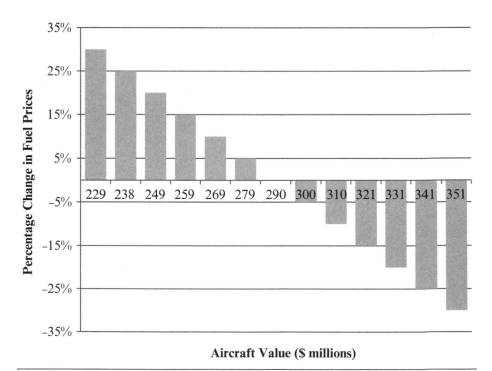

Figure 5.4 Sensitivity of theoretical A330-200 aircraft value to fuel prices

(1.7%), which pales in comparison to the $5.8 million decrease that happens when fuel price is increased by a relatively smaller 5% (see Figures 5.5 and 5.6).

Passenger Yield Sensitivity

As expected, passenger yield has the opposite effect on the theoretical value of aircraft than fuel prices and maintenance costs. Figures 5.7 and 5.8 show that as

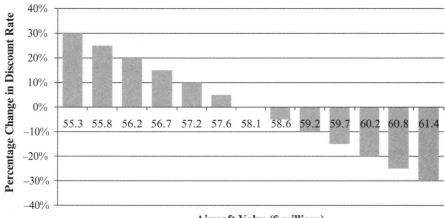

Figure 5.5 Sensitivity of theoretical A320-200 aircraft value to cost of capital

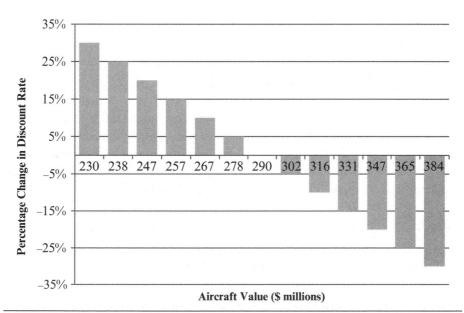

Figure 5.6 Sensitivity of theoretical A330-200 aircraft value to cost of capital

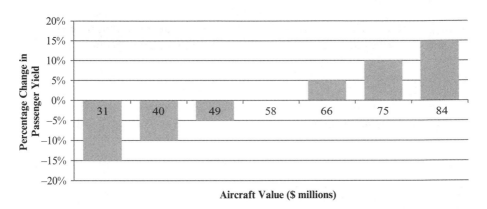

Figure 5.7 Sensitivity of theoretical A320-200 aircraft value to passenger yield

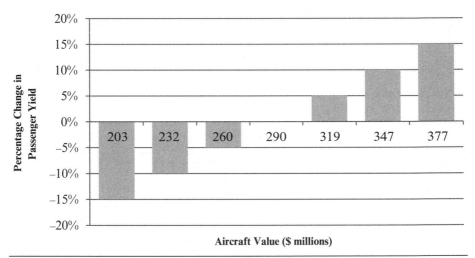

Figure 5.8 Sensitivity of theoretical A330-200 aircraft value to passenger yield

the passenger yield increases, the aircraft's value increases in tandem. The *passenger yield* is the average fare paid per mile per passenger.[7] Airlines enjoy revenue and incur cost over the lifespan of the aircraft. The corresponding increases in the aircraft's price and value associated with changes in the passenger yield make it the most influential factor on the value of the A320-200 and A330-200.

Maintenance Expense Sensitivity

The theoretical aircraft value is less sensitive to change in the total flight equipment maintenance costs (see Figures 5.9 and 5.10). A 30% increase in maintenance costs

---

[7] Yield or average fare is calculated by dividing passenger revenue by revenue passenger miles.

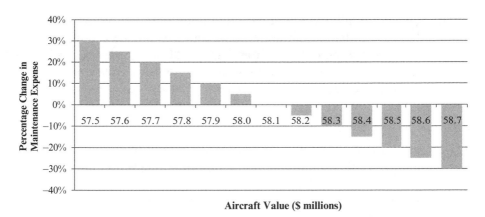

Figure 5.9 Sensitivity of theoretical A320-200 aircraft value to maintenance expenses

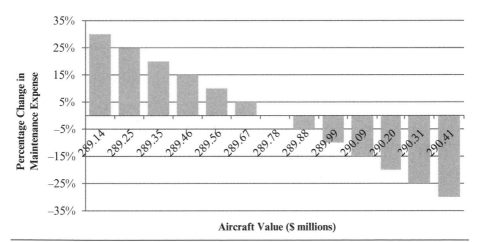

Figure 5.10 Sensitivity of theoretical A330-200 aircraft value to maintenance expenses

decreases the A320-200's value by less than $600,000, which represents a 1% drop in value. Alternatively, decreasing the maintenance costs by 30% increases the value of the aircraft by the same amount. For the larger wide-body A330-200, a 30% increase/decrease in maintenance costs decreases/increases the aircraft value by $636,457. Airbus' new wide-body (A350 XWB) is expected to have a 10% lower airframe maintenance cost and a 14% lower empty seat weight than competing aircraft.

Block Hour Sensitivity

Figure 5.11 is convex to the origin. As the number of hours that an aircraft and its components, including the engine and airframe, are in operation increases, the more rapidly the aircraft's value decreases. The condition of the airframe and engine components plays a significant role in appraising an aircraft, and thus increased use translates into increased wear and tear on the condition of the aircraft, hence decreasing its value. From Figure 5.11, it is illustrated that a 20% increase in the number of block hours that an A320-200 is operated decreases the aircraft's value by 1.75% ($1.01 million). Figure 5.12 details the A330-200.

Sensitivity Analysis Summary

The overall sensitivity of the theoretical aircraft value with respect to various factors is highlighted below. The coefficient values were calculated with @Risk, risk

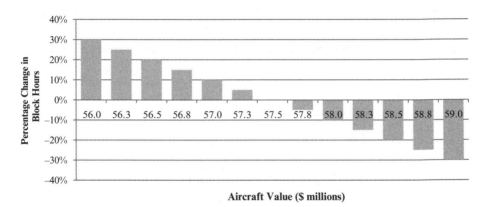

Figure 5.11 Sensitivity of theoretical A320-200 aircraft value to block hour changes

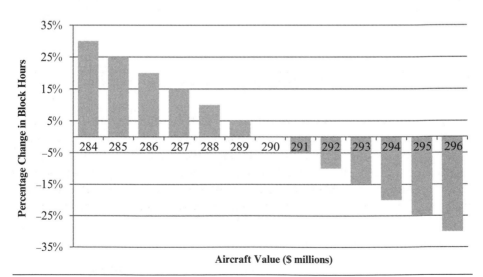

Figure 5.12 Sensitivity of theoretical A330-200 aircraft value to block hour changes

analysis software that performs the sensitivity analysis necessary through a Monte Carlo simulation.[8]

The coefficients in Figures 5.13 and 5.14 show the sensitivity of the theoretical value with respect to the variation of individual factors such as maintenance expense, block hours, cost of capital, and passenger yield. A negative value, for example, in total flight equipment maintenance shows that as the factor increases, the value of the aircraft decreases. The larger the coefficient values for the individual factors, the greater the relationship to the aircraft value, and the more sensitive the value of the aircraft is to changes in that factor. In Figures 5.13 and 5.14, passenger (pax) yield has the highest coefficient value, making it the largest contributor to the aircraft theoretical value. Also, passenger yield has a positive coefficient, which means that as passenger yield increases there is a highly correlated increase in the value of the A320-200 and A330-200.

Impact on Theoretical Aircraft Valuation of Input Changes over Lifespan of Aircraft

Similarly, Tables 5.6 and 5.7 show the changes in the aircraft value with respect to variation of individual input prices. Variation in aircraft value is calculated for the applicable growth rate contained in the tables while all other factors are held

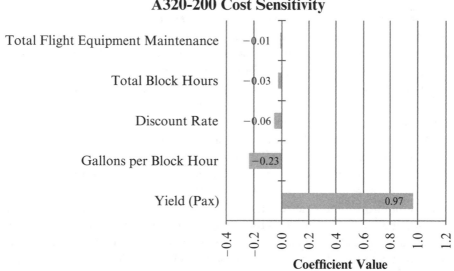

Figure 5.13 A320-200 theoretical aircraft value sensitivity analysis

---

[8] @Risk software is a Microsoft Excel add-in available from the Palisade Corporation.

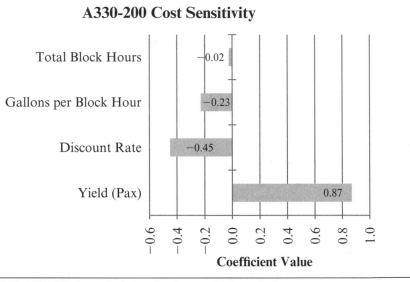

Figure 5.14 A330-200 theoretical aircraft value sensitivity analysis

constant. The factor studied is increased or decreased by a fixed percentage based on the previous year's value. Then, the theoretical aircraft value is estimated. For factors other than the cost of capital, a cost of capital of 12% is applied to obtain today's value of the periodic cash flows.

Tables 5.6 and 5.7 contain the theoretical aircraft values obtained by applying the different growth rates and are calculated for new aircraft only. Keeping the useful lifetime for an aircraft at 30 years, a one-year-old aircraft will generate less net cash flows (29 periods only). Therefore, the aircraft's theoretical value will be less. Calculating the value of the aircraft at each of the 30 periods, a valuation trend can be plotted. As Tables 5.6 and 5.7 show, the present value of the aircraft can vary greatly depending on the changes in the input variables.

It is also clear that tables and figures are helpful in making various financial decisions that might accompany the purchase or disposal of an aircraft as an asset. For example, suppose that an airline is employing an A320 on a specific route where the passenger yield has been dropping over some period of time. This could come about through increased competition or regulatory constraints, a decrease in demand, or a number of other factors. At the same time, maintenance costs, fuel costs, and personnel costs have all been increasing, and both of these trends are expected to continue. The airline could use the NPV equation with the appropriate extrapolations of the decreasing revenues and increasing costs (from historical data) and conclude that this aircraft will become non-profitable in the near future. At this juncture, the airline might decide to switch the aircraft to another route, retire the aircraft, attempt to lease it, or sell it. The airline would still use judgment

Table 5.6 Impact on theoretical aircraft value of the Airbus A320-200 by changing one factor and holding all others constant

Factor	Applied growth rate	Theoretical new aircraft value ($) Airbus A320-200
Discount rate	12%	77,781,963.66
	9%	99,205,431.77
	10%	91,028,573.62
	11%	83,948,914.28
	13%	72,378,664.80
Fuel cost (price per gallon)	2%	70,232,334.77
	1%	74,251,462.71
	1.50%	72,308,001.14
	3%	65,638,426.44
	5%	54,293,482.80
Maintenance expenses	3.75%	73,008,644.28
	1%	76,730,504.74
	5%	70,786,590.16
	8%	63,441,201.62
Passenger yield	1.25%	97,221,004.19
	1%	93,079,311.47
	1.50%	101,500,158.25
	2%	110,493,836.74
	3%	130,398,834.51
Block hours	0.10%	79,723,589.47
	0%	77,781,963.66
	0.05%	78,749,725.69
	0.50%	87,740,075.10
	0.75%	92,961,748.92

and experience in the final decision, but it would have quantitative evidence to support that decision.

Theoretical Value of Boeing Aircraft

Theoretical Aircraft Value vs. List Price

Boeing and Airbus are direct competitors in both the wide-body and narrow-body aircraft market segments. For purposes of this chapter, one narrow-body Boeing 737-700 and one wide-body Boeing 767-400ER were selected. Table 5.8 shows the high, low, and average prices of these aircraft, as well as the calculated theoretical

Table 5.7 Impact on theoretical aircraft value of the Airbus A330-200 by changing one factor and holding all others constant

Factor	Applied growth rate	Theoretical new aircraft value ($) Airbus A330-200
Discount rate	12%	187,074,341.29
	9%	238,596,282.72
	10%	218,931,529.78
	11%	201,905,443.30
	13%	174,079,755.17
Fuel cost (price per gallon)	2%	165,291,696.60
	1%	176,887,926.98
	1.50%	171,280,534.43
	3%	152,037,075.17
	5%	119,303,959.45
Maintenance expenses	12.45%	172,828,517.29
	9%	179,712,746.51
	11%	177,187,438.70
	14%	168,191,602.05
	15%	164,479,368.77
Passenger yield	1.25%	239,254,569.70
	1%	228,137,021.40
	1.50%	250,741,105.58
	2%	274,882,842.28
	3%	328,313,840.01
Block hours	0.10%	191,659,861.54
	0%	187,074,341.29
	0.05%	189,359,896.19
	0.50%	210,592,323.70
	0.75%	222,924,303.92

value and its percentage difference. In a similar trend to Airbus, the price difference between the narrow-body and wide-body products is approximately $100 million. The 767 was the first Boeing wide-body airliner with a two-person flight deck, significantly reducing crew costs by eliminating the need for a flight engineer, and subsequently increasing the aircraft's value to aircraft operators.

According to Boeing, the 737 fleet constitutes more than 90% of the combined fleets of the low-fare carriers around the world. This aircraft is favored by airlines across the globe because of advanced technology such as winglets, which allow airlines to save on fuel, extend its range, carry more payload, and reduce engine maintenance costs. The Boeing 737-700 had a theoretical NPV of $44.7 million, whereas the low list price was $59 million. This represented a 30.1% deficit in the theoretical vs. the average list price of the aircraft.

Table 5.8 Boeing aircraft prices ($ millions)

Aircraft type	High	Low	Average	Theoretical value	Difference between average and theoretical value
Boeing 737-700	69.5	58.5	64.0	44.7	30.1%
Boeing 767-400ER	161.5	169	161.5	150	7.1%

Source: Airline Monitor 2011 data.

The 767-400ER, however, had a theoretical NPV of $150 million compared to a low list price of $169 million, which represented a 7.1% deficit in the theoretical vs. list price, adding credibility to the use of the valuation methodology as a first value generator. Table 5.9 shows some of the non-financial characteristics of these two aircraft models. From this, it can be seen that despite the 767-400ER having a larger payload of 117 more passengers, the two aircraft remain comparable in both range and speed.

The assumptions and estimates of changes in certain factors for each aircraft model are given in Tables 5.10 and 5.11. The second column represents the cumulative overall growth rate for the 30-year period. This rate is an extrapolation of the previous 5-year growth rate for the factor in question. For example, the daily

Table 5.9 Boeing aircraft type specifications

	737-700	767-400ER
Launch year	1993	2,000
Normal seating	126	245
Range, miles (maximum payload)	3,440	5,625
Speed (Mach)	0.79	0.8
In service	705	38

Source: Boeing 2011 data.

Table 5.10 Forecasting factors for Boeing 737-700

Factor	Boeing 737-700		
	%	Year 2010	Year 2040
Daily utilization (hours)	0.1	10.75	11.08
Gallons per block hour	−0.05	697.47	687.08
Fuel cost ($ per gallon)	2	2.38	4.31
RPM (millions)	0.05	73,638.21	74,570.83
RTM (millions)	0.01	7,459.55	7,481.96

Source: OAG Form 41 data and Airline Monitor 2011 data.

Table 5.11 Forecasting factors for Boeing 767-400ER

| Factor | % | Boeing 767-400ER | |
		Year 2010	Year 2040
Daily utilization (hours)	0.1	13.29	13.70
Gallons per block hour	−0.05	1,746.91	1,720.90
Fuel cost ($ per gallon)	2	2.33	4.22
RPM (millions)	0.05	16,795.95	17,049.72
RTM (millions)	0.01	2,284.72	2,291.58

Source: OAG Form 41 data and Airline Monitor 2011 data.

utilization rate can be expected to grow about 0.1% for the 30-year period, gallons per block hour can be expected to decrease by about 0.5% over the same time period, and so forth. Figure 5.15 graphically represents the valuation trend of the Boeing 737-700 and Figure 5.16 does the same for the Boeing 767-400ER.

With the increase in maintenance (due to aging aircraft), operational expenses will increase accordingly. The volatility of fuel prices threatens airline profitability and their aircraft ownership demand. Airlines stored 1,167 aircraft in 2008. The total number of aircraft grounded was about 2,300, or 11% of the global air transport fleet of 20,293.[9] Many airlines such as US Airways, Delta, and American were forced to lay off employees and come up with a new source of revenue as the price of fuel skyrocketed. Operating expenses will also increase when market fuel prices increase.[10] In addition, if the aircraft is operated for longer hours per day, fuel consumption will increase, resulting in higher total fuel costs (but not per block hour). The changes in fuel cost are also dependent on the fuel efficiency of the aircraft. A continuous improvement in fuel efficiency reduces the gallons consumed per block hour. Rising fuel costs forced airlines to reduce aircraft fuel burn by coming up with innovative ideas to reduce fuel consumption. For example, many airlines now have single-engine taxi procedures to minimize fuel burn.

On the other hand, more ticket sales (thus increasing the load factor), or higher ticket prices, increase revenues. Non-ticket revenues from activities such as baggage fees, reservation change fees, frequent flyer award program mileage sales, and other ancillary and transportation fees have improved in the past few years as well.

---

[9] *Air Transport World*, February 25, 2009.
[10] On July 11, 2008, the price of crude oil reached $147.27 per barrel on the New York Mercantile Exchange, setting another record.

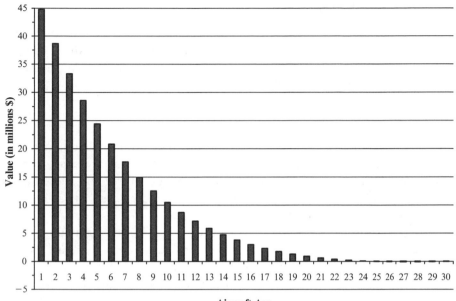

Figure 5.15 Theoretical aircraft valuation trend for Boeing 737-700

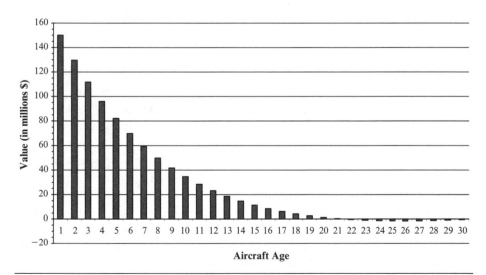

Figure 5.16 Theoretical aircraft valuation trend for Boeing 767-400ER

Aircraft Value Volatilities

In this section, we analyze the effects that the volatilities have on the theoretical value of Boeing aircraft and compare the varying effects with the Airbus competing models, highlighting the differing operating, technical, and design characteristics that may account for any differences.

Fuel Price Sensitivity

Given that fuel prices account for at least one-third of airline operating expenses, even a comparatively small change in fuel price can have a major impact on profitability and hence demand for aircraft. Owing to high jet fuel and interest costs, three major Indian airlines, Kingfisher, Jet Airways, and SpiceJet, have all reported heavy second-quarter losses in 2011.[11]

Rising fuel prices force airlines to reduce the number of flights to conserve fuel. Hence, higher fuel prices trigger airlines to reduce frequency and up-gauge to larger or more fuel efficient aircraft (Ferguson et al., 2009). This statement is true when looking at a market, but the number of larger gauge aircraft is somewhat fixed, especially in the short term, so a common result is higher fares along with the resulting decrease in passengers in an attempt to drive higher yields and help profitability. Over the long term, given that demand is at least partially elastic, higher fuel costs lead to a reduction in available seat miles or, at the very least, a decreased growth rate.

The Boeing 737-700 experiences a 4.5% ($2 million) drop in aircraft value when the fuel price is increased by 5% compared to a 7.25% ($3.04 million) decrease in the A320-200's value. The 737-700 is part of Boeing's Next Generation lineup of aircraft products that offer greater fuel efficiencies over previous versions, rendering it less sensitive to the volatile fluctuations of fuel prices. About 85% of all new 737s are built with fuel-saving winglets, particularly the -800 and -900 series. Of course, this is a capital budgeting decision and comes down to cost vs. benefits. Winglets cost about $750,000, and once fitted, they add 375-518 pounds to the weight of the aircraft.[12] Hence, if the average sector length is too short, airlines would not benefit from winglets.

This example further lends credibility to the move by aircraft manufacturers to redesign their products to become less sensitive to fuel prices; aircraft operators place a higher value on an aircraft that decreases in value by a lesser percentage based on fuel prices. The 767-400ER's theoretical aircraft value decreases by 4.8% ($9.7 million) when fuel prices are increased by 5%.

---

[11] Indo Asian News Service, December 15, 2011.
[12] Depending upon whether they were retrofitted or installed at the time of production.

Cost of Capital Sensitivity

The Boeing 737-700 is more sensitive than the wide-body 767-400ER to changes in the cost of capital. With a 10% increase in the cost of capital, the corresponding value of a 737-700 falls by $2.85 million, which is approximately 6.42%, and the 767-400ER falls by $19.6 million, a 7.78% change. The cost of capital is the minimum return expected for providing capital; as the risk associated with a purchase increases, the theoretical price decreases.

Passenger Yield Sensitivity

Due to the cyclicality of environmental economic conditions, the passenger yield experiences similar fluctuations. Continuing from previous discussions on passenger yield, the 737-700 experiences an $8.56 million decrease in value if the passenger yield is decreased by 5%; this is a 19.3% decrease in value. The 767-400ER's value falls by more than $26.5 million, which is a 10.5% decrease.

Maintenance Expense Sensitivity

Flight equipment maintenance expense has a minimal impact on the theoretical value of both Boeing aircraft. Increasing maintenance expense by 30% on a 737-700 decreases the aircraft price by a relatively minimum $284,360; this is less than 0.64% of the normal aircraft value. The wide-body 767-400ER is even less sensitive to changes in the maintenance expense. Increasing maintenance costs by 30% decreases the value by $843,557, which is approximately 0.33%.

Block Hour Sensitivity

If the number of block hours is increased on the 737-700 by 20%, then aircraft value drops by $711,431, which is 1.6%, compared to 1.75% for a similar increase for the Airbus A320-200. The Boeing 767-400ER for the same percentage increase drops in value by $2.64 million, which is 1.05% less.

Sensitivity Analysis Summary

The coefficient values for the various factors were calculated using @Risk software (see Table 5.12), allowing for comparisons to be drawn between the aircraft products. The factors for both Airbus and Boeing models display near identical sensitivities. The largest contributor to all four aircraft models was the passenger yield. For the A330 and 767, the coefficient value is 0.98, which means that for every x fraction of a standard deviation increase in passenger yield, the theoretical aircraft value will increase by $0.98x$ standard deviations.

Table 5.12 Theoretical aircraft value price change for 1% changes in input factors

	Discount rate	Fuel cost	Maintenance	Pax yield	Block hour
Narrow-body					
A320-200	−7.4	−6.16	−2.24	17.19	24.35
737-700	−7.4	−6.06	−2.32	18.48	27.57
Wide-body					
A330-200	−7.4	−7.56	−1.52	18.73	24.07
767-400ER	−7.4	−6.99	−1.95	17.75	24.06

Theoretical Aircraft Valuation Trend Comparison

A320-200 vs. 737-700

Figure 5.17 and Figure 5.18 depict the calculated aircraft values with the forecasted future cash flows. In both narrow- and wide-body segments, the total cash flows are discounted at 12% and useful life is considered at 30 years. In both instances, there is a value difference in the trends between Boeing and Airbus products. This value difference may be attributable to a variety of factors such as fuel consumption, seating capacity (class configurations), cargo capacity, whether or not belly space is containerized, maintenance cost, and the cost of capital.

For the narrow-body category illustrated in Figure 5.17, one factor to consider is the larger cargo capacity of the Airbus A320. The Airbus A320 is larger than the

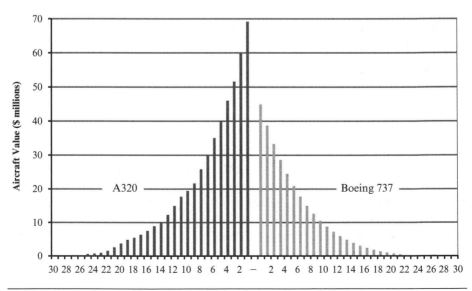

Figure 5.17 Aircraft valuation trend comparison: A320-200 vs. 737-700

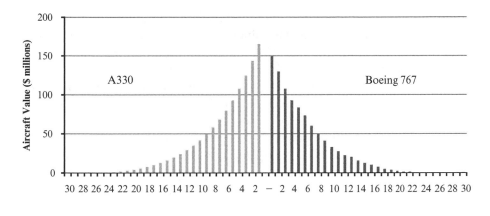

Figure 5.18 Aircraft valuation trend comparison: A330-200 vs. 767-400ER

Boeing 737-700, but smaller than the 737-800. This increased volume can generate higher revenue than the Boeing 737-700. As given in the revenue function from Chapter 4, the difference in the cargo volume contributes to the higher aircraft value of the Airbus A320 against the Boeing 737. Another contribution toward the A320 is it allows cargo pallets, which increases cargo loading efficiency, thus reducing labor costs and ground time. Another revenue disparity between the two aircraft is the passenger capacity; Airbus' one-class configuration accommodates 180 passengers while Boeing accommodates 149. The difference in the capacity will create a value difference in the aircraft comparison.

JetBlue founder David Neelman commented on the value difference, after the company's decision to place 80 orders for the Airbus A320 instead of the Boeing 737. According to JetBlue, the A320 had better fuel consumption, superior cabin technology, and wider cabins. Also, it is less narrow at the end of the aircraft. These non-financial characteristics can convert into higher passenger satisfaction levels and a preference over the Boeing 737. Furthermore, the highly computerized A320 operations save administrative time and labor cost.

A330-200 vs. 767-400ER

The value difference in the wide-body comparison between the A330 and 767 is significantly less than between the narrow-body A320 and 737. The Airbus A330-200 competes with the smaller Boeing 767-400ER. The wide-body category valuations depicted in Figure 5.18 are largely driven by the similar operating economics of both the Airbus A330 and Boeing 767, with revenues and operating costs resulting in similar cash flow profiles. The minute differences in value can be attributed to differences in seat capacity. The A330-200 in a normal three-class configuration accommodates 253 passengers, which is 8 more than the Boeing 767-400ER's normal configuration of 245. The Boeing 767, however, accommodates slightly more cargo with 144 m³ of space available, compared to 136 m³ for the A330. The A330 is more heavily utilized than the 767; as of September 2011, more than 429 A330-200 aircraft were in service compared to 38 Boeing 767-400ERs. Based on many of these aircraft characteristics, comparisons can be drawn between the A330, 767 and 777 families. However, of course, comparing the A330 to the Boeing 777 would result in a much different set of theoretical aircraft values.

Elasticity

Another way of looking at value changes is to use the well-known concept of elasticity. *Elasticity* measures the percent change in one factor relative to the percent change in another, so that it is a measure that is free of units. Point elasticity measures a relative change at a particular point, whereas arc elasticity measures the change over some larger amounts and is calculated as the average relative change.

The corresponding theoretical aircraft values at each level are computed for a +/− 1% increase or decrease in the input factor, and the arc elasticity of each factor for every aircraft model is calculated. From Table 5.12, block hour usage has the highest impact on the present value of the aircraft, with a 1% increase in block hours producing an approximately 24% increase in the present value of the aircraft. A real-world example of elasticity is Southwest Airlines, which has the highest block hour usage rate among the major airlines and is also consistently profitable.

As mentioned, passenger yield is also a major contributor to present value, and this shows in Table 5.12 as an approximate 18% increase in present value for a 1% increase in passenger yield. Table 5.12 also shows that fuel costs have a bigger impact on present value than maintenance costs. Finally, a 1% increase in the cost of capital produces a 7.4% decrease in the present value of the aircraft. The reason for this, of course, is the fact that we are comparing the present value of the aircraft as an asset to other possible investment opportunities in the economy, and as the rate of return on those investment opportunities increases, the value of the aircraft as an asset will decrease.

Summary

The developed aircraft evaluation methodology evaluates the aircraft's costs, revenue, capacity, and performance under a variety of inputs to develop a benchmark that can be used for airline valuation. It serves as a base figure for major financial decisions, including the sale/purchase of an asset or the theoretical economic value of the asset to be used in decision making. For example, it may give the decision maker a quantitative method with which to evaluate the impact of a specific decision, such as installing winglets to increase fuel efficiency. Under this methodology, the long-term aircraft value price was determined to be most sensitive to changes in passenger yield by conducting a range of analyses on the impact of various input factors on the theoretical aircraft price.

References

Airbus. (2011a). *Airbus A320 Family Specifications*. Retrieved from http://www.airbus.com/aircraftfamilies/passengeraircraft/a320family/.

Airbus. (2011b). *Airbus A340 Family Specifications*. Retrieved from http://www.airbus.com/aircraftfamilies/passengeraircraft/a340family/.

Airbus. (2011c). *Orders and Deliveries*. Retrieved from http://www.airbus.com/company/market/orders-deliveries/.

Benninga, S., & Sarig, H. (1997). *Corporate Finance: A Valuation Approach*. McGraw-Hill, New York, NY.

Boeing. (2011a). *Boeing 737-700 Technical Specifications*. Retrieved from http://www.boeing.com/commercial/737family/pf/pf_700tech.html.

Boeing. (2011b). *Boeing 767-400 Technical Specifications*. Retrieved from http://www.boeing.com/commercial/767family/specs.html.

Boeing. (2011c). *Orders and deliveries*. Retrieved from http://active.boeing.com/commercial/orders/index.cfm.

Ferguson, J., et al. (2009). Effects of fuel prices and slot controls on air transportation performance at New York Airport. Eighth USA and Europe Air Traffic Management Research and Development Seminar.

Khan, M. (1993). *Theory and Problems in Financial Management*. McGraw-Hill Higher Education, Boston.

U.S. Department of Transportation, Research and Innovative Technology Administration, Bureau of Transportation Statistics, Office of Airline Information. (2011). *Airline Fuel Cost and Consumption*.

Appendix to the Chapter

The prices below show an average price that reflects a range of available options and significantly diverges from the actual price.

Appendix Average price based on a range of options (not actual price)

Airbus: 2011	Price list	Boeing: 2010	Price list
A318	$65.20	737-600	$56.90
A319	$77.70	737-700	$67.90
A320	$85.00	737-800	$80.80
A321	$99.70	737-900ER	$85.80
A330-200	$200.80	747-8	$317.50
A330-200*	$203.60	747-8*	$319.30
A330-300	$222.50	767-300ER	$144.10
A340-300	$238.00	767-300ER	$164.30
A340-500	$261.80	767-300*	$167.70
A340-600	$275.40	767-300ER	$180.60
A350-800	$236.60	777-200ER	$232.30
A350-900	$267.60	777-200LR	$262.40
A350-1000	$299.70	777-300ER	$284.10
A380-800	$375.30	777*	$269.10
		787-8	$185.20
		787-9	$218.00

*Freighter version.
Prices are in millions of US dollars.
Source: Bloomberg, Airbus and Boeing Airplane Price List Comparison, May 23, 2011.

Web
Added
Value™

6

The Principles of Effective Cost Management and Capital Structure

It's just a god-awful time for this industry. This illustrates the uncertainty of capital markets to a T.

—Bob Mann, Independent airline consultant, responding to airline bankruptcies

Assessing an aircraft's value to an operator requires determining the potential cash flows the aircraft may generate over the life of the asset, as well as the impact of financing the aircraft on the company's financial statements. Hence, it is necessary to understand each element of the cash costs. An aircraft is expected to remain in service for 30 years or more. By understanding the costs of different resources, both physical as well as human capital, one can understand why airlines use different capital structures and business plans.

Determining the aircraft's generated cash flow in a specific part of an airline's operation over a long period of time brings a certain amount of risk that projected targets will not be met. Breaking down the cost into different components allows the analyst to assess the risks of changes to each component and how sensitive overall cash costs are and, therefore, what the cash flows would be with those changes. This chapter first describes what is usually meant by the various methods of financing fixed assets and then explores core elements of airline capital structure and finance before assessing the main aspects of an aircraft's crew costs as they relate to an airline's operation. The chapter is organized as follows:

Fixed Assets Financing

- Equity Financing
- Debt Financing

Strategic Labor Cost Management

- Financial Crew Cost Analysis
- Operational Crew Cost Analysis

Rules of Thumb

At the end of the chapter is a Summary for chapter review and References for further study.

Fixed Assets Financing

This chapter focuses on practical tools for the financial manager in determining an aircraft's proper cost breakdown. It includes the definitions of the different types of costs, review of capital structure alternatives, and the concepts of labor costs, financial leverage, and productivity.

The air transport industry is an extremely capital- and labor-intensive business. External sources of capital are a vital determinant of an airline's ability to acquire new aircraft, establish or expand a network, and remain profitable. Automobile manufacturers, the housing industry, and heavy equipment companies, in addition to the aircraft industry, are sensitive to the business cycles of related companies. Airlines, much like other transportation industries, repeatedly suffer when the economy is in a recession and benefit when the economy moves to recovery.

In order to introduce a new commercial airliner, the aircraft manufacturers require billions of dollars of capital in order to develop and manufacture the aircraft. This capital comes from a variety of sources, potentially including subsidies and launch aid. These capital resources have been argued as unfairly advantageous to respective manufacturers. For example, Boeing asserts that European governments provide billions of dollars to Airbus each time it develops a new airplane.[1] Airbus argues that Boeing receives government assistance through military contracts, which is then used for commercial aircraft.[2] Airbus and Boeing have both

---

[1] *The Seattle Times*, October 18, 2010.
[2] *Airport Journal*, July 2005.

sued each other through the World Trade Organization over subsidies to Boeing and launch aid to Airbus from their respective governments.

The aircraft industry requires massive capital investment. In fact, Airbus invested over $14 billion to develop the A380 in order to compete with Boeing's 747.[3] Miami International Airport underwent a $6.4 billion *capital improvement project (CIP)* aimed at expanding and redeveloping the airport. The CIP included a $2.85 billion, 3.6-million-square-foot North Terminal set to house American Airlines and its Oneworld alliance partners.[4] American Airlines will pay about 70% of the costs for the North Terminal (Magcale, 2007). Similarly, Delta Air Lines was on schedule with its $1.2 billion expansion of a 1.5-million-square-foot Terminal 4 at John F. Kennedy International that would replace the more than 50-year-old Terminal 3 for international passengers (see Table 6.1).[5]

Long-term assets should be financed with long-term sources of financing that may be internal as well as external. Airlines can raise the needed funds by issuing new equity or through the selling of corporate bonds, as well as commercial loans. Capital can also come from within the company through the use of profits reinvested in the company in the form of retained earnings. The capital structure of a company thereby presents how the company finances its overall long-term investment through some combination of long-term debt, preferred stock, and common equity.

Table 6.1 Airline and airport development costs

Project	Year	Cost (billions)
Aircraft manufacturers:		
Boeing 707	1957	1.3
Boeing 747	1970	3.7
Boeing 777	1994	7
Airbus A380	2005	14
Airbus A350	2012	15
Airport industry:		
JFK Terminal 8 (American)	2007	1.3
JFK Terminal 5 (JetBlue)	2008	0.75
JFK Terminal 4 (Delta)	2013	1.2
Miami International CIP	2011	6.5

Sources: Adapted from Miami Airport International, Delta, JetBlue, and American Airlines press releases.

---

[3] The Engineer. Airbus round off Paris air show with $14 billion of orders, June 22, 2001.
[4] Miami Airport International CIP Executive Summary, July 31, 2011.
[5] Delta Air Lines press release, July 19, 2011.

Equity Financing

Common Stock

Capital structure refers to the mix of sources from which the long-term funds required in a business may be raised. External equity financing takes the form of common stock and preferred stock. *Common stock* represents equity rights in a corporation, and each share provides an equal portion of ownership of a company. An important feature associated with common stock is par value. *Par value* is an arbitrary value assigned to stock before it is issued and represents a shareholders' liability ceiling. The next indicator of the value of common stock is *book value*, which is the value of common shareholders' equity divided by the number of shares outstanding.

$$\text{Book Value} = \frac{\text{Common Stockholders' Equity}}{\text{Number of Shares Outstanding}}$$

This source of financing has no end date, nor maturity date, and is the most frequently used form of stock an investor will encounter in the financial market. Stockholders are entitled to a share of the profits, either in the form of dividends or retained earnings. In addition, the stockholders have the right to vote in a company's general meeting for a board of directors as well as corporate policy. Equity in a company is a residual claim on a company's value that exists after paying its debts, so common stockholders are at the bottom of the totem pole in the event of a bankruptcy. Should a company go bankrupt, common stockholders are only paid after creditors and, frequently, preferred stockholders have received their share of any remaining assets (Miller & Rock, 1985). From the stockholder's point of view, purchasing common stock in a company is, therefore, riskier than debt or preferred shares, but usually outperforms both in the long run. Hence, common stock enjoy the following rights and privileges:

- Dividend rights: The right to receive dividend payments from earnings.
- Voting rights: The right to vote to elect directors and to approve fundamental transactions such as mergers, sale of assets, amendments to articles, dissolutions.
- Asset rights: The right to receive a proportionate distribution of assets on corporate liquidation.
- Preemptive rights: If a company plans to issue new shares, stockholders may have the right to purchase the new shares before they are issued to the public.

When a company issues stock it eliminates the drawbacks of the contractual claim on earnings and assets associated with debt financing. For example, on July 14, 2003, JetBlue Airways Corporation issued 2,600,000 shares of newly issued common stock, which brought the company approximately $122.4 million in proceeds, after deducting underwriting expenses.[6] In another example, Lufthansa obtained 42 million newly issued common shares of JetBlue in a private placement for $7.27 a share, or a total of about $300 million.[7] In 2008, Southwest Airlines authorized the repurchase of up to $500 million of the company's common stock.[8]

Common Stock Valuation

Suppose an investor wishes to value the common stock of WestJet Airlines. The airline is expected to continue paying indefinitely $0.20 dividend per share (D). If the investor determines the required rate of return (k) on this stock to be 5%, its value is:

$$P = \frac{D}{k}$$

$$P = \frac{0.20}{0.05} = \$4 \text{ per share}$$

If the last year dividend was $0.20 per share and dividends are expected to grow at an annual rate of $g = 3\%$ a year, then the value of the WestJets common stock is:

$$P = \frac{D}{k - g}$$

$$P = \frac{0.20}{0.05 - 0.03}$$

$$P = \$10 \text{ per share}$$

The value of WestJet's common stock increased sharply from $4.00 under the no growth assumption to $10 per share with assumed growth rates of 3% per year. Hence, a stock's value depends on its fundamentals such as its dividend and expected dividend growth.

Preferred Stock

A preferred stock is usually a hybrid of a bond and a common stock. Similar to a bond, a preferred stock generally has a dividend that must be paid out before dividends to common stockholders. Also similar to bonds, preferred shareholders usually do not have voting rights. Preferred stock come with different financial characteristics, and every company may use its discretion in setting its own rules for preferred stock. Nevertheless, they are generally characterized by fixed

---

[6] JetBlue Airways Corporation, July 14, 2003.
[7] Market Watch, December 7, 2007.
[8] Aero News Network, August 9, 2011.

dividend payments. Generally, preferred stock dividends tend to be considerably higher than dividends paid on common shares, in addition to the higher claim they grant the holder on assets and earnings of the company.

Many investors turn to preferred stock as a tool to set regular income via a preferred dividend. For example, in February, 2008, Mitsui Corporation acquired 80,000,000 shares of non-voting preferred shares of the Japan Airline Corporation, convertible into common stock for 20 billion Japanese Yen.[9] However, just as in the case of common stock shares, dividends on preferred shares also could be terminated. The cost of preferred stock is similar to common stock with constant dividends. Preferred stockholders receive a fixed dividend from the company, with dividend payments paid in perpetuity. In order to determine the cost of preferred stock, the amount of the dividend is divided by the price of the preferred stock:

$$k_{ps} = \frac{D_{ps}}{P_{ps}}$$

Conversely, to calculate the value of a preferred stock, use the equation for price of preferred stock:

$$P_{ps} = \frac{D_{ps}}{k_{ps}}$$

For example, suppose that DirectJet (a fictional name for discussion purposes) paid a dividend of $5.00 per share on preferred stock that is selling for $40.00 per share. Since the annual preferred dividend payments and the preferred stock price are known, the preferred stockholders' required rate of return on the preferred stock can be calculated:

$$k_{ps} = \frac{\$5.00}{\$40.00}$$

$$k_{ps} = 12.5\%$$

In the event of a liquidation, the holders of the *preferred stock* receive preferential treatment to *common stock* holders regarding unpaid dividends and the distribution of remaining assets.

Dividends

If we stop expanding for a year or two, we'll see a big cash build-up and that should be distributed to shareholders in the event the company can't get the price it wants for new aircraft.

---

[9] Mitsui, February 29, 2008.
[10] *Independent*, October 3, 2009.

—Michael O'Leary, Ryanair[10]

Stock dividends are income received by shareholders from the proceeds of a company. Airlines paying dividends are rare in the last several years because of the cyclical nature of the industry. The most recent dividend was announced by WestJet, paying five Canadian cents a share to the investors.[11] Investors receive a return on their investment through two means: a stock dividend and its capital gains (increase in stock price). However, common stock dividends may not usually remain constant. Dividends paid are recorded on a company's cash flow statement as a financing activity. The dividend (yields) and capital gains returns are added together to determine the total return on common stock (K_E).

As mentioned in the section above, common stock holders are eligible to receive dividends from the company's net profit if the company chooses to distribute dividends. Shareholders can receive those profits as payouts, i.e., dividends or repurchases, or the profits can be reinvested into the company for the benefit of the shareholders. Management must decide if the reinvested profits can return at least the cost of capital. If they do, then it's a good decision; if not, the capital should be returned to the shareholders.

As an example, assume a shareholder purchased a stock for $100 a share and received a $2.50 dividend at the end of the year. Hence, the dividend yield is:

$$K_E = \frac{D_1}{P_0} = \frac{2.50}{100} = 2.5\%$$

Now suppose that at the end of the first year, the stock is trading at $125 per share. When sold, $25 of capital appreciation, or a capital gain, is realized. Hence, the total return of the stock is:

$$K_E = \frac{D_1}{P_0} + \frac{P_1 - P_0}{P_0}$$

$$K_E = \frac{2.50}{100} + \frac{125 - 100}{100}$$

$$K_E = 27.5\%$$

The investor receives a 2.5% dividend yield and a 25% capital gains yield, which add together to give the investor a return of 27.5%. This return is required to gain investors because investors require compensation for the fact that they are foregoing consumption (time value of money) and for the risk involved in investing in the company. Companies must achieve enough profit (return on equity) to pay dividends and/or increase the value of the company. If not, investors will not invest in the company. As of September 20, 2011, the dividend yield of Southwest Airlines was 10%, GOL was 8%, and SkyWest was 6%.[12]

---

[11] Reuters, November 3, 2010.
[12] *Bloomberg Market Watch*, September 20, 2011.

Cost of Equity

> *Regardless, an investor who purchases an airline stock must be prepared to deal with a high risk of bankruptcy, in which case he could lose 100%. Add this risk to a commodity business with huge fixed costs and a gigantic capital base and I just don't see where the value will come from.*

— Andy Kern, Seekingalpha.com

Investors are not going to invest in an airline, or any other company, without expecting a minimum return on their investment. The return on investment that shareholders require from a company represents a company's cost of common stock. The cost of common stock (K_E) varies for each company. Investors will require different rates of return for each company they invest in, depending on the associated risks. Because the airline industry is considered a risky investment due to volatility and cyclicality, investors will likely require a greater rate of return on capital paid into Continental Airlines as compared to a company in a less risky industry such as United Healthcare.

Retained Earnings

There are two ways in which equity capital can be invested into a business: through the sale of common/preferred stock or through the company retaining earnings (Brigham & Gapenski, 2004). A company can either distribute net income to its shareholders through the payment of dividends, or it can keep part or all of its net income and invest back into the company as retained earnings. If a company decides to reinvest net income within the company, as has been the case with many airlines (such as JetBlue) that have historically paid no dividends, the investors must still be compensated for the opportunity cost of forgoing a dividend.

Remember that the rate of return for the investor is equal to the dividend yield plus the capital gains yield. If a company is not paying dividends, the capital gains yield must equal the investor's required rate of return. Therefore, the cost of retained earnings is equal to the required rate of return:

$$K_{RE} = k$$

The formula for cost of retained earnings is based on the value for cost of equity found, using the dividend discount model, as discussed earlier:

$$k = \frac{D_1}{P_0} + g$$

For example, suppose (fictitiously named) DirectJet decides that growth opportunities in the industry exist due to the capacity reductions by other U.S. airlines. As a result, the airline wants to hold most of its profits as retained earnings. The board of directors at the airline decides that next year's dividend (next dividend paid) will be only $0.10 per share. DirectJet expects to grow at a rate of 6% and its stock was trading at $14.77.

$$k_{RE} = \frac{\$0.10}{\$14.77} + .06$$

$$k_{RE} = .0668 = 6.68\%$$

The cost to DirectJet for using retained earnings to finance expansion is 6.68%.

Debt Financing

In addition to equity financing, companies may also use debt as part of their capital structure. The debt-to-equity ratio would probably be higher for the airlines because most airlines borrow heavily for their aircraft acquisition or capital leasing.

Debt financing can be either short term or long term. Short term debt financing usually applies to money needed for the day-to-day operations of the business, such as inventories or other operating expenses. Some other examples of short-term debt financing include bank loans and business lines of credit. Long-term debt financing usually applies to fixed assets such as aircraft, airport terminals, buildings, land, and machinery.

Airlines with heavy debt in relation to ownership equity are in greater danger of insolvency as compared to equity financing. However, the most powerful incentive for the use of debt in the capital structure is the tax deductibility of interest expenses. The motivation to borrow money increases with an airline's taxable income. On the negative side, the threat of financial distress and corporate bankruptcy is likely to increase as the level of debt in an airline portfolio increases.

A key ratio used to interpret the level of debt and determine a company's financing methods is the *debt-to-equity ratio*. This ratio indicates the relative proportion of debt used to finance a company's assets. A low debt-to-equity ratio indicates lower risk because shareholders have a claim on a larger portion of the company's assets. A higher debt-to-equity ratio usually means that a company has been either aggressive in financing growth with debt or funding losses with debt, and both often may result in insolvency.

Many airlines with heavy debt in their portfolios have never recovered from Chapter 11 bankruptcy, including Eastern Airlines, which had amassed $3.2 billion in debt and assets worth only $620 million when it ran out of cash in 1991. Eastern Airlines lost about $1.3 billion in only 22 months. In this unstable situation, there were a lot of disagreements between the former CEO, Frank Lorenzo, and the unions that further led to Lorenzo being forced to quit his job at Eastern Airlines (Weiss & Wruck, 1998). In 2007, Delta Air Lines filed for bankruptcy protection, since it was unable to restructure its $20 billion in corporate debt.

Pan American Airways and Trans World Airlines (TWA) also did not emerge from Chapter 11 bankruptcy. Pan American filed for liquidation, and TWA was acquired by American Airlines.

Bonds

Corporate fixed income debt instruments are known as *bonds*. The person who buys a bond from a company is the bond, or debt, holder. An indenture is a written agreement between the company and its bondholders that discloses all of the rights and privileges of bondholders as well as the terms of the bond. Bonds are essentially long-term loan agreements between a borrower and an investor; the terms of a bond obligate the borrower (issuer) to repay the amount of principal by maturity. Most bonds also require that the borrower pay the investor a specific amount of interest. A summary of the features of common stock, preferred stock, and bonds is given in Table 6.2.

In exchange for capital, the company agrees to pay the bondholder periodic interest payments, called *coupon payments*, until the bond has matured. A bond is a legally binding agreement between a lender and a borrower. Most corporations issue bonds in denominations of $1,000 (face value) with maturity between 10 to 30 years (Gitman, 2008). The maturity date is the date by which the par value must be repaid, and the payments are called "coupon payments" because when bonds were first issued, the bondholders would have to turn in a coupon they received with the bond in order to collect their interest payment. Nowadays, companies have much more modern systems of distributing interest payments; however, the original name remains.

The cost of debt (coupon rate) depends on the market interest rate, the airline's credit profile, and the company's tax rate and condition. The amount of the

Table 6.2 Features of common stocks, preferred stocks, and bonds

Common stock	Preferred stock	Bonds
Each share provides equal ownership	Hybrid of a bond and common stock	Debt instrument
Entitled to dividends (if company pays them)	Stockholders are granted high claim on assets and earnings	Interest is paid to bondholders before dividends are paid to stockholders
Riskier than debt or preferred shares	Generally, fixed dividend payments	Periodic interest payments, called coupon payments
Last to receive share of assets in case of bankruptcy	Dividends tend to be higher than dividends paid on common shares	First to receive interest and face value of bond in case of liquidation
Grants owners voting rights	No voting rights	No voting rights

coupon payment is based on two items, the face value of the bond and the coupon rate. An important risk associated with bonds is default risk. If the issuer defaults, investors receive less than the promised return on the bond. The greater the default risk, the higher the bond's coupon payments. Generally speaking, a company with a high level of debt compared to equity is thought to carry higher risk, and therefore, investors demand a higher rate of return. The Modigliani-Miller theorem (Modigliani & Miller, 1958) states that, in a perfect market (and ignoring the effect of taxes), a firm cannot create more value by using debt. Bonds are normally assigned quality ratings by ratings agencies, such as Moody's Investors Service and Standard & Poor's.

Face Value of a Bond

The *face value* of a bond is similar to the par value of a stock. Face value is the amount printed on the bond; bonds usually come with $100, $1,000, or $10,000 face values. The face value of the bond will be returned to the bondholder when the bond matures (Block, 1999). The maturity of a bond is the length of time remaining on the bond until the company must pay the face value to the bondholder. Bonds typically come with 10- to 30-year maturity periods. However, bonds can typically be bought or sold between the original investor and a third party at any time while the bond is still outstanding.

The coupon rate is the annual interest rate (i) at which the bondholder will receive coupon payments. For example, a bond with a face value of $1,000 and a coupon rate of 8% entitles the bondholder to $80 interest per year as their coupon payment. In much the same way that stocks are not always traded at their issued price (par value for stocks technically has a different meaning), bonds do not have to be sold at face value. There are three different types of bonds based upon their market value: par value bonds, premium bonds, and discount bonds, as shown in Table 6.3.

The actual price that a bond sells at is based on current market interest rates (k) for bonds of companies with similar risk. Bonds sell at a premium if the coupon rate (c) is higher than the market interest rate (k). Premium bonds have a built-in mechanism of capital loss. As the bond approaches maturity, the market value approaches face value; the market value of the premium bond decreases. Discount bonds, on the other hand, sell for below face value because the coupon

Table 6.3 Types of bonds based on market value

Discount bond	Par value bond	Premium bond
Bond's market value is less than face value ($c < k$)	Bond sells at face value ($c = k$)	Bond sells for (or market value is) greater than face value ($c > k$)

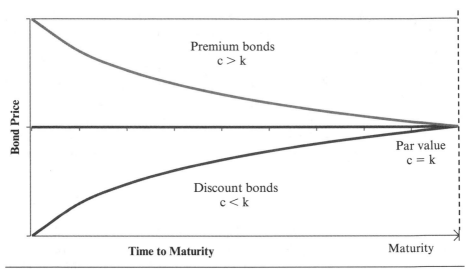

Figure 6.1 Bond value over time

interest rates are lower than the market interest rate for the perceived creditworthiness of the company at that time (Brealey & Myers, 2008). Discount bonds have a built-in mechanism of capital gains. As discount bonds approach maturity, their market value also approaches face value; the amount of the discount below face value shrinks (see Figure 6.1).

The value of a bond can be determined by using an annuity formula and adding the face value discounted by the market interest rate:

$$\text{Bond}_{\text{Market Value}} = \sum_{t=1}^{n} \frac{C}{(1+k)^t} + \frac{FV}{(1+k)^n}$$

$$\text{Bond}_{\text{Market Value}} = C\left[\frac{1}{k} - \frac{1}{k(1+k)^t}\right] + \frac{FV}{(1+k)^n}$$

where:

C = annual coupon payment
k = required rate of return, or market interest rate
t = each payment period starting at $t = 1$
FV = face value of bond
n = years to maturity

Note that bond prices vary inversely with market interest rates. Since the coupon payments are fixed, the higher the interest rate, the lower the present value of the expected coupon payments and, thus, the lower the price of the bond. Conversely, when the interest rate goes down, the price of bonds goes up. For example, consider a bond selling in 2009 for $1,000 with an annual coupon payment of $90 and a 10-year maturity. Suppose that immediately after the bond was issued, the interest rate dropped to 8%; as a result, the bond would appreciate to:

$$V_{\text{Bond}} = C \times \left[\frac{1}{k} - \frac{1}{k(1+k)^t} \right] + \frac{1000}{(1+k)^t}$$

$$V_{\text{Bond}} = 90 \times \left[\frac{1}{0.08} - \frac{1}{0.08(1+0.08)^{10}} \right] + \frac{1000}{(1+0.08)^{10}}$$

$$V_{\text{Bond}} = 90 \times 6.710 + 1000 \times 0.463$$

$$V_{\text{Bond}} = 603.90 + 463.00$$

$$V_{\text{Bond}} = 1,066.90$$

The purpose of bond valuation is to find out what price should be paid for a bond given the coupon payments, current discount rate, and remaining time to maturity. Hence, the value of a bond depends on the amount and timing of the coupon payments, the creditors' required rate of return, and the riskiness of these coupon payments.

Conversely, bonds can decrease in value; using the formula for the market value of a bond, the market value of a bond with five years until maturity, a face value of $1,000, and a coupon payment of $70 can be determined. Assume the market interest rate is 8%:

$$\text{Market Value of Bond} = \sum_{t=1}^{n} \frac{C}{(1+k)^t} + \frac{FV}{(1+k)^n}$$

$$V_{\text{bond}} = \frac{\$70}{(1+.08)^1} + \frac{\$70}{(1+.08)^2} + \frac{\$70}{(1+.08)^3} + \frac{\$70}{(1+.08)^4} + \frac{\$70}{(1+.08)^5} + \frac{\$1000}{(1+.08)^5}$$

$$V_{\text{bond}} = \$960.07$$

The bond is selling at a discount, since it is selling for $960.07 and the face value of the bond is $1,000. As interest rates change, so do bond prices; however, it is known that the bond will sell at a discount as long as the market interest rate remains above the coupon interest rate. However, how much of a discount the bond sells for is dependent on the time remaining until the bond matures.

Suppose the price of the bond is known, but the market interest rate is not known. The same formula can be used to find the interest a bond will yield its buyer, also known as the *yield to maturity*. Because this calculation is difficult to do by hand, most people use a financial calculator or a computer spreadsheet program to determine the yield to maturity. An example of yield to maturity is provided on next page.

Yield to Maturity

A bond has three years remaining until its maturity. The coupon payment is $80; face value is $1,000 and the bond is currently selling for $1,079.95.

What is the yield to maturity of the bond?

$$\text{Bond}_{\text{Market Value}} = \sum_{t=1}^{n} \frac{C}{(1+k)^t} + \frac{FV}{(1+k)^n}$$

$$\$1079.95 = \sum_{t=1}^{n} \frac{\$80}{(1+k)^t} + \frac{\$1000}{(1+k)^3}$$

$$k = 5.06\%$$

Cost of Debt (Bonds)

As mentioned, the interest rate on a bond is the rate of return for the investor and the cost of capital to the borrower. However, unlike the required rate of return on stocks, the rate of return is not the cost of a bond for a company. The cost of carrying debt is actually lower than the interest rate a company pays on its bonds. This is because the interest a company pays is tax-deductible. Any interest a company pays reduces the amount of taxes the company must pay on its earnings. Because interest is tax-deductible, financing a business through borrowing is usually cheaper than using equity.

The cost of debt, therefore, is the interest rate minus the tax savings that comes from interest being tax-deductible. We should bear in mind that the interest rate on a bond, k, is a combination of the risk-free rate of interest, default risk premium, liquidity premium, and inflationary risk premium. It is important to note that interest payments, as well as depreciation allowances, are tax-deductible expenses. The benefits of debt financing vs. equity financing favor a higher debt ratio as the tax benefits of debt typically mean that debt has a lower cost than equity. However, higher levels of debt increase the risk of default and may also carry higher costs:

- The first cost of higher debt derives from possible conflicts between a firm's shareholders and creditors.
- The second cost is the higher probability of financial distress (Thompson, 2007).

For example, an airline issues bonds with a coupon rate of 9% and has a marginal tax rate of 35%. What is the cost of debt?

$$K_d^{AT} = i(1-t)$$

where:

$$K_d^{AT} = \text{After tax cost of debt}$$
$$i = \text{coupon rate of bond}$$
$$t = \text{tax rate}$$

In effect, the government pays part of the cost of debt because interest is deductible (Block & Hirt, 2011). Therefore, if the airline can borrow at an interest rate of 9%, and if it has a marginal federal tax rate of 33%, then the after-tax cost of debt is 6.03%:

$$K_d^{AT} = 0.09 \times (1 - .33)$$
$$K_d^{AT} = 0.0603$$
$$K_d^{AT} = 6.03\%$$

The tax benefit of debt makes acquiring capital through debt financing more attractive to companies. In addition, bondholders have the right to be paid before shareholders, making bonds less risky than stocks. Because of the lower risk of a bond, the required rate of return is also lower for a bondholder than a shareholder.

Note that bond ratings from credit ratings agencies help investors determine a company's future potential risk of default. Bond ratings are extremely important in that a company's bond rating tells much about the cost of funds and the firm's access to the debt markets. Bonds that have a high credit rating and low likelihood of default are known as *investment-grade bonds*. Bonds that have a higher likelihood of default are called *speculative* or *non-investment grade*. The non-investment-grade, or "high-yield," bonds typically offer interest rates that are much higher than safer government and investment-grade issues. Bonds with a Standard & Poor's (S&P) rating of BB+ and below, or a Moody's rating of Ba1 and below, are called *below-investment-grade bonds*.

Strategic Labor Cost Management[13]

Profits are up, the share price is up and our members have improved the airline's bottom line by in-sourcing work from other carriers and finding new ways to boost productivity. The gains are there, it's time to share.

—James Little, TWU President

---

[13] Contributions to this section were made by Kelly Ison, an independent aviation consultant.

Labor accounted for 25.9% of the operating costs of the airline industry in 2010, although labor cost varies across the industry; for example, labor costs are 31.3% of all operating costs at AMR, but only 22.9% at Delta and 22.5% at United and Continental.[14] Automation and downsizing are naturally the first strategy used for airlines to reduce the labor costs and increase labor productivity.[15]

In the post-deregulation period of the late 1970s, airlines faced heavy price competition from startup airlines. Competition from low-cost carriers, high fuel prices, and the ability of passengers to search for the cheapest fare have put considerable pressure on airlines to cut costs. In an effort to cut costs and stay profitable, airlines quickly became interested in minimizing the aircraft crew. The aircraft crew is a combination of the flight crew (captain, first officers, flight engineers, and relief pilots) and the cabin crew (flight attendants). Boeing's first two-pilot commercial aircraft was the 737 and the manufacturer successfully examined the possibility of the two-crew flight deck for the 757 and 767 design as well. Boeing launched the 757 program in April 1979, FAA certification was awarded July 30, 1982 and United was the first airline to receive the aircraft in January 1983.

This section provides guidance on how to measure the cost of human resources in the airline industry. These costs are a significant cash cost of operating an aircraft; thus, improving productivity and efficiency greatly impacts an airline's profit. To determine the potential cash flows of an aircraft, it is necessary to analyze the total cost of crews. These costs have many components, which can vary substantially from airline to airline. Further complicating the cost analysis is the fact that different airlines staff aircraft differently and pay their crews according to different formulas. Even within the same airline, a variety of different pay formulas may be utilized.

Financial Crew Cost Analysis

If the Wright brothers were alive today Wilbur would have to fire Orville to reduce costs.

—Herb Kelleher, Southwest Airlines[16]

There are two major types of crew costs analysis that can be undertaken: *financial* and *operational*. The financial analysis uses high-level information generally available from investor information, government filings, or third parties. The focus of the financial analysis is normally on the entire company as a unit and measures total output and cost ratios.

---

[14] Massachusetts Institute of Technology, Airline Data Project, 2011.

[15] World Press, *CBS*, May 19, 2011.

[16] *USA Today*, June 8, 1994.

Ratios

These ratios and measurements can be fine-tuned to suit the purpose of the analysis and are more useful for broad comparisons of companies. Some common ratios included in the analysis are:

- Block hours per employee
- Available seat miles (ASM) per employee[17]
- Revenue passenger miles (RPM) per employee[18]
- Total revenue or passenger revenue per employee, etc.

These ratios provide a general picture, but they do not account for differences in aircraft size, fleet makeup, stage length, or other variables that would allow an accurate forecast of a prospective aircraft's specific crew cost.

Operational Crew Cost Analysis

Conducting an *operational crew cost analysis* is useful because it takes a departmental approach and deconstructs crew costs into its various components. The challenge of operational crew cost analysis for non-airline managers is that it relies on a company's internal information. Although government and industry groups maintain filings for participating carriers, useful information is not always readily available to outsiders. Since there are many different methods for calculating crew pay, it is helpful to have a common denominator that allows an *apples-to-apples* comparison of crew costs across the industry. A generally accepted method for this comparison is to reduce those costs to an amount per aircraft block hour. A *block hour* is the time between an aircraft's movement from the departure gate and the time it arrives at the destination gate, specifically the time between removing nose wheel blocks at the departure and adding the blocks at the arrival gate.

Although the following section does not provide a comprehensive list of an individual airline's crew pay, work rule, and benefit structure, it outlines the steps for calculating each element of the operational crew cost analysis for the desired airline and/or aircraft to make meaningful comparisons. The basic formula is:

$$CC/BH = \left[\frac{\frac{\lambda}{BH}}{\frac{ASM}{BH}} \right] \times ASM$$

where:

CC = flight crew salaries, benefits, and training expenses
BH = block hour

---

[17] Or ASK.
[18] Or RPK.

Each of these elements under CC can be broken down into various components that include compensation and pay, productivity, benefits, and fringe costs.

Compensation and Pay

Pay, typically stated as a rate per flying hour (or something similar), is the simplest to quantify, but arriving at a total pay rate for the aircraft is not always straight-forward. As previously stated, airlines use varying methods to calculate crew pay. Most crew pay is somewhat variable, based on the amount that the crew flies per month (usually block hours). Rates are normally different for each of the crew members, depending on position (captain, first officer, etc.). Calculating accurate pay rates requires summing the actual pay rate for each position that can be found in the airline's *collective bargaining agreement (CBA)*, human resources depart-ment, or other internal documents. In order to illustrate the calculations, the published rates for a captain, first officer, and cabin crew are given in Table 6.4.

Modifications to the published pay rates can include items such as:

- *Pilot seat position:* Captains, first officers, engineers, and relief pilots can all specify different pay rates. In some cases relief pilots are simply extra captains or first officers and are paid their normal rate. It is important to determine the flight crew complement for the aircraft and type of operation for its typical mission. For example, a flight scheduled for more than 8 hours must include a number of relief pilots, based on the scheduled block hours for the flight.

Table 6.4 Published pay rates for flight and cabin crew

Longevity	Captain	FO	Cabin crew
1	$134	$25	$20
2	$135	$66	$22
3	$136	$72	$25
4	$137	$78	$29
5	$138	$83	$31
6	$139	$85	$34
7	$140	$89	$36
8	$141	$92	$36
9	$142	$95	$37
10	$143	$96	$37
11	$144	$97	$37
12	$144	$98	$37

Source: Compiled from Form 41.

- *Aircraft type*: Many airlines pay different rates for different aircraft types. Although more typical for flight crew, cabin crew rates can also vary by aircraft type.
- *Crew member longevity*: Pay rates frequently increase with the amount of time the crew member has been employed with the airline. Each position's longevity can vary with each flight, so it is customary to average the longevity of each position.
- *Cabin crew position*: Cabin crew members can be paid differently for their positions on the flight. For example, the lead position, sometimes called the "purser" or simply "lead," can carry an hourly override of some amount, which can vary with aircraft type or type of operation.
- *Special qualifications*: These can include any special rate adjustments for flight or cabin crew. Some adjustments include language qualifications for international flights or an hourly override for transoceanic, international, or night operations.

Once differences are accounted for, the adjusted pay rate for each position is added to produce a *total pay rate*. Utilizing the published rates given previously and any company adjustments, the total pay rate calculation for an airline operating a Boeing 767 aircraft with one relief pilot can be made:

Flight Crew

Captain (½ day rate and ½ night rate, 12 years longevity)	$144
First Officer (½ day rate and ½ night rate, 6 years average longevity)	$85
Relief Pilot (½ day rate and ½ night rate, 6 years average longevity)	$85
International Override ($6 × 3 pilots)	$18
Flight Crew Total Pay Rate	**$332**

Cabin Crew

Lead Flight Attendant ($6 lead override, 6 years average longevity)	$40
Flight Attendant (6 years average longevity)	$34
Flight Attendant (6 years average longevity)	$34
Flight Attendant (6 years average longevity)	$34
Flight Attendant (6 years average longevity)	$34
Language Qualification ($6 × 2 Flight Attendants)	$12
International Override ($5 × 5 Flight Attendants)	$25
Cabin Crew Total Pay Rate	**$213**

Productivity

Pay rate alone is not enough to accurately forecast the *crew cost per block hour* or to compare these costs between different airlines. It is necessary to account for any differences in efficiency caused by dissimilar route systems, fleet makeup, company structure, utilization, staffing levels, work rules, scheduling, and other issues.

A key factor to the flight crew's productivity is the productivity of the aircraft itself. Anytime the aircraft is not being flown represents lost productivity on the part of the crew. Maximizing the number of block hours that the aircraft is flying vs. parked serves to maximize the productivity of the aircraft and the crew. For example, Southwest Airlines in 2010 had a daily utilization per aircraft of 13.67 block hours and an airborne time of 8.79 hours per aircraft.[19]

Any time that the aircraft spends not in operation (i.e., when the aircraft is parked at the gate for any or all of the following to occur) is referred to as *turn-around time*:

- Passenger boarding and deplaning
- Cargo loading and unloading
- Fueling
- Galley servicing
- Cabin cleaning
- Potable water replenishment
- Pre-flight checks

The aircraft is often the costliest asset of an airline, making the maximization of its productivity (and its flight crew) a critical factor. One of the first steps to analyzing this productivity is to separate crew pay hours from crew or aircraft block hours. The *crew pay hour* is an hour a crew member is paid for, while a *crew block hour* is an hour the crew member actually operates the aircraft. Therefore, a crew member generates both *pay* and *block hours* for taxiing the aircraft out for departure, the flight time, and taxiing in at the destination. A flight may be scheduled for more time than it actually takes to complete the trip on a particular day. In that case, crews are often paid the greater of actual aircraft block hours or scheduled aircraft block hours. In addition to scheduling considerations, this allows pilots to save aircraft block time when possible without reducing the hours for which they are paid. For example, changing to an altitude with more favorable winds could allow a flight from Charlotte, NC, to London's Gatwick Airport to be completed in 8 hours instead of the scheduled 9 hours. In this case, the flight generated 9 pay hours with only 8 block hours.

A variety of other activities and decisions may create pay hours at a different rate than block hours. Some of these include sick time, vacations, paid training time, penalty or "rig" time based on CBA rules, deadhead time, or guarantee time to compensate reserve crew members for on-call time. In short, any hour paid to

---

[19] Massachusetts Institute of Technology Airline Data Project, 2011.

crew members without a corresponding block hour must be taken into account. As an example, following the pay rate calculation, the flight would generate 8 aircraft block hours and the following crew block hours and pay hours:

Flight Crew Block Hours (8 × 3 Flight Crew Members)	24
Cabin Crew Member Block Hours (8 × 5 Cabin Crew Members)	40
Total Crew Block Hours	**64**
Flight Crew Pay Hours (9 Pay Hours × 3 Flight Crew Members)	27
Cabin Crew Pay Hours (9 Pay Hours × 5 Cabin Crew Members)	45
Total Crew Pay Hours	**72**

The ratio of *pay hours to block hours* (PTBH) for this flight is 72/64 or 1.13. This ratio is a generally accepted measure of crew productivity and will be the productivity multiplier in the *operational crew cost analysis*. Calculating the PTBH for this flight, however, is statistically too small of a sample to paint an accurate picture of the aircraft's and airline's characteristics. A year's data is much better because it captures seasonal changes, but a few months of data can also be statistically significant if a full year's data is not available.

In addition to low statistical significance, an individual flight calculation does not account for the other factors that generate pay hours at a different rate than block hours. Often, calculating each flight and each factor such as sick time, vacation, etc. over a year's time is too cumbersome to be useful. Therefore, it is more practical to total the year's crew pay hours and crew block hours for the target group, whether an airline, a specific aircraft type, or other subgroup, and then divide crew pay hours by crew block hours to produce the PTBH:

$$PTBH = \frac{CPH}{BH}$$

Continuing the hypothetical airline's 767 crew cost analysis, according to information received from the hypothetical finance department for the most recent 12 months, flight crew block hours are 176,749, and flight crew pay hours are 250,984:

$$FPTBH = \frac{\text{Flight Crew Pay Hours}}{BH}$$

$$FPTBH = \frac{250,984}{176,749} = 1.42$$

Likewise, for the cabin crew, the finance department reports block hours of 294,582, and pay hours of 409,468:

$$KPTBH = \frac{\text{Cabin Crew Pay Hours}}{BH}$$

$$KPTBH = \frac{409,468}{294,582} = 1.39$$

Plugging in PTBH/BH as the measure of productivity in the basic formula produces the following modification:

$$\text{Crew Cost per BH} = \text{Pay Rates} \times \frac{\text{PTBH}}{\text{BH}} + \text{Benefits and Fringe Costs}$$

Benefits and Fringe Costs

Benefits and fringe costs include insurance, parking, transportation, company-paid retirement contributions, expenses, company-paid uniforms, or other items the company pays on behalf of the employee. Employer taxes based on payroll, both direct and indirect, are also included; an employee's contribution is included in payroll, as is employee retirement plan contributions. It is not unusual for this calculation to be roughly the same for each department since benefits, taxes, and retirement contribution percentages may not vary widely between employee groups. Therefore, it may not be necessary to separate data for flight and cabin crews.

$$\text{Benefits Rollup} = \frac{\text{Payroll before Benefits and Fringe}}{\text{Benefits and Fringe}}$$

The calculation takes total payroll costs before benefits and fringe costs and divides that number by total benefits and fringe costs to arrive at the percentage of benefits and fringe costs to payroll cost. For the hypothetical airline, its payroll department reports that for the latest 12 months employee payroll is $1,278,583,959 with benefits and fringe at $409,146,867:

$$\text{Benefits Rollup} = \frac{\$1,278,583,959}{\$409,146,867}$$

$$\text{Benefits Rollup} = 30\%$$

This crew cost analysis uses the benefits and fringe percentage as an inflator to "roll up" the hourly cost. In fact, this percentage is referred to as the *benefits rollup*.

In the hypothetical airline example, total pay rate for the flight crew is $332 and PTBH is 1.42, resulting in a cost per block hour of $471.44 before accounting for the benefits and fringe costs. Mathematically, the benefits rollup calculation would add 30% of the result of the formula to that point to produce the total crew cost per block hour. Multiplying $471.44 by 1.30 is the same as calculating 30% of $471.44 and then adding it to $471.44, but eliminates the addition step. For ease of calculation then, "+ Benefits and Fringe Costs" becomes "$x(1 + \text{Benefits Rollup})$." The formula modification becomes:

$$\text{Total Pay Rate} \times \text{PTBH} = x(1 + \text{Benefits Rollup}) = \text{Crew Cost/BH}$$

Total Aircraft Crew Cost Per Block Hour

For the flight crew cost per block hour:

$$FCC = \$332 \times 1.42 \times 1.30$$
$$FCC = \$612.87$$

Repeating the calculation for the cabin crew:

$$KCC = \$213 \times 1.39 \times 1.30$$
$$KCC = \$384.89$$

Adding the flight crew cost per block hour of $612.87 to the cabin crew cost per block hour of $384.89 produces the aircraft crew cost per block hour of $997.76:

Flight Crew Cost per Block Hour	$612.87
+ Cabin Crew Cost per Block Hour	$384.89
Aircraft Crew Cost per Block Hour	$997.76

For every 767 aircraft block hour the hypothetical airline flies, it can expect to pay $997.76 for crews.

The aircraft crew costs can then be added to other costs per block hour for various aircraft models and a table indicative of total costs per block hour can be generated (see Tables 6.5 and 6.6). The block hour costs for each aircraft can also be contrasted with other performance and operational metrics (including seat capacity, speed and range) to find the most suitable aircraft choice for the particular airline's needs.

Rules of Thumb

For U.S. carriers, some historical rules of thumb apply. These rules of thumb, by their nature, are not exact and do not apply to any one airline, but provide a reasonableness test of the analysis. If the results of the analysis are significantly different than these, it is important to understand why, because there may be either data or calculation issues.

Crew members fly an average of approximately 1,000 pay hours per year, or 85 pay hours per month. The average block hours are 660 per year and 55 per month. Network carriers average PTBH = 1.55 while low-cost carriers average PTBH = 1.40, and regional airlines average 1.30 (see Table 6.7).

Table 6.5 Total cost per block hour for narrow-body aircraft

	737-500	737-700	737-800	A318	A319	A320	A321
Flying labor cost	$600.16	$653.50	$635.88	$410.51	$507.31	$498.45	$292.44
Fuel cost	1,625.24	1,660.25	1,831.15	1,530.99	1,632.13	1,785.27	1,967.06
Other costs	89.31	97.18	38.81	103.84	71.41	68.58	96.46
Total flying cost	**$2,314.71**	**$2,410.93**	**$2,505.84**	**$2,045.35**	**$2,210.85**	**$2,352.31**	**$2,355.97**
Direct maint.—Airframe	270.41	248.92	190.04	205.43	336.53	296.00	314.52
Direct maint.—Engines	132.78	178.58	147.43	60.40	199.88	228.18	182.28
Total direct maintenance	403.19	427.50	339.19	265.83	536.41	530.73	496.68
Maintenance burden	144.99	93.06	209.22	64.33	135.53	151.75	94.33
Total maintenance costs	**$548.18**	**$520.56**	**$548.42**	**$330.15**	**$671.93**	**$682.48**	**$591.01**
Depreciation	124.36	241.48	293.27	92.43	120.26	186.62	258.97
Aircraft rent	461.43	152.53	368.93	405.41	471.11	309.36	231.13
Total cost per block hour	**$3,448.68**	**$3,325.50**	**$3,716.46**	**$2,873.34**	**$3,474.15**	**$3,530.76**	**$3,437.07**

Source: Adapted from Airline Monitor 2011 data.

Table 6.6 Total cost per block hour for wide-body aircraft

	767-400	777-200	747-400	A330-200	A330-300
Flying labor cost	$999.25	$1,279.95	$929.24	$721.91	$407.74
Fuel cost	4,072.05	5,157.88	7,684.94	4,153.50	4,350.57
Other costs	38.48	816.64	123.39	14.60	14.51
Total flying cost	$5,109.78	$7,254.48	$8,737.57	$4,890.00	$4,772.82
Direct maintenance—Airframe	405.37	490.12	542.53	534.57	288.56
Direct maintenance—Engines	195.44	574.33	272.79	302.13	220.58
Total direct maintenance	600.80	1,064.45	815.32	836.69	509.14
Maintenance burden	315.70	625.27	379.69	167.65	273.75
Total maintenance costs	$916.50	$1,689.72	$1,195.01	$1,004.34	$782.89
Depreciation	540.35	755.44	748.06	246.36	209.75
Aircraft rent	84.70	160.46	238.90	634.34	34.74
Total cost per block hour	$6,651.34	$9,860.09	$10,919.54	$6,775.04	$5,800.20

Source: Adapted from Airline Monitor 2011 data.

Table 6.7 Approximate historical averages for U.S. carriers

Hours	Per year	Per month
Crew member pay hours	1,000	85
Crew member block hours	660	55
CC/β =		
Network carriers	1.55	
Low-cost carriers	1.40	
Regional carriers	1.30	

Exploring the reasons for a company's particular PTBH is beyond the scope of this book, but such an exploration would likely include these factors:

- **Route structure:** The mix of long- and short-haul, domestic, international, and transoceanic routes.
- **Company structure:** Hub-and-spoke system or point-to-point, number and type of aircraft in the fleet, number and location of crew bases.
- **Work rules:** These may or may not be contained in the CBAs of the company's employee groups. Work rules also include government regulations and company practices.

Summary

This chapter evaluated the various elements of cash costs that an aircraft operator may face, as well as the potential impact of various capital structure decisions. Using the analytical framework described for both debt and equity financing of long-term fixed assets allows the manager to evaluate the best long-term financing alternatives. Equity considerations may include the use of common or preferred stock, whether to pay dividends to shareholders, and whether to tap into retained earnings when a use of proceeds may justify it. The cost of equity for airlines will reflect the higher degree of earnings volatility and cyclicality as compared to other industries.

Debt financing, in the form of loans or bonds, is likely an appropriate part of the airline's capital structure. Bond value over time can be determined using a pricing formula, and investors will consider the market value of the bond and the yield to maturity, among other factors such as the underlying credit of the airline and the ratings assigned by the credit ratings agencies.

Strategic cost management of an aircraft operator's labor costs involves both financial and operational considerations. Aircraft crew consists of flight crew (pilots and flight engineers) and cabin crew (flight attendants, pursers, etc.). There are two types of aircraft crew cost analysis. The appropriateness of each depends on the information needed from the analysis. Financial crew cost analysis uses ratios to compare companies. Operational crew cost analysis uses internal data to measure the components of crew cost. Converting airline and crew data into common formats is as much art as science.

The watchword here is *consistency*. As long as conversions and computations are consistent for each airline, then the data will present an accurate comparison. Shortcuts such as CC/β can serve as useful measurements for quick comparisons, either between groups or between time frames. Rules of thumb provide reasonableness checks to highlight the possibility of data or calculation issues.

References

Block, S. (1999). A study of financial analysts: Practice and theory. *Financial Analysts Journal, 55,* 86–95.

Block, S., & Hirt, A. (2011). *Foundations of Managerial Finance.* 14th ed. McGraw-Hill.

Brealey, R., and Myers, S. (2008). *Principles of Corporate Finance.* 9th ed. McGraw-Hill/Irwin.

Brigham, E., and Gapenski, L. (2004). *Financial Management: Theory and Practice.* Thomson.

Gitman, L. (2008). *Principles of Managerial Finance.* 12th ed. Addison Wesley.

Magcale, J. (2007). Daily World News. December 23, 2007

Miller, M., & Rock, K. (1985). Dividend policy under asymmetric information. *Journal of Finance, 40*(4), 1031–1051.

Modigliani, F., & Miller, M. (1958). The cost of capital, corporation finance and the theory of investment. *American Economic Review 48*(3).

Thompson, D. (2007). A critique of "deepening insolvency," a new bankruptcy tort theory. *Stanford Journal of Law, Business and Finance, 12*(2), 536.

Weiss, K., & Wruck, K. (1998). Chapter 11's failure in the case of Eastern Airlines. *Journal of Financial Economics, 48,* 55–97.

Aircraft Secured Bond Transactions and Securitization

The airline business is crazy. I've not been enamored with the industry in general. You can't depend on anybody and anything. It's dog-eat-dog and one thing or another from one minute to the next. I don't like what I see.

—Robert Brooks, Hooters Air owner, 2006

Continued demand from emerging markets such as Asia-Pacific and Latin America will keep demand for commercial aircraft strong, with global passenger traffic projected to rise 6% annually for 2011-14. Boeing's long-term forecast for 2011 anticipates delivery of 33,500 new aircraft over the next 20 years valued at about $4.0 trillion.[1] Demand for commercial aircraft is driven by emerging markets in Brazil, China and India, with airlines in developed markets such as Europe and the United States enjoying moderate growth. In China, the number of passengers should more than triple and airline fleets will double in size by 2020. These significant increases mean that airlines now have to acquire new and additional aircraft. Traditionally, airlines have acquired new aircraft through operating leases, capital leases, or through debt financing.

This chapter will detail the two structures for aircraft lease securitization: the enhanced equipment trust certificate market, which is widely utilized by airlines

---

[1] Boeing. Current Market Outlook 2011–2030.

to finance their aircraft capital requirements, and the pooled aircraft lease portfolio securitization structure. The rating process and the criteria for aircraft backed securitization and for enhanced equipment trust certificates are discussed. The discussion includes conventional equipment trust certificates, pass-through certificates, and specific enhanced equipment trust certificate features relating loan-to-value, call features, appraised values, and cross-collateralization. This chapter covers the following topics:

Aircraft Secured Bond Products

- Asset-backed Securities
- Conventional Equipment Trust Certificates and Pass-through Certificates

Bankruptcy Protection Issues

- Chapter 11 Reorganization
- Chapter 7 Liquidation

Aircraft Lease Securitization

- Aircraft Lease Portfolio Securitizations
- Enhanced Equipment Trust Certificate
- Tranching
- Liquidity Facility
- Cross-default

Ratings Agencies

- Standard & Poor's
- Moody's Investors Service
- Fitch Ratings
- Altman Bankruptcy Index

At the end of the chapter is a Summary for chapter review and References for further study.

Aircraft Secured Bond Products

Airlines traditionally acquire aircraft through operating lease, capital lease, or debt financing. Bonds are a type of debt security that is issued in the capital markets in a format that allows investors to freely trade the instrument without regard to authorization or consent by the issuer, as may be the case in private loan transactions. Bonds can be issued in a public registered format under the Securities Act of 1930 and its amendments, in a private format under a Rule 144A exemption to registration with the Securities and Exchange Commission, or as a pure private (Regulation D) transaction.

In order to attract the highest level of potential investors to a transaction and create price tension in the marketing of the bonds at issuance, issuers tend to issue bonds that are eligible for the Barclays Bond Index as well as bonds that are rated by the credit ratings agencies. By ticking the box on these two items, the bonds will be eligible for investment by a larger group of institutional investors, particularly fund managers or asset managers. Other institutional investors include insurance companies and banks.

Secured bonds and securitization provide a dependable source of aircraft funding for the industry. Securitization is a method by which a company packages its illiquid assets as a new security to diversify risk and increase liquidity. Simply put, it is the creation and issuance of debt securities, or bonds, whose payments of principal and interest are derived from cash flows generated by separate pools of assets. Securitization is used by businesses to create securities based on financial assets such as loans and credit cards. Securitization is also used by institutions to cover non-financial assets such as aircraft and buildings. In addition to aircraft, other assets that can be used to collateralize these securities include: manufactured housing loans, equipment leases and loans, accounts receivables, and other assets. Financial institutions sell pools of loans to a *special-purpose vehicle (SPV)*, whose sole function is to buy such assets in order to securitize them. The SPV, which is usually a corporation, then sells them to a trust that repackages the loans as interest-bearing securities and actually issues them.

To immediately realize the value of a cash-producing asset such as trade receivables and leases, the company puts these assets under the legal control of the investors through a special intermediary through the use of a mortgage lien or pledge of the shares of the SPV (the day-to-day control of the asset remains with the operator, who continues to operate the asset as before). In other words, the regular stream of payments expected from a lease (in this case, the lease is the asset) can be utilized to support interest and principal payments on debt securities. By securitizing the lease, the originator (the aircraft owner) receives the payments stream as a single large payment rather than as individual payments spread out over the time of the lease.

Assets with expected payment streams are known as *asset-backed securities.* In reality, the securitization of aircraft assets incorporates a package of several assets and their attached leases, and the analysis looks to the current and future lease streams during the useful economic life of the aircraft with a level of over-collateralization (a haircut) in the form of the equity risk retained by the issuer or sold to an equity investor. The profile of these assets is further improved by credit enhancements provided by the originator. Credit enhancements are structural features incorporated into the transaction that enhance the credit profile of the transaction. These may include an unfunded credit facility covering interest payments for a certain period of time, a loan-to-value ratio providing a buffer to the value of the asset or a residual value guarantee, among others.

Aircraft securitizations are an extension of a spectrum of financing forms that range from single aircraft leases or secured debt to large multi-airline pools. The different financing vehicles available are dependent on whether the reliance is on either the airline's creditworthiness or on the value of the aircraft:

- **Reliance on airline's creditworthiness:** *Equipment trust certificates* (ETCs) and *pass-through certificates* (PTCs) used for financing a single aircraft or multiple aircraft for a single airline as well as *enhanced equipment trust certificates* (EETCs), which first look to the underlying credit of the airline and then up-tier the credit ratings of the securities based on the value and type of the underlying collateral.
- **Reliance on aircraft value:** Multi-airline EETCs that allow for small portfolio securitizations and aircraft lease portfolio securitizations.

Before deregulation and, subsequently, bankruptcy reform in the U.S. in 1994, the traditional aircraft financing methods favored the credit side of the spectrum, primarily through loans and mortgages from the banking sector. After airline credit deteriorated, these traditional sources of financing that relied on corporate credit also deteriorated. New structures evolved in this new market that moved across the spectrum to a higher reliance on asset value and structure for the repayment of debt.

Deregulation in the U.S. in 1978 led to an increase in the number of aircraft in the market. One of the biggest gainers from deregulation was the aircraft manufacturing industry. Manufacturers increased their production rates and low-cost carriers were created that expanded the customer base. The North American market grew to become the largest single aircraft user market in the 1980s. This created a large need for capital expenditures as airlines sought to grow and had a substantial need for capital to pay for the new aircraft. This also had an impact on the residual values of these assets as more and more planes joined the national fleet.

United States and Japanese banks began to slow the levels of their airline and aircraft lending in the 1980s. Combined with the heavy manufacturer order books, less lending drove U.S. airlines to tap into alternative sources of capital in the bond markets. Initially, ETCs and PTCs were the primary forms of structured finance, where airlines would seek to finance individual aircraft through the capital markets while still maintaining recourse against the airline/borrower in the event of default. Those basic structures evolved into (EETCs) and aircraft *asset-backed securities* (ABS), which came from adding pools of aircraft, with more than one aircraft type, and then issuing several tranches of debt on a non-recourse basis.[2] Aircraft leasing and its growth have driven the large number of ABS transactions as lessors seek financing for their fleets through these pooled aircraft securitizations.

Asset-backed Securities

In 2005, the U. S. Securities and Exchange Commission (SEC) created Regulation AB, which provided the final rules and definition of ABS as securities that are backed by a discrete pool of self-liquidating financial assets. Asset-backed securitization is a financing technique in which financial assets, in many cases themselves less liquid, are pooled and converted into instruments that may be offered and sold in the capital markets.[3] However, the vast majority of aircraft ABS transactions were not executed as registered deals. Rather, these deals are usually sold to investors in a private format under a Rule 144A exemption to registration with the SEC, or as a pure private transaction under Regulation D. As an early example, in 1998, *Canadian Regional Aircraft Finance Transaction (CRAFT)* was launched partly as an aircraft securitization agency to provide lease and loan financing for customers buying Bombardier's CRJ and Dash 8 aircraft.[4]

The modern securitization market originated in the 1970s, when the Government National Mortgage Association (Ginnie Mae), a wholly owned U.S. federal government corporation, guaranteed a pool of mortgage loans for the first time. For a number of years, mortgage-backed securities were almost exclusively a product of government-sponsored entities such as Freddie Mac, the Federal National Mortgage Association (Fannie Mae), and Ginnie Mae. Since the mid-1980s, non-mortgage-related securitizations grew to include many other types of financial assets, such as credit card receivables, auto loans, and student loans. The asset types that have been securitized have homogenous characteristics, including similar terms, structures, and credit characteristics, with proven histories of performance, which in turn facilitate modeling of future payments and, thus, the analysis of yield and credit risks.[5]

Auto loans form the second largest sector and are categorized into prime, non-prime, and sub-prime auto ABS. Prime auto ABS are collateralized by loans made to borrowers with strong credit histories. Non-prime auto ABS consist of loans made to lesser credit quality consumers. Sub-prime borrowers will typically have lower incomes, tainted credit histories, or both.

---

[2] Wachovia Aircraft-Backed Debt Securities, September 2005.
[3] Securities and Exchange Commission: Asset-Backed Securities; Final Rule (17 CFR Parts 210, 228, et al.).
[4] Standard & Poor's Presale Report, CRAFT No. 1 Trust 1998—A, page 3.
[5] Staff Report: Enhancing Disclosure in the Mortgage-Backed Securities Markets, January 2003.

Securities collateralized by credit card receivables were first launched in 1987 and form the third largest sector. Credit card holders may borrow funds on a revolving basis up to an assigned credit limit and then pay principal and interest as desired, along with the required minimum monthly payments. Generally, mortgage-backed securities are attractive and safe investments, which provide a stream of income coupled with potential capital gain.

Student loans are the fourth major sector of the ABS market and are of two types: the *Federal Family Education Loan Program* (FFELP) and *private student loans*. FFELP loans are the most common form and are guaranteed by the U.S. Department of Education. A second and faster growing portion of the student loan market consists of non-FFELP or private student loans.[6]

Pros of Asset-backed Securities

There are several important benefits of issuing an ABS:

- A significant advantage of ABS is that they enable the banks and financial institutions to remove risky assets from their balance sheets by having another institution assume the credit risk. In a case of insolvency or financial default, the holders of ABS securities would suffer capital loss rather than the originator. This allows banks to invest more of their capital in new loans or other assets and possibly have a lower capital requirement.[7]
- Loan originators are able to bring together a pool of financial assets that otherwise could not easily be traded in their existing form. By pooling together a large portfolio of illiquid assets, they can be converted into instruments that may be offered and sold freely in the capital markets.[8]
- Originators earn fees from originating the loans, as well as from servicing the assets throughout their life.
- To the investor, investments in financial securities are backed by assets. The risk of a complete loss of capital is very low since the assets used to back the security can be sold to compensate for any capital losses due to defaults.
- Investors gain a diversified investment in a pool of loans, which can be more appealing than a standard fixed-income investment or corporate bond.

---

[6] U.S. Department of Education, Office of Federal Student Aid.

[7] Ayotte, Kenneth, and Gaon, Stav, Asset-backed securities: Costs and benefits of bankruptcy remoteness, *Review of Financial Studies,* September 14, 2010.

[8] Henzler, Filip. (2008). The Private Equity Securities Market: Alternative Routes to Liquidity: Securitizing Private Equity.

- For the original debtors (recipients of the auto loan, residential loan, or student loan), after their loans are sold or traded in the market, nothing changes except that the payments will go to the investors instead of the financing company.

Cons of Asset-backed Securities

There are several arguments against ABS:

- Securitizations are expensive and often require large-scale structuring for all involved parties. A major disadvantage for the investor lies in the fact that the performance of an ABS is solely dependent on the cash flows pertaining to the assets. For example, in case of mortgage-backed securities, the value of the security is determined by the frequency and regularity of the payments by mortgage holders.[9] The majority of revolving ABS is subject to some degree of early amortization risk stemming from specific early amortization events or payout events that cause the security to be paid off prematurely.[10]
- The recent mortgage and financial crisis pointed out that analysis of risk within the ABS market had a critical flaw in that many investors were not fully aware of the risk in the underlying mortgages within the pools of securitized assets and overrelied on credit ratings assigned by rating agencies, which, in many cases, turned out to be wrong. Loan originators retained no residual risk for the loans they made, but collected substantial fees on loan issuance and securitization, which does not encourage improvement of underwriting standards. The SEC approved new rules that took effect in 2012, which require banks and other financial firms that issue ABS to review the quality of the underlying assets, including mortgages, credit card debt, and student loans. The banks then must disclose their findings to investors and explain any discrepancies.[11]

---

[9] *EconomyWatch.* (2010). Backed Securities Advantages and Disadvantages.

[10] Fixed income sectors: Asset-backed securities: A primer on asset-backed securities. Dwight Asset Management Company, 2005.

[11] Securities and Exchange Commission: Disclosure for Asset-backed Securities; Final Rule (17 CFR Parts 229, 232, 240 and 249).

Conventional Equipment Trust Certificates and Pass-through Certificates

The simplest forms of aircraft financing in the U.S. are secured debt and debt issued in leveraged leases to an airline. A growing percentage of the world fleet of commercial aircraft is leased by commercial aircraft leasing companies. ETCs are a basic form of financing that depends entirely on the creditworthiness of the airline and involves the financing of a single aircraft at a time for that airline in a fashion similar to a typical mortgage.

In this type of secured debt transaction, the airline and the owner of the aircraft issue equipment notes called ETCs as agreements with a security trustee. This trust certificate is sold to investors in order to finance the purchase of an aircraft by a trust managed on the investors' behalf. The trust then leases the aircraft to an airline, and the trustee routes payments through the trust to the investors. Upon maturity of the note, the airline receives the title for the aircraft.[12] This is not considered a true lease since the aircraft is ultimately owned by the airline until the leasing period ends.

For these kinds of transactions, it is required that the holders of the ETC have the first priority benefits when it concerns the interest of the aircraft and any related collateral. Depending on the agreed stipulations, the holders of the ETC may also have the benefits of Section 1110 in the event of the airline's bankruptcy. The availability of the benefits of Section 1110, the status and effectiveness of the ownership, and security interests in the aircraft are discussed and settled prior to entering into an ETC transaction.[13] This represents an advantage that EETCs have over conventional ETCs (from the perspective of creditors); EETCs are automatically covered by Section 1110 protection, which stipulates that underlying aircraft will be available for seizure within 60 days following an uncured default.

ETCs are a desirable way to finance aircraft because of the possibility of trading the equipment notes and are advantageous, considering the protection available from airline bankruptcy for the trustees.

Pass-through Certificates

PTC offerings are an extension of the secured debt financings where different equipment notes issued for various aircraft within the airline are bundled into new securities.[14] A PTC certificate is given to an investor against certain mortgaged-backed securities that remain with the issuer and usually include a single type of

---

[12] Morrell, Peter S. (1997). *Airline Finance.*

[13] 11 U.S.C. § 1110—Aircraft Equipment and Vessels.

[14] The term "pass-through" means the issuing company has received money from the borrower and passed it to the investor.

asset. A critical component when bundling the different equipment notes is to ensure that they have identical payment terms.

For each aircraft, the airline issues equipment notes in various series with payment terms that correspond to those desired for the respective PTCs.[15] Each pass-through SPV purchases the corresponding equipment notes along with the proceeds from the sale of the same PTC. The purchasers of each series of PTCs hold the entire beneficial interest in the pass-through trust.

These certificates hold the same benefits as the single aircraft ETCs issued and are similar except for the larger pool of aircraft. As in the ETC methodology for secured financing, at the end of the leasing period, the airline owns the aircraft. Legal opinions on the validity and enforceability of the PTCs must be obtained prior to entering into such a financing agreement.

Typically, PTCs are sold in arm's-length transactions to disinterested third-party investors. For each pass-through trust, these certificate holders constitute the owners of the trust. This ownership structure ordinarily does not raise the types of risks arising because of the owner participant's role in a leveraged lease that would result in additional opinions and requests. For example, assume a banker sells $100,000,000 of PTCs in USD$10,000 denominations. Monthly collections of interest and principal are remitted to certificate holders, except for a portion of the annual principal that is kept by the administrator or banker as a servicing fee (see Figure 7.1).

Bankruptcy Protection Issues

Under Chapter 11 of U. S. Code Title 11, an aviation company can file for bankruptcy protection that allows it to restructure/reorganize.[16] Under Chapter 7 of the same Bankruptcy Code, if the company ends operations, all non-exempt assets are liquidated and the proceeds are distributed to the creditors.[17]

Chapter 11 Reorganization

If we went into the funeral business, people would stop dying.

—Martin R. Shugrue, Vice Chairman, Pan Am

Chapter 11 bankruptcy proceedings allow the trustee, who may be the debtor, to operate the debtor's business. A Chapter 11 filing means that the business intends to continue trading while the bankruptcy court supervises the company's debt

---

[15] Structured Finance: Aircraft Securitization Criteria, Standard & Poor's, 1999.

[16] 11 U.S.C. § 1121—The Plan.

[17] 11 U.S.C. § 726—Collection, Liquidation, and Distribution of the Estate.

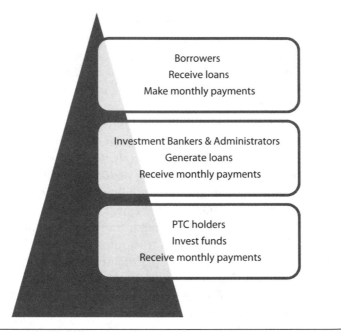

Figure 7.1 Structure of PTCs

and contractual obligations. Both creditors and owners must vote approval of the reorganization plan before the reorganization can be confirmed by court action and become effective. The court does have the power to cancel all or some of the company's debts, including unsecured loans, vendor and customer contracts, and real estate leases.

Emerging from Chapter 11 bankruptcy may take months or several years, depending upon the size, complexity, and terms of the bankruptcy. Chapter 11 gives the debtor a fresh start, subject to the debtor's fulfillment of its obligations under its plan of reorganization. Thus, Chapter 11 is often the choice of large businesses looking to restructure their debt; this particular chapter in the Bankruptcy Code places no limit on the amount of debt. The rate of successful Chapter 11 reorganizations is estimated at 10% or less. If the company is unable to recover from its debt, the ownership of the reorganized company will transfer to the company's creditors. The largest Chapter 11 filing by an aircraft corporation was in 2002 when UAL Corporation filed with over $25 billion in assets. Delta followed in 2005 with $22 billion in assets.[18] UAL Corporation and its subsidiaries emerged from bankruptcy

---

[18] New Generation Research Inc.—Bankruptcy Data.

protection four years after filing, in 2006, while Delta emerged from Chapter 11 protection two years after it filed, in 2007 (see Table 7.1).[19]

The key component of Chapter 11 reorganization as it relates to aircraft finance is Section 1110 of the Bankruptcy Code. Once a debtor files for bankruptcy, the Code's automatic stay (as outlined in Section 362) prevents a secured creditor from repossessing its collateral as long as the collateral is "adequately protected." However, following a default, Section 1110 generally limits to 60 days the period in which airlines must decide whether to become current under the obligations owed to secured aircraft creditors or return the aircraft to the secured creditors. There are several potential options for the airline under this Code section:

- Under Section 1110(a), the debtor may make an election to keep the automatic stay in place. However, in so doing, the company must pay the debtor the monetary remedies due (even if it is not affirming the underlying financing terms).
- Section 1110(b) allows a debtor to agree, jointly with the creditor, to an extension beyond the 60 days under a "1110 Stipulation." This would need to be negotiated, and some monetary implications may result.

Table 7.1 United States airline bankruptcy filings, 2005–2011

U.S. airline	Year	Bankruptcy action	Ceased operations
Delta	2005	Chapter 11	—
Comair	2005	Chapter 11	—
MAXjet	2007	Chapter 11	12/24/2007
Aloha Airlines	2008	Chapter 7	3/31/2008
Gemini Air Cargo	2008	Chapter 7	8/12/2008
Sun Country	2008	Chapter 11	—
Air Midwest	2008	Chapter 7	6/30/2008
Frontier Airlines	2008	Chapter 11	—
ATA Airlines	2008	Chapter 7	4/2/2008
Skybus	2008	Chapter 7	4/5/2008
Primaris Airlines	2008	Chapter 11	—
Mesa	2010	Chapter 11	—
Gulfstream International Airlines	2010	Chapter 11	—
Arrow Air	2010	Chapter 11	—
American Airlines	2011	Chapter 11	—

Source: Air Transport Association and company annual reports.

---

[19] Delta News Release, April 30, 2007.

- Section 1110(c) allows the creditor to repossess the aircraft, and the debtor must immediately return it upon delivery of a written demand notice.

Section 1110 terms mean that a creditor in this U.S. Code construct may have a high degree of certainty over an event of default. The airline will either *affirm* or *reject* the individual aircraft within 60 days such that a creditor will either continue to receive monies owed or the aircraft itself will be promptly returned, easing repossession concerns.

While there are definite benefits of this provision of the Code to creditors of airlines and other aircraft debtors, the airlines also benefit from this provision. Creditors have recognized through many applications of this provision that U.S. bankruptcy law allows for prompt payment or return of the subject collateral to the creditor. As such, creditors have been able to offer U.S. aircraft debtors more favorable terms to reflect this reduced level of risk. The internationalization of this provision is also evidenced in many of the provisions of the UNIDROIT Convention on International Interests in Mobile Equipment (also known as the Cape Town Convention).

Chapter 7 Liquidation

Chapter 7 (sometimes referred to as *straight bankruptcy*) of U. S. Code Title 11 governs the liquidation process that occurs when a company or individual files (or is forced by its creditors to file) for bankruptcy in a federal court. Chapter 7 is available to individuals, married couples, corporations, and partnerships. However, debtors engaged in business would usually not prefer the option of liquidation; Chapter 11 might be a better option for persons associated with corporations and partnerships.

Under Chapter 7, the business ceases all operations unless the operations are continued by a court-appointed trustee. The trustee is usually appointed almost immediately, with extended powers to examine the business' financial affairs and generally sell all the assets and distribute the proceeds to the creditors. Fully secured creditors, such as collateralized bondholders or mortgage lenders, have a legally enforceable right to the collateral securing their loans or to the equivalent value, a right that cannot be voided by bankruptcy.

For an individual filing Chapter 7, a discharge of all qualified debts usually occurs within four months.[20] A corporation or partnership, however, does not receive a similar discharge of debts; instead, the entity is dissolved. The debts of the corporation or partnership theoretically continue to exist until all applicable statutory periods of limitations expire.[21]

---

[20] 11 U.S.C. § 721—Collection, Liquidation, and Distribution of the Estate.
[21] 11 U.S.C. § 727(a)(1)—Discharge.

Aircraft Lease Securitization

Aircraft lease securitization has become an important source of capital for airlines as well as aircraft operating lessors. Over the past few years, many aircraft leasing companies have engaged in portfolio securitizations as a means of accessing new sources of capital.[22] Usually, aircraft lease securitization takes one of the following two structures: aircraft lease portfolio securitization or EETCs.

The second structure includes the utilization of EETCs, which is a unique methodology employed mostly within the limits of the aviation industry. The EETCs are a result of the enhancement of the creditworthiness of the traditional ETCs. The main difference between the ETC structures and the portfolio securitizations is that the securitizations are not directly linked to the credit quality of a particular airline (see Table 7.2).

Aircraft Lease Portfolio Securitizations

Aircraft lease portfolio securitizations depend on the value of the aircraft and attached leases that involve a large number of airlines and several aircraft. The airlines are typically located in different geographic regions of the world, which provides the benefit of diversification of risk. The aircraft asset risk is greatly

Table 7.2 Characteristics of ETCs, PTCs, and EETCs

	ETCs	PTCs	EETCs
Size	Small ($25–$65 million)	Small to medium ($60–$300 million)	Large (up to $1 billion)
Liquidity	Low	Medium to low	Above average
Collateral age	Average to old	Average to young	Less than average to very new
Aircraft diversification	Maybe	Maybe	Low to high
Rating enhancement (from senior unsecured)	S&P: 2 notches (HY) 1 notch (HG)	S&P: 2 notches (HY) 1 notch (HG)	S&P and Moody's: Tranche A: 6-8 notches Tranche B: 2-6 notches Tranche C: 0-4 notches
	Moody's: 2 notches for all	Moody's: 2 notches for all	

Source: Enhanced Equipment Trust Certificate (EETC) Primer, J.P. Morgan U.S. Corporate Research, January 2006.

---

[22] William C. Bowers, Aircraft Lease Securitization: ALPS to EETCs, 1998.

diversified in comparison to other securitization methodologies due to the combination of airlines and aircraft models. Diversification also has varying degrees of consequences. Within this form of securitization, the process itself may vary significantly, depending on the portfolio size and the legal implications of the airlines and aircraft operating in diverse geographic regions and under multiple laws and structures. The type of financial asset being securitized can also vary, and structures may be expanded to include operating leases, tax-oriented finance leases, and loans.

Aircraft lease portfolio securitization refers to the securitization of the receivables generated from the leases of the planes in the SPV. This is like any other kind of securitization, relying on a diversified portfolio of aircraft on operating leases to a number of airlines. These airlines could be in most countries (certain exclusions such as North Korea, Iran, and other countries exist where there is a concern over the possibility of aircraft repossession in the event of default), and the ratings of the debt securities issued are based on the existence of a worldwide aircraft leasing market and the estimated residual values of all the aircraft in the portfolio.

The ratings agencies and the ultimate investors in these types of securitization look to a variety of factors in assessing the risk and ultimate pricing of the transaction. As a general matter, the securitization of the portfolio is not simply a net present value analysis of the individual leases attached to the aircraft that contributed to the SPV underlying the transaction. Rather, the analysis goes to the aircraft itself and the future rental generation capacity of the asset. Similar to the analysis one would do in a REIT to the underlying cash generation capacity of the portfolio of real estate over its useful life, the aircraft lease portfolio securitization looks to the aircraft assets as the *moveable real estate* that will generate cash flows into the securitization waterfall, where they will be applied against the various expenses and debt service costs of the transaction.

Each of the aircraft that are contributed to the SPV will have a stream of cash flows that are currently contracted at the close of the transaction. At the closing of the deal, the SPV will have acquired each of the aircraft, and each individual lease attributable to each plane would need to be novated such that the SPV, as the new owner of the assets, would receive the payments from the airline lessees. There would be an assigned servicer to the special-purpose company as well. This servicer is usually an established aircraft lessor that has the blessing of the ratings agencies to act in that capacity.

Servicer analysis is an integral part of the ratings criteria, and certain servicers with less experience may need to be supplemented by the addition of a contracted *backup servicer* in the event of default. The servicer's duties are to make sure the aircraft are leased, meet maintenance requirements, are re-leased upon lease expiration, etc. The cash flow generation of the planes depends not only on the type and quality of the aircraft, but also the track record of the servicer in getting planes re-leased quickly and at attractive rates.

The ratings agencies and investors will look at the servicer quality, the aircraft the SPV will own, and the initial lessee pool, among other factors. The general perception is that narrow-body aircraft in such securitizations are preferable to wide-body pools of planes. The reason for this is that there is a larger installed base into which the aircraft may be re-leased and the fact that during most cyclical downturns, the first aircraft to be pulled out of service are the wide-body planes used on intercontinental routes by legacy carriers. Another point of note is that the younger the aircraft in the securitization pool, the better. The reason is that younger aircraft have a longer remaining useful life, which translates into a longer period of time that the planes may be leased out to generate cash flows to service debt (which also means that the planes will have a higher residual value).

In terms of lessees, investors and the agencies know that better credit lessees also are usually accompanied by lower cash flows from the contracted leases, reflecting the better credit quality of those airlines. As such, there is a trade-off between having high-quality lessees and lower cash flows to service debt. The real key to lessee analysis is maximizing diversification in the airline lessees, as well as geographic diversity. The logic is that the threat of multiple airlines across geographies defaulting in the same time frame is diminished with greater numbers in these factors. Diversity in aircraft type can also be helpful, but that is also a function of the target pool. For example, diversifying a pool of narrow-body 737-700s and -800s by adding older 747-200s is not helpful.

Once the cash inflows are analyzed, sensitivities are modeled using Monte Carlo simulation. The modeling will assume that a certain number of defaults will occur at once, and the cash flows are then analyzed to see what cash will be available under different stress scenarios to meet the expenses of paying the servicer, meet interest and principal payments, and so on. The cost elements of the securitization are laid out in an explicit securitization "waterfall," which outlines the priority of each payment. A sample securitization waterfall is provided in Table 7.3.

The first international portfolio securitization was a transaction called ALPS 92-1. ALPS 92-1 constituted a portfolio of 14 aircraft on lease to 14 lessees in 12 countries (excluding the U.S.) with an aggregate appraised value of USD$521 million. All lease securitizations prior to ALPS 92-1 involved large portfolios of *small ticket* items, making this the first securitization of *big ticket* items with values greater than USD$15 million. The structure of the ALPS 92-1 transaction was such that its debt was to be paid from aircraft sales 18 months prior to the maturity date. The ALPS 92-1 deal was required to create a sinking fund by selling aircraft throughout this period.

The primary credit risk in an aircraft securitization is a reduction in cash flows due to a combination of airline delinquency and a reduction in the value of the aircraft. In the case of ALPS 92-1, if it could not meet any of the required goals, the aircraft would be sold at levels sufficient to pay the senior debt. This

Table 7.3 Indicative securitization *waterfall* priority of payments after collections

Priority	Payments
1	Required Maintenance Payments and Expenses
2	Interest on Class A Notes, Senior Hedge Payments, Senior Liquidity Facility Undrawn Fees
3	Senior Liquidity Facility Drawn Fees and Replenishments of Senior Liquidity Facility for Previous Draws
4	Monoline Insurance Premium (if applicable)
5	Class A Notes Minimum Principal Repayment
6	Maintenance Support Account Reimbursements
7	Interest on Class B Notes and Junior Liquidity Facility Undrawn Fees
8	Junior Liquidity Facility Drawn Fees and Replenishments of Junior Liquidity Facility for Previous Draws
9	Class B Notes Minimum Principal Repayment
10	Class E Holder Contribution Reimbursements/Cure Advances
11	Interest on the Class E Notes
12	Share Capital Margin Payments
13	Subordinate Hedge Payments
14	Discretionary Modification Payments
15	All Outstanding Class A Notes
16	All Outstanding Class B Notes
17	Additional Monoline Insurance Premium (if applicable)
18	All Outstanding Class E Notes

Note: In the event of default, such a priority of payments may shift into a default priority of payments.

financial structure forced aircraft sales within a limited period and required that sales proceeds be held in low-return investments. Each country in which a lessee was located was completely vetted, and each lease was carefully reviewed to ensure that it met certain legal standards. Similar standards were applied to the aircraft deliveries, adding to the time period between the initial funding and the transfer of the last aircraft.[23]

ALPS 94-1 was the second ALPS transaction of a portfolio of aircraft on operating leases. It had the same legal structure as ALPS 92-1, but differed otherwise. First, it was larger in size; this portfolio constituted leasing 27 aircraft to 22 lessees in 14 countries (excluding the U.S.) with a base value of USD$998 million. The aircraft in ALPS 94-1 had a lower average age and the special-purpose company was given more flexibility in selling aircraft to pay down the debt, although the aircraft were required to be sold once their lease term expired. If a lessee defaulted,

---

[23] Bowers, William C. Aircraft Lease Securitization: ALPS to EETCs, 1998.

then a new lease and aircraft would have to be substituted in the portfolio from a designated backup pool of aircraft.

The financial structure of ALPS 94-1 involved three multi-tranche classes of investment-grade senior debt. The debt was partially amortizing, with each class of debt having an expected repayment based on the assumption that the aircraft would be sold at the end of their leases and the sales proceeds would repay the debt. The expected maturity dates for ALPS 94-1 were not as rigid as its predecessor. Also noteworthy in the financial structure was that a failure to repay principal on the said date was not to be considered as a default. A default was considered to have occurred only if all principal was not paid by the final maturity date. However, if any class of debt was not paid within one year after its expected maturity, the interest rate on that class would increase in order to motivate ALPS 94-1 to sell the aircraft rather than leasing them. A default could also occur due to a failure to pay interest on the senior debt.

In 1996, Lehman Brothers closed its refinancing of GPA's original aircraft securitization—ALPS 92-1. This deal was known as ALPS 96-1. The passage of time had revealed several weaknesses in the ALPS 92-1 deal. One was the inability of the structure to deal with a fall in aircraft values, and another was the cost involved in moving the aircraft from GPA's books to the ALPS portfolios. The refinancing was modeled on the ALPS 94-1 GPA securitization and involved the issue of USD$383,531,750 144A (most aircraft lease portfolio securitizations rely on this safe harbor from the SEC registration requirements) PTCs in four tranches. The 10-year notes had an average life of 6 years.

Under the original ALPS 92-1 transaction, remarketing of the 14 aircraft in the ALPS 92-1 portfolio was to begin 18 months prior to maturity of the instruments. The portfolio included four 737-300s on lease to Malev, Istanbul Airways, British Midland, and Asiana; a 737-500 on lease to China Southern Airlines; a 747-200 with Philippine Airlines; a 757-200 with Transwede; two 767-300ERs, one with Spanair and another on lease through Whirlpool Financial Corp.; two MD-83s, one with TWA and another with British West Indian Airlines; an A300B4 with Air Jamaica; an A320-200 with Canadian Airlines; and a Fokker 100 on lease to Portugalia. However, the sharp fall in aircraft values since the deal was signed in 1992 meant that this remarketing exercise became inappropriate.

In this dynamic environment, securitization provides a dependable source of aircraft funding for the industry. Securitization is the packaging of assets and/ or cash flows backed by credit enhancement and liquidity support into a tradable form through the issuance of securities that are secured by the assets and serviced from the cash flows generated by the assets. For example, a company may obtain new capital through asset securitization by selling its account receivables. Securitization gives potential borrowers access to international capital markets, thus increasing the availability of funding. In most cases, securitization produces a lower cost of funds and enables a borrower to diversify away from traditional bank sources of financing into the capital markets.

Airline Default and Credit Risk

In the cyclic world of commercial aviation, marked by a series of upturns and downturns closely linked to the world economy, the risk of airline default on leases and loans is an important consideration for lenders, investors, and the airlines themselves. Lenders that finance an aircraft purchase or invest in ABS face the risk that the airline will default on its loans, particularly during periods of high oil prices when airline operating expenses for jet fuel increase significantly. If the airline defaults on the loan, the lender then has to go through the process of repossessing the aircraft and trying to sell it to another airline. This presents additional problems since airline bankruptcies tend to occur during times of economic downturns, and it is exactly the time when the market for used aircraft is depressed.

Taking into account these risks, the unregulated practice of credit swaps began. Credit swap refers to a credit default swap, where a contract is created between parties to transfer the credit exposure of a fixed-income product. Credit swaps are often used by financial institutions to protect against debt losses. Credit default swaps pay the buyer face value if a borrower fails to meet its obligations, less the value of the defaulted debt.[24] This cost of protecting airlines from default increases and decreases over time; as oil and jet fuel prices attain new highs, the cost of this protection increases.

Asset Risk

Asset risk involves the risk that market changes or poor investment performance of a financial asset will create. The asset risk typically involved with an airline is that of aircraft value. Operating leases do not keep the residual value risk with the airline. Aircraft lease securitizations will generally have annual reviews to update their base values; EETC securities do not have annual reviews. EETCs are more exposed to market value risk, where the stress on aircraft values will keep market values below base values for an extended period.

Repossession Risk

When an airline defaults on its financial obligations to lenders, the lessor/lender has to decide whether to repossess the aircraft. Under the United States Uniform Commercial Code, a lessor may repossess an aircraft under default without

---

[24] Harrington, Shannon D. (February 23, 2011). *Airline Credit Swaps Climb for Second Day as Oil Reaches $100. Bloomberg Business Week.*

judicial process if it will not breach the peace.[25] In many cases, allowing continued operations may be a preferred option to repossession. Even where an airline is not making lease rental or debt payments, it may be preferable for the lessor or lender to allow continued operations, at least for a fixed period of time so that aircraft and engine records, manuals and technical logs can be recovered in an orderly manner; collection of these records may not be feasible when an aircraft or engine is seized at short notice.[26] A successful repossession requires that airframe, maintenance and engine records are recorded in their entirety while ferry flight, storage and aircraft remarketing post-repossession can all be carried out under a feasible schedule.

Quality of Servicer

An important element in aircraft lease securitization is the quality of the servicer of the portfolio, in monitoring the performance of the lessees and in re-leasing and selling the aircraft both at the normal expiry of leases and in the case of lease defaults (Bowers, 1998). The servicer of the portfolio may be employed in a range of capacities including, but not limited to, post-default management and workout, asset valuation, insurance, customer service, collateral perfection and management, collections, loss, and litigation.

Enhanced Equipment Trust Certificates

By the mid-1990s, the combination of the improved status of secured creditors in an airline's reorganization filing with the bankruptcy court and the availability of tax equity created the PTC or ETC. The tax investor (typically a financial institution without sufficient assets to create a dent in its tax bill) needed a long-term lease to depreciate the aircraft. However, at the same time, U.S. banks were pulling out of the financing markets. The bond markets were ideal to source long-term funding at a fixed interest rate. While the financial fortunes of the airlines were worsening, their capital needs were increasing. As their credit ratings slid to sub-investment grade or high-yield corporate ratings, they needed additional structural enhancements to increase the credit quality of the bonds, and the EETC was created.

The EETC structure is a type of financing that has less to do with the market and more to do with the need for capital.[27] Under the EETC structure, the note-holder has two sources of ultimate recovery should a default occur: the collateral

---

[25] U.C.C. § 2A-525—Lessor's Right to Possession of Goods.

[26] International Bureau of Aviation. (2011). *Repossession*.

[27] Coggeshall, *Airfinance Journal*, November 2007.

backing of the bond/notes and a claim on the airline itself.[28] As such, EETCs are not non-recourse, unlike most aircraft pooled asset-backed securitizations.

The addition of an unfunded bank line to cover the cost of repossessing the aircraft and remarketing it to obtain the proceeds to repay the creditors was the enhancement needed to gain the additional credit quality in the transaction, resulting in a cost savings in the interest rate. Additional means of increasing the credit quality include:

- *Lower the advance rate* or *loan-to-value* below 100% of the appraised value. By lowering the loan-to-value ratio, more overcollateralization is created—a buffer that allows for more certainty of recovery of principal in the unlikely event of the airline's default and rejection of the mortgage or lease with the issuer.
- *Residual value guarantee.* While not commonly used, certain insurance companies, banks, or manufacturers may provide investors with an insurance product enabling them to put the aircraft back to the insurance provider should it be worth less than the insurance amount and recover any shortfall under the outstanding principal.
- *Monoline insurance cover.* The 2003 to 2007 period saw a large number of issuers take advantage of a risk arbitrage product provided by the monoline insurance community. The monolines were in the business of providing investors with an unconditional guarantee to repay the investors. Their rating was Aaa/AAA by Moody's and S&P. As the underlying transaction rating was either A2/A or Baa1/BBB+, the spread differential for the issuer between the unguaranteed transaction and the Aaa/AAA guaranteed one was higher than the cost of the guarantee. Given the events of 2008 and the downgrades of the monoline insurance companies, this arbitrage no longer exists.
- *Cash liquidity reserve.* In order to bridge shortfalls in cash flows under a lease or mortgage, a cash reserve may be incorporated to pay for all amounts due under the transaction.
- *Cross-subordination.* EETCs are typically issues with several levels of debt or tranches. Each tranche is junior in claim to the collateral of the more senior tranche(s). Under "normal" par recovery circumstances, aircraft can be liquidated to pay off the full principal value of each equipment note, so Class A EETCs recover the full value of Series A equipment notes, etc. However, cross-subordination unlocks value for A tranches by allowing them to recover Series B and C equipment note principal if aircraft recoveries are deficient. In the "distressed recovery" example, the recovered balance of Series A notes was only USD$65MM,

---

[28] Shpall, Joel. Up in the air: Finding value in aircraft EETCs, March 2010.

less than the Class A EETC balance of USD$90MM. But by claiming the value of the subordinate tranches, the Series B and Series C notes, Class A EETC holders recover par—at the expense of Class B and C EETC holders, who recover nothing from the aircraft value.

- *Cross-default.* In the event of default under any existing indenture, the notes may cause a default under other indentures to which the cross-default provision applies. This is further described below. It should also be noted that such clauses may now also be accompanied by cross-collateralization.

Cross-collateralization

As EETCs continue to mature, new provisions have been built in over time to assist with market placement and to address issues for investors and the airline seeking to lower its debt pricing. One such innovation was *cross-collateralization.* After JetBlue's 2004 transaction and Continental's 2007-1 EETC, EETC transactions can provide for cross-collateralization of indentures so that, in the event of default, the defaulted equipment notes underlying an EETC may first cross-default other indentures and, under a cross-collateralization provision, share in the proceeds from any dispositions under one or more of the various indentures. EETCs can also be utilized for small portfolio securitization transactions called *multi-airline EETCs* (see Table 7.4).

Table 7.4 EETC milestones

Year	Event
1994	• Northwest issues first EETC.
1996	• Continental issues first EETC with both owned and leased aircraft • Northwest issues first EETC utilizing prefunding.
1997	• Fed Ex becomes first investment-grade EETC issuer. • Fed Ex issues first EETC backed by cargo aircraft collateral. • Atlantic Coast Airlines issues first EETC backed by turboprop aircraft collateral. • Continental issues first EETC backed by regional jet collateral. • United issues first floating rate EETC.
1998	• Continental issues first EETC with bullet tranche.
1999	• Iberia becomes first non-U.S.-based EETC issuer.
2001	• Delta widens pricing, but successfully closes post-9/11 on a pre-9/11 syndicated EETC.
2004	• JetBlue issues EETC under revised template where interest due on the junior notes is payable prior to principal on the senior notes.
2009	• Continental issues first EETC with full cross-default under the mortgages.

Source: Adapted from Enhanced Equipment Trust Certificate (EETC) Primer, J. P. Morgan U.S. Corporate Research, January 2006.

Airlines that incur millions of dollars of new debt through EETCs lose some degree of financial flexibility. The risks associated with the loss of flexibility could reduce an airline's credit rating for unsecured debt. In these financings, airline credit is typically undiversified but the aircraft portfolio may consist of one model of plane or several, allowing some credit for diversifying asset risk.

EETCs have become the predominant capital markets vehicle for U.S. airlines to finance aircraft and they have generally withstood market ups and downs. In 2007, EETCs were strong, with $4.2 billion in offerings from Continental, United, Southwest, Northwest, and Delta. However, in 2008, as financial markets worsened, EETCs began disappearing. This lack of issuance lasted through mid-2009, at a point where it was thought that the structure would never come back or would take years to return after major structural modifications. In July 2009, Continental Airlines offered an EETC of $390 million and American Airlines offered EETCs of $520 million to test the market. Soon after, in October 2009, Continental and United offered EETCs of $644 million and $659 million, respectively. United and Delta Air Lines pursued EETC offerings in November 2009 of, respectively, $810 million and $689 million.[29]

In 2009, airlines were pressured to offer investors more favorable economics than the 2007 EETCs in order to spark a return of investors to the market. The coupons on the senior A tranche in the first two of the 2009 EETCs were 9% and 10.37%, while the A tranche in the 2007 EETC ranged between 6% and 7%. Nevertheless, the airlines were able to reduce the offered coupon on the A tranche in later transactions in 2009, as the EETC market continued to improve. Furthermore, the EETCs had much shorter debt maturities than their predecessors in 2009. The tranche maturity in the 2007 EETCs ranged between 12 and 15 years, whereas in 2009, the EETCs ranged between 6 and 9 years.

Key characteristics for financings that allow a higher rating are:

- Debt tranching, providing for various levels of overcollateralization.
- Dedicated liquidity facilities, which usually pay interest only while an aircraft is being repossessed and sold.
- Soft amortization scheduling, so that interest is paid on a fixed schedule but principal is legally not due until the final maturity date.
- Reliance on a secure legal mechanism to assure access to the collateral on a timely and predictable basis.

Tranching

EETC tranching before 2009 had different levels of strict subordination; in early 2009, EETC arrangers said that investors preferred simplicity in EETC structures.

---

[29] *Airfinance Journal*, May 2010.

This concern contributed to the simplification of the tranching of EETCs. Continental and American offered only a single A tranche of EETCs in July 2009. However, as the EETC market continued to improve in the second part of 2009, Continental, United and Delta offered two tranches. The first EETCs generally included a strict subordination payment; waterfall payments of principal and interest on senior tranches were paid before any payments were made on junior tranches. The two July 2009 offerings each only had one tranche, while the later 2009 EETCs had multiple tranches, preserving the modified 2004 waterfall. If the airline wanted to grant a liquidity facility for a subsequently issued tranche, it would have to supply security to the liquidity provider outside of the EETC deal, such as a lien on additional aircraft or a letter of credit.

Liquidity Facility

A liquidity facility covering interest on the applicable tranche for a number of interest periods is usually provided for the most senior tranche, and it may be provided for one or more junior tranches in order to obtain an enhanced rating for EETCs. During 2008 and 2009, some financial institutions, which previously appeared as liquidity providers for EETCs, were either downgraded or left the air finance markets. Of six EETC transactions that took place in 2009, three of the liquidity providers were affiliated with one of the underwriters of the transactions, and in the other three, the same foreign bank was engaged as the liquidity provider acting through a New York branch. Also, all of the EETCs in 2009 were configured as prefunded agreements; the proceeds from issuance of EETCs were placed in escrow to be used to purchase equipment notes in accordance with subjecting one or more aircraft to the EETC transaction at a future date. Due to this problem, the availability of depositories was constrained while the pool of liquidity providers in 2009 was reduced.

EETCs add a dedicated source of liquidity support to pay interest and tranche the debt to increase the likelihood of repaying principal on the securities that have been rated higher than the airline's unenhanced ETC rating. The liquidity facility in the U.S. financings must cover 18 months of debt service and the tranched debt can achieve ratings up to three full rating categories above the airline's Section 1110 unenhanced ETC rating. One of the more attractive features to investors of market junior tranches introduced in 2007 EETCs was to provide holders of junior tranches of EETCs the right to buy out senior series of equipment notes issued under certain individual aircraft indentures. However, due to the EETC arrangers' concerns about the simplification and making the senior tranche more attractive to investors, this buyout right was eliminated in the 2009 EETCs. Nevertheless, junior tranches did retain the right to buy out in whole the tranches of the EETC to which they were junior in an airline bankruptcy.

Cross-default

Cross-default and selective redemption was not provided among the aircraft indentures in a deal until 2007. In case of a bankruptcy, the airline could pick and choose which of the aircraft in an EETC to keep or to abandon. In order to hinder the airline's aptitude in a bankruptcy to abandon aircraft selectively, the 2007 structure included a limited cross-default among the indentures, providing that in the event of default under any indenture existing at the final maturity date, the notes having the latest maturity date would cross-default all of the other indentures. The limited cross-default to apply to all indentures at any time was broadened in the 2009 transactions and the latest structure obliterated the right of airlines to do selective redemptions of equipment notes relating to individual aircraft that the airlines deem more desirable to pull from the collateral pool.

Ratings Agencies

Credit ratings agencies play a crucial role in the financial system and specifically play a crucial role in the airline world. The main concern of any creditor is whether a borrower is likely to meet its contractual agreement. Therefore, investors depend on the credit rating agencies for independent evaluations.

The credit rating agencies offer judgments and assess the creditworthiness of a corporation's debt issues, serving as a financial indicator to investors as to the likelihood that a borrower will pay principal and interest, on time and in full. Credit ratings are assigned by the credit rating agencies: Moody's Investors Service, Standard & Poor's, and Fitch Ratings have the majority of the world market share of credit rating business.[30] Each agency applies its own methodology in measuring creditworthiness and uses a specific rating scale to publish its ratings opinions. These three agencies assign letter designations to their rating opinions. For example, AAA represents high credit quality ranging from prime and high grade at the top of the scale to substantial risks and in default at the bottom of the scale[31] (see Table 7.5).

Standard & Poor's

Standard & Poor's (S&P) is a U.S.-based division of The McGraw-Hill Companies that began in 1860 as a book, detailing the financial and operational state of U.S. railroad companies. McGraw-Hill acquired the S&P company in 1966. Since its

---

[30] See Partnoy (1999, 2002); Richardson & White (2009); Sylla (2002); White (2006, 2007).
[31] Morgan Stanley Smith Barney. (2009). Bond Perspectives: An Educational Look at Bond Credit Ratings.

Table 7.5 Rating scales for long-term corporate obligations

	Moody's	S&P	Fitch
Highest Ranking	Aaa	AAA	AAA
	Aa	AA	AA
	A	A	A
	Baa	BBB	BBB
	Ba	BBB−	BB
	B	BB+	B
	Caa	BB	CCC
	Ca	B	CC
	C	CCC	C
		CC	RD
		C	D
Lowest Ranking		D	

inception, Standard & Poor's has grown to become a credit rating agency that issues both long- and short-term credit ratings on more than $32 trillion in outstanding debt. Standard & Poor's is also widely known for maintaining one of the most widely followed indices of large-cap American stocks, the S&P 500. [32]

Standard & Poor's ratings range from AAA to D, with pluses and minuses. An obligor rated as AAA has extremely strong capacity to meet its financial commitments. An obligor rated SSD (selective default) or D has failed to pay one or more of its financial obligations (rated or unrated) when it came due. For some borrowers, a credit watch is issued that indicates whether it is likely to be upgraded, downgraded, or uncertain (see Table 7.6).

Moody's Investors Service

Moody's was founded in 1909 in a similar way to Standard & Poor's: a book was published about railroad securities, using letter grades to assess their risk. Later, in 1914, Moody's Investors Service incorporated extended coverage to U.S. municipal bonds. By 1924, Moody's ratings covered nearly 100% of the U.S. bond market. In the 1970s, Moody's expanded into commercial debt and began the practice, along with other ratings agencies, of charging bond issuers for ratings as well as charging investors[33] (see Table 7.7).

---

[32] Standard & Poor's. (2006). *A history of Standard & Poor's.*
[33] Moody's Corporation, Moody's History: A Century of Market Leadership (2011).

Table 7.6 Standard and Poor's rating scale for long-term corporate obligations

Rating	Description/Criteria
AAA	Highest rating, extremely strong capacity to meet financial commitments
AA	Very strong capacity to meet financial commitments
A	Strong capacity to meet commitments but somewhat susceptible
BB+	Considered highest speculative grade by market participants
BBB	Adequate capacity to meet financial commitments, but subject to adverse economic conditions
BBB–	Considered lowest investment grade by market participants
BB	Less vulnerable in the near term but faces ongoing uncertainties
B	More vulnerable in the near term but faces ongoing uncertainties
CCC	Currently vulnerable and dependent on favorable business, financial and economic conditions to meet commitments
CC	Currently highly vulnerable
C	Bankruptcy petition or similar, but payments of commitments continue
D	Payments default on financial commitments

Source: Adapted from Standard & Poor's.

Table 7.7 Moody's rating scale for long-term corporate obligations

Rating	Description/Criteria
Aaa	Highest quality with minimal credit risk
Aa	High quality with very low credit risk
A	Upper-medium grade and subject to low credit risk
Baa	Moderate credit risk
Ba	Subject to substantial credit risk
B	Subject to high credit risk
Caa	Of poor standing and subject to very high credit risk
Ca	Likely in, or very near, default with some prospect of recovery
C	Lowest class, typically in default with little prospect of recovery

Source: Adapted from Moody's Investors Services.

Fitch Ratings

Fitch Ratings is one of three Nationally Recognized Statistical Rating Organizations designated by the U.S. Securities and Exchange Commission in 1975, along with Moody's and Standard & Poor's. The organization is dual-headquartered in

Table 7.8 Fitch's rating scale for long-term corporate obligations

Rating	Description/Criteria
AAA	Lowest expectation of default risk
AA	Very low default risk
A	Low default risk
BBB	Expectations of default risk are currently low
BB	Elevated vulnerability to default risk
B	Material default risk is present, but a limited margin of safety remains
CCC	Default is a real possibility
CC	Default of some kind appears probable
C	Default is imminent or inevitable, or the issuer is in standstill
RD	Restricted default
D	Default and bankruptcy

Source: Adapted from Fitch Ratings, Ltd.

London and New York, with 50 offices worldwide. Fitch Ratings is dedicated to credit opinions, research, and data. Fitch Ratings' long-term credit ratings are assigned on a similar alphabetic scale from AAA to D (see Table 7.8). Fitch's short-term ratings indicate the potential level of default within a 12-month period and range from the highest quality grade F1+ to grade D (in default).[34]

Altman Bankruptcy Index

Although not used within the securitization context, it should be noted that, similar to the credit ratings from the ratings agencies, Altman, between 1946 and 1965, developed a z-score model that continues to be used to predict bankruptcy and other financial stress conditions.[35] The lower a company's z-score, the higher its probability of bankruptcy. The z-score developed by Altman is a combination of five common business ratios, weighted by coefficients. The formula's approach has been used in a variety of industries and contexts; however, the z-score was originally designed for predicting the bankruptcy likelihood of publicly held manufacturing companies with assets of more than $1 million (Altman, 1968).

---

[34] Fitch Inc., Fitch Ratings: Overview (2011).

[35] John Stephen Grice & Robert W. Ingram, Tests of the generalizability of Altman's bankruptcy prediction model. *Journal of Business Research* Volume 54, Issue 1, October 2001, pages 53–61.

Summary

This chapter has detailed various aspects of aircraft lease securitization, including the two main types of structures for aircraft lease securitization: the EETC and the pooled aircraft ABS structure and the methodologies they employed. As the price of fuel goes up, aircraft leasing companies focus on improving fuel efficiency of their fleet, and as the aircraft are coming off lease, leasing companies are not only likely to take a hit on lease rates but also may have difficulty finding airlines to take delivery of aircraft.

Securitization of aircraft leases has enjoyed significant acceptance as a means of financing in the airline industry. The various risks associated with an airline defaulting or filing for bankruptcy were covered, along with the bankruptcy structures available to airlines. Credit ratings are used to assess corporations' creditworthiness. Some of the main companies that provide those ratings are Standard & Poor's, Moody's, and Fitch Ratings.

References

Altman, E. (September 1968). Financial ratios, discriminant analysis and the prediction of corporate bankruptcy. *Journal of Finance.*

Bowers, W. (1998). *Aircraft lease securitization: ALPS to EETCs, Guide to capital markets.* Pillsbury Winthrop Shaw Pittman LLP, New York, NY.

Cowan, C. (2003). American Securitization Forum. Before the Subcommittee on Finacial Institutions and Consumer Credit, United States House of Representatives.

EconomyWatch. (2010). Backed securities. Retrieved from http://www.economy-watch.com/finance/high-finance/backed-securities.html.

Grice, J., & Ingram, W. (October 2010). Tests of the generalizability of Altman's bankruptcy prediction model. *Journal of Business Research, 54*(1), 53-61.

Harrington, S. (February 23, 2011). Airline credit swaps climb for second day as oil reaches $100. *Bloomberg Business Week.*

International Bureau of Aviation. (2011). Feature: Repos on the rise. *Airfinance Journal,* Retrieved from http://www.airfinancejournal.com/Article/2770272/Feature-Repos-on-the-rise.html.

McGrail, S., & Littlejohns, A. (1998). *Aircraft Financing.* 3rd ed. London: Euromoney Publications.

Morgan Stanley. (2009). Bond perspectives: An educational look at bond credit ratings. Retrieved from http://morganstanleyindividual.com/markets/bond-center/school/credit/bp_cr_ratings.pdf.

Morrell, P. (2007). *Airline Finance*. 3rd ed. Surrey, UK: Ashgate Publishing.

Spreen, W. (2007). *Marketing in the International Aerospace Industry*. Surrey, UK: Ashgate Publishing.

Standard and Poor's. (2001). Structured finance: Aircraft securitization criteria. Retrieved from http://www.as777.com/data/business/data/Rating%20 Process%20for%20Aircraft%20Portfolio%20Securitizations.pdf.

Streeter, M., & Hamid, T. (2006). Enhanced Equipment Trust Certificate (EETC) Primer. Airline Credit Research. J.P. Morgan Securities, Inc.

Tarullo, D. (March 26, 2010). Lessons from the crisis stress tests. Federal Reserve Board International Research Forum on Monetary Policy. Washington, D.C.

United States Securities and Exchange Commission. (2003). Staff Report: Enhancing disclosure in the mortgage-backed securities markets.

United States Securities and Exchange Commission. (2005). Asset Backed Securities; Final Rule 17 CFR Parts 210, 228, et seq.

United States Securities and Exchange Commission (2010) Form F-3. Retrieved from http://www.law.cornell.edu/ucc/2A/2A-525.html.

United States Uniform Commercial Code. (2010) Section (§) 2A-525-Lessor's Right to Possession of Goods.

8

General Aviation
Aircraft and Appraisal

There are 52 million intraregional business trips per year, 40 million of which are by car. Our target is the business traveler who drives between intraregional markets where there is no or limited air service. We will be competing with the automobile. We expect that we will stimulate growth for both scheduled airlines and DayJet because we are pulling people out of the car. We are providing a new model of travel that is cost effective when considering the true cost of travel which includes hotels, mileage, and time lost by being in an automobile.

—John Staten, Chief Financial Officer, DayJet, 2006

The increasing global demand for business aviation and general aviation operations has generated a subsequent increase in general aviation sales, fixed-base operators, and their appraisals. Most appraisals are conducted in order to render an opinion of the market value of physical assets, which includes industrial, commercial, municipal, and personal properties.

It is generally up to the appraiser to help the client identify the appropriate definition of value to be used (i.e., market value, orderly liquidation value, or forced liquidation value) in order to achieve the intended use of the appraisal.

Property appraisal experts provide detailed property analyses and valuations using several potential methods, including comparable sales, replacement cost, and income approaches. The appraisal process obtains a professional opinion of the value of an airplane that simultaneously assists the prospective buyer in obtaining financing for the purchase. A clear preference exists among general aviation appraisers to assess a general aviation aircraft's value that is primarily based on sales comparison. This chapter focuses on the *general aviation* category of aircraft that are certified under FAR 23, and operated under FAR 91 or 135, as well as the fixed-base operators that service these aircraft. The unique aspects of appraising general aviation aircraft are also introduced to identify the basics of the aviation appraisal process that go into rendering a professional opinion of the present fair market value of an aircraft. The chapter is organized as follows:

General Aviation Aircraft

- General Aviation Aircraft Manufacturers

Appraisal Standards and Requirements

- American Society of Appraisers
- International Society of Transport Aircraft Trading
- Appraisal Company Requirements

General Aviation vs. Commercial Aviation Appraisal Methods

- Aircraft Bluebook Values
- Scope of Appraisal

Diminution of Value Assessment

- Diminution of Value Scope of Work

Fixed-base Operators

- Scope of FBO Appraisals

At the end of the chapter is a Summary for chapter review and References for further study.

General Aviation Aircraft

The many varieties and models of aircraft in use worldwide make it important to identify an aircraft's category under the Federal Aviation Regulations (FAR). General aviation aircraft are certified under FAR 23, which identifies general aviation aircraft as having a seat configuration, excluding pilot seats, of nine or less; a maximum certificated takeoff weight of 12,500 pounds or less; and intended for non-acrobatic or limited acrobatic operation. Identifying the proper use for the aircraft guides the appraiser in identifying the correct maintenance items, equipment, and markets to be considered in the appraisal process.

The uses for general aviation aircraft are fairly broad and encompass corporate, personal, charter, and experimental aircraft and flight instruction. Generally, any non-military or non-scheduled private and commercial flight falls under the umbrella of general aviation. According to the FAA, as of September 2011, active general aviation aircraft including piston engine, turboprop, turbojet, rotorcraft, and experimental aircraft are based in the United States under either FAR 91 or 135.[1] There are also more than 320,000 general aviation aircraft in the worldwide fleet.[2] Each type of general aviation aircraft (piston, turboprop, jet, and rotorcraft) is designed to satisfy one or more broadly defined mission categories (personal, business, corporate, and utility).

The majority of general aviation aircraft are used for instructional, personal, business, and corporate missions, as shown in Figure 8.1. The first affordable small aircraft was the Aeronca C-2 produced in 1929. It was powered by a 36-horsepower engine built by Aeronca and sold for under $2,000. Soon after, American engine manufacturers began to produce small affordable aircraft engines.[3] In general aviation, the business category is differentiated from corporate aviation based on who is flying the aircraft; if the owner is flying the aircraft for non-personal reasons, it is considered under the business category (Spenser, 1978). If it involves the use of a professional pilot who is compensated for the work, it is considered under the corporate category.

General aviation received remarkable recognition in the late 1920s with the transatlantic flight of Charles Lindbergh.[4] The general aviation industry contributes an estimated $150 billion annually to the U.S. economy. These general aviation

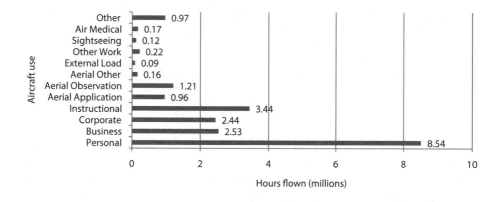

Figure 8.1 General aviation hours flown by use
Source: Compiled from FAA General Aviation data.

---

[1] FAA General Aviation and Part 135 Activity Surveys, CY 2011.
[2] Ranging from two-seat training aircraft to intercontinental business jets.
[3] The Centennial of Flight Commemoration, National Aeronautics and Space Administration (NASA), 2003.
[4] The Centennial of Flight Commemoration, National Aeronautics and Space Administration, 2003.

aircraft fly to approximately 4,000 airports with paved runways in the U.S., while the number of similar airports served by commercial airlines and aircraft is under 600. The data also shows that general aviation aircraft fly approximately 166 million passengers about 27 million flight hours each year, of which approximately 67% are for business purposes.[5]

General Aviation Aircraft Manufacturers

In a shift from the world of commercial aircraft manufacturing that remains dominated by a few industry giants, there are a number of general aviation aircraft manufacturers, big and small, with a variety of products focused on either flight training, corporate and business use, or personal flying. In the United States, more than 5,400 communities depend on general aviation for their air transportation needs.[6] We can now briefly analyze some of the product offerings of the larger general aviation manufacturers that serve the general aviation uses, namely Hawker Beechcraft, Cirrus, Piper, Cessna, and Gulfstream.

Hawker Beechcraft

Hawker Beechcraft, founded in 1932, operates out of Wichita, KS, and leads the industry with a global network of more than 100 factory-owned and -authorized service centers. The company manufactures aircraft designed for two general aviation uses, the corporate-flown aircraft (Hawkers) and those certified for single-pilot flight (Beechcraft) (see Tables 8.1 and 8.2). Hawker Beechcraft produced its first general aviation aircraft during the 1930s, the Model 17, a classic Beechcraft "Staggerwing" designed especially for the business traveler. In 1964, Beechcraft introduced the Model 90 Beech King Air family, which currently maintains a market share of more than 90% in its class.[7] During World War II, more than 90% of all U.S. Army Air Corps bombardiers and navigators were trained in derivatives of the Beechcraft Model 18.[8]

In 1980, Beech Aircraft Corporation became a subsidiary of Raytheon. Hawker Beechcraft delivered 418 business and general aviation aircraft in 2009 adding to the company's record of over 54,000 aircraft built since 1932. Of these, more than 36,000 aircraft are flying today in a variety of missions globally. The company's current lineup of products includes the flagship Hawker 4000, which serves the super-midsize business jet market, the midsize Hawker 900XP and similarly equipped Hawker 750 and 400XP. On the Beechcraft side of operations,

---

[5] General Aviation Manufacturers Association (GAMA), *2009 Statistical Data Book*.
[6] General Aviation Manufacturers Association (GAMA), 2011.
[7] Flightglobal. Hawker Beechcraft shows trio of aircraft as its prospects improve. March 8, 2011.
[8] Hawker Beechcraft company profile and 2010 data.

Table 8.1 Technical characteristics of Hawker Beechcraft aircraft

Aircraft	Range (nm)	Speed (kt)	Capacity	Wingspan	Length
Beechcraft Baron	244	202	4-5 pax	37' 10"	29' 10"
Beechcraft Bonanza	221	176	4-5 pax	33' 6"	27' 6"
Beechcraft King Air	947	313	9-11 pax	57' 11"	46' 8"
Beechcraft Premier 1A	826	434	6-7 pax	44' 6"	46'
Hawker 200	1,050	473	5-6 pax	45' 7"	46'
Hawker 400XP	876	465	7-9 pax	43' 6"	48' 5"
Hawker 750	1,978	465	9 pax	51' 4"	51' 2"
Hawker 900XP	2,600	465	9 pax	54' 4"	51' 2"
Hawker 4000	2,855	484	8-10 pax	61' 9"	69' 6"

Source: Compiled from available Hawker Beechcraft 2010 data.

Table 8.2 Financial characteristics of Hawker Beechcraft aircraft

Aircraft	Unit cost ($)	Cost per mile ($)	Cost per hour ($)	Cost per seat mile ($)
Beechcraft Baron	742,700	1.07	180	0.18
Beechcraft Bonanza	1,350,700	1.55	300	0.25
Beechcraft King Air	7,038,300	3.43	995	0.38
Beechcraft Premier 1A	6,934,700	2.66	1,030	0.38
Hawker 200	7,495,000	2.73	1,115	0.39
Hawker 400XP	7,775,000	3.29	1,360	0.41
Hawker 750	13,309,200	4.10	1,625	0.51
Hawker 900XP	16,023,800	3.91	1,580	0.49
Hawker 4000	22,908,900	4.20	1,760	0.52

Source: Compiled from available Hawker Beechcraft 2010 data.

the company manufactures the King Air series, Premier 1A, the single-engine piston Beechcraft Bonanza, and the twin-engine Beechcraft Baron.

The corporate aircraft manufactured by Hawker Beechcraft range in unit cost from the $7.5 million Hawker 200 to the $23 million Hawker 4000. The Beechcraft lineup caters to single pilots and falls on the lower end of the price spectrum for Hawker Beechcraft, ranging from the $742,700 Beechcraft Baron to the $7 million Beechcraft Premier 1A.[9]

---

[9] Hawker 2010 sales figures.

Cirrus

Cirrus, a member of the global portfolio of Bahrain-based Arcapita companies, has been a long-standing leader in personal aviation aircraft. Headquartered in Duluth, MN, since its founding in 1984, this manufacturer's lineup of aircraft includes two main design families, the SR 20 and SR 22. The SR 20 and SR 22 families of all-composite airplanes incorporate innovative and advanced performance and safety technologies, including the unique Cirrus Airframe Parachute System (CAPS), a parachute system designed to protect occupants in the event of an emergency by gently lowering the aircraft to the ground after deployment. All Cirrus aircraft are made in the U.S., with authorized sales centers covering export markets in 60 countries worldwide. Cirrus' latest addition to the market, in development as of 2011, is the Cirrus Vision Jet (SF 50), which already has nearly 500 production positions reserved.[10] Table 8.3 shows the technical characteristics of Cirrus' aircraft, and Table 8.4 examines the financial characteristics.

The SR 20 and SR 22 are similar in design, with the SR 22 essentially being a more powerful version of the SR 20. The SR 22 has a larger wing, higher fuel capacity, and higher power engine, giving it an additional 264 nm of range and 30 kts of cruise speed. The in-development SF 50 is expected to offer double the speed of the SR 20 and fly more than twice the number of passengers, suitable for the personal use market.[11]

Table 8.3 Technical characteristics of Cirrus aircraft

Aircraft	Range (nm)	Speed (kt)	Capacity	Wingspan	Length
SR 20	785	155	3 pax	38' 4"	26'
SR 22	1,049	185	3 pax	38' 4"	26'
SF 50 (in development)	1,100	300	7 pax	38' 4"	—

Source: Compiled from available Cirrus 2010 data.

Table 8.4 Financial characteristics of Cirrus aircraft

Aircraft	Unit cost ($)	Cost per mile ($)	Cost per hour ($)	Cost per seat mile ($)
SR 20	289,900	1.75	253	0.58
SR 22	449,900	1.93	308	0.64
SF 50 (in development)	1.72 M	—	—	—

Source: Compiled from Conklin & de Decker (2010), vol. II data.

---

[10] Cirrus Aircraft company profile.
[11] Cirrus Vision SF 50 Jet Update, October 2010.

Piper

Piper Aircraft grew under the vision of William T. Piper, who introduced the Piper Cub in 1937. The Piper Cub, a single-engine and high-wing two-seater, was the first inexpensive training aircraft produced in large numbers. Since then, the company has produced more than 144,000 aircraft, 85,000 of which are still flying. Along with Beechcraft and Cessna, Piper is considered one of the "Big Three" in the field of general aviation manufacturing. With over 70 years of aircraft manufacturing experience, Piper Aircraft, as a general aviation manufacturer, offers a complete line of aircraft from rugged, reliable trainers to high-performance turboprops.[12]

The technical characteristics displayed in Table 8.5 outline the wide variety offered by Piper's main product lines. With ranges that span from 522 nm for the Archer LX to 1,343 nm for the Mirage and Matrix aircraft, speeds that similarly span from 128 kts to 260 kts, and a comfortable capacity range from 3 to 6, the Piper family of products meets the needs of numerous general aviation operators and a variety of missions. Financial characteristics of the company are shown in Table 8.6.

Cessna

Cessna has undergone similar operations to Piper, having manufactured general aviation aircraft for more than eight decades from humble beginnings as a small aircraft company in Wichita, KS.[13] Since then, the company has grown into the largest general aviation aircraft manufacturer (by sales), having sold and delivered

Table 8.5 Technical characteristics of Piper aircraft

Aircraft	Range (nm)	Speed (kt)	Capacity	Wingspan	Length
Meridian	1,000	260	6 pax	43'	29' 7"
Mirage	1,343	213	6 pax	43'	28' 11
Matrix	1,343	213	6 pax	43'	28' 11"
Seneca V	828	197	6 pax	38' 11"	28' 7"
Seminole	700	162	4 pax	38' 7"	27' 7"
Arrow	880	137	4 pax	35' 5"	24' 8"
Archer LX	522	128	3 pax	35' 6"	24'

Source: Compiled from available Piper 2010 data.

---

[12] Piper Aircraft company profile, 2010.
[13] Just before World War I, Clyde Vernon Cessna, a self-taught exhibition pilot, briefly operated his first aircraft company, one he founded with the purpose of building and selling small, relatively inexpensive aircraft for personal use.

Table 8.6 Financial characteristics of Piper aircraft

Aircraft	Unit cost ($)	Cost per mile ($)	Cost per hour ($)	Cost per seat mile ($)
Meridian	2.07 M	3.44	861	0.69
Mirage	998,000	3.27	593	0.65
Matrix	869,000	3.15	572	0.63
Seneca V	849,000	3.53	598	0.71
Seminole	644,000	2.90	438	0.97
Arrow	300,000	2.18	285	0.73
Archer LX	229,000	2.12	254	0.71

Source: Compiled from Conklin & de Decker (2010), vol. II data.

more than 192,000 aircraft since its establishment in 1927.[14] In 2010, Cessna Aircraft delivered 512 aircraft, almost twice as many as Cirrus Design (264) in the same period.[15] The Federal Aviation Administration estimates that the U.S. general aviation aircraft fleet will grow to 270,920 aircraft in 2031. This is equal to an average annual growth of about 1%.[16]

The company, a subsidiary of the U.S. conglomerate Textron, has become synonymous with small, piston-powered aircraft, but also produces a Cessna Citation family of business jets, of which over 5,000 are currently in operation around the world.[17] Cessna manufactured more general aviation aircraft than any other company and almost twice as many as Cirrus Design in 2010 (see Figure 8.2). In third place, Hawker produced 214 aircraft followed by Piper, Bombardier, Embraer, Diamond Aircraft, Gulfstream, Dassault, and Pilatus.[18]

More than 43,000 Cessna 172 Skyhawks, first flown in 1955, have been built, making it the most successful mass-produced light aircraft in history. The 172 Skyhawk was an overnight sales success, with more than 1,400 aircraft built in its first full year of production. Production of the Skyhawk stopped for 11 years after 1986, resuming in 1997. Tables 8.7 and 8.8 show that Cessna's products cover a range of performance and financial metrics. The $269,500 Cessna 172 offers roughly 700 nm of range at 122 knots in comparison to the $21.7 million Citation X aircraft, which flies more than four times faster and further (525 kts and 3,070 nm).

---

[14] The Cessna Aircraft Corporation officially became incorporated in September of 1927.
[15] General Aviation Manufacturers Association (GAMA), 2011.
[16] Federal Aviation Administration (FAA), 2011.
[17] Cessna company profile and operating figures 2010.
[18] General Aviation Manufacturers Association, 2010.

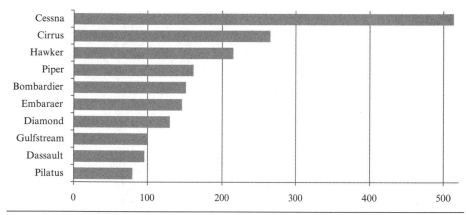

Figure 8.2 General aviation aircraft manufacturers: 2010
Source: Compiled from GAMA.

Table 8.7 Technical characteristics of Cessna aircraft

Aircraft	Range (nm)	Speed (kt)	Capacity	Wingspan	Length
Cessna 172 Skyhawk	696	122	3 pax	36' 1"	27' 2"
Cessna 182 Skylane	927	145	3 pax	36'	29'
Cessna 206 Stationair	690	151	6 pax	36'	28' 3"
Cessna 350 Corvalis	1,395	191	4 pax	35' 10"	25' 2"
Cessna Citation Mustang	1,150	340	5 pax	43' 2"	40' 7"
Cessna Citation Encore+	1,780	428	8 pax	54' 9"	48' 11"
Cessna Citation XLS+	1,858	441	9 pax	56' 4"	52' 6"
Cessna Citation Sovereign	2,847	458	9 pax	63' 4"	63' 6"
Cessna Citation X	3,070	525	9 pax	63' 11"	72' 4"

Source: Compiled from data available on Cessna, 2010.

Gulfstream

The company that eventually evolved into Gulfstream started in the late 1950s when Grumman Aircraft Engineering Company, known for military aircraft production, developed a marketable business aircraft—the twin turboprop Gulfstream I. Following the high success of the program, Grumman began producing a twin turbojet named the Gulfstream II. Grumman later separated the company's civil and military aircraft production to improve efficiency. In 1977, the Gulfstream line of products was sold to American Jet Industries, a company renamed as Gulfstream American. In the 1990s, General Dynamics, another giant

Table 8.8 Financial characteristics of Cessna aircraft

Aircraft	Unit cost ($)	Cost per mile ($)	Cost per hour ($)	Cost per seat mile ($)
Cessna 172 Skyhawk	269,500	1.85	205	0.62
Cessna 182 Skylane	390,300	2.14	268	0.71
Cessna 206 Stationair	533,400	2.39	336	0.48
Cessna 350 Corvalis	558,200	2.09	358	0.70
Cessna Citation Mustang	3.07 M	4.09	1,266	1.02
Cessna Citation Encore+	9.15 M	6.34	2,498	0.91
Cessna Citation XLS+	12.45 M	7.36	2,978	0.92
Cessna Citation Sovereign	17. 6 M	8.37	3,414	0.93
Cessna Citation X	21.7 M	11.08	5,215	1.39

Source: Compiled from Conklin & de Decker (2010), vol. II data.

in the defense industry, purchased Gulfstream and renamed its products using Arabic numerals instead of Roman numerals to differentiate aircraft.[19]

Gulfstream chose to focus entirely on the business jet segment of aircraft manufacturing, establishing itself as the aircraft of choice for many Fortune 500 corporate operators (see Tables 8.9 and 8.10). The G150 was the first business jet to be certified by the FAA for Stage 4, the industry's most stringent noise standards. The flagship of the fleet, the Gulfstream G650, is the only traditional business jet capable of flying 7,000 nautical miles (12,964 km) non-stop at 0.85 Mach or 5,000 nautical miles at 0.90 Mach. The G650 has a maximum operating speed of 0.925 Mach, making it the fastest civil aircraft in the world. The G650 can also climb to

Table 8.9 Technical characteristics of Gulfstream aircraft

Aircraft	Range (nm)	Speed (Mach)	Capacity	Wingspan	Length
G150	3,000	0.85	6-8 pax	55' 7"	56' 9"
G200	3,400	0.80	8-10 pax	58' 1"	62' 3"
G250	3,400	0.85	8-10 pax	63'	66' 10"
G350	3,800	0.85	12-16 pax	77' 10"	89' 4"
G450	4,350	0.88	12-16 pax	77' 10"	89' 4"
G500	5,800	0.87	14-18 pax	93' 6"	96' 5"
G550	6,750	0.87	14-18 pax	93' 6"	96' 5"
G650	7,000	0.90	11-18 pax	99' 7"	99' 9"

Source: Compiled from available Gulfstream 2010 data.

---

[19] Gulfstream company history.

Table 8.10 Financial characteristics of Gulfstream aircraft

Aircraft	Unit cost ($)	Cost per mile ($)	Cost per hour ($)	Cost per seat mile ($)
G150	15.05 M	7.42	2,998	1.06
G200	23.32 M	10.45	4,225	1.31
G250	24 M	10.38	4,399	1.3
G350	34.90 M	14.12	5,982	1.01
G450	39.90 M	14.18	6,007	1.01
G500	51.8 M	15.19	6,434	0.84
G550	59.8 M	15.26	6,467	0.85
G650	64.5 M	—	—	—

Source: Compiled from Conklin & de Decker (2010), vol. II data.

a maximum altitude of 51,000 feet, allowing it to avoid airline traffic congestion and adverse weather.[20] This makes the G650 a viable replacement for commercial aviation travel by Fortune 500 companies.

Appraisal Standards and Requirements

In the late 1980s, the U.S. government and the appraisal industry began standardizing the Uniform Standards of Professional Appraisal Practice (USPAP). No matter the aircraft type, a complete knowledge of the current and potential market is crucial to accurate valuation. A full appraisal is one that includes an inspection of the aircraft and its maintenance records. These quality control standards are binding and applicable to all American Society of Appraisers aviation appraisers.

Since 2006, USPAP has been updated in two-year cycles, which begin on January 1 of even-numbered years. USPAP provides a minimum set of quality control standards for the conduct of appraisal in the U.S., but does not attempt to prescribe specific methods to be used. Rather, USPAP requires that appraisers be familiar with and correctly utilize those methods that would be acceptable to other appraisers familiar with the assignment at hand and acceptable to the intended users of the appraisal. In addition to the control standards, USPAP includes 32 Advisory Opinions, which are non-obligatory.[21]

In the U.S. aircraft appraisal industry, there are two organizations that are nationally recognized and adhere to a recognized industry standard. The organi-

---

[20] Gulfstream G650 Product Specification Data.
[21] Adapted from The Appraisal Foundation, USPAP, 2010-2011.

zations that represent members of the aircraft appraisal industry are the American Society of Appraisers and the International Society of Transport Aircraft Trading.

American Society of Appraisers

The American Society of Appraisers (ASA) is a multidiscipline organization of appraisers founded in 1936. ASA is the oldest and only major appraisal organization representing all of the disciplines of appraisal specialists. ASA members perform appraisals ranging from business valuation to gems and jewelry, machinery and technical specialties, personal property, and real property.

Membership into the organization occurs on two levels: Accredited Member and Accredited Senior Appraiser. The Accredited Senior Appraiser designation is assigned after completing five years of documented appraisal experience, testing in the associated field or specialty, the submission of two appraisal reports to the society's International Board of Examiners for review, successful completion of the Principles of Valuation education program, and successful completion of the 15-hour USPAP course. The lesser designation, Accredited Member (AM), requires only two years of documented appraisal experience in addition to the other requirements. However, appraisers at all levels of the ASA are subject to a mandatory re-accreditation process every five years.[22]

International Society of Transport Aircraft Trading

The International Society of Transport Aircraft Trading (ISTAT) has more than 1,900 members worldwide and was founded in 1983. ISTAT is involved in operating, manufacturing, maintaining, selling, purchasing, financing, leasing, and appraising aircraft.[23] ISTAT is governed by its bylaws and the volunteer ISTAT Board of Directors, which is composed of and elected by the members. Within ISTAT is a core group of professional aircraft appraisers who work cooperatively for the elevation of the appraisal profession within the world aviation community. ISTAT has established four professional status categories:

- Appraiser
- Senior Appraiser
- Appraiser Fellow
- Appraiser Emeritus

The Appraiser categories are awarded to individuals who have a minimum number of years of experience in aviation-related business.

---

[22] American Society of Appraisers 2010 Certification Requirements.
[23] International Society of Transport Aircraft Trading, 2011.

For appraisers, the value of a general aviation aircraft is found by analyzing the historical aircraft values, physical condition, and adjusting the historical value accordingly to come up with a fair market value. Since the historical value pertains to the past, it does not necessarily reflect the actual value of the aircraft in question at a given time. Availability of credit is another factor that could impact the value of aircraft. Major lenders are adapting to the 20-year rule. That is, the age of the aircraft and term of the loan cannot exceed 20 years.[24]

A good appraisal generally should provide the client with a detailed examination and report of airframe, engines, props, instrumentation, avionics, and all related systems; a review of aircraft documentation, logbooks, and associated records; and a computer analysis of relevant value data.[25]

Appraisal Company Requirements

Not all aviation appraisals are created equally. Appraisal companies range in size from single-person entities and family-owned businesses to large-scale multinational corporations. Family-owned businesses like M&B Aviation based in Fort Worth, TX, are able to provide appraisal services to a wide assortment of clientele, ranging from individuals and small and large corporations to flight departments, lending companies and banks.[26]

As a starting point, all credentials should be verified. It is important when selecting the company to conduct an appraisal that all certifications, membership and standards are current, updated and relevant in order to render an accurate and useful appraisal. Older appraisal companies like Airport & Aviation Appraisals Inc., founded in 1984, are able to capitalize on a significant amount of experience and years in operation; companies with extended lifespans like this have likely developed relationships with aircraft brokers, dealers, service providers and manufacturers.[27] These relationships provide invaluable assistance in supplying current and accurate information to the client during the appraisal process and generally result in a faster and more accurate appraisal.

General Aviation vs. Commercial Aviation Appraisal Methods

The purchase, sale, and use of general aviation aircraft are significantly different from that of commercial aircraft aviation. When an aircraft is purchased for

---

[24] Janssens, C. *Aircraft Bluebook Price Digest*, August 18, 2010.
[25] National Aircraft Appraisers Association, 2010.
[26] M&B Aviation, LLC company profile.
[27] Morristown Municipal Airport Services Directory.

commercial operations, its purchase and use is viewed as a long-term physical asset by the company involved. The aircraft is consequently appraised utilizing a method that takes into account the book value of the aircraft depreciation, obsolescence, and the condition of its components. Commercial aviation appraisal, by the nature of its operations, has to involve assessing an additional component: determining the revenue generation that will occur through the use of the aircraft over time becomes a factor to be included in the appraisal process.

General aviation aircraft are typically not viewed in this manner; the majority of general aviation aircraft are used for personal use (as shown in Figure 8.1), and not as long-term revenue generators; therefore appraising a general aviation aircraft does not necessitate looking at the revenue-generating potential of the aircraft, but instead the book value of the aircraft and the condition of its components.

Many factors exist in both the general aviation and commercial aviation worlds that can impact the value of aircraft. The number of cycles (takeoffs and landings), avionics, and compartment configuration influence value directly. Other factors like the absorption of aircraft and aircraft spare parts into the marketplace can have significant impact on value. Each possible influencing factor must be addressed by the appraiser in order to determine a credible opinion of value.

A clear preference exists among commercial and general aviation appraisers for the basic valuation tools used to assess an estimate of an aircraft's value. These techniques primarily use a sale comparison and sometimes a combination of cost and aircraft specifics to establish a range of imputed aircraft value. The cost approach considers the current cost of replacing the aircraft less depreciation. The income approach to valuation is more adaptable to commercial aircraft appraisals since it is based on the aircraft's net income potential; it uses the current value of the aircraft's future income potential to estimate its value.

Aircraft Bluebook Values

The limited number of general aviation aircraft transactions, coupled with a lack of standardized sales reporting data, makes it a critical step in the appraisal process to employ the baseline analysis. The main sources of baseline aircraft values for the aviation industry can be found within four aircraft bluebooks: *Aircraft Bluebook Price Digest, Aircraft Value Reference, Airliner Price Guide* (dedicated to commercial aircraft), and *International Bluebook*. The values shown in the aircraft bluebooks are intended only as a guide and to provide a foundation from which to begin appraisal of an aircraft; prices are not to be considered to reflect all factors involved in the appraisal process of any particular aircraft.

None of the aviation industry bluebooks should be expected to give the simple calculation accuracy typical of the U.S. automotive bluebooks. A number of issues contribute to the difficulty in presenting a clear figure for a make/model/year,

such as lack of central reporting of aircraft sales for either tax or license requirements, the complexity of individual aircraft value calculations, the timing of sales
(long time frames from offer to closing, during which the market can go up or
down substantially), multiple synchronous closings for jet aircraft in particular,
international currency sales, and non-disclosure-of-price terms included in many
transaction documents.[28]

Aircraft Bluebook Price Digest

The *Aircraft Bluebook Price Digest* has been in existence for 55 years and is available in a standard print format and on a CD-ROM. Its data are updated every
quarter to include the latest market values on more than 3,000 model years of
identification and values for business and general aviation aircraft. The *Aircraft
Bluebook Price Digest* shows the published rates for the factory new list standard
price, factory new list average equipment price, average retail price, average
wholesale price, and the computed price across a range of metrics and usage calculations. The prices are based on historical data and do not represent the current
market conditions such as supply and demand, the level of economic activities, or
fuel prices. The price of fuel and the level of economic activities have profound
impacts on the aviation market. These factors have direct impact on potential buyers and the marketplace.

The *Aircraft Bluebook Price Digest* also includes tables for avionics, airworthiness directives, conversions, and overhauls as well as the Bluebook Scale.[29] The
Bluebook Scale is used throughout the industry to rate the exterior and interior of
aircraft. A rating of 10 means the aircraft is new and a rating of 1 means that the
aircraft is not fit for occupation or flight without extensive work.[30]

Aircraft Value Reference

The *Aircraft Value Reference (Vref)*, published by the Aircraft Value Analysis
Company (AVAC), is updated semi-annually in April and October. Since its
introduction in 1991, the *Vref* has been used extensively by aircraft brokers and
financial institutions to provide estimates of the future value of aircraft. AVAC also
reports on metrics and figures related to valuation, including the fact that there
are approximately 17,000 business jets in service, of which nearly 3,000 are being
advertised for sale.[31]

---

[28] JetList. *Private Jet Sales Buyers Guide.*
[29] *Aircraft Bluebook Price Digest*, 2010.
[30] The full Aircraft Bluebook Rating Scale is available from *Aircraft Bluebook Price Digest* in various
formats.
[31] *Aircraft Value Reference*, vol. 1, *Current & Future Values & Lease Rates (2010–2030)*, 38.1, April 30,
2010.

Airliner Price Guide

The *Airliner Price Guide (APG)* was established in 1985 to provide the average new price, used retail price, and used wholesale price for most commercial aircraft. In addition to aircraft values, the *APG* provides engine values, technical data, and background information. The hardcover publication is updated and published twice annually, while an online version is intended to provide real-time updated values. The *APG* is published by ACI Aviation Consulting, a subsidiary of Brasie, Inc., which through its portfolio of subsidiaries offers an array of aviation consulting services.[32]

International Bluebook

The *International Bluebook* is a free service that offers general bluebook figures online for private and corporate aircraft. Calculations are not available for an individual aircraft, but are provided as a free service through jet aircraft dealers and jet aircraft multiple listings on Internet sites.[33]

Scope of Appraisal

There are several motivations for getting an aircraft appraised, including to safeguard against excessive tax assessments or capital gains. Most aviation appraisals are ordered to determine an accurate estimation of the market value, but other specific conditions may be included in the scope of work, for example the aircraft's engine condition and hours of usage. Specific conditions are to be clearly stated in the scope of work contract between the appraiser and client.

A primary focus of the appraiser is to determine the initial dimensions that the appraisal should encompass after the question of intended use has been answered. Most sellers and buyers do not know how to determine a price on the aircraft that they want to sell or to buy. Further, the appraisal can assist in expediting the sale of the aircraft because the buyer and seller know the fair market value and relative condition of the aircraft through the independent appraisal. The intended use of the appraisal determines what is verified and appraised pertaining to the aircraft.

If the aircraft appraisal is to be used for financing or a sale, then a proper appraisal of the airworthiness of the aircraft should be conducted. Likewise, if an appraisal is to be used for insurance claim purposes, a likely additional dimension would be indicating not only airworthiness, but also the extent of damage to the aircraft. Once the intended use and intended users of the appraisal are clearly established, the purpose of the appraisal can be determined and preliminary work conducted.

---

[32] ACI Aviation Consulting Company Info., 2010.
[33] *International Bluebook Reference Guide*, 2010.

Asset Identification

The item to be appraised must always be clearly identified and verified to ensure that the correct items and components are being evaluated. For aircraft engines and other components, the manufacturer serial number makes identification of the proper asset a relatively simple task and allows the aircraft manufacturer, model, year, and date of manufacturing as well as any related documentation to be correctly identified, cross referenced, and accounted for. When this phase is complete, the asset can be correctly evaluated in accordance with the appraisal contract agreement.

Special attention has to be paid to correctly identifying and assessing aircraft engines and other power plant parts. In the course of normal maintenance operations, loaner parts are often swapped out to allow for uninterrupted operation of an aircraft. If an appraiser values an aircraft with a particular engine and discovers post-appraisal that the engine was a loaner while the actual subject engine was being overhauled, then an erroneous value would have been developed on the engine, resulting in an incorrect appraisal. Similar to the engine, avionics and related flight instruments should be inventoried to ensure they are properly accounted for.

Physical Inspections

A physical inspection is not always required or possible. However, inspecting the subject aircraft and its associated records may be a helpful tool in carrying out the appraisal. Coordinating a physical inspection requires careful planning as aircraft records are not required to be kept with the aircraft and therefore may be in another location (often a maintenance facility or primary base of operations).[34] This means that travel to several locations is often an unstated requirement to conducting a proper inspection. During the planning stages, any safety and security concerns applicable to the conduct of the inspection must be noted and carefully addressed, including release forms, escorts, limited camera use, and pre-approval from the relevant authorities for photos. Also, due to enhanced aviation security measures, it is anticipated that inspectors may sometimes be turned away, making a physical inspection impossible. Table 8.11 highlights critical items that should be included in a physical inspection.

Review of Records

Generally, the older the aircraft and more heavily utilized it is, the greater the number of accompanying records. Reviewing the records must be achieved in

---

[34] The exterior will be inspected for damage, corrosion, loose or missing fasteners, paint condition, airframe condition, and tire condition.

Table 8.11 Physical components of aircraft that are critical for appraisal

Critical items	Description
Aircraft serial number	This is a required data plate on the exterior of the aircraft.
Aircraft registration number	The current registration number should be painted on the exterior of the aircraft.
Airworthiness certificate	These items are required to be inside aircraft. In addition to supporting identification and ownership, these items should also help verify aircraft equipment.
Aircraft registration	
Weight and balance	
Operation handbook	
Wings	Overall condition (hail damage, hangar rash, paint condition, etc.).
Empennage	Overall condition (hail damage, hangar rash, paint condition, etc.).
Fuselage	Overall condition (hail damage, hangar rash, paint condition, etc.).
Windows	Are they new, used or crazing?
Engines	If required, verify serial number.
Interior	Overall condition (seats, headliner, carpet, equipment).
Interior	How many seats, and in what configuration?

Source: Compiled from sample appraisal reports.

a systematic manner that identifies critical items. Records common to general aviation aircraft operations include airframe maintenance records, engine maintenance records, propeller maintenance records, computer-generated maintenance schedules, and FAA forms. Aircraft appraisers must thoroughly search logbooks and all available records for latest airworthiness directives, damage history, and maintenance history of components. The purpose of reviewing the records is to identify the critical items, noted in Table 8.12, which are directly related to the history and utilization of the aircraft.

Maintenance Records

Although aircraft owners are required to keep and maintain proper maintenance records for the airframe, engine, propeller, and appliances, general aviation aircraft maintenance records are not always kept up to date, and this in turn may have a negative impact on the final appraised value of the aircraft. The records must contain detailed reports on the type of maintenance performed, the date of completion, the mechanic's signature, the FAA certificate, and the certificate number of

Table 8.12 Records to be reviewed during aircraft appraisal

Critical items	Description
Serial numbers	Do the serial numbers match that of the subject aircraft?
Continuity	Continuity of records from date of production.
Language	What language are the records in?
Damage history	Do the records mention any damage history?
Inspection history	Dates and part(s) for major and minor inspections.
Replacement history	When was the last paint and interior replacement?
Equipment	When was the installation and approval of equipment?

Source: Compiled from sample appraisal reports.

the person approving the aircraft for return to service. The records should also contain the inspections required, pursuant to the Code of Federal Regulations.[35]

Sometimes maintenance records or logbooks may be missing or incomplete by accident or intentionally. Regardless of intent, a missing logbook may mean that the aircraft's history is not available for scrutiny, and factors in the aircraft's past cannot be taken into account when assigned a value. This means that any damages or lapses in maintenance can be conveniently hidden through the destruction of logbooks—even though logbooks are a key part of the appraisal process. The following considerations provide an example of the range of valuable information that can be found in maintenance records/logbooks and which have a direct impact on the price and value that will ultimately be derived:

- Age of the aircraft
- Aircraft limitations
- Paint and interior condition
- Inspection methods used and current status
- Status of airworthiness directives and service bulletins
- Aging aircraft/corrosion requirement
- Noise classification and potential airport restrictions
- Engine status—overhauls, interim inspections, life-limited items
- Anticipated operating costs—fuel, oil, routine maintenance
- Anticipated extraordinary costs

A notable entry that can be found in the maintenance records/logbooks that ultimately becomes a key component of a general aviation aircraft's value to its operator is the noise classification and potential airport restrictions, particularly with older models. Since 1968, with an amendment to the Federal Aviation Act of 1958,

[35] Code of Federal Regulations, Title 14, § 91.409.

the FAA has been authorized to develop both noise regulations and standards. The FAA established a classification system of Stage 1, 2, 3, and 4 that categorizes aircraft based on their weight, number of engines, and amount of noise they produce. Stage 1 aircraft are the noisiest and are being phased out; Stage 1 aircraft are not approved for commercial use in the United States. In 2004, the FAA created a Stage 4 classification, which paralleled a 2002 ICAO standard; this applies to all aircraft designs post-2006 and imposes a requirement that designs must produce noise levels 10 decibels lower than Stage 3.[36]

General and commercial aviation aircraft that have Stage 4 classification avoid noise restrictions and may also be subject to lower usage charges relating to the noise levels generated. This reduces the operating cost of the aircraft and, hence, increases its value to the operator. The G150 referenced earlier in this chapter was the first business jet to meet the stringent Stage 4 noise classification.

Diminution of Value Assessment

Applicable to the appraisal of aircraft and aircraft-related items is the concept of diminution of value. *Diminution of value* refers to the loss in value that occurs whenever an aircraft or its components are involved in any type of accident or incident. In aviation, the diminution concept has been used to set aircraft prices, but is considered a separate issue for valuation. Diminution value depends on personal judgment and physical inspection; it is a negotiated figure based on the opinion of industry experts and professionals with experience in selling, buying, and trading aircraft.

The end product of a diminution of value assessment is comprised of a detailed written report that depicts the overall condition of the aircraft and its components, the full scope and type of damage that occurred, as well as a representation of any perceived diminution of value. The purpose of the assessment is to verify the extent of the damage, the general physical condition of the aircraft and its components, and what, if any, potential there is for a diminution of value.

Diminution of Value Scope of Work

Diminution of value assessments are typically required by owners, operators, and lawyers to discover the financial implications following a damage or loss event. In order to form a proper diminution of value assessment, a required checklist covering the information needed has to be followed. Table 8.13 highlights some of the items that are to be included in the checklist. The list is not comprehensive, and many other factors and variables should be included in the assessment, such as the

---

[36] Federal Aviation Administration Airport Noise and Capacity Act of 1990.

date and severity of the damage; the stage of flight that the incident occurred in; any personal injuries, deaths, or FAA violations; the status of the repair work; and whether the items were replaced with new or remanufactured parts. These factors are to be considered independently and not lumped into an arbitrary percentage of total value, as factors not related to the incident (aircraft age, for example) also influence the value of the aircraft. Again, the focus is on how the damage will affect the current and future values of aircraft, equipment, or business operations, and the diminution of value assessment is not used as a tool to determine the airworthiness or serviceability of the aircraft.

The final diminution of value assessment should include the scope and magnitude of the damage, with any structural damage fully detailed. The repair section should include the method of repair, its regulatory compliance, and the repair center or service. The amount of time that has passed, and any maintenance performed since the incident, may be recorded and detailed. Any previous incidents and maintenance records should be reviewed and included in the final report.

As indicated by the checklist in Table 8.13, diminution is a highly subjective and controversial concept when applied to general aviation. There exists no specific technique or principles that can be applied to every case in order to determine the diminution value. Numerous intangible factors like the damage characteristics often come into play during a negotiation; those types of factors have effects that are hard to isolate because every airplane used in general aviation has a different history and, consequently, a different perceived value. Ultimately, the buyer is the final judge of the total "value" of the aircraft, including the diminution factor. Depending on the nature of the damage, the appraiser may be called upon to provide expert witness testimony during a trial or court-ordered proceeding.

While intangible factors cannot be eliminated entirely from diminution of value, evaluations should be carefully guided by objective criteria. An appropriate method to determine market value is to conduct an investigation of the aircraft

Table 8.13 Components of diminution of value assessment

Required items	Description
Photographs	A complete set showing areas of damage before and after repairs (interior and exterior).
Description of incident	A complete description and factual accounting of the incident.
Repairs	All repair work orders/invoices with complete and detailed description of repair(s), including photographs.
Logbook entries	A copy of all logbook entries including: current aircraft times, engine's hours, vendor work orders, weight and balance manuals, current equipment list, maintenance task and work cards, and any FAA Form 337s generated due to an incident.

Source: Compiled from sample appraisal reports.

and logbooks, review specific issues regarding the repairs, compile all of the damage event's elements and subsequent maintenance history, and then apply the conclusions to market activity for the specific aircraft, utilizing current USPAP standards. The American Society of Appraisers is expanding its classes to include an overview of damage diminution.

Fixed-base Operators

Fixed-base operators (FBOs) include the private or publicly-held businesses that operate at an airport and cater primarily to general aviation (some FBOs also handle commercial airline customers) as well as passengers by providing a range of services not limited to fueling, aircraft rental, parking, aircraft maintenance, and flight instruction. For general aviation, an FBO often provides the necessary support at large and small airfields, including fueling and line services (approximately 98% of the fuel consumed by general aviation aircraft is pumped by FBOs).[37]

Over the past several years, a rapid growth of FBOs occurred in the United States, with many operators moving from small single-location entities to comprehensive regional, national, and international chains through acquisition and mergers. This industry consolidation came at a time when a record number of business jet deliveries and large backlogs simultaneously occurred. FBO companies are constantly acquiring other FBOs, evolving rapidly to provide more services to general aviation traffic. Signature Flight Support, for example, owns and operates 115 facilities and has acquired numerous other FBOs over the years, including Hawker Beechcraft's fuel and line service operations for $128.5 million. These acquisitions have made Signature Flight Support's parent company, BBA Aviation, the simultaneous holder of the most non-U.S. FBOs and of the most FBOs overall.[38]

This trend of constant FBO acquisitions and expansions means that a similar trend of appraisals of FBOs will continue to occur. Proper appraisals of the FBO must be carried out in order for a value to be assigned to the property (tangible or otherwise). It should be noted that because appraising an FBO (in contrast to acquiring an aircraft) involves assessing an entire business, the process is consequently more extensive.

Scope of FBO Appraisals

Similar to general aviation aircraft appraisal, FBO appraisals are intended to be consistent with the USPAP. A critical step in acquiring an FBO, or making the decision to invest in existing facilities, is to carry out an appraisal of the tangible assets and support equipment to determine the fair market value and ultimately

---

[37] Aviation Resource Group International (ARGI) 2009 Survey.
[38] Aviation International News 2008 FBO Survey.

the cost of acquisition. It may also become necessary to appraise an FBO's operations in order to justify a loan for expanding operations, determining a base value for setting up an employee stock ownership plan (ESOP), or establishing a buy-sell agreement between several owners. In addition to the tangible assets and support equipment that may be appraised, an FBO may also require a separate or joint valuation of the business enterprise and/or the real property, which may include items such as office furniture and equipment.

The equipment and value of the tangible items that will be found in the FBO vary significantly, based on the FBO's size and scope of operations. Support equipment is a broad category that includes the equipment found at the FBO, repair facilities, and airport. Support equipment may include fuel trucks, fuel tanks, repair platforms, maintenance testing tools, avionic test equipment, tugs, and waste disposal equipment. Assessing the FBO's premises often includes assessing buildings, hangars, offices, aprons, parking lots, and tie-down areas.

In addition, determining an FBO's value often involves a comprehensive review of its operational and financial records to gain a retrospective and prospective view on the various elements of its revenue generation. Current and potential future income generators increase the acquisition costs for a buyer, whereas liabilities tend to decrease the value and, as a result, the cost of acquisition.

Summary

General aviation aircraft makes a significant contribution to the economy and is vital to the national interest. General aviation aircraft includes business jets, turboprops, piston twins, piston singles, rotorcraft, and home-built aircraft that cover a large range of activities, including private flying, flight training, air ambulance, police aircraft, aerial firefighting, and air charter. As a result of global economic problems, total shipments for 2010 were 2,015 aircraft, down 11.4% from 2009. General aviation and aircraft appraisal, in part due to its broad scope of operations and aircraft, is a complex and time-consuming process that needs to be carried out by a certified appraiser.

Many guidelines for carrying out an appraisal of an aircraft or FBO exist, and a variety of techniques and practices can be employed. When selecting an aircraft for valuation there is no single method that works in every situation. Appraisal experts, at the end of the process, provide detailed property analyses and valuations using several methods, including comparable sales, replacement cost, and income approaches. This chapter highlighted some of the factors that have to be considered when conducting an aviation appraisal.

References

Airworthiness Standards. (2011). Normal, Utility, Acrobatic, and Commuter Category. *Code of Federal Regulations.* § 23.3.

The Appraisal Foundation. (2010). Uniform Standards of Professional Appraisal Practice. 2010-2011 ed.

Aviation International News. (2008). FBO Survey.

Cessna. (2010a). Company Overview. Retrieved from http://www.cessna.com/about/about-cessna-overview.html.

Cessna. (2010b). *Cessna 172 Skyhawk Specifications.* Retrieved from http://www.cessna.com/single-engine/skyhawk/skyhawk-specifications.html.

Cessna. (2010c). *Cessna 182 Skylane Specifications.* Retrieved from http://www.cessna.com/single-engine/skylane/skylane-specifications.html.

Cessna. (2010d). *Cessna 206 Stationair Specifications.* Retrieved from http://www.cessna.com/single-engine/stationair/stationair-specifications.html.

Cessna. (2010e). *Cessna Corvalis Specifications.* Retrieved from http://www.cessna.com/single-engine/cessna-400/cessna-400-specifications.html.

Cessna. (2010f). *Cessna Citation Encore Specifications.* Retrieved from http://www.cessna.com/citation/encore/encore-specifications.html.

Cessna. (2010g). *Cessna Citation Mustang Specifications.* Retrieved from http://www.cessna.com/citation/mustang/mustang-specifications.html.

Cessna. (2010h). *Cessna Citation Sovereign Specifications.* Retrieved from http://www.cessna.com/citation/sovereign/sovereign-specifications.html.

Cessna. (2010i). *Cessna Citation X Specifications.* Retrieved from http://www.cessna.com/citation/citation-x/citation-x-specifications.html.

Cessna. (2010j). *Cessna Citation XLS Specifications.* Retrieved from http://www.cessna.com/citation/citation-xls/citation-xls-specifications.html.

Cirrus Aircraft. (2010a). Company Overview. Retrieved from http://cirrusaircraft.com/about/.

Cirrus Aircraft. (2010b). Cirrus SR20 Models. Retrieved from http://cirrusaircraft.com/sr20/.

Cirrus Aircraft. (2010c). Cirrus SR22 Models. Retrieved from http://cirrusaircraft.com/sr22/.

Cirrus Aircraft. (2010d). Vision SF50. Retrieved from http://cirrusaircraft.com/vision/.

Conklin & de Decker. (2010). Aircraft Variable Cost. Retrieved from http://www.conklindd.com/CDALibrary/ACCostSummary.aspx.

Federal Aviation Administration. (2009). General Aviation and Part 135 Activity Surveys - CY 2009. Retrieved from http://www.faa.gov/data_research/aviation_data_statistics/general_aviation/CY2009/.

General Aviation Manufacturers Association. (2009). Statistical Databook and Industry Outlook. Retrieved from http://www.gama.aero/files/GAMA_Databook_2009.pdf.

Hawker Beechcraft. (2010a). Company Overview. Retrieved from http://www.hawkerbeechcraft.com/about_us/.

Hawker Beechcraft. (2010b). *Beechcraft Baron*. Retrieved from http://www.hawkerbeechcraft.com/beechcraft/baron_g58/.

Hawker Beechcraft. (2010c). *Beechcraft Bonanza*. Retrieved from http://www.hawkerbeechcraft.com/beechcraft/bonanza_g36/.

Hawker Beechcraft. (2010d). *Beechcraft King Air 350i*. Retrieved from http://www.hawkerbeechcraft.com/beechcraft/king_air_350i/.

Hawker Beechcraft (2010e) *Beechcraft Premier 1A*. Retrieved from http://www.hawkerbeechcraft.com/beechcraft/premier_ia/.

Hawker Beechcraft. (2010f). *Hawker 200 Business Jet: Overview*. Retrieved from http://www.hawkerbeechcraft.com/hawker/200/.

Hawker Beechcraft. (2010g). *Hawker 400XP Business Jet: Overview*. Retrieved from http://www.hawkerbeechcraft.com/hawker/400xp/.

Hawker Beechcraft. (2010h). *Hawker 750 Business Jet: Overview*. Retrieved from http://www.hawkerbeechcraft.com/hawker/750/.

Hawker Beechcraft. (2010i). *Hawker 900XP Business Jet: Overview*. Retrieved from http://www.hawkerbeechcraft.com/hawker/900xp/.

Hawker Beechcraft. (2010j). *Hawker 4000 Business Jet: Overview*. Retrieved from http://www.hawkerbeechcraft.com/hawker/4000/.

Jet Sales 101. (2010). Retrieved from http://www.jetlist.com/jet_sales_101.php.

M&B Aviation. (2010). M&B Aviation Certified Aircraft Appraisal. Retrieved from http://www.mbaviationappraisal.com/appraisal/index.php.

National Aircraft Appraisers Association. (2011). Aircraft Appraisal. Retrieved from http://www.plane-values.com/appraisalsoverview.php.

National Air Transport Association. (2009). *General Aviation Factbook*. Retrieved from http://nata.aero/data/files/NATA%20publications/NATA_factbook.pdf.

Piper Aircraft. (2010a). *Archer LX Price and Equipment*. Retrieved from http://www.piper.com/home/pages/ArcherPriceStandardEquipment.cfm.

Piper Aircraft. (2010b). *Arrow Price and Equipment*. Retrieved from http://www.piper.com/home/pages/ArrowPriceStandardEquipment.cfm.

Piper Aircraft. (2010c). Company Profile. Retrieved from http://www.piper.com/home/pages/AboutUs.cfm.

Piper Aircraft. (2010d). *Meridian Price and Equipment.*

Piper Aircraft. (2010e). *Mirage Price and Equipment.*

Piper Aircraft. (2010f). *Matrix Price and Equipment.*

Piper Aircraft. (2010g). *Seneca V Price and Equipment.*

Piper Aircraft. (2010h). *Seminole Price and Equipment.*

Spenser, J. (1978). *Aeronca C-2: The Story of the Flying Bathtub.* Washington, D.C.: Smithsonian Institution Press. 71.

9

Aircraft Leasing and Finance

We have selected the Boeing Next-Generation 737-800 as a cornerstone of our growing commercial aircraft lease fleet. The 737-800 represents an opportunity for our wide range of airline clients to operate this most economical, fuel efficient and versatile 150–189 passenger airplane, on a wide variety of airline missions profitably.

—Steven Hazy, Chairman and CEO of Air Lease Corporation

For airlines, the acquisition of commercial aircraft is often the most expensive investment decision and requires external sources of funding. For this reason, airlines employ a variety of innovative financing tools in acquiring aircraft without draining their cash reserves. Aircraft leasing provides a viable alternative to the outright purchasing of aircraft for cash-strapped airlines operating with very low margins and dealing with uncertain travel demands. The decision to lease is a function of a company's fiscal practices and tax obligations, as airlines seek to protect their balance sheets.

The benefits of the depreciation of a major capital asset such as aircraft may appeal to certain airlines, whereas expensing all costs related to aircraft operations through an operating lease may be of greater value to others. Further, some airlines will opt to lease aircraft for operational reasons such as fleet management in the short or medium term. A variety of leases and lease combinations that have evolved out of the necessity to acquire aircraft are detailed in this chapter, along with an overview of the current leasing market:

Commercial Aircraft Leasing

Characteristics of Aircraft Leasing

- Advantages of Aircraft Leasing
- Disadvantages of Aircraft Leasing

Classification of Leases

- Operating Lease
- Financial (Capital) Lease
- Cross-border Aircraft Leasing
- Sale and Leaseback
- Dry and Wet Leases

Financial Considerations for Aircraft Leasing

- Buy vs. Lease Analysis

Business Jets Market and Fractional Ownership

Major Commercial Aircraft Leasing Companies

At the end of the chapter is a Summary for chapter review and References for further study.

Commercial Aircraft Leasing

The growth in air traffic and reducing risks by portfolio diversification are the principal factors driving demand for leased aircraft. In newly growing economies such as Brazil, Russia, India, and China (BRIC), economic growth facilitates strong derived demand for air travel and impetus for airlines to expand their fleets. The BRIC countries represent four of the world's largest emerging markets with over 40% of the world's population and 15% of global GDP.[1] This makes the BRIC markets a potential powerhouse for years to come. In emerging markets, as well as the Middle East, ambitious construction plans for new airports provide impetus for commercial aircraft leasing companies.

At Abu Dhabi airport, the newest terminal (Terminal 3) opened in January 2009 and is expected to serve 12 million passengers annually.[2] To meet the future demand for air travel, the Chinese government is planning to build 45 additional

---

[1] Center for Asia Pacific Aviation Report, May 2011.
[2] Abu Dhabi International Airport, Annual Report.
[3] China Expands Number of Airports. *Fresh News Daily*, February 25, 2011.

airports, at a cost of about \$228 billion over the next five years.[3] China Southern Airlines, operating a fleet of more than 300 aircraft from its hub in Guangzhou, is accelerating its pace of international expansion. On June 28, 2011, China's ICBC Financial Leasing Company signed an agreement with Airbus for a total of 88 A320 family aircraft, valued at \$7.5 billion at list prices, to be delivered between 2012 and 2015.[4] In another transaction, ICBC signed a contract with Bombardier for \$8 billion to lease aircraft.

Another BRIC giant, India, enjoyed 19% traffic growth in 2010. Many Indian carriers are growing their fleets as demand booms—growth that is expected to last for many years. Air India plans to lease 40 new planes from Bombardier and Airbus to meet increased demand for air travel.[5] Kingfisher Airlines plans to lease both wide- and narrow-body aircraft to meet an unanticipated increase in demand.[6] Brazilian airline GOL serves about 55 destinations and mainly operates a fleet of more than 100 aircraft. Nearly all are leased Boeing 737s.

The downturn in the global economy, reduction in corporate profitability, and a higher unemployment rate force airlines to reduce capacity and retire aircraft. Aircraft leasing may provide significant flexibility to airlines to meet these and other unexpected changes in market conditions. For example, in 2008, several airlines were forced to return their leased aircraft due to deteriorating global economic conditions. To cut costs, Air India restructured and canceled some of its routes as well as returned several leased aircraft.[7] In the face of falling demand, and in order to cope with higher fuel prices, several airlines including American Airlines, Delta, United, and Continental announced significant reduction in capacity.[8]

Leasing companies and aircraft manufacturers have developed many innovative financing methods to satisfy the needs of the airline industry. These include different kinds of leases, equipment trust certificates, and government export credit. Airlines are steadily leasing more aircraft and owning fewer. Many airlines around the world are not enthusiastic about buying new planes because of the uncertainly and volatility in the air transport market. Airlines that utilize leasing enjoy the flexibility it provides, which also allows them not to be as restricted from a liquidity standpoint. Conversely, lessors globally are placing more orders for new aircraft in anticipation of higher future demand. Over 30% of the world's aircraft are leased, and it is expected that this market share will grow to 40% by 2016 (Mann, 2009). Figure 9.1 shows the percentage of various aircraft fleets that

---

[4] Centre for Asia Pacific Aviation Report, June 2011.
[5] Reuters, January 17, 2011.
[6] Vijay Mallya, Kingfisher CEO, June 6, 2011.
[7] *Wall Street Journal*, November 11, 2009.
[8] *CNN Money*, June 27, 2008.

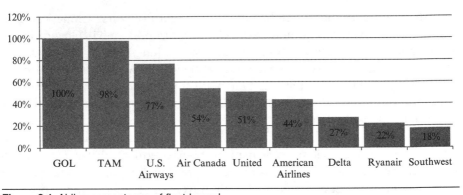

Figure 9.1 Airline percentages of fleet leased
Source: Company 2010 annual reports, 10-Ks, and 20-F filings.

Table 9.1 Airline fleet compositions

Airline	Total operating fleet	Total leased aircraft	Operating lease	Financial (capital) lease
GOL	125	125	86	39
TAM	151	148	144	4
Air Canada	205	111	77	34
American Airlines	620	272	202	70
Delta	815	224	111	113
Ryanair	250	75	55	20
Southwest	548	97	92	5

Source: Company 2010 annual reports, 10-Ks, and 20-F filings.

are leased, and Table 9.1 displays the number of aircraft operated under financial (capital) and operating leases by selected airlines.

Low-cost airlines such as GOL Linhas Aéreas constantly seek ways to cut costs and generate additional revenues. Leasing a significant portion of their fleets is an innovative way to reduce costs by always having the most modern, fuel-efficient aircraft while minimizing the impact of these large investments on their balance sheets. TAM and GOL are two major airlines operating out of Brazil. TAM is Brazil's largest airline, with 44.4% domestic market share in Brazil and 89.6% for the international market. Of its leased aircraft, an overwhelming majority (97%) of the aircraft leases held by TAM are operating leases.

GOL is one of the most profitable low-cost airlines in the world and the second largest airline in Brazil, with a 35.4% market share.[9] The airline leases 100%

[9] GOL offers more than 940 daily flights to 63 destinations that connect all of the important cities in Brazil and 13 major destinations in South America and the Caribbean.

of its current operating fleet (see Figure 9.1). GOL operates 86 of its 125 leased aircraft under operating leases and 39 under financial leases. With an extensive domestic and regional network, GOL is expected to continue increasing its services and routes, having entered an agreement to acquire rival low-cost carrier Webjet for $61.4 million. Webjet is Brazil's fourth largest airline, with a 5.2% market share in May 2011.[10]

Aircraft leasing could be a cost-effective tool for airlines to finance their fleet. With availability of leasing opportunities, airlines are able to invest in and modernize aircraft to meet future demand without the cash flow burden of down payments or large equity outlays to fund the non-debt portion of an aircraft purchase. Of course, there are advantages and disadvantages to leasing aircraft. Airlines have to make sure that they investigate both the benefits and weaknesses before consummating any transactions (see Table 9.2).

Table 9.2 Leased vs. owned Boeing aircraft for major airline fleets

Airline	Owned	Leased		
		Operating	Financial	Unknown
Air Canada	8	25	9	—
American Airlines	348	202	70	—
Delta	414	50	100	—
GOL	—	86	39	—
Ryanair	151	55	20	—
Southwest	451	—	—	67
United	264	—	—	294
US Airways	4	—	—	88

Source: Compiled from company 2010 annual reports, 10-Ks, and 20-F filings.

Table 9.3 Leased vs. owned Airbus aircraft for major airline fleets

Airline	Owned	Leased		
		Operating	Financial	Unknown
Air Canada	—	52	25	—
Delta	128	30	—	—
United	84	—	—	64
US Airways	60	—	—	172

Source: Compiled from company 2010 annual reports, 10-Ks, and 20-F filings.

---

[10] National Civil Aviation Agency of Brazil (ANAC), May 2011.

Characteristics of Aircraft Leasing

Airlines seeking to add new aircraft to their fleet are frequently faced with the question of whether to buy or to lease the aircraft. Lease transactions are often designed to circumvent an airline's need to appropriate up-front capital. The final decision whether to lease an aircraft or not is based on how different factors can contribute to the attractiveness of aircraft leasing.

Advantages of Aircraft Leasing

Many airline financial managers believe that there are benefits in leasing vs. the traditional purchasing of an aircraft. Leasing an aircraft offers significant potential advantages over purchasing that same aircraft, such as the following:

Flexibility and Speed of Delivery

The main advantages of leasing are the flexibility and speed of delivery to airlines when it comes to fleet planning and adjustments. Fleet size can be adjusted based on any changing conditions that the airline faces. As an airline's needs evolve, the fleet can be adjusted faster and with increased flexibility. This flexibility allows airlines to enter new markets with reduced risk; if a route is unprofitable, the airline can put the aircraft on another more profitable route or return it. The increased flexibility also comes in handy during times of economic downturn; airlines can respond to unprofitable overcapacity quickly when traffic is decreased.

Ability to Introduce New Aircraft Types and Models

Leasing allows airlines to access newer, fuel-efficient aircraft and replace older, fuel-thirsty aircraft, particularly during times of rising fuel costs. Newer model aircraft offer increased operational reliability and reduced operating costs. Technology advances can also be capitalized on by leasing newer aircraft. For example, the A320neo will incorporate the latest generation engines and wing tip devices to deliver 15% in fuel savings.[11] These savings are expected to contribute to the A320neo becoming a cornerstone of leasing companies and fleets seeking to further reduce costs and increase efficiency. IndiGo became the first A320neo customer, placing a massive order for 150 aircraft, which will become available in 2016.

Leasing newer aircraft protects airlines from technological obsolescence. With ownership, airlines face the risk that new technology will render their flight equipment obsolete within a few years. If that happens, an airline may be left with

---

[11] Airbus A320neo to enter service in 2016. *Flightglobal.com.*

equipment that no longer meets its needs and, consequently, is difficult to sell. Leasing allows airlines to remain competitive on the technological front by replacing or upgrading equipment.

Airlines Can Receive Aircraft without Pre-delivery and Installment Payments

To purchase aircraft from Boeing or Airbus, airlines need to provide cash deposits and pre-payments. Leasing permits acquisition of equipment immediately and preserves bank credit lines or airline cash for other uses. Also, financing an aircraft for ownership through loans often requires a large down payment in advance. Leasing, on the other hand, generally only requires a first and last payment for delivery of the aircraft.

Conserve Working Capital and Improve Cash Flow

An aircraft lease can minimize the cash flow required to provide regular commercial airline service. Retaining working capital reflects positively on the company's ability to pay its short-term debts and the overall financial health of the airline. The fixed nature of lease expenses eliminates uncertainty about the future cost of the aircraft. The operating leasing model involves the lessor accepting the risk of aircraft residual values, and the lessee is free from concern about the aircraft's residual value after the lease term ends.

Off-balance-sheet Treatment

Under an operating lease, an airline is afforded the ability to exclude leased equipment from its liabilities on its balance sheet. This frees up the company's lines of credit, as the aircraft is not seen as a long-term debt on the balance sheet, but rather as an ordinary expense. The reduced debt on the balance sheet helps the airline maintain a healthy debt-to-asset ratio, which makes the airline more favorable to lenders.

However, it should be noted that when analyzing airline credit, many lenders and analysts will adjust for this factor by looking at alternative credit ratios. For example, rather than looking at a company's leverage as debt divided by EBITDA, they will instead tweak the ratio to adjusted debt divided by EBITDAR (adding back the operating rental expense to EBITDA as if it were an interest payment). The adjusted debt in the numerator will take the on-balance-sheet debt and add the present value of the future lease obligations to that figure. Alternatively, the adjusted debt can be eight times one-year's operating lease expense plus the on-balance-sheet debt, where the eight times multiple represents an approximation for the average life of the leased financing tenor. Another credit metric that adjusts for off-balance-sheet items would be EBITDAR divided by interest plus rent, instead of EBITDA divided by interest, to represent the interest coverage ratio for an airline.

Disadvantages of Aircraft Leasing

Some of the arguments against leasing aircraft, which can help airline managers to make a decision, involve the following:

Conditions of Return

Aircraft that are leased must be returned in a pre-agreed condition. Should an aircraft fail to meet the return conditions owing to higher than expected utilization or extreme wear and tear, an airline will likely face a penalty. When an airline owns an aircraft, it can fly the aircraft as much as needed without the risk of penalties.

Early Return Penalties

If an aircraft is returned prior to the agreed return date, the airline often is still responsible for the remaining lease payments. Some contracts may grant the lessee the option to terminate the lease for a predetermined early return penalty.

Operating Restrictions

Leases may place certain restrictions on where an aircraft can be based, as well as under what conditions the aircraft may be operated. Restrictions may include geographic regions to which an airline is not permitted to fly. A lease may also restrict where the airline can base or how it can operate the aircraft.[12]

Tax Disadvantages

Operating leases do not allow the benefit of writing off an aircraft to a zero tax basis, since the lease payments are accounted for as expenses. This may result in higher short-term taxes for the airline if the aircraft depreciation allowance exceeds the lease payment deduction.

In recent years, new forms of leases appeared in which lessors offer some services together with the aircraft, and these are called *wet* and *dry leases* (Gavazza, 2010). Wet and dry leases, in turn, may have variations based on the conditions and terms of the arrangement between the lessee, lessor, and any third parties, which are covered in detail in the next section.[13]

---

[12] Conklin & de Decker. Lease pros and cons: The things you should know, 2010.
[13] Lease classifications are defined in the FAA Advisory Circular AC 91-37A—Truth in Leasing.

Classification of Leases

A *lease* is a contract whereby the owner of an aircraft (the lessor) grants to another party (the lessee or airline) the exclusive right to the use of the aircraft for an agreed period of time, in return for the periodic payment of rent.[14] Aircraft leasing has become one of the major sources of portfolio formation in the industry in recent years (Morrell, 2009). Leases involving commercial aircraft are categorized according to general classification criteria: operating, financial (capital), cross-border, sales/leaseback, or wet leases.

Operating Lease

In an operating lease, the aircraft is under lease for a relatively short period of time compared to the useful life of the aircraft. The airline does not record the aircraft as an asset or a liability on the balance sheet. If the lease is a capital lease, the lessee treats the leased asset as though it were. Under an operating lease, a lease rental payment is an expense to the lessee (Ely, 1995). With the useful life of many aircraft reaching 30 years or more, an operating lease is relatively short (usually less than 10 years). Because of its flexibility, almost all airlines use operating leases as a component of their capital structure.

With an operating lease, the airline does not assume the risk of ownership, and thus the aircraft does not show up on the balance sheet. The aircraft is returned to the lessor at the end of the contractual period. This type of lease presents a significant advantage to a lessee, as the residual value risk is shifted to the lessor (see Table 9.4).[15] In addition, the relatively short time period for which the aircraft is leased offers the operator tremendous flexibility in its fleet capacity. Increased flexibility makes the operating lease advantageous for satisfying short-term increases in passenger traffic or yield associated with new and developing markets. In 2008, there were 950 Airbus and Boeing aircraft in service with airlines in China. By the end of May 2011, there were about 575 A320 family (A318, A319, A320, and A321) aircraft in operation with 13 Chinese airlines.[16] Some 44% of those aircraft, or 418 planes, were on operating leases, with more than 31 companies leasing aircraft to Chinese airlines.[17]

Operating leases may have several disadvantages based on the terms. Restrictions may be placed on where and how the aircraft can be flown as part of the lease agreement. If an airline's need for the aircraft changes and the aircraft is returned to the lessor early, the lessee may still be responsible for any remaining

---

[14] FAA Advisory Circular AC 91-37A—Truth in Leasing.
[15] The residual value is the risk that the fair value of the equipment will be less than originally estimated.
[16] Airbus Press, 2011.
[17] *Orient Aviation*, November 2007.

Table 9.4 Operating lease characteristics

Item	Treatment
Lessee's accounting	Off-balance-sheet
Lessor's accounting	Varies
Residual value risk	Lessor
Time period	Relatively short compared to useful life of aircraft

lease payments. Leases do not allow the benefit of writing off an aircraft to a zero tax basis, since lease payments are marked as an expense, which may result in higher short-term taxes. Also, terms of an operating lease make an airline contractually committed to either return the aircraft in a certain condition or to compensate the lessor based on the actual condition of the airframe, engines, and parts upon return (see Table 9.5).

To illustrate the effect of not having an aircraft show up on an airline's balance sheet, let's say that DirectJet needs one additional aircraft, which costs $60,000,000. The airline has the option of financing the aircraft with debt (purchasing it outright) or leasing it under an operating lease. Table 9.6 shows the effect that purchasing the aircraft with debt (typical of many airlines) would have on the airline's balance sheet. Table 9.7 shows the effect on the balance sheet of an operating lease.

Table 9.5 Advantages and disadvantages of an operating lease

Advantages	Disadvantages
Less capital intensive than purchasing	Lease may place restrictions on operations
Residual value risk shifted to lessor	Return conditions may lead to penalties and additional fees
Lease payments can be written off as an expense	Lessee may still be required to make payments if aircraft is returned early
Lease period can be relatively short	Lessee loses tax advantage of writing off aircraft to zero tax basis

Table 9.6 Balance sheet example for aircraft purchased with debt

Assets		Liabilities	
Aircraft	$60,000,000	Debt	$110,000,000
Other assets	$200,000,000	Equity	$150,000,000
Total	$260,000,000	**Total**	$260,000,000

$$\text{Debt asset}_{Debt-Financing} = \frac{110}{260} = 42\%$$

Table 9.7 Balance sheet example for aircraft under an operating lease

Assets		Liabilities	
Aircraft	$0	Debt	$50,000,000
Other assets	$200,000,000	Equity	$150,000,000
Total	**$200,000,000**	**Total**	**$200,000,000**

$$\text{Debt asset}_{\text{Lease-Financing}} = \frac{50}{200} = 25\%$$

Financial (Capital) Lease

Airlines may choose to lease aircraft for a long period rather than short term for a variety of reasons. In a capital lease, the airline bears some of the risks of ownership and enjoys some of the benefits. In the U.S., operating leases are also called *true leases*, and finance leases are known as *capital leases*. The airline enjoys the depreciation expenses and deducts the interest expense component of the lease payment from the taxable income each year. To be considered a capital lease, the Financial Accounting Standards Board (FASB) requires that at least one of these conditions is met:

- The lease contract provides for a transfer of ownership by the end of the term.
- The lease contract contains a bargain purchase option.
- The lease term is at least 75% of the asset's economic life.
- The present value of the minimum lease payments is at least 90% of the asset's fair value.

Under a capital lease, the present value of the lease expense is treated as debt and shows up on the company's balance sheets (Pulvino, 1998; Miller & Upton, 1976; Littlejohns & McGairl, 1998). Key differences exist in the lease accounting standards issued by FASB and the IASB. Currently, FASB's standard (SFAS 13) for capitalizing leases has four criteria, only one of which needs to be met by the lessee (Grossman & Grossman, 2010).

An example of the treatment of an aircraft that is acquired through a capital lease on an airline's balance sheet is shown in Table 9.8. The lease payments show

Table 9.8 Balance sheet example for aircraft under a financial (capital) lease

Assets		Liabilities	
Aircraft	$60,000,000	Debt	$110,000,000
Other assets	$200,000,000	Equity	$150,000,000
Total	$260,000,000	Total	$260,000,000

up as a liability on the airline's balance sheet. Having the aircraft show up on the balance sheet as an asset has long-term tax implications for the airline. An airline can receive the tax benefits of interest and depreciation expenses.[18] Table 9.9 summarizes the primary characteristics of the financial lease and Table 9.10 translates these characteristics into the primary advantages and disadvantages of this form of leasing to the airlines.

Under a capital lease, the airline is considered the owner of the aircraft, which allows the airline to reap the tax benefits of ownership. Capital leases, owing to the long lease terms, are often non-cancelable near the useful life of the aircraft. One unique feature of the capital lease is that the airline is able to customize the aircraft's various specifications, including engine selection and layouts, similar to a straight purchase. The cost of leasing under a capital lease approaches the cost of buying the aircraft outright. However, cost savings available to leasing companies owing to their better credit ratings and bulk purchase discounts with the various aircraft manufacturers may be transferred to the airline, albeit on a smaller scale.

Table 9.9 Financial (capital) lease characteristics

Item	Treatment
Airline's accounting	On-balance-sheet
Lessor's accounting	Varies
Interest in residual value	Generally to lessor, may also be shared
Cross-border	Common in order to take advantage of tax incentives
Leveraged	Frequent, but tax laws may sometimes make leveraged leasing uneconomic
Cancelable	Not common, but may be allowed after a certain period for a fee.

Table 9.10 Advantages and disadvantages of a financial (capital) lease

Advantages	Disadvantages
Airline receives tax benefits of interest and depreciation expense	Airline bears the risk of ownership
Airline can specify features and specifications of aircraft	Aircraft cannot be returned if financial conditions worsen
Lessor savings due to better credit ratings and discounts from manufacturers may be transferred to airline	Cost of lease approaches cost of buying aircraft if lease term nears useful life of aircraft

---

[18] In the U.S., the tax ownership in a capital lease is the *lessee*, whereas in the UK and Ireland the *lessor* in a finance lease is regarded as the owner for tax purposes.

Cross-border Aircraft Leasing

Differential income tax rates between the lessor and the lessee can make leasing attractive because it can generate more tax benefits.

—Robert Kolb

Leases often occur cross-border, meaning that the two parties involved in the lease have their registered offices in different countries, under different accounting regulations and tax laws. A significant advantage to a cross-border lease (CBL) is that it allows both parties to take advantage of tax benefits owing to disparities in international accounting laws governing the transaction (Park, 2007). In some cases, both lessee and lessor are able to write off the tax commitments in a CBL agreement and thus generate tax-deductible expenses. Therefore, one of the major objectives of cross-border leasing is to reduce the overall cost of financing by reducing taxable income (Mehta, 2005). The countries involved in a CBL must have different rules for determining whether the lessor under a CBL tax lease is the owner of the leased aircraft for tax purposes and thereby eligible to claim depreciation tax allowances. Ireland, Bermuda, and the Netherlands have historically been prime locations for cross-border leasing.

Ireland, Japan, France, the UK, Sweden, Denmark, Germany, and other countries have engaged in cross-border leasing. As an example, assume that an Irish lessor signs a capital lease agreement with an airline in the U.S. to lease a 737-800. Under Irish tax rules, the Irish lessor would claim tax depreciation in Ireland. Since the lease is not a true lease under U.S. rules, the airline would be entitled to claim ownership of the asset for tax purposes in the United States. Hence, the tax benefits are claimed by both parties.

Sale and Leaseback

Financial leases may be structured in a number of ways, the most common being as a sale and leaseback and a leveraged lease. These types of leases involve selling an airline's aircraft to an outside purchaser (generally a lending institution), who will then lease the aircraft back to the airline. One obvious benefit to the airline is the freeing up of capital for expansion and other expansion projects. A typical sale and leaseback agreement is long term, at least 15 years (Ray & Rowley, 2007).

In a typical sale and leaseback transaction, the carrier initially owns the aircraft, then sells it and simultaneously leases it back from a lessor. This arrangement not only changes the airline's aircraft ownership structure, but generates a cash inflow from the sale of the aircraft that can be used to pay debt associated with that aircraft. The end result of a sale and leaseback transaction is that the airline continues the use of the aircraft while generating cash from its sale. Recent sale and leaseback transactions include Air Berlin entering into a $1 billion 12-aircraft agreement (five A320s, three A321s, and four 737s) with GE Capital Aviation Services. Those aircraft were slated to be delivered in 2012.[19] American Airlines entered into a sale-leaseback arrangement with AerCap, to finance up to 35 Boeing 737-800s scheduled for delivery in 2013-2014.[20] GOL also closed a sale-leaseback deal with AWAS and took delivery of one new Boeing 737-800 Next Generation.[21]

Converting physical assets into liquid capital through sale and leaseback transactions tends to enhance a company's financial position and profitability. Sale and leaseback transactions can improve a company's current and debt-to-equity ratios, and reduce depreciation expenses. Since the aircraft is never out of operation during this process, there is no revenue loss associated with an aircraft being out of the fleet. The aircraft is no longer financed through a financial institution under terms of a loan or other arrangement, which allows the airline to free up its lines of credit for use in the most effective way. There also exist several tax advantages in a sale and leaseback transaction. Under some jurisdictions, the lease payments become allowed tax deductions.

There are also unique disadvantages to sale and leaseback transactions. When an aircraft sells one of its aircraft in such a transaction, it loses any residual value benefits that may exist. The airline runs the risk of losing the flexibility associated with ownership of the aircraft since it no longer possesses the title to the aircraft and may be subject to operating restrictions outlined in the leasing contract. See Table 9.11 for more details.

Leveraged Leases

The leveraged lease is a variation of a sale and leaseback where a third-party lender is involved. Under a three-party leveraged lease, the lessor borrows some of the funds necessary to finance the aircraft being leased to the lessee. The lender holds the title to the leased aircraft while the lessor enjoys the tax benefits of ownership

Table 9.11 Advantages and disadvantages of sale and leaseback

Advantages	Disadvantages
Improves debt-to-equity ratios	Loss of flexibility associated with ownership
Reduces depreciation expense	Loss of any residual value benefits
Aircraft remains in operation throughout transaction	Operating restrictions may be placed on aircraft per terms of lease
Lease payments may become allowed tax deductions	Higher financing costs

---

[19] *Air Transport Intelligence News*, March 23, 2011.
[20] *Investment Weekly News*, Atlanta, July 30, 2011.
[21] *Airfinance Journal*, July, 2011.

(depreciation), and the lessee claims the full amount of the lease payment as expenses. The lessor and lessee together seek to finance 50 to 90% of the aircraft cost through borrowing. The lessor actually invests only 10 to 50% of the cost of the aircraft, but is entitled to 100% of the tax benefits of ownership.[22] Also key to these transactions is the fact that when lessors buy aircraft from airlines in a sale and leaseback transaction, they avoid pre-delivery payments.

Dry and Wet Leases

A *dry lease* is for a basic aircraft without insurance, crew, or maintenance. The typical dry lease may occur in two different forms, either as an operating lease or a finance (capital) lease. The primary difference between the two forms of dry leases is in their treatment on the lessee's balance sheet. A dry lease is classified by the lessee as either a capital lease or an operating lease for accounting purposes.

Wet leasing an aircraft provides an airline with the physical aircraft and everything needed to operate it, including crew, maintenance, and insurance. Wet leases are also often more descriptively referred to as aircraft, crew, maintenance, and insurance (ACMI) leases. A wet lease may be employed for a variety of reasons. Among these is the fact that an aircraft may be needed in service to take advantage of many possible scenarios, including a temporary increase in demand, before additional crew can be hired or trained. Iceland Express, which operates additional flights and routes to North America during the summer months from its Reykjavik base, is a prime example. In order to operate these flights, Iceland Express wet leased two Boeing 757s and four 737s from its sister company Astraeus Airlines for the 2011 summer months.[23]

A wet lease is also advantageous when an aircraft is out of service for an extended period of time and needs to be replaced before it can return to normal service. Many airlines regularly wet lease. For example, TAM wet leases two Airbus A330s to South African Airways.

Seasonal increases in demand remain a common cause for wet leasing, as well as large-scale global events including the Olympics. During such times, airlines often have to wet lease additional aircraft to deal with the increased influx of travelers to a particular region or country where special events occur.

Wet leases also allow airlines to circumvent political issues. For example, Egyptian government policy restricts EgyptAir from flying to Israel under its own name. Flights between the countries are operated by Air Sinai, which has aircraft wet leased from EgyptAir. Wet leases would be more likely on an ad-hoc basis, where the leasing airline does not have a particular type of aircraft in its fleet or

---

[22] European Legal Alliance Aircraft Lease Agreements, 2005.
[23] *Air Transport Intelligence News*, May 18, 2011.

does not have enough aircraft. To satisfy this potential demand for a variety of aircraft types, companies like Air Atlanta Icelandic wet lease everything from Boeing 747s to Lockheed Tristars.

A wet lease also allows an airline a means of testing out new routes and destinations without the long-term financial burden of an aircraft should the route not be satisfactory. A wet lease without crew is occasionally referred to as a *moist lease*.[24]

Another variety of wet leases, although not frequently used, is the *damp lease*. The sole difference between an ACMI lease and a damp lease is in the treatment of cabin crew. Under ACMI leases, the lessor provides the cabin crews whereas under a damp lease, the lessee supplies the crew members. Wet and damp leases are a small fraction of all aircraft leases (Gavazza, 2010).

The lessor of a wet leased aircraft will provide one or more crews, their salaries, and any related allowances. The lessor is also responsible for all maintenance of the aircraft and insurance, usually including hull and third-party liability. The lessor makes money by charging the lessee per block hour of use, with a minimum number of block hours per month. Regardless of aircraft use, the lessee will be charged for the minimum number of block hours. Wet leasing is a short-term leasing solution, often less than a year, but more than one month. An exception to this was Etihad Airways, which wet leased two Airbus A300-600 freighters from Maximus Air Cargo in June 2009 and extended the wet lease until August 2012. These aircraft were used to operate both scheduled and charter services between the Middle East, the Indian subcontinent, East Africa, and China.[25]

Financial Considerations for Aircraft Leasing

Airlines leasing aircraft tend to benefit from economic downturns that result in falling aircraft values. Conversely, leasing companies suffer from falling aircraft values, although as more airlines turn toward leasing to hold up their balance sheets, individual leasing companies may experience upswings in demand and revenue. The decision between leasing and buying an aircraft impacts the balance sheet and financial ratios, as well as any consequential impacts on investors and future lending capacity.

Buy vs. Lease Analysis

The lessee will rely primarily on analyzing the net present value (NPV) cash flow over the expected useful life of the aircraft that will occur from either a purchase

[24] GlobalPlaneSearch.com.
[25] *Air Transport Intelligence News*, January 11, 2011.

or a lease in order to determine the *net advantage to leasing (NAL)*. The NAL of an aircraft is a powerful tool to help managers make the decision between purchasing and leasing. The NAL is determined by comparing the NPVs of the cash outflows associated with purchasing the aircraft to leasing the same aircraft.

In interpreting the cash flows, the lessee identifies the maximum price it is willing to pay, while the lessor establishes the minimum price that it is willing to accept. The gap between these maximum and minimum prices for the lease represents the feasible range along which both parties will be willing to accept the particular lease. However, the specific price is a matter of negotiation and may fall anywhere within this range. For example, Figure 9.2 shows that if a lessee determines that the maximum price it is willing to pay is $7,835, and the lessor's minimum that it will accept is $7,285, then the feasible range of prices that can be agreed on by both parties will occur somewhere between these prices. However, the final price is a product of negotiations and thus may fall anywhere within that range.

Evaluation by Lessee

A lessee's financial evaluation of a lease comes from determining the present value of the lease and the present value of any alternatives. The present values are then compared side by side to determine the most cost-effective one. Every buy vs. lease scenario is different, and all relevant metrics must be considered. Many lessees take the financial evaluation into account in conjunction with the non-financial advantages and disadvantages associated with either purchasing or leasing the aircraft. However, from a purely financial standpoint, the most cost-effective

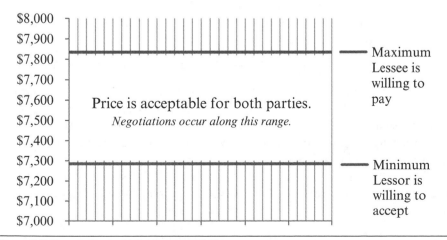

Figure 9.2 Range along which lease negotiations occur

solution is the most appropriate. In order to illustrate this, consider the following example:

> DirectJet is considering the purchase of an aircraft that is expected to have no salvage value at the end of its useful life. Typically, the expected useful life of an aircraft is 20+ years, but in this example, the useful life of the aircraft is capped at 10 years. DirectJet will depreciate the cost of the aircraft on a straight-line basis, and can borrow $80,000,000 (the purchase price) at 10% on a simple interest loan to buy the aircraft. Alternatively, DirectJet can lease the same aircraft for $8,000,000 annually. DirectJet's tax rate is 40% and annual maintenance costs associated with ownership are estimated at $4,000,000. Which alternative should DirectJet choose?

The first step for DirectJet is to identify the relevant cash inflows and inflows of each decision:

- *Interest payments*: If DirectJet buys the aircraft, it will borrow $80,000,000. The airline must pay this principal in full after 10 years. With a 10% interest rate on the principal, the airline pays $8,000,000 in interest for the first year. Table 9.12 shows the amortized schedule of payments, interest, and other ownership costs.
- *Maintenance costs*: On an after-tax basis, a maintenance expense of $4,000,000 per year would be:

$$\$4,000,000(1-0.40) = \$2,400,000$$

- *Depreciation*: If DirectJet owns the fleet, it will depreciate $80,000,000 over 10 years. This gives a straight-line depreciation of $8,000,000 per year. Depreciation tax saving is $3,200,000.[26]
- *Lease payments*: With the lease alternative, the lease payment of $8,000,000 is due annually.

The after-tax cost of the lease is $8,000,000(1-0.40) = $4,800,000 annually.

The cash flows are discounted at DirectJet's after-tax cost of capital. With a 10% borrowing rate and a 40% tax rate, the airline's after-tax cost of borrowing is 6%. Using these numbers results in a present value of the costs of $76,731,060.

Similarly, DirectJet would now analyze the cash flows associated with the cost of leasing, shown in Table 9.13.

The NPV of the lease payments, using the cash flows found previously and after-tax cost of capital of 6% is $52,992,626. In present value terms, leasing saves

---

[26] The depreciation tax saving is equal to the depreciation times the tax rate.

Table 9.12 Ownership costs and associated cash flows for the DirectJet example

Year	Payment	Interest payment	After-tax interest payment	Maintenance cost	After-tax maintenance cost	Depreciation tax savings	Net cash flow
1	$13,019,632	$8,000,000	$4,800,000	$4,000,000	$2,400,000	$3,200,000	12,000,000
2	$13,019,632	$7,498,037	$4,498,822	$4,000,000	$2,400,000	$3,200,000	11,698,822
3	$13,019,632	$6,945,877	$4,167,526	$4,000,000	$2,400,000	$3,200,000	11,367,526
4	$13,019,632	$6,338,502	$3,803,101	$4,000,000	$2,400,000	$3,200,000	11,003,101
5	$13,019,632	$5,670,389	$3,402,233	$4,000,000	$2,400,000	$3,200,000	10,602,233
6	$13,019,632	$4,935,465	$2,961,279	$4,000,000	$2,400,000	$3,200,000	10,161,279
7	$13,019,632	$4,127,048	$2,476,229	$4,000,000	$2,400,000	$3,200,000	9,676,229
8	$13,019,632	$3,237,790	$1,942,674	$4,000,000	$2,400,000	$3,200,000	9,142,674
9	$13,019,632	$2,259,605	$1,355,763	$4,000,000	$2,400,000	$3,200,000	8,555,763
10	$13,019,632	$1,183,603	$710,162	$4,000,000	$2,400,000	$3,200,000	7,910,162
PV cost of owning at 6%							$76,731,060

Table 9.13 Cost of leasing and associated cash flows for the DirectJet example

Year	Lease payment	After-tax lease payment	Maintenance cost	After-tax maintenance cost	Net cash flow
1	$8,000,000	$4,800,000	$4,000,000	$2,400,000	$7,200,000
2	$8,000,000	$4,800,000	$4,000,000	$2,400,000	$7,200,000
3	$8,000,000	$4,800,000	$4,000,000	$2,400,000	$7,200,000
4	$8,000,000	$4,800,000	$4,000,000	$2,400,000	$7,200,000
5	$8,000,000	$4,800,000	$4,000,000	$2,400,000	$7,200,000
6	$8,000,000	$4,800,000	$4,000,000	$2,400,000	$7,200,000
7	$8,000,000	$4,800,000	$4,000,000	$2,400,000	$7,200,000
8	$8,000,000	$4,800,000	$4,000,000	$2,400,000	$7,200,000
9	$8,000,000	$4,800,000	$4,000,000	$2,400,000	$7,200,000
10	$8,000,000	$4,800,000	$4,000,000	$2,400,000	$7,200,000
NPV cost of leasing at 6%					**$52,992,626**

the difference in the two outflows, or $23,738,432. This difference is the NAL. This example shows the financial advantage of a lease over ownership when evaluated financially by the lessee.

Evaluation by Lessor

The lessor's perspective involves evaluating the lease to determine what the lease payment must be in order to achieve a target rate of return on the investment. The lessor must obtain a higher rate of return on the lease because the lessor must bear all risk associated with the lease, such as finding a buyer for the aircraft at the end of the operating lease. The payment is a function of the present value of the cash flows taken into account with a rental factor and is calculated by using the following formula:

$$\text{PMT} = \frac{AC_{\text{Price }t}}{\text{Discount}_{\text{Factor }e}}$$

$$\text{Discount}_{\text{Factor }e} = \frac{1}{i} - \frac{1}{i(1+i)^n}$$

$$\text{PMT} = AC_{\text{Price }t} \times \left[\frac{(1+i)^n - 1}{i(1+i)^n} \right]$$

where:

PMT = periodic rental payment
i = interest rate per period
n = number of periods

In another example, a leasing company, LeaseCo, is planning on entering nego-tiations with DirectJet to supply an $80,000,000 aircraft. The lessor has to conduct a financial evaluation of the lease as well as alternatives. LeaseCo may sell the aircraft for cash to the airline, sell it on credit terms, or lease the aircraft to DirectJet. The following presents the cash flows for the alternatives and determines which is most advantageous to the lessor. In this example, the aircraft is depreciated using the *Modified Accelerated Cost Recovery System (MACRS)* for tax depreciation, which may be either straight-line or declining balance.[27] Table 9.14 outlines the cash flows if LeaseCo opts to purchase the aircraft in cash and the NPV of the arrangement as revenues are generated through a 10-year lease to DirectJet.

Table 9.15 outlines the cash inflows if LeaseCo purchases the aircraft on credit by making a down payment of $24,000,000 and future yearly payments of $11,200,000, while leasing to DirectJet under the same conditions.

Another consideration in buying vs. leasing analysis is the deteriorating effect that buying has on an airline's balance sheet. In some instances, purchasing the aircraft is not a viable option after the future effects have been taken into con-sideration. For example, DirectJet is contemplating changing its fleet ownership structure to add a $20 million aircraft. The aircraft's economic life is seven years; however, the aircraft will only be kept for three years, owing to high maintenance costs. The resulting balance sheet from purchasing with debt is shown in Table 9.16.

Table 9.14 Cash flow associated with cash purchase for the LeaseCo example

Year	Payment	MACRS	Depreciation tax savings	Lease revenue	After-tax cash flow
0	$80,000,000	0	0		($80,000,000)
1		$11,432,000	$4,572,800	$8,000,000	$12,572,800
2		$19,592,000	$7,836,800	$8,000,000	$15,836,800
3		$13,992,000	$5,596,800	$8,000,000	$13,596,800
4		$9,992,000	$3,996,800	$8,000,000	$11,996,800
5		$7,144,000	$2,857,600	$8,000,000	$10,857,600
6		$7,136,000	$2,854,400	$8,000,000	$10,854,400
7		$7,144,000	$2,857,600	$8,000,000	$10,857,600
8		$3,568,000	$1,427,200	$8,000,000	$9,427,200
9				$8,000,000	$8,000,000
10				$8,000,000	$8,000,000
NPV					$4,696,149

[27] The depreciation percentages listed in IRS Publication 946 are used to generate the declining bal-ance schedule for seven years.

Table 9.15 Cash flow associated with credit purchase for the LeaseCo example

Year	Payment	Interest	Depreciation	Depreciation tax savings	Lease revenue	Net cash flow
0	$24,000,000					($24,000,000)
1	$11,200,000	$5,040,000	$11,432,000	$4,572,800	$8,000,000	($3,667,200)
2	$11,200,000	$4,032,000	$19,592,000	$7,836,800	$8,000,000	$604,800
3	$11,200,000	$3,024,000	$13,992,000	$5,596,800	$8,000,000	($627,200)
4	$11,200,000	$2,016,000	$9,992,000	$3,996,800	$8,000,000	($1,219,200)
5	$11,200,000	$1,008,000	$7,144,000	$2,857,600	$8,000,000	($1,350,400)
6			$7,136,000	$2,854,400	$8,000,000	$10,854,400
7			$7,144,000	$2,857,600	$8,000,000	$10,857,600
8			$3,568,000	$1,427,200	$8,000,000	$9,427,200
9					$8,000,000	$8,000,000
10					$8,000,000	$8,000,000
NPV						$535,052

Table 9.16 Balance sheet effect of aircraft purchased with debt for the LeaseCo example

DirectJet Balance Sheet December 2012			
Assets		Liabilities and net worth	
Current assets	20	Current liabilities	15
Fixed assets	330	Long-term debt	265
Total assets	350	Equity	70
		Total debt & equity	350

$$\text{Debt ratio} = \frac{\text{Total Debt}}{\text{Total Assets}}$$

$$\text{Debt ratio} = \frac{\$280}{\$350} = 80\%$$

With this transaction, we can consider the deteriorating effect that this would have on the debt ratio of the airline. An 80% debt ratio is considered very high for a non-financial company, and it may cause lenders to be reluctant to lend to such a risky company. An alternative solution to purchasing the aircraft would be to undertake an operating lease on the aircraft. The lease qualifies as an operating lease since the three-year term that the airline is planning to operate it is for less than 75% of the economic life of the aircraft. However, despite this balance sheet differential due to existing accounting rules, most creditors will look to the underlying creditworthiness of the airline by normalizing for operating leases to look at adjusted financial ratios, as noted earlier.

Business Jets Market and Fractional Ownership

Fractional ownership serves as the middle ground between ownership and leasing, offering the advantages of aircraft ownership at a reduced cost. By definition, it is considered to be a percentage share in an expensive asset. Typically, a secondary company handles the management of the asset on behalf of the owners. The owners, in exchange, pay a monthly or annual fee for the management and the variable costs of operating the aircraft. Originally seen as the next major development in business aviation, declining business travel and falling aircraft residual values have dealt heavy blows to this particular segment.

In similar fashion to the rest of the aviation industry, the fractional ownership market is dominated by four major players: CitationAir, Flexjet, Flight Options, and NetJets. Of these, NetJets is the industry's most powerful player as well as its pioneer since 1998, with more than half of the market share (Thurber, 2009). The primary advantage of fractional ownerships lies in its lower barriers to entry when compared to the financial requirements for aircraft purchases and leases. This made fractional ownership a quick and easy way for companies to obtain an aircraft or additional aircraft without the operating and financial burdens.

Summary

A lease is a contract that allows an airline the use of an aircraft for a given period of time. The leasing or purchasing of aircraft is a complex process, and examining types of leases should lead to a better understanding of the options available to the parties involved. There are two major types of aircraft lease: a capital lease and an operating lease. If an airline needs an aircraft for a short period of time, it may have no better option than to lease the aircraft. For start-up airlines, which may be in a weaker financial position, or established carriers that prefer to maintain flexibility, leasing may be an attractive option.

Finally, leasing may be a less expensive alternative than borrowing money to purchase an aircraft. Leasing is not always financially superior to purchasing because a lease can place restrictions on the operations of the aircraft, and with a lease, airlines may not enjoy favorable tax advantages. Hence, the outcome of each option depends on market conditions and the airline's specific financial and operational position.

Appendix: Major Commercial Aircraft Leasing Companies

The airline leasing industry is largely dependent on the commercial aviation industry, driven by its sensitivity to economic cyclicality. Growth in the leasing industry is consequently largely attributable to passenger yield, low-cost carrier growth and expansion, and the reduction of risk it offers to traditional legacy carriers. Although fleet compositions change rapidly in the leasing market based on the laws of supply and demand, the top 50 leasing companies have a combined fleet size in excess of 6,700 and are poised to continue growing as the commercial aviation sector recovers. The aircraft leasing business is dynamic, capital intensive, and, in marked similarity to the commercial aircraft manufacturing industry, dominated by two major players, GECAS and ILFC, which together account for more than 50% of the assets. GECAS is a subsidiary of the General Electric conglomerate, and ILFC is a wholly owned subsidiary of the insurance giant AIG. The top lessors, including ILFC, GECAS, RBS Aviation Capital, and BOC Aviation, each have strong corporate parents, which further benefits their operations.

General Electric Capital Aviation Services

General Electric Capital Aviation Services (GECAS) is the leasing industry's front-runner, offering a full range of commercial, regional, cargo, government, military, and VIP aircraft. GECAS typically offers three- to five-year dry lease contracts on its fleet of Boeing, Airbus, Embraer, and Bombardier aircraft. GECAS reaps the benefits of leasing a significant number of the fleet that are equipped with engines from GE Aviation, another subsidiary of General Electric. An important benefit to General Electric is that this has allowed GECAS to also offer engine leasing under a full range of operational and financial services, including short-term rentals, engine exchanges, operating leases (including sale/leaseback), and structured, long-term finance options.

International Lease Finance Corporation

The International Lease Finance Corporation (ILFC) began operating in 1973 and is a wholly owned subsidiary of American International Group (AIG). It is GECAS' direct competitor in the duopolistic leasing market. ILFC offers the full line of Boeing and Airbus aircraft to its lessees in more than 130 countries.[28] ILFC was previously able to borrow cheaply as a result of the triple-A credit rating attached to AIG before the 2008 financial crisis. Post-crisis, ILFC's unsecured debt credit rating has been determined to be evolving (BB), stable (B1), and negative (BBB-) by Fitch, Moody's, and S&P, respectively, which restricts access to debt markets and results in unattractive funding costs.[29]

CIT Aerospace

Founded in 1908, CIT is a bank holding company with a division called CIT Aerospace that is taking a two-pronged approach: two aircraft leasing units catering to two segments of the industry. CIT Aerospace not only leases to commercial aircraft operators, but also to the business aviation segment of the industry and further offers financing solutions such as cash flow and asset-backed loans through its *transportation lending* unit.[30] Through its business aviation unit, it provides fractional share financing and leasing to NetJets' customers. CIT Aerospace's commercial fleet of 300 aircraft is leased and financed to 115 customers in 50 countries.[31]

---

[28] International Lease Finance Corporation Company Profile.
[29] International Lease Finance Corporation 10-Q, May 2011.
[30] CIT Annual Report 2010.
[31] CIT Aerospace Company Fact Sheet.

RBS Aviation Capital

RBS Aviation Capital is headquartered in Ireland and was founded in 2001 after the Royal Bank of Scotland (RBS) acquired IAMG, a small Irish lessor.[32] RBS Aviation Capital has 100 commercial airline customers in 38 countries. RBS Aviation Capital is scheduled to be sold in a formal auction after being identified as a non-core business as part of the Royal Bank of Scotland's 2009 restructuring plan.[33]

Babcock & Brown Aircraft Management

Babcock & Brown Aircraft Management (BBAM) currently operates as the manager of 340 aircraft, including FLY Leasing Limited's 60 aircraft, out of San Francisco, CA. The company began operations in 1989 as a division of Babcock & Brown, a global investment and financing group. After the liquidation of Babcock & Brown in 2009, former senior executives of Babcock & Brown Aircraft Management acquired the majority of the aviation assets and formed a new privately held company, BBAM.[34] In April 2010, FLY acquired 15% of BBAM and BBAM's management team acquired an approximately 4% stake in FLY.[35]

Ansett Worldwide Aviation Services

Ansett Worldwide Aviation Services (AWAS), headquartered in Dublin, Ireland, has a fleet of 206 Boeing and Airbus aircraft leased to over 90 customers in 44 countries. AWAS was purchased by private equity firm Terra Firma in 2006 and went on to acquire the Pegasus Aircraft Finance Company in 2007.[36] AWAS seeks to continuously have a younger, more fuel-efficient fleet; the average age of its aircraft was 7.8 years at the end of 2010, compared to 8.1 years at the end of 2009.[37]

Aviation Capital Group Corporation

Aviation Capital Group (ACG) owns, manages, and leases 245 single- and twin-aisle Airbus and Boeing aircraft under operating leases. ACG is a wholly owned subsidiary of Pacific Life Insurance Company.[38] ACG was founded in 1989 and is headquartered in Newport, CA, with additional offices in Seattle, London, Chile, China, and Singapore.[39]

---

[32] G. Collinson. Eastern interest in RBS Aviation Capital sale. *The Journal for Asset Finance*, July 25, 2011.

[33] Formal sale of RBS Aviation Capital begins. *Air Finance Journal*, July 25, 2011.

[34] FLY Leasing, Press Release: B&B Air invests in its manager and repurchases shares, April 29, 2010.

[35] FLY Leasing Annual Report, 2010.

[36] Terra Firma Company Profile, 2011.

[37] AWAS Aviation Capital Limited Annual Report, 2010.

[38] Aviation Capital Group Annual Report, 2010.

[39] Company Profile: Aviation Capital Group Corporation. *Bloomberg Business Week*, August 1, 2011.

Boeing Capital Corporation

As a wholly owned subsidiary of the Boeing aircraft manufacturing company, Boeing Capital Corporation's primary mission is to support other business units by providing asset-backed leasing and lending services to Boeing customers worldwide. The company's portfolio includes aircraft held under capital, operating, and leveraged leases. Boeing Capital Corporation was founded in 1968 as McDonnell Douglas Finance, which changed names following Boeing's acquisition of McDonnell Douglas in 1997.[40]

Table 9.17 and Figures 9.3 and 9.4 give some statistics on the top aircraft leasing companies.

Table 9.17 Aircraft leasing companies ranked by total fleet value

Rank	Company	Total fleet value ($m)	Total fleet value change	Total fleet	Average fleet value ($m)	Average fleet value change
1	GECAS	33,403	1.50%	1,502	22.2	0.40%
2	ILFC	31,522	−19.70%	1,068	29.5	−5.00%
3	AerCap	8,413	69.40%	321	26.2	3.20%
4	CIT Group	8,250	−3.70%	300	27.5	−2.10%
5	RBS Aviation Capital	7,878	−3.00%	253	31.1	−2.60%
6	BBAM	7,786	19.40%	340	22.9	−
7	BOC Aviation	6,932	24.30%	161	43.1	0.20%
8	Aviation Capital Group	4,740	−5.60%	243	6,023	77.40%
9	AWAS	4,518	−5.10%	206	21.9	−0.90%
10	Macquarie AirFinance	4,052	47.20%	157	25.8	3.10%
11	Aircastle Investment	3,237	11.30%	135	24	1.80%
12	Pembroke Group	3,152	83.10%	129	24.4	−6.30%
13	Boeing Capital	2,758	−21.40%	258	10.7	−1.00%
14	Sumisho Aircraft Asset Management	2,397	3.60%	77	31.1	−3.40%
15	Doric Asset Finance	2,340	7.70%	23	101.7	−1.70%
16	Hong Kong Aviation Capital	2,312	−	68	34	34.00%
17	MC Aviation Partners	2,227	27.20%	77	28.9	1.10%
18	ALAFCO	1,830	12.50%	48	38.1	1.20%
19	AerVenture	1,769	55.40%	47	37.6	−3.00%
20	DAE Capital	1,729	27.70%	39	44.3	3.30%

Source: Airline Business, February 2011.

---

[40] Boeing Annual Report, 2010.

Figure 9.3 Top ten aircraft leasing companies by fleet value

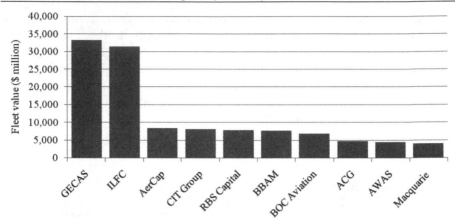

Source: Compiled from Airline Business, February 2011.

Figure 9.4 Top ten aircraft leasing companies by fleet size

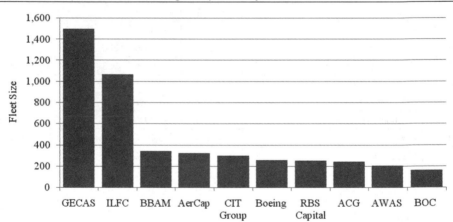

Source: Compiled from Airline Business, February 2011.

References

ANAC. (May 2011). Advanced Comparative Data.

Ely, K. (1995). Operating lease accounting and the market's assessment of equity risk. *Journal of Accounting Research, 33*, 397–415.

European Legal Alliance. (2005). Aircraft Lease Agreements: International Legal Requirements.

Gavazza, A. (2010). Asset liquidity and financial contracts: Evidence from aircraft leases. *Journal of Financial Economics 95*, 62–84.

Grossman, A., & Grossman, S. (2010). Capitalizing lease payments. *The CPA Journal, 80*(5), 6.

ILFC. (May 10, 2011). Form 10-Q.

Kolb, W., & Rodriguez, J. (1992). *Financial management.* D. C. Heath and Company, Lexington, MA.

Littlejohns, A., & McGairl, S. (1998). *Aircraft Financing.* 3rd ed. Euromoney Books, London, UK.

Mann, D. (2009). Aviation finance: An overview. *Journal of Structured Finance, 15*(1), 109.

Max, R., & Strotman, R. (1991). Sale/Leaseback: Financing tool for the '90s. *The CPA Journal, 61*(4), 48.

Mehta, A. (2005). *International Taxation of Cross-Border Leasing Income.* IBFD Publications, Amsterdam, The Netherlands.

Miller, M., & Upton, C. (1976). Leasing, buying, and the cost of capital services. *Journal of Finance 31*, 761–786.

Morrell, P. (2009). *Airline Finance*, 3rd ed. Ashgate, Aldershot, UK.

Park, E. (2007). Lease classification of aircraft leasing. Sloan School of Management, MIT, Boston, MA.

Pulvino, T. (1998). Do asset fire sales exist? An empirical investigation of commercial aircraft transactions. *Journal of Finance, 53*, 939–978.

Ray, J., & Rowley, J. (May 2007). The financial advantages of sale—Leaseback. TRIRIGA.

Stickney and Weil. (2007). Glossary of financial accounting: An introduction to concepts, methods, and use. 12th ed. 791, Southwestern College Publishing, Boston, MA.

Thurber. (2009). NetJets Announces Major Pilot Layoffs. Bloomberg Business Week, November 17.

10

Airline Fleet
Selection Process

Airbus earns a record 418 firm orders valued at $44 billion in list prices, with the largest order coming from AirAsia for 200 A320neo aircraft valued at $18.2 billion.

—Airbus Paris Air Show, July 2011 results

With a large population and robust economic growth, Asia is well on its way to becoming one of the largest air transportation markets in the world. The Boeing Commercial Airplane Group predicts the world's biggest growth in air travel over the next 20 years will occur in India and China. Embraer forecasts world demand for regional jets at $200 billion in 20 years (Bloomberg, 2010). In today's challenging airline environment, one of the most critical decisions is that of trying to match the right amount of capacity for a specific market. The fleet selection of an airline is an important driver of productivity and cost. Generally, larger aircraft are more cost efficient than smaller aircraft. The smaller seat capacity associated with smaller aircraft affects cost and productivity. This is the essence of airline fleet planning, a complicated and cross-functional activity that requires a deep understanding of technical and commercial airline areas.

Airline fleet planning is the process of guiding aircraft selection, acquisition, and management. Through this process, an airline manages aircraft capacity to anticipate changes in market demand and the economic environment. Fleet planning determines the types and number of aircraft the airline should acquire. In selecting the right aircraft types, airlines must consider several important issues such as payload, range, fuel burn, aircraft utilization, financing cost, operating cost, and compatibility with the rest of the fleet. Airline fleet selection also depends on how competitive the airline operating environment is, the desired airline image, and the anticipated load factor amongst others. This chapter provides a detailed discussion of the steps in the fleet selection process:

Network Planning and Aircraft Selection

- Operating Environment
- Market Forecast and Route Analysis
- Analyzing the Competitive Dynamic

Choosing an Aircraft Type

- Aircraft Selection Methodology
- Detailed Aircraft Performance
- Cost Efficiency
- Payload vs. Range

Modeling Techniques and Issues

- Assessing Aircraft Profitability—Cost Components
- Assessing Aircraft Profitability—Revenue Components
- Sensitivity Analysis

At the end of the chapter is a Summary for chapter review and References for further study.

Network Planning and Aircraft Selection

The airline fleet selection problem has been a topic of academic research and industrial interest for many years (Smith & Johnson, 2006). Aircraft selection and fleet planning can take various forms. In an ideal world, a long-term strategic plan guides airline management to marry a company's network growth plans with fleet requirements. The management team would do a bottom-up analysis of every season and evaluate destinations where it feels it could increase passenger flows or take market share from competitors, and then it would seek to have the right aircraft type operating on the route to ensure strong operating profits even at lower load factor levels.

Narrow-body, single-aisle planes are suitable for short- and medium-haul routes, such as the Airbus A319, A320, and A321; Boeing 717, 727, 737, and 757; and McDonnell Douglas DC-9, MD-80, and MD-90. Wide-body, twin-aisle passenger planes are suitable for serving a long-haul network, such as the Airbus A300, A310, A330, A340, and A380; Boeing 747, 767, 777, and 787; Lockheed 1011; and McDonnell Douglas DC-10 and MD-11. The Airbus A350 will also fit long-haul

needs, while regional jets in varying sizes have allowed carriers to also match traffic
levels on short- and medium-haul routes with smaller jet aircraft instead of turboprops. However, the airline business is cyclical as well as seasonal, and many times
aircraft orders are made at a time of robust growth, only to fall victim to the realities
of a manufacturer's order book whereby planes are delivered several years later—
potentially at a cyclical trough. Such market realities often impact the availability
of aircraft when they are needed by airlines such that an ideal aircraft type may not
necessarily be available or available at an affordable price. A snapshot of the active
fleet compositions of several global airlines between Boeing and Airbus narrow- and
wide-body aircraft is given in Table 10.1.[1]

Operating Environment

*We are delighted to add Thailand to our growing network and we look forward to bring-
ing new travel and business development opportunities, both for the tourism operators
in the region as well as the many expats who travel home to Australia frequently.*

—Brett Godfrey, Virgin Blue Airlines Group CEO, 2009

The air transport environment is exposed to ferocious competition. In addition,
the industry is very cyclical; when the global economy is doing well, passenger
traffic increases. Conversely, when the global economy moves into a recession,
air traffic decreases and travel pattern shifts from costly long-haul trips to less

Table 10.1 Active airline fleet composition

Airline	Boeing		Airbus		Total active fleet
	Narrow-body	Wide-body	Narrow-body	Wide-body	
Air France	—	74	145	36	255
ANA	2	122	27	—	151
BA	19	125	86	—	230
Delta	436	126	126	32	720
GOL	101	—	—	—	101
JetBlue	—	—	119	—	119
Lufthansa	59	30	132	73	294
Ryanair	272	—	—	—	272
Singapore	—	71	—	37	108
Southwest	560	—		—	560
United	96	111	152	—	359

Source: Air Transport Intelligence and ACAS data.

---

[1] As of October 1, 2011.

expensive short- and medium-haul trips (IATA Economic Briefing, 2008). In this market, getting more flights out of an aircraft is essential to airlines as revenues are reduced.

In reality, airline managers have to evaluate both the long-term strategic aircraft needs of the company while also managing short-term fleet requirements. For example, an airline may place an order with Boeing for 787 aircraft to handle future route operations on city-pairs where there is anticipated long-haul demand. These destinations may already be served by the airline with another wide-body aircraft or are cities targeted for future growth. However, production delays with the 787 program subsequently would require the fleet managers to try to backfill capacity by either delaying aircraft retirements or seeking operating leases of another aircraft type in order for the airline to operate on those desired routes.

In developing new aircraft, there will always be some risk of delays in production. If this were to happen at a time in the cycle where the airline may actually feel it best to constrict its network, to reduce costs vs. the initially planned growth, then the airline may actually seek to cancel orders where possible.

Airlines may also face periodic grounded aircraft (AOG) situations due to maintenance problems or regulatory requirements. For example, SAS decided to ground its fleet of 27 Bombardier Q400 turboprop aircraft in October of 2007 after three incidents in two months where the landing gear collapsed on landing. As a result, there was a short-term and immediate need to replace the missing aircraft with leased capacity of a different type so the airline could continue to fly its route network. In 2008, Southwest Airlines grounded 43 planes, or about 8% of its fleet, after inspections found cracks in some of the fleet;[2] the move caused about 300 flight cancellations and delays.

However, core fleet decisions are taken by management after thorough analysis of the cost and revenue implications of utilizing specific plane types on the planned route network. The analysis is done in an interdisciplinary manner, tapping into subsets of the management team, to determine:

1. Total cost of providing service on any given route
   - *Flight operations:* Considerations could include the future crew requirements of aircraft in terms of required number of employees or training needs. If shifting aircraft type, then pilots and flight attendants would need retraining or potential flight certification on the new type, and so on.
   - *Maintenance:* Evaluation of the future repair needs, the required downtime of the particular aircraft time at different intervals, impact of engine choice on existing operations, need to adjust spare parts inventory, and other factors.

---

[2] Associated Press, March 12, 2008.

- *Finance:* Responsibility for calculating the aggregate cost implications of new aircraft additions, and ultimately paying for and financing the potential deposits, progress payments, and the final delivery of new planes—buy vs. lease decisions, qualifying aircraft for government-subsidized financing through export credit agencies, and evaluation of the ultimate cost on an annualized basis to the company.

2. Treatment of market entry by other airlines
   - *Cost of barriers to entry:* Barriers may prevent airlines from serving new markets and therefore benefit existing airlines that already operate in the market by protecting their existing revenues from new entrants. There are a number of barriers to entry that can affect new entrants:
     - o Limits on takeoff and landing slots at airports. That is one reason why a number of low-cost airlines are flying out of secondary airports.
     - o The existence of long-term leases, giving airlines the exclusive use of airport gates.
     - o Rules prohibiting flights of less than a certain distance.
     - o High start-up costs.
     - o Regulatory barriers such as limits on foreign ownership and limits on foreign airlines.
   - *Price controls:* Cost of barriers to exit can also be substantial in the airline industry.
     - o Grounded aircraft and flight equipment do not generate any revenue; disposing them under distress could be very difficult, so there may be pressure to continue to operate the fixed-cost base in the hopes of offsetting the marginal or variable costs of flying.
     - o There may also be the added pressure of losing slots and gates at airports if they are not flown, which may impact the long-term market on certain routes.

3. Revenue projections[3]
   - *Sales and marketing:* Evaluation of revenue growth opportunities and ultimately filling the seats that need to be sold.

---

[3] Japan Air Lines (JAL) cut more than 90 international and domestic routes as part of its effort to accelerate its restructuring by shutting down unprofitable air routes such as flights from Narita to San Francisco, Milan, Indonesia's Denpasar, and Kona on the Island of Hawaii, and from Kansai International Airport in Osaka to Bangkok, Beijing, Guangzhou, and Hong Kong (Breitbart, April 4, 2010).

- *Revenue management:* Estimating what yields may be achievable for new routes as well as for continued operations on existing city-pairs.
4. Other cost or regulatory implications
   - *Human resources and legal:* Issues that may be raised could include the future fleet impact on any union contracts such as pilot scope clauses or addressing the economic impact of any potential import duties (for example in Russia there have been times where an import levy has been imposed or seat configurations have been limited on non-Russian-manufactured aircraft).

Fleet assignment determines which aircraft type is assigned to a given flight segment to maximize profit (Gao, Johnson, & Smith, 2009). Before determining the appropriate aircraft type, an assessment of the market demand must occur. Typically, airlines will already have an operating history to evaluate, and historical passenger trends may be analyzed. For example, if the passenger flows for a given city-pair show that there is an opportunity for the airline to profitably add capacity, then additional frequency may become justified.

Similarly, companies may wish to defend market share in a particular region to keep out competitors. This is often evident with legacy network carriers' efforts to prevent low-cost carriers from entering a given market. In those situations, a tactical decision may be made to add capacity even when it may be unprofitable in order to defend one's market position or in order to economically "bleed" a new entrant. All of these factors, in their totality, create the operating environment.

The operating environment can be impacted by exogenous events. For instance, if oil prices have spiked, the cost structure of every flight would be negatively impacted and may result in an overall capacity reduction. For example, SkyTeam (Delta Air Lines, Air France, KLM, and Alitalia) planned to cut capacity between the U.S., Canada, and Europe by about 8% in the fall of 2011 in response to significantly higher fuel prices and fluctuating seasonal demand.[4]

Regulatory changes, such as the broadening of traffic rights in an open skies agreement, could lead to airlines adding capacity to affected markets in a rush to broaden market share. Deregulation of airlines in the U.S. led to many new entrants and expansion of airlines beyond their historical boundaries. There may also be considerations such as governmental or airport subsidies that may have an economic impact on providing air services to certain markets.

For an airline manager, digesting all of the variables is a critical job. As a starting point, the existing route network would be analyzed to see how

---

[4] Air Transport World (ATW), May 20, 2011.

demand patterns evolved during the last several seasons, asking these types of questions:

- If passenger flows increased, then at what cost? For example, is a given route performing well in terms of passenger numbers and load factors, but at a very low yield?
- Are there increased travelers due to temporary reasons such as special events or because of unseasonal weather patterns?
- Is the route characterized as leisure or a business city-pair, where frequency is needed to meet the needs of the corporate customer?

Once there is a thorough understanding of the historical passenger demand, the management team must forecast the potential pool of passengers and estimate the numbers that will fly the airline based on the timing of each flight. Revenue management and sales then need to provide their opinions on potential yields.

Market Forecast and Route Analysis

When analyzing an existing route, managers first look to estimate the total number of passengers. This is done by first looking at the passengers carried by the company itself. What is important to note is that there usually will be a different approach between low-cost carriers and network airlines in this analysis. The network carriers may have inflated passenger flows if there are connections offered at one of the two points of travel. It is best to first segregate the true origination and destination (O&D) travelers first, and then to also look at the addition of connecting travelers.

Global distribution systems (GDS), such as Sabre, Galileo, and Apollo, and alliance partner data would be a resource to the manager who is totaling the number of passengers. Governmental, airport, and third-party service providers would supply additional passenger traffic figures. For example, in the U.S., the Bureau of Transportation Statistics, a division of the U.S. Department of Transportation, collects traffic data from domestic and foreign carriers flying to the United States. The International Air Transport Association (IATA), comprised of 230 international airlines, provides monthly traffic data and statistics from its participating members about a variety of international routes. Traffic data is also available from the Airports Council International, which compares passenger traffic to aircraft movements for more than 1,350 airports globally.

Looking at the existing pool of airline passengers is only a start to the process. Airlines, especially low-cost carriers, would then look at how much traffic may be stimulated further from the market. This would be done by looking at the catchment area of each airport. Looking at the total population pool and evaluating travel patterns on other modes of transport would allow the team to estimate potential new air travelers. For example, in a given region, there may be migrant workers who have historically opted for ship or bus travel as a less expensive alternative to air travel. Low-cost carriers would look to displace those travelers and to attract them to the airline instead through a cost-effective offering. This would be part of the process of forecasting the overall market demand.

Analyzing the Competitive Dynamic

Once a route seems to have economic potential, the competitive landscape needs to be assessed. If the route has already been under operation for the company, its statistical trends are important:

- Has the route been growing, or have passenger numbers declined?
- How has the overall capacity on the route performed?
- Are there additional flights that have been added recently, or have competitors withdrawn?
- At what times are competitors operating their flights, and at what frequency levels?

Other qualitative factors also will need to be considered: Are there entrenched competitors that may possess a home market or service advantage based on the airline's products or frequent flier program?

In order to answer this question, let's look at an example: Delta's decision to begin operations on a Reykjavik-New York route on June 1, 2011 through Keflavik and JFK airports. At that point, Delta became the only U.S. carrier to serve Iceland non-stop from the United States. Free from any competing U.S. airline in Keflavik, Delta appeared to be looking at a potential opportunity to capitalize on this market from a U.S. perspective. The decision to undertake this new route can be critically analyzed from a variety of standpoints in an effort to determine the economic potential of the route, as well as any particularities including the competitive landscape and statistical trends.

The competition on this route would mainly occur on two fronts. The primary competitor would be Icelandair, the flag carrier of Iceland and the dominant player on the route. Icelandair served the market from an O&D perspective, but also has historically offered one of the lowest cost methods of traveling to continental Europe by connecting at its Keflavik hub. This is an important consideration in that Icelandair is able to manage its capacity on the route more effectively than a carrier that may only target the natural O&D flows on the route. Icelandair may fill its aircraft by enticing additional passengers to fly on the route by revenue managing the seat capacity of the connecting/via travelers.

The low-fare carrier Iceland Express, which operates flights to the U.S. through its wet lease partner, Astraeus, would be the other significant competitor to commercial aviation operations in Iceland, including Delta's plan. The airlines are structured differently and, consequently, rely upon a variety of city-pairs in maintaining and capturing the commercial aviation market share for that region. Icelandair seeks to tap into the large East Coast catchment area around New York, Boston, and Washington, getting those travelers to connect via Iceland to mainland Europe by offering passengers a quick connection or via a stopover in Iceland for no additional charge.

Delta appeared to be capitalizing on a New York-Iceland passenger flow while Iceland Express, the main low-cost carrier with service in the area, was targeting point-to-point service—largely geared toward Icelanders traveling to the United States. Figures 10.1 and 10.2 show the route maps of Icelandair and Iceland Express. Thus, for Delta, the competition on a New York-Keflavik route would come from Iceland Express, which flies into Newark Liberty International Airport twice per week during the winter months and seven times a week during the summer, as well as the direct competition from Icelandair with its daily flights into JFK.

After the appropriate city-pairs are determined, it is important to consider the most appropriate airport in the area to operate out of. In a 2007 FAA Air Service Demand Report, the catchment area market share of JFK (where Delta will operate its Keflavik route) was determined to be 46%, based on passenger surveys, in

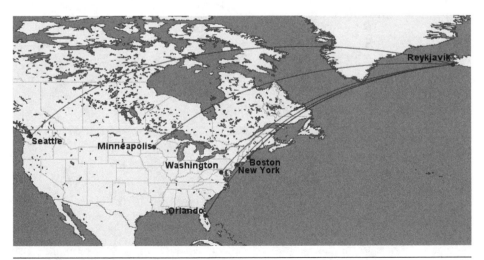

Figure 10.1 Icelandair: United States—Iceland routes[5]
Source: Icelandair route maps.

---

[5] As of June 14, 2011.

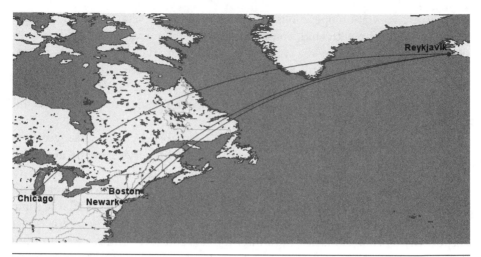

Figure 10.2 Iceland Express: United States—Iceland routes[6]
Source: Iceland Express route maps.

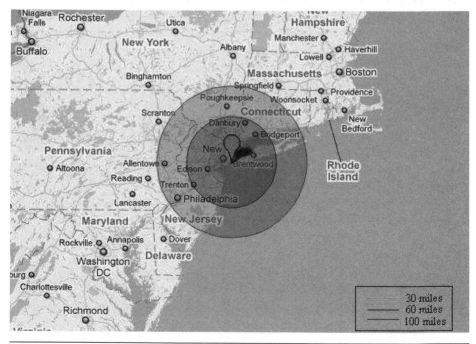

Figure 10.3 JFK International Airport catchment area

---

[6] As of June 1, 2011.

addition to having a $30 billion economic impact on New York. In Figure 10.3, the innermost ring is a 30-mile radius around JFK International, which encompasses much of New York City, with secondary 60-mile and 100-mile rings. This theoretical method bases the airport catchment area on distance, with the majority of customers coming from the innermost ring. An airport's catchment area in reality, particularly in the case of JFK and New York, is a combination of varying customer bases as well as the effects of the other commercial airports in the area.

The New York metropolitan area is serviced by three primary commercial airports: John F. Kennedy International Airport (JFK),[7] LaGuardia International (LGA),[8] and Newark Liberty International Airport (EWR).[9] The presence of two alternative airports may either simplify or complicate the decision process for an airline in selecting a particular route. In the case of the New York metropolitan airports where each airport has an identifiable niche, determining the airport of O&D for an international flight to Keflavik International is made easier. Another consideration in determining which airport to operate out of is whether or not the carrier already has operations in that particular airport. Delta has a significant presence at JFK, with the airline being ranked first in total number of passengers for the twelve-month period prior to February 2011 by the Port Authority of New York, which is responsible for the airport's operations.

The Keflavik Airport offers the opportunity for a U.S. carrier to serve an entire country with one route. As the sole major international airport in a country surrounded by the Atlantic Ocean, the theoretical catchment area (shown in Figure 10.4) for international travel spans the majority of the population, which was estimated to be slightly more than 300,000 inhabitants in 2009, according to World Bank data. It may also be argued that Delta could subsequently draw Icelandic passengers to JFK to connect them to Delta's expansive connection opportunities throughout the U.S. and beyond.

A final consideration in assessing the strategic landscape is the competitive dynamic between carriers. For example, Delta and Icelandair were not alliance partners. If they were, it may have made sense to share cost and revenue on a jointly planned route to draw out the respective strengths of each airline partner. When Delta flies to Paris, its SkyTeam partner, Air France, has a large asset in offering many selections for connecting travelers, improved customer experience through access to the home country airline's lounges and infrastructure, and other advantages.

On the flip side, airlines may choose to flex their own competitive muscle when deciding to enter a new route. In this case, it may not be clear that there is

---

[7] Over 90 airlines operate out of JFK, and the airport handled 46,514,154 passengers in 2010.

[8] La Guardia is the smallest of the New York metropolitan area's three primary commercial airports.

[9] Newark is the third largest hub for United Airlines, after Houston's George Bush Intercontinental Airport and Chicago's O'Hare International.

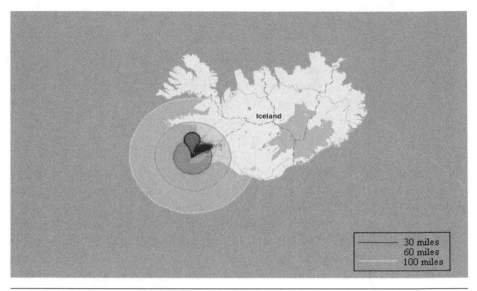

Figure 10.4 Keflavik International Airport catchment area

significant O&D demand out of the U.S. to Iceland, which presumably would be Delta's competitive advantage vs. the Icelandic carriers. However, Delta does operate a significant amount of flights from JFK to Europe, and Icelandair's connecting traffic to mainland Europe via Keflavik could bleed some of Delta's passengers. The U.S. airline may wish to add a route to simply take market share away from the two Icelandic airlines, making it a more difficult and less profitable operating environment. By making the route less hospitable, the competing airlines may have to re-evaluate growth strategies on their end. This may be uneconomic for the airline for a period of time, but if the competitive response is coming from a larger or better capitalized airline, it may ultimately succeed in having the competition retreat.

Choosing an Aircraft Type

Although factors such as an aircraft's safety record, passenger comfort and amenities, the cost and future residual values, and even the potential availability of delivery slots all influence the decision making behind fleet selection, the process of network planning on a route by route basis is one of the main drivers for determining the appropriate aircraft type to use on each route. Bear in mind that the total passenger demand on an O&D basis may be stated in many different ways. One large plane could carry all of the passengers at one time. Alternatively, a fleet of smaller aircraft could carry the same number of passengers, but at different times during the day. Passengers may be able to get from one point to the other by connecting at a network airline's hub or may be able to get to their final destination on a direct non-stop flight.

Numerous arrangements between aircraft manufacturers and airlines are almost a certainty in the selection process. Airlines not only select the seat configurations, they select engines and other aircraft specifics. Due to poor financial performance of the airline industry, high seating densities in the aircraft are likely to continue. Airline seats may be equipped with a reclining mechanism for increased passenger comfort, reclining either mechanically or electrically. Airlines also select the power plant. For example, Singapore Airlines selected the Rolls-Royce Trent 900 engine to power its nine additional Airbus A380-800s, which were delivered in 2010 and 2011. Etihad Airways purchased 78 GEnx-1B engines to power its 35 Boeing 787 Dreamliner aircraft.[10] If the characteristics of the route show a decidedly business-oriented traveler trend, then frequency and providing a non-stop service become extremely important. As business travelers also usually offer the airline increased yield, the company may now opt for smaller gauge aircraft. Alternatively, the airline may wish to take advantage of the lower unit operating costs of a larger aircraft instead. That decision may also need to be made in consideration of whether the airline has the necessary slots to operate at the desired airports and at the correct times. For example, it may make sense to have multiple morning flights into London to satisfy business demand to and from continental Europe; however, Heathrow and the other London airports are some of the busiest in the world, and slots are difficult to come by. Therefore, the option of operating a wide-body from one route to connect to other flights may be the only viable option at airports such as Narita (NRT), Haneda (HND), London Heathrow (LHR), or Chicago O'Hare (ORD).

Once the estimated demand for the carrier has been determined, the fleet team will need to assess what the current aircraft fleet of the airline is capable of handling. The existing fleet and future fleet plan would be applied to the desired route network first before looking for incremental lift and adding capacity. This is where the process of fleet selection begins.

Aircraft Selection Methodology

One of the greatest challenges facing the aircraft industry is the need to adjust the aircraft supply to the limited airport and runway capacities. Very large aircraft, such as the A380, impact the industry greatly. The immense capacity of the aircraft opens up opportunities to transfer more passengers through airports without increasing the number of aircraft. They are beneficial in the hub-and-spoke system, enabling increased service of passengers between major congested hubs. The main reason SIA and UAE use the larger A380s is because of economies of

---

[10] Travel Blackboard, July 1, 2010.

scale—to operate bigger aircraft with fewer flights and generate more revenue. According to SIA spokesperson Christina Hollenweger, "We have a load factor of 67% for the existing B777-300ER flights, which is not good for a long distance service. So using a single A380 will earn us more money for passengers and cargo."[11]

Narrow-body aircraft are ideally suited for short-haul networks and allow airlines to redeploy the wide-body aircraft to long-haul destinations. An airline will have a planned route network that it feels meets its goals in the short, medium, and long term. Hopefully, this has been arrived at by also taking into consideration the fleet that the carrier already has and which it can reasonably access as it seeks profitable growth.

Now the question becomes what additional aircraft should be chosen. As expected, the most important factor is to make sure the plane can actually fly the distance required with a full complement of passengers, crew, luggage, and cargo. Samples of gauge aircraft with manufacturers' estimates of range at maximum takeoff weight (MTOW) are given in Tables 10.2 and 10.3. Samples of range comparisons are given in Table 10.4.

Detailed Aircraft Performance

The appropriate gauge of the aircraft is the next factor to consider. Generally speaking, the larger the capacity of the aircraft, the lower the operating cost per person. The reason for this is that the marginal cost of carrying one extra passenger is spread over a larger base. Of course, there may be exceptions to this general rule of thumb, such as, if one is looking at a comparison between a new and older aircraft that may not be as fuel efficient, two competing gauge aircraft with differing number of engines that may increase long-term maintenance requirements, or comparable size planes that may have differing crew requirements (e.g., a McDonnell Douglas MD-80 with two pilots vs. a Boeing 727 with two pilots and a flight engineer). However, for purposes of this analysis, consider that the aircraft offerings are comparably aged with a similar crew and similar engines from Western manufacturers of aircraft where such anomalies are held in check. Tables 10.5 and 10.6 give an approximation, in general terms, of how the cost per available seat mile (CASM) varies, depending on the size and type of plane.

Cost Efficiency

Armed with technical and operating data, an airline can undertake further analysis of aircraft choices by looking at the trade-off between key metrics, including CASM, seat capacity, and range (see Figures 10.5-10.13). Figures 10.5-10.6 compare the seat capacity of different aircraft types and their corresponding CASM.

---

[11] The A380 justifies its size by its superior CASM. *Business Traveler*, April 9, 2009.

Table 10.2 Boeing aircraft range comparison at maximum takeoff weight

Aircraft	Wingspan	Length	MTOW (lbs)	Fuel capacity (lbs)	Capacity (2-class configuration)	Cruise speed	Range
737-700	112' 7"	110' 4"	154,500	6,875	126	0.785	3,400 nm (with winglets)
737-800	112' 7"	129' 6"	174,200	6,875	162	0.785	3,115 nm (with winglets)
737-900ER	112' 7"	138' 2"	187,700	7,837	180	0.78	3,265 nm (with winglets and 2 aux. fuel tanks)
747-400	211' 5"	231' 10"	875,000	57,285	524	0.85	7,260 nm
747-400ER	211' 5"	231' 10"	910,000	63,705	524	0.86	7,670 nm
747-8	224' 7"	250' 2"	975,000	64,055	467 (3-class)	0.86	8,000 nm
767-400ER	170' 4"	201' 4"	450,000	23,980	304	0.80	5,625 nm
777-200	199' 11"	209' 1"	545,000	31,000	400	0.84	5,240 nm
787-8	197'	186'	502,500	—	210	0.85	7,650 nm

Source: Boeing aircraft technical data.

Table 10.3 Airbus aircraft range comparison at maximum takeoff weight

Aircraft	Wingspan	Length	MTOW (lbs)	Fuel capacity (lbs)	Capacity (2-class configuration)	Cruise speed	Range (nm)
A318	111' 11"	70' 2"	150,000	6,400	107	0.82	3,250
A319	111' 11"	111' 0"	166,400	6,400	124	0.82	3,700
A320	111' 11"	123' 3"	172,000	6,400	150	0.82	3,300
A321	111' 11"	146'	206,100	6,350	185	0.82	3,200
A330-200	197' 10"	193'	524,700	36,750	253	0.86	7,250
A330-300	197' 10"	208' 11"	513,700	25,765	293	0.86	5,850
A340-300	197' 10"	208' 11"	609,600	37,150	295	0.86	7,400
A350-900	212' 5"	219' 5"	590,800	36,456	314 (3-class)	0.85	8,100
A380-800	261' 8"	238' 7"	1,235,000	84,600	525 (3-class)	0.85	8,300

Source: Airbus aircraft technical data.

Table 10.4 Embraer and Bombardier aircraft range comparison at maximum takeoff weight

Aircraft	Wingspan	Length	MTOW (lbs)	Fuel capacity (lbs)	Capacity	Cruise speed	Range (nm)
CRJ200ER	69' 7"	87' 10"	51,000	14,305	50	0.74	1,345
CRJ700	76' 3"	106' 8"	72,750	19,450	78	0.78	1,434
CRJ900	81' 6"	119' 4"	80,500	19,450	86	0.80	1,350
ERJ 140ER	65' 9"	93' 4"	44,312	9,109	44	0.78	1,250
ERJ 145LR	65' 9"	93' 4"	48,501	11,322	44	0.78	1,550
E-170	85' 4"	98' 1"	79,300	20,580	80	0.82	1,800
E-175	85' 4"	103' 11"	83,000	20,580	88	0.82	1,800
E-190	94' 3"	118' 11"	105,400	28,600	114	0.82	1,800

Source: Embraer and Bombardier aircraft technical data.

Table 10.5 Selected Boeing aircraft operating cost comparison

Aircraft	Crew cost per block hour	Fuel cost per block hour	Other costs	Maintenance cost per block hour	CASM	Total cost per block hour
737–700	$602.09	$1,365.35	$86.69	$397.09	5.66¢	$2,806.80
737–800	$686.35	$1,570.12	$51.92	$651.01	5.75¢	$3,536.54
737–900	$710.38	$1,549.71	$42.64	$526.00	4.67¢	$3,233.05
747–400	$1,204.14	$5,985.22	$105.54	$1,260.20	4.85¢	$9,443.76
757–200	$660.86	$2,111.01	$67.40	$1,081.64	6.18¢	$4,503.71
757–300	$740.66	$2,334.79	$33.78	$902.22	5.17¢	$4,675.02
767–200	$793.72	$2,732.44	$62.57	$1,457.11	7.01¢	$5,648.48
767–400	$903.12	$3,831.50	$67.17	$1,054.91	5.55¢	$6,416.10
777–200	$1,203.82	$4,127.54	$120.80	$1,716.41	6.16¢	$8,061.08

Source: Adapted from available Airline Monitor 2010 data.

Table 10.6 Selected Airbus aircraft operating cost comparison

Aircraft	Crew cost per block hour	Fuel cost per block hour	Other costs	Maintenance cost per block hour	CASM	Total cost per block hour
A300	$1,041.75	$3,301.53	$118.25	$1,203.87	8.27¢	$8,658.58
A318	$307.43	$1,021.45	$126.02	$223.03	4.74¢	$1,889.06
A319	$557.82	$1,281.35	$68.58	$527.40	6.62¢	$3,045.27
A320	$576.13	$1,456.65	$60.92	$694.25	5.85¢	$3,354.15
A321	$271.36	$1,549.87	$89.86	$559.46	4.05¢	$2,978.61
A330	$980.97	$3,497.56	$17.23	$783.26	4.48¢	$6,002.74

Source: Adapted from available Airline Monitor 2010 data.

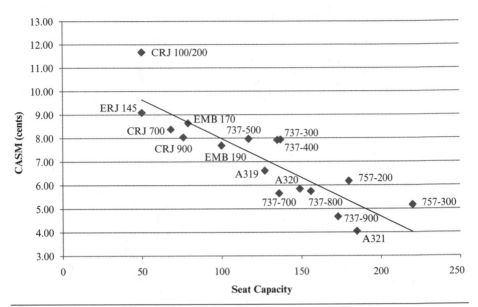

Figure 10.5 Narrow-body aircraft CASM vs. seat capacity
Source: Adapted from Airline Monitor 2010 and manufacturers' sources.

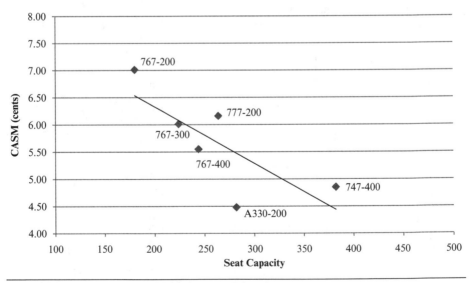

Figure 10.6 Wide-body aircraft CASM vs. seat capacity
Source: Adapted from Airline Monitor 2010 and manufacturers' sources.

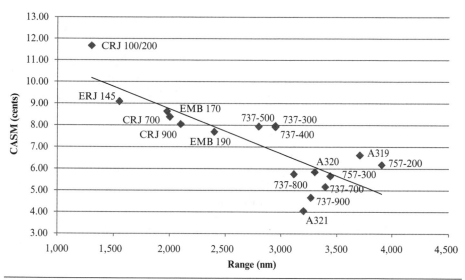

Figure 10.7 Narrow-body aircraft CASM vs. range
Source: Adapted from Airline Monitor 2010 and manufacturers' sources.

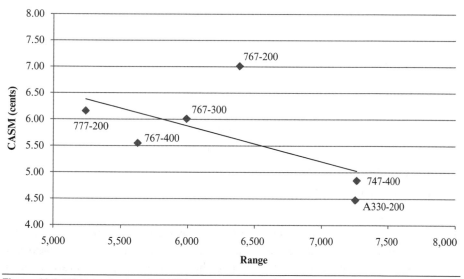

Figure 10.8 Wide-body aircraft CASM vs. range
Source: Adapted from Airline Monitor 2010 and manufacturers' sources.

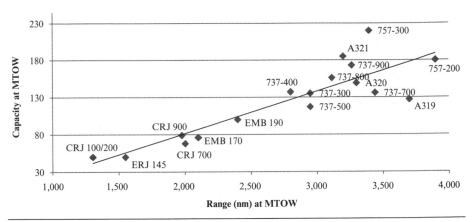

Figure 10.9 Narrow-body aircraft seat capacity vs. range at MTOW
Source: Adapted from Airline Monitor 2010 and manufacturers' sources.

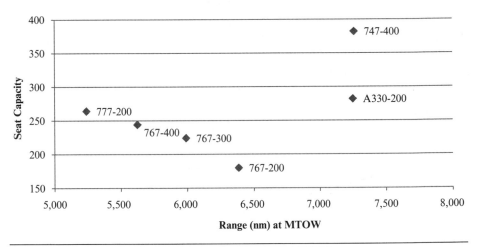

Figure 10.10 Wide-body aircraft seat capacity vs. range at MTOW
Source: Adapted from Airline Monitor 2010 and manufacturers' sources.

For example, an airline that has identified the need for a 50-seat aircraft on a particular route can choose between the EMB 145 and CRJ100/200. However, in comparing the seat capacity and CASM of these two makes of aircraft, with all other factors being equal, the EMB 145 is the more cost-effective option, capable of carrying the same number of passengers for two cents less per average seat mile.

An airline can compare the range of an available aircraft model to the CASM to determine which model offers the best trade-off between operating cost and performance. In these categories, we can see pockets of aircraft operating at similar ranges for similar costs. Lower range regional aircraft have the highest CASM

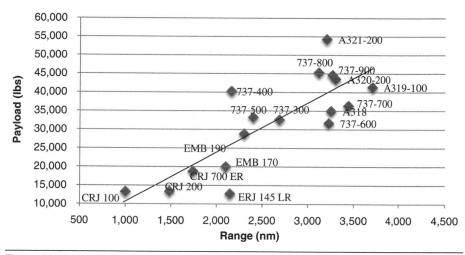

Figure 10.11 Narrow-body aircraft payload-range comparisons
Source: Adapted from manufacturer technical specifications.

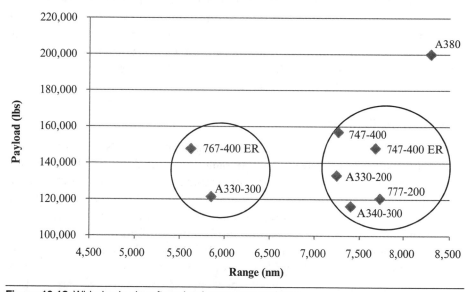

Figure 10.12 Wide-body aircraft payload-range comparisons
Source: Adapted from manufacturer technical specifications.

compared to long-range aircraft. Therefore, a holistic view that takes into account all performance and operating metrics, including landing fees and fuel capacity, has to be used when deciding which aircraft is suitable for operations.

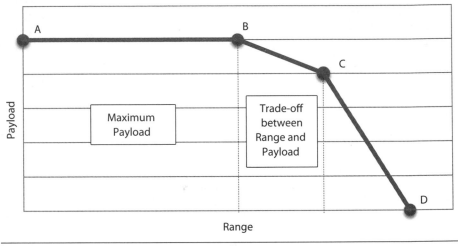

Figure 10.13 Aircraft payload-range trade-off chart

These comparisons also show the trend in airline manufacturer approaches to designing aircraft to operate within niche markets and cost metrics. In Figure 10.9, seat capacity and range are positively related. The more people the aircraft seats, the further it can fly. Intuitively, this makes sense for the purpose of completing long-haul international flights. Shorter regional flights that occur more frequently reduce the need for extensive seat capacity.

Payload vs. Range

An intuitive trade-off occurs between an aircraft's range and its payload. For this reason, individual aircraft have a variety of ranges based on the payload. An aircraft's maximum payload is determined by the maximum zero fuel weight (if given) minus the empty weight, less all justifiable aircraft equipment, and less the operating load, consisting of minimum flight crew, food and beverages, and supplies and equipment related to food and beverages, but not including disposable fuel or oil. The maximum payload can be determined by the MTOW less the empty weight, less all justifiable aircraft equipment, and less the operating load (consisting of minimum fuel load, oil, and flight crew). Weights for flight crew members, oil, and fuel load are listed under applicable federal aviation regulations.[12] Various payload/range combinations for a variety of aircraft models are given in Tables 10.7, 10.8, and 10.9.

Figure 10.11 highlight various payload-range comparisons of several narrow-body aircraft. From this we can see that the 737 Classic family (-300, -400, and -500 series) have comparable payload-ranges, whereas the 737NG family of

---

[12] 14 CFR 119.3.

Table 10.7 Selected Airbus aircraft payload vs. range comparisons

Aircraft	Payload (lbs)	Range (nm)
A318	34,973	3,250
A319-100	41,392	3,700
A320-200	43,555	3,300
A321-200	59,401	3,200
A330-200	133,009	7,250
A330-300	121,626	5,850
A340-300	116,311	7,400
A380	199,818	8,300

Source: Airbus aircraft technical specifications.

Table 10.8 Selected Boeing aircraft payload vs. range comparisons

Aircraft	Payload (lbs)	Range (nm)
737-300	32,639	2,685
737-400	40,256	2,160
737-500	33,287	2,400
737-600	31,702	3,225
737-700	36,387	3,400
737-800	45,283	3,115
737-900	44,622	3,265
747-400	157,399	7,260
747-400ER	148,099	7,670
767-400ER	148,099	5,625
777-200ER	120,450	7,725

Source: Boeing aircraft technical specifications.

Table 10.9 Selected Embraer/Bombardier aircraft payload vs. range comparisons

Aircraft	Payload (lbs)	Range (nm)
CRJ100	12,800	980
CRJ200	13,099	1,477
CRJ700ER	18,797	1,739
ERJ145LR	12,755	2,076
EMB 170	20,062	2,100
EMB 190	28,836	2,300

Source: Embraer and Bombardier aircraft technical specifications.

aircraft have increased their payload-range trade-offs. In the wide-body market, there exist two payload-range groupings, with the A380 significantly surpassing both of these groups. The first group of wide-body aircraft comprises the A330-300 and 767-400ER which offer similar payload and range characteristics; the second group is dominated in both payload and range by Boeing products (747-400 and 777-200). The next aircraft to be produced by Airbus, the A380, surpasses all Boeing products in terms of range and payload.

Note that payload vs. range is dependent on a number of factors, including weather conditions, altitude, speed, and fuel. No aircraft has a particular number that measures its ultimate range; range is highly subjective to a variety of factors. Payload in particular is limited by the maximum structural landing weight of the particular aircraft. For individual aircraft, as the need for increased range (and increased fuel) exceeds MTOW, payload has to be reduced in order to carry enough fuel for the particular trip without exceeding the MTOW. Normally, an aircraft's payload-range trade-off chart follows the pattern in Figure 10.13.[13] Four critical points for any aircraft's range-payload trade-off can be identified and interpreted. At any point along the AB line, the aircraft is at its maximum payload weight. This represents the range that the aircraft can fly at maximum payload. At point B, the aircraft is at its maximum payload (and MTOW), but not at full fuel capacity. Any additional fuel will increase range, but because the aircraft is already at MTOW, the payload has to be reduced. At point C, the aircraft has maximum fuel, MTOW, and a reduced payload. Increasing range at this point means reducing payload by increasing amounts until point D, where the maximum range of the aircraft is achieved with maximum fuel and minimum payload.

Modeling Techniques and Issues

Aircraft selection focuses on marrying the appropriate plane type to serve the demand on the routes being flown. The financial analysis that accompanies aircraft selection will not only look at the operating economics of the individual plane, but it will also look at the aggregate impact across the fleet and overall company profitability. A thorough evaluation of this process and its modeling methodology are found in Chapter 4.

Assessing Aircraft Profitability—Cost Components

The optimal selection embodies the best arrangement of the airline's daily scheduling, arrivals, departure routes, cockpit commonality, and fleet composition, which

---

[13] Detailed Aircraft Technical characteristics, including payload-range charts for individual aircraft, are available from the aircraft manufacturer.

maximizes revenue and minimizes cost. In order to calculate the profitability of the various aircraft types, the finance team will evaluate the total costs of the aircraft, based on the individual cost structure of the aircraft operator. This process looks at the direct operating costs when the plane is being utilized, such as fuel, employees needed to operate the plane, maintenance needed, etc. It will also incorporate a holistic analysis of the potential utilization, load factors, and potential projected yields to consider whether the airline will be able to deploy the aircraft profitably. As mentioned in Chapter 4, the costs associated with operations include:

- Direct operating costs:
  a. Fuel and oil
  b. Maintenance
  c. Landing fees
  d. En route and navigation fees
  e. Handling fees
  f. Crew expenses
  g. Traffic-related direct operating costs
  h. Passenger and cargo commissions
  i. Airport load fees
  j. In-flight catering
  k. General passenger-related costs
- Indirect operating costs:
  a. Aircraft standing charges
  b. Flight crew pay
  c. Cabin crew pay
  d. Maintenance
  e. Handling costs
  f. Overheads
  g. Sales costs
- Administration:
  a. General management
  b. Real estate costs, etc.

With the goal of profitability, fleets and their respective schedules seek to achieve the following objectives while minimizing costs (listed above):

- Customer satisfaction
- High aircraft utilization
- Optimized load factors
- High frequency
- Maximization of connections

When calculating estimates, there are many operating realities that need to be factored in. For example, the crew costs could be impacted by the number of pilots and flight attendants required or regulatory and labor contract requirements to carry additional staff for given flight times or distances. For a given airline, different aircraft types may attract different union scope clause treatment based on the number of passengers, which could impact such operational costs.

One of the reasons Embraer enjoyed such early success in penetrating the U.S. regional jet market was precisely the fact that the nature of union contracts at many major U.S. carriers allowed for lower cost regional jet pilots to be deployed if the number of passengers carried was less than certain milestones. The original scope clauses in most cases limited the number of airframes in addition to the number of seats. Table 10.10 is a compilation of various airline scope clauses, the majority of which have increased the number of allowed units and aircraft seats over time. Embraer's early success was largely attributable to the fact that its various aircraft products from the 30-seat EMB 120 to the latest E-Jets family were designed to fit the scope clauses of most airlines.

With the advent of regional jets, the pilots who previously were used by subsidiary or affiliate carriers flying smaller turboprop planes on shorter routes could be deployed longer distances on regional jets to defray the costs previously associated with using mainline pilots.

Other factors are the navigation and landing fees that may vary by aircraft type and size. As an example, the British Airport Authority, owner of London's Heathrow Airport (LHR), charges landing fees based on *maximum total weight authorized*, *engine Nox* emissions, and noise certification values for all flights. An aircraft's landing fee at LHR is therefore a combination of:

- Air navigation fees of £75.61 with an additional £1.03 per metric ton
- Emission charge on aircraft over 8,618 kg of £6.09 per kilogram of Nox
- Noise charges, as outlined in Table 10.11

Table 10.10 North American carrier scope clauses pre-9/11

Airline	Allowed number of airframes	Seat restrictions
American	67	45-70
Continental	unlimited	up to 59
Delta	70	up to 70
Northwest	54	50-69
United	390	up to 50
US Airways	70	69 max

Source: Company press releases, SEC filings, and industry sources.[14]

---

[14] Retrieved from Bombardier Regional Jet Market Reports.

Table 10.11 Landing fee noise charges at London Heathrow Airport

Aircraft	Noise category					
	Chapter 2	Chapter 3 high	Chapter 3 base	Chapter 4 high	Chapter 4 base	Chapter 4 minus
Less than 16 metric tons			£1637.35			
MTOW > 16 metric tons	£4,912.05	£4,912.05	£1,637.35	£982.41	£818.68	£491.21
MTOW > 16 metric tons (night period)	£12,280.13	£12,280.13	£4,093.38	£2,456.03	£2,046.70	£1,228.03

Source: Heathrow Airport April 2011 Conditions of Use.

Management will also add the indirect costs that would need to be paid whether the aircraft is used or not, such as the acquisition and financing costs of the plane, plus the required insurance. One may choose to attribute the variable costs on a per-seat-mile basis as well to aid in the comparison between types. The aircraft acquisition costs may be factored into this calculation as well, by taking the estimated financed cost and spreading it over the anticipated utilization of the plane, which will be based on block hours.

Assessing Aircraft Profitability—Revenue Components

The revenue generation capability on a route-specific basis may be calculated by looking at projected passenger flows, load factors (which compare capacity to the actual number of passengers occupying the seats), the route distances, amount the aircraft will be used, and anticipated yield and mix of passengers.

Thus, revenue generation is determined by first looking at total capacity, which is arrived at by multiplying the number of miles or kilometers a day the plane is operated (which is itself a function of the utilization—measured in block hours flown—and flight speed), the number of seats each aircraft has, and the distances the aircraft is flying. Capacity is measured in either *available seat miles* (ASM) or *available seat kilometers* (ASK). For example, a Boeing 737-700 two-class configuration with 126 seats flown on six 600-mile segments a day (3600 miles per day) would generate a seat capacity of 453,600 ASM, which is 126 multiplied by 3600.

Next, how many passengers are being flown on those flights is determined. This may be done by making an assumption about projected load factors or calculating the estimated production. Production is measured in *revenue passenger miles* (RPM) or *revenue passenger kilometers* (RPK) and is defined as one revenue-paying passenger—as opposed to someone flying for free—flying one mile. Load factors, measured as a percentage, are calculated by dividing production by capacity (RPM divided by ASM).

Finally, the analyst needs to estimate the projected yield of the passengers. Yield is measured by aggregate passenger revenues divided by total production (total RPM), which will be expressed in cents per mile. One may also evaluate the yield at an individual passenger level, which involves looking at the ticket price and estimated ancillary fees paid and then dividing by the mileage for that segment flown.

Yield is an important measure of profitability. If there is a passenger mix that is tilted toward business travelers booking at higher price points, the yield will be higher. This may be the case if the fleet is configured into multiple classes rather than planes that have one large economy class. Evaluating a fleet decision may involve an analysis of the trade-offs between increased seat capacity vs. fewer seats, but adding a premium class that may attract higher yielding passengers.

One method to financially model revenue projections would be to multiply the factors above:

Passenger Revenue = Capacity (in ASM) × Load Factor (%) × Yield (cents per mile)

It should be noted that in the example if we simply were to multiply yield by load factor, we would arrive at *PRASM* (*passenger revenue per available seat mile*), which is measured in cents per mile and is a reflection of the unit revenue of the airline:

PRASM (cents per mile) = Yield (cents per mile) × Load Factor (%)

In modeling the projected profitability of a potential new fleet addition, the revenue generation is offset by the direct costs of operating the plane, to determine whether the addition of new aircraft will make financial sense. Of course, a detailed financial model is usually made to encompass all of the factors covered in this chapter and in Chapter 4 and would also look at some of the fixed costs of the airline, SG&A expenses, and any other costs that might be attributable as well. This may be done on an individual aircraft basis to create a bottom-up analysis by tail number.

Sensitivity Analysis

A sensitivity analysis can then be run to see what may happen if yield assumptions are lower than estimated if load factors do not meet expectations, etc. Some other factors to consider in running sensitivity analyses would include:

- Maximizing the utilization of the aircraft and fleet by flying more or "sweating the assets": the fixed costs of the fleet, such as the purchase price of the planes, are spread out over longer block times.
- Matching aircraft with routes while considering variations in stage lengths: generally, the longer the distance flown, the greater the fare that is charged; however, this needs to be analyzed by also recognizing that the greater the number of cycles, the greater the number of passengers flown and the greater the number of tickets sold. For example, one aircraft may fly for a longer segment length and fly for five hours at an average ticket price of $500 vs. the same plane being used on two two-hour segments at an average ticket price of $300. The latter would give the airline a lower utilization of the aircraft (four hours vs. five hours), but if the airline were to have identical loads, it would have two $300 fares over the same period of time, or $600 per average ticket instead of $500.
- Configuring seats: there are trade-offs between outfitting a new aircraft with more seats vs. two- or three-cabin configurations with premium

seating, where there may be an increase in yield but fewer seats to sell, and cargo capacity may also be impacted. Emirates, the largest customer for the A380, has an ultra-long-haul configuration of 489 seats: 14 in first class, 76 in business, and 399 in economy, with 13 tonnes of bellyhold capacity for cargo. Singapore Airlines' A380 seat map shows 471 seats in total in three classes: 12 first class, 60 business, and 399 economy.

- Accurately measuring potential aircraft switching costs: shifting aircraft types or manufacturers may result in significant costs from training flight crews and pilots to implementing new maintenance procedures and training staff to completely replacing spare parts inventories, etc.
- Choosing between the economic profile of smaller aircraft offering greater frequency with multiple flights vs. one larger aircraft carrying the same number of passengers on one flight: offering a shuttle service with multiple frequencies offers greater flexibility, especially for business travelers, and may command a revenue premium vs. one frequency on a larger aircraft; however, operating simply one flight on a larger plane will offer lower unit costs with one set of crew, one plane being utilized just once, fewer crew members, one landing fee, etc.
- Potential differences in financing costs: for example, choosing an aircraft type with a small installed base vs. one with many established users will impact a lender or investor's view of the long-term marketability of that aircraft to other airlines and, thus, impact the potential collateral value. Other considerations may be the availability of subsidized government financing for purchasing or leasing an aircraft type (i.e., availability of export credit agency finance, etc.).

Summary

The process of fleet selection needs to be extremely detailed as it is connected to the very essence of the airline. The fleet represents the core product offering to customers. From a financial perspective, it is also what will drive the fixed asset base of the airline for many years.

Aircraft selection begins with a consideration of the route network itself. By analyzing where the airline flies today and where it seeks to grow, fleet management decisions may be taken to marry the needs of the airline. The route network analysis will draw from many internal constituencies within management. The goal will be to analyze the cost and revenue implications and to sensitize the potential permutations of the use of the aircraft across the route network. CASM vs. seat capacity and CASM as compared to the range of potential plane choices will be considered.

The overall implications of any fleet decisions on the cost structure will be balanced by the potential opportunity to serve more passengers or to increase yield. Better fuel efficiency may be offset by a higher financing cost for a newer plane, but the passengers may also have better seating, which may help the airline in the competitive environment. Aircraft are very expensive to purchase or lease and, in this asset-intensive business, choosing the right aircraft is a key determinant of success or failure.

References

Air Transport Association of America. (1967). Standard method of estimating comparative direct operating costs of turbine powered transport airplanes. Retrieved from http://adg.standford.edu/aa241/cost/atamethod.html.

ATA briefing.

Bloomberg. (July 19, 2010). Embraer sees world demand for regional jets at $200 billion in 20 years. Retrieved from http://www.bloomberg.com/news/2010-07-19/embraer-sees-world-demand-for-regional-jets-at-200-billion-in-20-years.html.

Bombardier. (2011). CRJ jetSense: Scope clauses continue to allow larger regional aircraft. Retrieved from http://www.crj.bombardier.com/CRJ/en/crjstory.jsp?langId=en&crjId=revolution&lastId=range.jsp?crjId=705.

Gao, C. E., Johnson, E., & Smith, B. (2009). *Transportation Science, 43*(1), 2–15.

Heathrow Airport Limited. (2011). Conditions of use including airport charges from 1 April 2011. Retrieved from http://www.heathrowairport.com/assets/Internet/Heathrow/Heathrow%20downloads/Static%20files/ConditionsOfUse_LHR.pdfI.

IATA Economic Briefing. (2008). The impact of recession on air traffic volumes. http://www.iata.org/whatwedo/Documents/economics/IATA_Economics_Briefing_Impact_of_Recession_Dec08.pdf.

Liebeck, R., et al. (April 1995). Advanced subsonic airplane design and economic students. NASA CR-195443.

Ross, T. (1998). *Designing for minimum cost: A method to assess commercial aircraft technologies*. Purdue University Press, Lafayette, IN.

Smith, B., & Johnson, E. (2006). *Transportation Science, 40*(4), 497–516.

Export Credit Agencies and Aircraft Finance

In June, the WTO ruled on the U.S. complaint and found Airbus benefited from $4 billion in support from European governments to launch the A380 superjumbo jet. The WTO ruled very clearly at the end of June that all government money provided to Airbus for... development of new aircraft was an illegal subsidy and must stop...

—Bloomberg News, 2010

Many airlines, leasing companies and other aircraft purchasers require long-term financing to effect the sale from the manufacturer. As many customers fall into the lower levels of the credit spectrum, and as airline operators have to grapple with a high fixed-cost base as a necessary dynamic of their business, there is a need for lower cost financing sources to help bridge the gap between purchaser needs and the strong desire for manufacturers to sell aircraft and parts.

Aircraft producers wish to boost export sales and their customers have a need to finance these purchases. National governments, recognizing the ability of aircraft manufacturing to increase high-value exports and to create jobs at home, have used their governmental export credit agencies (ECAs) to provide financing support in these cases. Often, these agencies are tasked with providing financing when no other source of capital may be available for the sale and subsequent export. However, creditworthy airlines and lessors have also taken advantage of agency programs to secure lower cost financing. The role of ECAs and their respective programs that support aircraft sales are covered in this chapter:

Background of Aircraft Export Credit Finance

- Export Credit Agencies throughout the World
- Overview of Large Aircraft Sector Understanding Rules
- ECA Finance Supported by the U.S., EU, Brazil, and Canada

Cape Town Convention

- Overview of UNIDROIT Convention
- ECA Financing and the Cape Town Treaty

The 2011 Aircraft Sector Understanding

- Export Credit Rules and the New Aircraft Sector Understanding
- Grandfathered Transactions

Financing Alternatives Utilizing ECA Support

- How Aircraft Financiers Utilize the ECA Guarantee to Lower Borrowing Costs
- Loan and Bond Instruments and Structures

At the end of the chapter is a Summary for chapter review and References for further study.

The E.U. claims Boeing received $24 billion in illicit aid, including $16 billion in grants from NASA and $2.1 billion in export tax discounts, plus subsidies from the Pentagon. The panel also is likely to condemn $5.7 billion in aid for Boeing's 787 Dreamliner.

—The Telegraph, September 2010

Background of Aircraft Export Credit Finance

Access to credit is a major issue for exporters. National governments have a vested interest in boosting exports and supporting strategic industries. In an effort to increase trade, various countries have long-established governmental agencies that assist foreign trade and promote exports by assisting foreign purchasers.

As one may imagine, aircraft are some of the higher value items that a country will wish to promote abroad. As such, ECAs in different regions have long provided financing support to aircraft manufacturers in an effort to boost cross-border sales. Although there are many ECAs supporting numerous industries across the globe, there is a concentration in aircraft manufacturing with Airbus and ATR in the European Union, Boeing in the United States, Embraer in Brazil, and Bombardier in Canada. Although Russia, Japan, and China are also growing aircraft manufacturing capacity, the amount of aircraft exported from these countries is either limited, with the majority of planes sold to domestic carriers, or production is in preliminary stages.

The dominant ECAs, when it comes to aircraft finance, are:[1]

- Brazil: Brazilian Development Bank, Banco Nacional de Desenvolvimento Econômico e Social (BNDES), or Seguradora Brasileira de Credito à Exportação (SBCE)
- Canada: Export Development Canada (EDC)
- France: Compagnie Française d'Assurance pour le Commerce Extérieur (COFACE)
- Germany: Euler Hermes Kreditversicherungs-AG (Hermes)
- United Kingdom: Export Credits Guarantee Department (ECGD)
- United States: Export-Import Bank of the United States (U.S. Ex-Im Bank)

ECAs play a vital role of getting new projects financed so the developing economy can grow and enjoy economic prosperity. ECAs finance or underwrite about $55 billion of business activity in developing countries. Without this help, many projects would go unfunded.

Ex-Im Bank's financing support of our acquisition of 777-300ER aircraft is critical to TAAG's success in achieving a strongly competitive position in the Africa-to-Europe marketplace.

—Dr. Pimentel Araujo, Chairman of TAAG Angola Airlines

Export Credit Agencies throughout the World

ECA-supported aircraft financing can take many forms. Often, the national government of the aircraft manufacturer will use its ECA to offer government-supported or -guaranteed loan financing to the export customer. In 2009, Germany joined France in offering credit to buyers of new Airbus planes to overcome the reluctance of world banks to lend money, thereby underwriting the plane manufacturer's sales. AerCap issued the first European ECA-backed bond in 2009, guaranteed by the UK's ECGD with approximately $225 million raised to finance three A330s.[2] Another example of ECA support was to Chilean carrier LAN in the form of a $300 million export credit loan to purchase eight A320s in October 2011.[3] Russia's flag carrier, Aeroflot, financed three Airbus A330s with an export

---

[1] Some of these entities are not government agencies or institutions, but private sector companies that manage sovereign export credit products.

[2] Leahy calls for more ECA bonds. *Airfinance Journal*, October 24, 2011.

[3] LAN closes $300m ECA deal. *Airfinance Journal*, October 26, 2011.

credit-backed finance lease in 2011. Emirates, in September 2011, secured export credit financing guaranteed by France's COFACE and the U.S. Ex-Im Bank for two A380s and two 777-300ERs, worth a combined $1.3 billion.[4]

ECA support may take the form of a direct loan or, more commonly, a guarantee or an insurance product to be provided in connection with a loan, which a financial institution such as a bank will then use to supply the aircraft buyer with a financing package at prices reflecting the government support. This may mean that the airline or lessor buying a plane will be able to secure lower cost financing by virtue of having a loan with a U.S. or European governmental guarantee rather than paying the credit risk premium reflected by its own creditworthiness. In return for this support, the ECA charges an up-front exposure fee or risk premium to the airline and will usually take security in the collateral and impose certain financial covenants, much as any commercial secured creditor would.

Overview of Large Aircraft Sector Understanding Rules

The OECD's Large Aircraft Sector Understanding (LASU) has been in effect since 1986 to provide standard financing terms for the export sales of large aircraft, initially defined as aircraft having more than 70 seats or comparably sized freighter aircraft. When ECA loans or loan guarantees were provided, LASU rules required that the buyer pay a minimum of 15% of the cost in cash, allowing 85% to be financed for a term not exceeding 12 years by the ECA. Under a gentlemen's agreement, ECA financing was also limited to exports outside of so-called *home countries* where aircraft were produced. This meant that aircraft purchased by operators in France, Germany, the United Kingdom, and the United States were never allowed to take advantage of ECA support under this informal arrangement, as these markets represented the manufacturing sites for Boeing and Airbus. A separate agreement between the ECAs also prohibited Spain from enjoying ECA financing benefits, as Spain also had aircraft manufacturing operations that supported Airbus.

This point has caused significant friction and political infighting within airlines in Europe. Take the example of EasyJet and Ryanair, two European low-cost carriers that actively compete with one another. Ryanair has had been a longtime Boeing 737 operator and, despite its strong track record of profitability, has been able to repeatedly secure U.S. Ex-Im Bank supported financing, as it is headquartered in Ireland. This arrangement is in contrast to EasyJet, which operates a fleet of both Airbus and Boeing aircraft, but is not able to enjoy the same level of ben-

---

[4] Walid, T. Emirates says J.P. Morgan to finance purchases from Airbus, Boeing. Bloomberg News, September 27, 2011.

efits of government-supported aircraft finance because it happens to be domiciled in the UK, a *home country* rule nation.

The difference in aircraft finance costs between two airlines can, as a result, be quite substantial, which also impacts the overall cost structure of the airlines and can create an uneven competitive dynamic. However, even as a *home country* airline, EasyJet may have been able to indirectly benefit from ECA financing, if any of its leased aircraft were supported by the ECAs. The U.S. Ex-Im Bank allows an operating lessor to lease its ECA-supported Boeing aircraft to a European *home country* airline after the fourth anniversary following delivery (but never into the U.S.) as long as it does not constitute more than 25% of the overall U.S. Ex-Im Bank supported aircraft. The European ECAs have similar covenants, but may allow the lease to be to any *home country* airline following its delivery in Toulouse or Hamburg. In 2011, Air France became the first "home country" airline to request export credit support in the form of a refinanced export credit loan on one of its A380s.[5] It should be noted that neither Canada nor Brazil followed the *home country* rule.

ECA finance is limited to non-military commercial aircraft used in passenger or cargo configurations. These may include helicopters and smaller executive aircraft, as well as engines, spare parts, and other equipment and, in some instances, certain service contracts.

ECA Finance Supported by the U.S., EU, Brazil, and Canada

Under original LASU rules, the French and German ECAs would initially provide conditional insurance that would have government support for up to 95% of the debt amount as opposed to U.S. Ex-Im Bank's and ECGD's 100% government guarantee program. (For the sake of clarity, the debt amount, which this percentage is multiplied against, would be no more than 85% of the net purchase price.) Over time, all of the European ECAs migrated to a unified unconditional guarantee program (known as the *harmonized agreement*) so that after 2003, the European ECAs and U.S. Ex-Im Bank had a similar product on offer to the customers of Airbus, Boeing, ATR, and other manufacturers in these regions. European ECAs (France's COFACE, the UK's ECGD, and Germany's Euler Hermes) have also pre-agreed export credit guarantees for all A320 aircraft assembled in China.[6]

Historically, another material distinction between the European ECAs and the U.S. had been that the Europeans gave customers the opportunity to fix the interest rates of the financing at no cost and no obligation to actually take that fixed rate at delivery. This meant that up to three years prior to the actual aircraft delivery

---

[5] Air France Applies for export credit. *Airfinance Journal*, July 12, 2001.
[6] ECA guarantees for all China-built Airbus aircraft. *Airfinance Journal*, October 11, 2011.

date, the airline or lessor buying an Airbus or ATR product could have the option of a fixed interest rate at no cost. As the first set of reforms came to market, this free option of fixing rates in advance was removed, bringing the Europeans and the Americans further in line with one another's product offerings.

The two other major export credit providers in the aircraft realm have been BNDES through its BNDES-Exim program and Canada's EDC. The BNDES-Exim program was started as FINAMEX in 1991 to provide long-term trade financing to boost Brazilian exports. The updated program name was established in 1997 when the Brazilian Development Bank underwent reforms to boost its stature and accessibility. After 1997 financing tenors were also extended to 12 years, and up to 30 months for pre-export lines of credit. According to Embraer, in 2010, 53% of the company's commercial aviation deliveries were supported by BNDES, as compared to 32% in 2009.[7] For the period 1996 through 2008, approximately 28% of the total value of export sales was financed by the BNDES-Exim program.[8]

Separately, Brazil also historically offered another export credit scheme, the ProEx program. ProEx offered customers of Embraer, and other Brazilian exporters, interest rate adjustments in an effort to offset Brazil's historically higher country risk premium, as compared to the U.S., Canada, or Europe. Brazil was attempting to bridge the gap between itself and other export-supported financings, where the country offering a guarantee may enjoy a better sovereign credit standing, leading to a lower comparable rate of finance for the ultimate end user of the guarantee. Foreign customers that purchased selected products made in Brazil, such as Embraer aircraft, received the benefits of interest rate discounts to offset this potential differential. The ProEx program was at the heart of a long-running dispute between Brazil and Canada over subsidies for Embraer and Bombardier. Four cases were ultimately brought to the World Trade Organization (WTO) for adjudication between 1996 and 2001, one by Canada and three by Brazil. Eventually a series of rulings by the WTO against ProEx led to multiple revisions, with the latest revision resulting in the ProEx III program, which was ultimately approved by the WTO in July 2001 as it was no longer viewed as the provision of an illegal subsidy.[9] Similarly, Brazil's cases against Canada's EDC in the WTO also resulted in changes to the way the EDC program offered government-supported financing to Bombardier customers.[10]

Founded in 1944, Canada's EDC program is a source of market-based financing, export credits, and other financial support for airlines purchasing Bombardier

---

[7] Embraer-Empresa Brasileira de Aeronáutica 2010 Form 20-F filing.

[8] Embraer-Empresa Brasileira de Aeronáutica 2008 Form 20-F filing.

[9] World Trade Organization. (2001). Brazil—Export Financing Program for Aircraft, Second Recourse by Canada to Article 21.5 of the DSU. Report of the Panel, July 26, 2001.

[10] World Trade Organization. (2002). Canada—Export Credits and Loan Guarantees for Regional Aircraft. Report of the Panel, January 28, 2002.

passenger aircraft. EDC support for a non-Canadian airline wishing to make a purchase from Bombardier may occur through a series of varying guarantees, lines of credit, and loans. This support to the Canadian aerospace sector is estimated to exceed $5 billion with an additional $2.5 to $3.5 billion per year.[11] In the event that EDC has been unable to support the financing, another resource that may be employed to facilitate the sale is the Canada Account—a special account created in 2003 whose sole purpose is to support specific export projects that are seen to be in the national interests of Canada, but beyond the scope and risk tolerance of EDC's normal corporate loans. The combination of these programs allowed Bombardier to make more attractive offers to potential customers by guaranteeing financing to airlines that needed to borrow money in order to purchase aircraft. EDC's general rule is to finance up to 85% of the value of the sale. As an example, in 2011, UK low-cost carrier Flybe announced that its latest Q400 purchase was financed using an 85% loan-to-value ratio, using export credit from EDC. Loans through EDC may be direct to the airline or via a different financial institution. In practice, EDC usually provides support through direct loans as it sources funding at a lower cost than LIBOR through the Canadian Treasury and is able to run its operations profitably for the Canadian taxpayer.

EDC, in a calculated response to the threat of competition offered by Embraer and BNDES, extended its reach of financing resources to Bombardier and its customers. In 2009, EDC announced that CAD$173 million (USD$160 million) in loans was being made available to Bombardier in a coordinated effort to complete an order for up to eight Q400s and CRJ900s for Scandinavian Airlines (SAS) through the EDC program. Funding for this program came through the Canada Account, where, with the authorization of the Minister of International Trade and concurrence of the Minister of Finance, a special allowance may also be granted. Funding through the Canada Account is still negotiated, executed, and administered by EDC; however, the risks are assumed by the federal government. The account has been used four times in $100+ million loans since 2001, at rates better than those available commercially, for the following aircraft sales:

- Air Wisconsin, December 2001
- Northwest Airlines, December 2002
- Comair, July 2004
- Comair and Atlantic Southeast Airlines, April 2005

Airlines can take advantage of a range of guarantees when another financial institution is to be involved in the financing of the aircraft sale. A loan guarantee from EDC offers an airline the ability to have an increased amount available to borrow from another financial institution. Through the bank guarantee

---

[11] Siegel, E. (2009). EDC and Canadian aerospace: Working together to address the challenges and opportunities of global trade, October 14, 2009, Export Development Canada, Ottawa, Canada.

program, EDC provides cover to a Canadian or international bank that is financing the export for an airline operating out of a developing market. The amount financed determines some of the conditions of the guarantee. For amounts under $10 million, financing is guaranteed for 95 or 100% cover on 85% of the contract.

EDC will provide 100% cover when the bank is financing on an uncovered basis the down payment or local costs. The uncovered bank financing is repayable not fewer than two years subsequent to the repayment start date of the guaranteed facility, and the uncovered bank financing is at least equal to 15% of the contract value. The bank determines and retains the loan interest rate in cases where the financing is less than USD$10 million. However, if the financed amount is over USD$10 million, EDC and the bank jointly determine the interest rate.[12]

EDC established lines of credit that give airlines access to financing in 27 countries across Africa, the Middle East, Asia-Pacific, Europe, and Latin America. These lines of credit allow repeat aircraft buyers to take advantage of predetermined financing terms including currency, length of credit, and fixed or floating interest rate preferences that streamline the financing process. If a line of credit has been established with a foreign institution, EDC lends money to the financial institution, which then lends to the airline.

As part of the financing process, all ECAs assesses the creditworthiness of the borrower/investor and conduct a financial analysis of the transaction before approving a proposal to support an airline purchasing aircraft from the supported manufacturer. The basis of this assessment includes reviewing years of financial statements and reports, the company profile, bank references, any existing relationships between the manufacturer and the airline, contract estimates, payments, terms, and delivery schedule. Often, a feasibility study from the manufacturer will also be analyzed, showing how the intended use of the aircraft type will help the airline in its business and operations. An information memorandum from the airline containing this material is submitted to the ECA, alongside the application and applicable fees. The review process between the ECA, the airline, and in many cases the financier is iterative as the assigned case officer from the ECA works through the material and develops an approval package. While the package is prepared and submitted for approval, the financing institution assisting the airline or lessor will also work in parallel on the actual financing instrument itself, be it a loan, bond, etc., so that the capital may be provided to the aircraft purchaser once the government support is ultimately received.

---

[12] Export Development Canada. (2010). Bank Guarantee Program Terms and Conditions.

Cape Town Convention

Overview of UNIDROIT Convention

ECAs have been actively involved with industry groups such as the Aviation Working Group and governmental bodies in improving the aircraft financing markets. One of the major initiatives for these groups has been furthering the Cape Town Convention on International Interests in Mobile Equipment and the Aircraft Equipment Protocol, which was adopted on November 16, 2001 by UNIDROIT to reduce the risk of asset-based financing and leasing transactions.[13] The purpose of the Cape Town Treaty is to help standardize, on an international level, the registration of ownership and security interests in mobile assets such as aircraft and engines. Aircraft financiers may register their financial interest in equipment through the use of the International Registry of Mobile Assets, located in Ireland.[14] The International Civil Aviation Organization is the supervisory authority of the International Registry and creates a database of the priority of interests that is recognized internationally by all ratifying states. This facilitates cross-border leasing and financing of all aviation assets as it eases the ability to demonstrate the legal claim on collateral that a financier may have. The treaty came into full effect on March 1, 2006.

In countries where the treaty is not adopted, there may be differing laws that apply to each transaction. This situation can complicate the ability of lenders and other creditors in establishing their right to their collateral, which leads to higher risks. Under this convention, there are declarations that a nation may make to specify how the application of the laws will occur in their respective country. The declarations may impact asset-based financing and leasing transactions, and the aircraft finance community has been actively educating and encouraging nations to declare in a manner that is most conducive to meeting the requirements of international finance. Generally, once there is an event of default, in the case of an aircraft or other asset covered by the treaty, it is easier to repossess the subject collateral within a predefined time frame.

For example, following the filing of a restructuring order with the courts, the airline will have a predefined time frame under which to affirm or reject a lease. This allows a creditor the ability to quickly take possession and control of the rejected leased aircraft, and then export and deregister it. This reduces risk to

---

[13] International Institute for the Unification of Private Law, UNIDROIT. (2005). Protocol to the Convention on International Interests in Mobile Equipment on Matters Specific to Aircraft Equipment.

[14] International Registry of Mobile Assets permits individuals and organizations to register financial interest in assets using the MSN (manufacturer's serial number). Its role is to electronically record international interests in aircraft objects, thereby establishing priority of interests.

financiers, which also correlates to reduced cost of finance to the end user, even though the newly implemented laws have not been tested in most of the countries that have ratified Cape Town.

ECA Financing and the Cape Town Treaty

The Cape Town Treaty is being ratified by many countries, often through the inducement by certain ECAs of reduced exposure fees or risk premium charged to airlines as part of a financing. For example, in 2003, the U.S. Ex-Im Bank began to offer to reduce its exposure fee by one-third on aircraft financings for airlines in countries that sign, ratify, and implement the treaty. At that time, the minimum exposure fee on any aircraft finance transaction by the U.S. Ex-Im Bank was a flat 3% of the total transaction amount for most applicants. This discount allowed some airlines to reduce their cost of the U.S. Ex-Im Bank fee to 2%, thereby significantly reducing the overall financing cost to the carrier from approximately 48 basis points per annum to 32 basis points (assuming a 6.2-year average life of the loan and no net present value of the fees). Consequently, airlines would lobby their governments to enact changes to their national aircraft finance laws to benefit from this financial incentive. The OECD and Brazil's 2011 Aircraft Sector Understanding adopted the idea to provide "Cape Town discounts" by all of the major ECAs when countries ratify the Cape Town Treaty and adopt the appropriate set of qualifying declarations. An up-to-date listing of the countries that have ratified the treaty may be viewed on the website of the International Registry.[15]

The 2011 Aircraft Sector Understanding

Export Credit Rules and the New Aircraft Sector Understanding

As international trade evolved, the ECAs have also adapted their rules accordingly. The financing landscape offers airlines, leasing companies, and other purchasers of aircraft a largely harmonized set of rules between the major global ECAs. This evolution took many years, but the revised rules from the 2011 Aircraft Sector Understanding (ASU), which went into effect on February 1, 2011, implemented many of the suggestions that the finance community, manufacturers, and counsel had sought for many years. The 2011 ASU was adopted by the countries of the OECD and Brazil and superseded both the 2007 ASU and the 1986 LASU. The "new" 2011 ASU agreement is colloquially referred to as *NASU* by practitioners. A comparison is drawn between the rules in Tables 11.1 and 11.2.

---

[15] As of July 6, 2011, the International Registry of Mobile Assets asserted that 46 countries and regional economic organizations have ratified.

Table 11.1 Comparison of ASU 2007 bifurcated system and ASU 2011 single system

	ASU 2007 bifurcated system		ASU 2011 single system
	Cat. 1	Cat. 2/3	All aircraft
Risk categories	5	15	8
Pricing in terms of spread or fee	Up-front fee	Annual spread	Annual spread and equivalent up-front fee; NPV-based conversion model
Payments	Quarterly	Semi-annual	Quarterly (option for semi-annual with 15% surcharge on MPR with prior notification)
Maximum official support	85%	85%	80% for BBB– up 85% for BB+ to C
Maximum term	12 years	15 years for Cat. 2 10 years for Cat. 3	12 years (15-year option with 35% surcharge on MPR on an exceptional basis and with prior notification)
Risk mitigants (RMs)	0 for BB and up 1 for BB– to B+ 2 for B to B– 3 for CCC to C	No RMs	Two types of RMs: A and B 0 for BB and up 1 (1 A) for BB– 2 (1A + 1B) for B and B+ 3 (2A + 1B) for B– 4 (3A+ 1B) for CCC to C (Option to replace one A risk mitigant with 15% surcharge on MRP with prior notification)
Cape Town Convention discount	Differentiated maximum: 5% for BBB– up 10% for BB+ to B+ 15% for B to B– 20% for CCC to C	Flat 10% maximum for all borrowers	Flat 10% maximum reduction in MPR for all borrowers
Minimum direct lending interest rates	Standard for pure cover. Direct lending only in exceptional circumstances with prior notification CIRR-1	Choice of CIRR-2 or swap rates	Market interest rate (7-year swap for 12-year fixed, 6-year swap for 10-year fixed, LIBOR for floating) + margin benchmark (based on commercially funded pure cover transactions) (CIRR only for aircraft less than USD 35 million with prior notification)
Minimum premium rates (MPR)	Pure cover up-front fees fixed	Direct lending annual spreads updated annually (based on historical 1st lien bank loan LGDs)	MPR = risk-based rates (RBR) updated annually (based on historical 1st lien bank loan LGDs) + market-reflective surcharges (MRS) updated quarterly based on corporate bond market median credit spreads (MCS)

Source: Aviation Working Group, London, UK.

Table 11.2 Comparison of 2007 ASU and 2011 ASU up-front fees (MPR)

Risk category	Risk classification	MPR, non-Cape Town Convention			MPR, Cape Town Convention		
		2007 ASU C1 up-front, %	2011 ASU C1 up-front, %	MPR increase	2007 ASU C1 up-front, %	2011 ASU C1 up-front, %	MPR increase
1	AAA to BBB–	4.00	7.72	93%	3.80	6.95	83%
2	BB+ to BB	4.75	10.44	120%	4.28	9.4	120%
3	BB–	5.50	11.03	101%	4.95	9.93	101%
4	B+	5.50	11.85	115%	4.95	10.67	115%
5	B	6.25	13.38	114%	5.31	12.04	127%
6	B–	6.25	13.50	116%	5.31	12.15	129%
7	CCC	7.50	14.45	93%	6.00	13.01	117%
8	CC to C	7.50	14.74	97%	6.00	13.27	121%
			Average:	106%		Average:	114%

Source: 2011 Sector Understanding—Aviation Working Group, London, UK.

Pre-2007 ASU Rules[16]

- LASU among U.S., UK, Germany, France, Spain (Boeing, Airbus)
- WTO framework between Brazil and Canada (Embraer, Bombardier)
- LASU: 3% fee (discretionary increases for weaker credits) and market pricing for non-LASU financings
- No universal risk classification process (LASU)
- Discretionary structural flexibility: wraps, stretched overall amortization repayment (SOAR) loans allowed (LASU)
- Only U.S. Ex-Im Bank provided discount for Cape Town (1/3) (LASU)
- Home market rule observed (LASU), except by Brazil and Canada

2007 ASU[17]

- LASU added Brazil and became relevant for Canada and Japan
- Embraer, Bombardier, MJET[18], ATR operating under OECD framework
- Increased premium based on risk classification:
  o 4.0–7.5% (Category 1)
  o Spread 16–249 basis points (Category 2)
- Bifurcated system, including pricing
  o Category 1, large aircraft—5 classes, 12-year term
  o Category 2, other aircraft—15 classes (includes 737-600, A318), 15-year term
- Mandatory structural risk mitigants for Category 1 but not Category 2; no wraps, no SOARs for either
- Variable maximum Cape Town Convention discounts:
  o Category 1, 5–20%
  o Category 2, 10% often deemed
- Home market rules same as pre-2007

2011 "New" ASU (Referred to as NASU)[19]

- Single set of rules apply to all OECD countries plus Brazil
- Further increased premium based on risk classification plus market adjustments
- Initial 7.72–14.74%; 137–257 basis points[20]

---

[16] Aviation Working Group, London, UK.
[17] Aviation Working Group, London, UK.
[18] The practical effect of this was for the Japanese to provide re-insurance to U.S. Ex-Im Bank for the B777 and the content that Japan contributed to that aircraft.
[19] Aviation Working Group, London, UK.
[20] These figures may change each month based on market adjustments that are required.

- Single system, including one risk classification process for all borrowers
  - o 8 risk classes
  - o 12-year term
- Increased mandatory structural risk mitigants required; no wraps, no SOARs
- 10% maximum discount for Cape Town Convention
- Home market rules same as 2007, unless C-series competition (matching contemplated)[21]

Grandfathered Transactions

The new ASU's set of rules does not affect transactions on deliveries that were already a part of the previously agreed upon set of rules in place prior to the 2011 ASU, which may be classified as either "grandfathered" (governed under the 2007 ASU) or "great grandfathered" (governed by the 1986 LASU). In the case of "great grandfathered" aircraft, notification had to be submitted to the OECD Secretariat, as well. As a practical matter, the grandfathering provisions are applicable to aircraft with firm contracts in place prior to December 31, 2010 and with deliveries as outlined in Table 11.3.

Financing Alternatives Utilizing ECA Support

How Aircraft Financiers Utilize the ECA Guarantee to Lower Borrowing Costs

As a general matter, ECA support offers aircraft financiers the ability to provide funding to the aircraft purchaser at government-subsidized rates. Instead of taking the credit risk of the airline or leasing company, the lender or creditor providing

Table 11.3 Great grandfathered and grandfathered contract/delivery requirements

Great grandfathered—LASU	Grandfathered—2007 ASU
Firm contracts by 04/30/2007	Firm contracts concluded by 12/31/2010
Deliveries originally scheduled through 12/31/2010	Cat. 1 aircraft delivered by 12/31/2012
	Cat. 2 & 3 aircraft delivered by 12/31/2013

Source: Aviation Working Group, London, UK.

---

[21] The "home country rule" in the 2011 and 2007 ASU is a gentlemen's agreement. Canada and Brazil have not historically followed this agreement; the assumption is that if EDC or BNDES were to offer ECA support for an aircraft to be operated in France, Germany, Spain, the UK, or the U.S., then the ECAs in those countries would feel justified in "matching" that support to win a transaction to level the playing field.

debt finance is benefitting from a government guarantee. Thus, the debt financing will reflect the borrowing costs of the ECA home country rather than the company or individual purchasing the asset. For example, if an airline in an emerging market such as Ethiopia were to purchase an aircraft, it would have to pay a portion of the purchase price in cash—much as someone purchasing a home would pay a down payment in equity. The airline would then seek to raise debt for the balance of the purchase price.

If there were no ECA support, the airline would need to work with a lender such as a bank that would look at the historical and projected financial performance of the company. Is the airline going to be able to generate enough income from the asset and from other sources to repay the loan over the span of financing tenor? The lender would also evaluate the potential value of taking a mortgage on the aircraft and what the legal ramifications would be on trying to perfect the security interest. An analysis of the ability to repossess, remarket, or dispose of the plane in the event of default would also need to be made. As a creditor, the first set of analysis would be on the financial viability of the carrier and its ability to service the debt. The collateral issues would be the second analysis to make sure that the lender could recoup any potential losses in a default by repossessing the plane and selling it. These analyses would also look at the potential geopolitical environment, and where the plane may operate, to assess any potential risk of loss that may arise as a result of natural disaster, population trends, war, etc. Once all factors are considered, the lender may adjust tenors or the advance rate/loan-to-value that it is ultimately comfortable with for the particular transaction.

In the case of the ECA, a similar process will be followed to analyze the risks of the transaction; however, this will be done mostly by the ECA and the airline in close partnership. The benefit of this process is that the ECA is accustomed to evaluating firms that may not otherwise have access to financing due to various circumstances. These factors may include the company's location in a region where lenders may not normally wish to lend but potentially where an ECA may have a political motivation to assist another foreign government's airline, a short operating history, etc. However, when the analysis is completed, and if the ECA agrees to extend credit to assist the manufacturer's sale, then the actual cost of the financing benefits from the governmental guarantee. The debt financing would have the risk of the ECA that has agreed to serve as intermediary and not the airline or other purchaser itself. The cost of the financing would similarly reflect this risk, so in the case of a U.S. Ex-Im Bank loan, the cost would reflect the fact that the full faith and credit of the U.S. government stood behind the debt, among other factors.

In a volatile financial environment, other factors may include the breadth of (or lack of) financial relationships, overall liquidity/illiquidity, the pricing differential between bonds vs. loans, and the ability of the lender to source 12-year funding. The U.S. Ex-Im Bank's guarantee would cover the full principal balance as well as the interest due to a creditor. In the event of a default, and following a grace period, the lender could simply take its claim to the U.S. Ex-Im Bank for payment of outstanding principal and accrued but unpaid interest under the loan, rather than worrying about how to repossess its collateral and recover the principal by disposing of the plane in the market. Of course, there is an element of structure in these financings and a potentially short waiting period in the event of default. As such, these financings do not simply price at the same level as a similarly dated U.S. Treasury bonds or notes, which feature bullet maturities and pay promptly, but they are far closer to that level than the transaction pricing that would carry the risk of the purchaser itself.

In return for this benefit, the aircraft purchaser also would need to pay an exposure fee to the ECA to offset some of the risks that the ECA would be taking. The exposure fees are governed by the 2011 ASU, as are other elements of the financing. The ECA would also have collateral rights to the plane in the event of default and may also seek other forms of guarantees in the case of state-owned national carriers. However, as a general matter, ECA finance offers airlines a lower cost of borrowing at longer tenors (up to 12 years, with a potential for up to 15 years in certain circumstances) and higher advance rates (up to 85% loan-to-value) than they would be able to normally secure from commercial lenders. This is particularly true for those airlines or other buyers residing in emerging markets or nations where commercial lending is restricted or offered at a much higher price point due to the higher potential sovereign risks. However, even creditworthy airlines with access to alternate sources of capital, such as Ryanair, still avail themselves of ECA financing when they are able to do so, as the cost is generally more attractive.

Loan and Bond Instruments and Structures

Adjustable Floating Rate Notes

As noted, ECA guarantees may be used to offer government support and guarantees to a loan structure. The bank loan would have a guarantee from the ECA so that in the event of default, the lender may seek payment from the ECA instead of waiting in line with other creditors over a potentially long period of time in an unfamiliar jurisdiction. Another advance has been the *adjustable floating rate note (AFRN)*, which has been used primarily by the U.S. Ex-Im Bank. This structure was formulated to utilize the ECA guarantee to tap into the deep, liquid market of traditional money market funds that would typically invest in U.S. Treasury notes and other sovereign debt by creating a bond instrument supported by the ECA guarantee.

The first such structure was formed by J.P. Morgan for Hainan Airlines. The transaction broke up the typical 12-year maturity into shorter tenor strips. Upon maturity of each tranche, the transaction would be remarketed into the prevailing market conditions. By breaking up the 12-year tenor of the financing into a series of shorter maturities, the transaction could be placed with money market funds buying Treasury notes, which were, at the time, limited to investing in short-maturity profiles inside of 5 years. The idea was to help bridge the pricing difference between traditional ECA-supported loans, which were priced off of LIBOR plus a spread, and the pricing of a national government's debt offerings.

According to the U.S. Ex-Im Bank, under the AFRN structure, the Ex-Im Bank permits the airline to document a 12-year Ex-Im Bank guaranteed floating rate aircraft transaction as a series of shorter but *extendable* Ex-Im Bank guaranteed floating rate loans and notes, which in the aggregate will provide for a 12-year repayment term. The AFRN structure requires the margin on the interest rate on the floating rate loan to be reset at predetermined dates based upon the prevailing spread over U.S. Treasury bills for similar financings that would carry the guarantee of the U.S. Ex-Im Bank.[22]

The AFRN structure was designed to create a synthetic instrument to closely mimic Treasury notes—the U.S. Ex-Im Bank guarantee carries the full faith and credit of the United States, just as a Treasury note does, albeit with less liquidity and a structural difference in that the potential waiting period to get paid in the event of default is longer. Given these differences, the pricing of AFRNs would always be at a premium to the securities issued by governments. However, this structure does help to bring pricing lower by tapping into a liquid investor base and diversifying away from bank balance sheets that have a higher cost of funding than nations. The narrowing of this gap was further aided by the fact that the first AFRN was also physically deposited with the Depository Trust Company. This deposit provided clearing and settlement efficiencies and aided in the tradability of the fixed-income instrument, similar to any typical corporate bond issued in the U.S. dollar institutional capital markets.

Following the original capital markets execution in 2000 for Hainan Airlines, the U.S. Ex-Im Bank, as well as ECGD, has allowed issuer clients to convert their initial loans to a capital markets take-out in order to allow them to take advantage of the deeper investor base. Thus, several issuers including Emirates, Ryanair, GECAS, LAN Chile, Aercap, and GOL Airlines have used this investor base to fund their aircraft deliveries with both Airbus and Boeing.

Private Export Funding Corporation

If an aircraft purchaser wishes to obtain a fixed-rate financing and is benefitting from a U.S. Ex-Im Bank guarantee, the airline or lessor may apply for a fixed-rate financing from the Private Export Funding Corporation (PEFCO). PEFCO was established in 1970 with the assistance of the U.S. Ex-Im Bank to supplement the

---

[22] United States Export-Import Bank, 2000 Annual Performance Report.

export financing then available through the U.S. Ex-Im Bank and from commercial banks and other lenders.

The benefit initially was to bridge the financing gap at a time when commercial banks weren't able to provide a fixed-rate product to their issuer clients. PEFCO offered that ability and has since widened its product range to include a broad range of financing programs as a direct lender and as a secondary market buyer of export loans originated by lenders (PEFCO does not buy loans directly from exporters).[23] PEFCO's stock is collectively owned by some of the largest commercial lenders, financial services companies, and industrial companies, including 23 banks, six industrial companies, and two financial services companies. The largest shareholders are J.P. Morgan with 16.7% and Bank of America with 13% of the shares.[24]

Effectively, the mandate of PEFCO is to fund new loans on its balance sheet. Once funded, it will turn to the capital markets and, through its commercial paper and term note issuance programs, issue debt out of its trust to fund itself in the institutional capital markets. In effect, PEFCO acts as a conduit to its clients. PEFCO's lending activities and programs mirror the U.S. Ex-Im Bank's various short-, medium- and long-term guarantee and insurance programs. For example, PEFCO's Long-Term Loan Program is designed around the terms of the U.S. Ex-Im Bank's Long-Term Guarantee program. As mentioned, PEFCO also has access to commercial paper to fund short-term liquidity needs. The advantage of PEFCO is that even with a profit margin built in, it can provide one of the most cost-effective fixed-rate options to a borrower by passing on the relatively low cost of funds it achieves in the capital markets to the aircraft purchaser.

In addition, it allows aircraft purchasers to pre-fix the rate on the U.S. Ex-Im Bank loan, typically following receipt of the final commitment of the guarantee by the board. PEFCO effectively enters into a forward starting swap with a financial institution to fix the rate for the aircraft purchaser. This enables the aircraft purchaser to fix the interest rate without using its own credit capacity with the financial community. In 2010, PEFCO's outstanding aircraft loans were valued at $3.4 billion, with three new aircraft loan commitments for the year totaling $291 million.[25]

Stretched Overall Amortization Repayment Loans

When airlines and manufacturers requested that the terms of export credit loans be lengthened beyond the 12-year limit, ECAs sometimes used *mismatch* or SOAR

---

[23] Private Export Funding Corporation. (2010). Company Profile.
[24] Private Export Funding Corporation Presentation. (2010). Trade Finance Solutions for Exporters and Lenders.
[25] Private Export Funding Corporation. (2010). Annual Report.

loans, whereby commercial lenders supplemented an ECA-supported loan with a commercial loan to provide loan economics typically associated with a longer repayment term. The way a SOAR loan works is that there is a commercial loan that shares *pari passu* in the security/collateral of the ECA-supported loan, but without the ECA guarantee. This loan, typically from a bank, accretes in value over the 12-year tenor of the ECA financing. Effectively, on each interest payment date, the airline makes its normal payment of interest and principal on the 12-year ECA financing, but the accreting commercial loan provides a portion of the payment that equates to the difference between what would have been owed under the usual 12-year financing tenor and a (usually) 15-year amortization profile. Thus, the airline gets a 12-year financing with a 15-year amortization profile through the use of this supplemental commercial financing.

As an example, the U.S. Ex-Im Bank used an asset-based lease structure that included a SOAR loan in support of a $113 million long-term guarantee to support the export of four B737-700 aircraft plus two spare engines made by CFM International to Compania Panamena de Aviacion (COPA) in Panama.[26] SOAR loans were a feature used by some airlines in financings before the 2007 ASU rules. Under the 2007 ASU, and subsequently the 2011 ASU, the maximum tenor can no longer be stretched using commercial debt that shares *pari passu* in the security/ collateral of the ECA-supported loan. Thus, any SOAR or mismatch debt must now be subordinated, which, from a commercial point of view, makes it less attractive for lenders except for the most creditworthy airlines and lessors.

Summary

Governmental ECAs provide financing support to aircraft operators and manufacturers in an effort to increase high-value exports. Long-established governmental agencies and some private sector programs assist foreign trade and promote exports by assisting foreign purchasers. These agencies often provide financing, when no other source of capital may be available, through a variety of programs that offer lower cost financing. The dominant ECAs, when it comes to aircraft finance, predominantly exist in the countries where various aircraft manufacturers are located: Brazil, Canada, France, Germany, the U.S., and the UK. ECAs typically offer a government-supported or -guaranteed loan financing to the export customer.

---

[26] Ex-Im Bank supports $132 million U.S. aircraft sale to Panama—Largest ever Ex-Im Bank transaction to this country. Export-Import Bank of the United States. February 2, 2000 press release.

Recent developments in ECA finance have come about as a result of the new 2011 ASU (NASU) as well as the increased adoption of the Cape Town Treaty. These agreements, coupled with new financing structures such as AFRNs, have continued the evolution of the ECA aircraft financing markets. Consequently, many airlines and lessors have been able to obtain more attractive financing tenors, rates, and terms than otherwise would be available to them.

References

Aviation Working Group. (2011). Aircraft Sector Understanding—Overview and Summary. London, UK. Retrieved from http://www.awg.aero/export_credit_rules.htm.

Department of Foreign Affairs and International Trade. (August 5, 2009). Government of Canada Provides Support to Bombardier. Retrieved from http://www.global tradealert.org/measure/canada-financial-support-bombardier.

Embraer. (May 1, 2009). Embraer—Empresa Brasileira de Aeronautica, 2008 Form 20-F. 38.

Embraer. (April 19, 2011). Embraer—Empresa Brasileira de Aeronautica, 2010 Form 20-F Filing. 41.

Export Development Canada. (2011). Canada Account Transactions. Retrieved from http://www.edc.ca/english/disclosure_9239.htm.

International Institute for the Unification of Private Law, UNIDROIT. (2005). Protocol to the Convention on International Interests in Mobile Equipment on Matters Specific to Aircraft Equipment.

International Registry of Mobile Assets. (2011). Listing of Ratified Countries. Retrieved from https://www.internationalregistry.aero.

Private Export Funding Corporation. (2010a). Annual Report. Retrieved from http://www.pefco.com/pdf/PEFCO-AR2010.pdf.

Private Export Funding Corporation. (2010b). Company Profile. Retrieved from http://www.pefco.com/about/overview.html.

Private Export Funding Corporation. (2010c). PEFCO Company Shareowners. Retrieved from http://www.pefco.com/about/shareowners.html.

Siegel, E. (October 14, 2009). *EDC and Canadian Aerospace: Working Together to Address the Challenges and Opportunities of Global Trade*. Export Development Canada, Ottawa, Canada.

United States Export-Import Bank. (2000). Annual Performance Report 2000, Washington, D.C.

World Trade Organization. (July 26, 2001). Brazil—Export Financing Program for Aircraft, Second Recourse by Canada to Article 21.5 of the DSU, Report of the Panel.

World Trade Organization. (January 28, 2002). Canada—Export Credits and Loan Guarantees for Regional Aircraft, Report of the Panel.

APPENDICES

Appendix A Top 20 Commercial Airline Leasing Companies

Rank	Company	Total fleet value ($m)	Total fleet value change	Total fleet	Average fleet value ($m)	Average fleet value change
1	GECAS	33,403	1.50%	1,502	22.2	0.40%
2	ILFC	31,522	−19.70%	1,068	29.5	−5.00%
3	AerCap	8,413	69.40%	321	26.2	3.20%
4	CIT Group	8,250	−3.70%	300	27.5	−2.10%
5	RBS Aviation Capital	7,878	−3.00%	253	31.1	−2.60%
6	BBAM	7,786	19.40%	340	22.9	—
7	BOC Aviation	6,932	24.30%	161	43.1	0.20%
8	Aviation Capital Group	4,740	−5.60%	243	6,023	77.40%
9	AWAS	4,518	−5.10%	206	21.9	−0.90%
10	Macquarie AirFinance	4,052	47.20%	157	25.8	3.10%
11	Aircastle Investment	3,237	11.30%	135	24	1.80%
12	Pembroke Group	3,152	83.10%	129	24.4	−6.30%
13	Boeing Capital	2,758	−21.40%	258	10.7	−1.00%
14	Sumisho Aircraft Asset Management	2,397	3.60%	77	31.1	−3.40%
15	Doric Asset Finance	2,340	7.70%	23	101.7	−1.70%
16	Hong Kong Aviation Capital	2,312	—	68	34	34.00%
17	MC Aviation Partners	2,227	27.20%	77	28.9	1.10%
18	ALAFCO	1,830	12.50%	48	38.1	1.20%
19	AerVenture	1,769	55.40%	47	37.6	−3.00%
20	DAE Capital	1,729	27.70%	39	44.3	3.30%

Source: Airline Business, February 2011.

Appendix B Top 4 Commercial Aircraft Manufacturers, 2011

	Boeing	Airbus	Embraer	Bombardier
Historical orders	21,361	11,098	1,908	2,920
Historical deliveries	17,877	6,882	1,660	2,686
Commercial aircraft revenue (USD millions)	31,834	37,527	2,858	8,600
Current commercial aircraft	737NG 747-8 767-200ER 767-300ER 767-400ER 777-200ER/LR 777-300/-300ER 787-8/-9	A318 A319 A320 A321 A330-200 A330-300 A340-500/-600 A380	ERJ 135 ERJ 140 ERJ 145 EMB 170 EMB 175 EMB 190 EMB 195	CRJ100/200 CRJ440 CRJ700/705 CRJ900/1000 CS100 CS300 Challenger 800 Q100/200/300/400

Appendix C Top 20 Airlines, 2011

Rank	Airline	Active fleet	RPM (millions)	Employees	Revenue (USD millions)
1	Delta Air Lines	717	193,169	80,000	31,755
2	American Airlines	614	125,450	66,525	19,843
3	United Airlines	359	102,503	46,262	23,229
4	Emirates	161	90,803	30,258	14,807
5	Lufthansa	292	80,572	57,157	27,603
6	Continental Airlines	336	79,718	35,301	14,011
7	Southwest Airlines	561	78,047	34,901	12,104
8	Air France-KLM	254	77,774	60,686	14,521
9	China Southern Airlines	342	69,176	65,085	11,317
10	Qantas	142	66,337	32,629	14,842
11	British Airways	229	65,880	36,178	13,167
12	Cathay Pacific	126	60,017	21,592	11,523
13	US Airways	339	58,977	30,900	11,908
14	China Eastern Airlines	248	57,882	44,153	11,016
15	Air China	278	53,558	24,459	12,203
16	Singapore Airlines	104	52,693	13,793	8,855
17	Ryanair	275	52,009	8,069	4,807
18	Air Canada	201	51,875	23,200	10,428
19	Korean Air	143	37,626	17,395	9,889
20	Japan Airlines	122	37,121	16,000	16,018

Appendix D World Airline Vital Statistics, 2011

Rank	Airline	Active fleet	RPM (millions)	Load factor	IATA code	Country
1	Delta Air Lines	717	193,169	83.01%	DL	USA
2	American Airlines	614	125,450	81.89%	AA	USA
3	United Airlines	359	102,503	84.11%	UA	USA
4	Emirates	161	90,803	80.00%	EK	UAE
5	Lufthansa	292	80,572	79.41%	LH	Germany
6	Continental Airlines	336	79,718	83.93%	CO	USA
7	Southwest Airlines	561	78,047	79.28%	WN	USA
8	Air France-KLM	254	77,774	80.46%	AF	France
9	China Southern Airlines	342	69,176	79.23%	CZ	China
10	Qantas	142	66,337	80.10%	QF	Australia
11	British Airways	229	65,880	77.57%	BA	UK
12	Cathay Pacific	126	60,017	83.44%	CX	China
13	US Airways	339	58,977	82.38%	US	USA
14	China Eastern Airlines	248	57,882	77.98%	MU	China
15	Air China	278	53,558	80.25%	CA	China
16	Singapore Airlines	104	52,693	78.47%	SQ	Singapore
17	Ryanair	275	52,009	—	FR	Ireland
18	Air Canada	201	51,875	81.69%	AC	Canada
19	Korean Air	143	37,626	76.20%	KE	South Korea
20	Japan Airlines	122	37,121	68.91%	JL	Japan
21	All Nippon Airways	154	36,296	67.46%	NH	Japan
22	EasyJet	185	34,876	87.00%	U2	UK
23	Thai Airways	91	34,595	73.64%	TG	Thailand
24	Qatar Airways	101	34,262	75.53%	QR	Qatar
25	TAM	152	31,967	71.93%	JJ	Brazil
26	Iberia	104	31,840	82.23%	IB	Spain
27	Turkish Airlines	148	29,795	73.65%	TK	Turkey
28	JetBlue	167	28,279	81.39%	B6	USA
29	Air Berlin	126	28,120	76.99%	AB	Germany
30	Aeroflot	108	24,341	77.10%	SU	Russia
31	Virgin Atlantic	37	23,710	82.53%	VS	UK
32	Malaysia Airlines	95	23,511	76.24%	MH	Malaysia
33	Alaska Airlines	117	23,457	83.28%	AS	USA
34	Saudi Arabian Airlines	140	21,164	64.73%	SV	Saudi Arabia
35	Etihad Airways	61	20,754	74.00%	EY	UAE

Continues

Appendix D *Continued*

Rank	Airline	Active fleet	RPM (millions)	Load factor	IATA code	Country
36	LAN	70	20,597	78.25%	LA	Chile
37	Alitalia	150	20,445	70.48%	AZ	Italy
38	Thomson Airways	59	20,327	88.91%	BY	UK
39	SkyWest Airlines	314	20,227	79.31%	OO	USA
40	China Airlines	68	20,037	80.96%	CI	Taiwan
41	Hainana Airlines	85	19,984	81.73%	HU	China
42	AirTran Airways	140	19,578	81.36%	FL	USA
43	GOL	104	19,016	68.90%	G3	Brazil
44	Swissair	65	18,344	82.29%	LX	Switzerland
45	Thomas Cook Airlines	40	17,016	93.12%	MT	UK
46	Jet Airways	85	16,760	78.58%	9W	India
47	Virgin Australia	80	16,712	79.09%	DJ	Australia
48	Asiana Airlines	71	16,591	76.87%	OZ	South Korea
49	Transaero Airlines	68	16,338	83.66%	UN	Russia
50	Air New Zealand	48	16,049	81.79%	NZ	New Zealand
51	WestJet	96	15,613	79.92%	WS	Canada
52	TAP Portugal	55	14,696	74.18%	TP	Portugal
53	EVA Air	53	14,680	76.72%	BR	Taiwan
54	SAS	137	14,600	75.18%	SK	Sweden
55	Shenzhen Airlines	103	14,586	81.84%	ZH	China
56	Jetstar Airways	60	14,480	77.98%	JQ	Australia
57	South African Airways	50	13,100	70.62%	SA	South Africa
58	Garuda Indonesia	83	12,716	68.79%	GA	Indonesia
59	EgyptAir	61	12,673	71.53%	MS	Egypt
60	Condor Flugdienst	23	12,358	89.01%	DE	Germany
61	Philippine	36	12,313	76.65%	PR	Philippines
62	Air India	117	12,170	64.89%	AI	India
63	Finnair	65	11,944	76.50%	AY	Finland
64	Vietnam Airlines	70	11,861	77.16%	VN	Vietnam
65	Aeromexico	53	11,577	77.41%	AM	Mexico
66	AirAsia	54	11,495	75.93%	AK	Malaysia
67	El Al Israel Airline	38	11,472	81.45%	LY	Israel
68	Austrian	43	10,870	76.81%	OS	Austria
69	Air Europe	39	10,612	79.32%	UX	Spain
70	Shanghai Airlines	63	10,215	75.71%	FM	China

Rank	Airline	Active fleet	RPM (millions)	Load factor	IATA code	Country
71	Xiamen Airlines	79	10,076	77.05%	MF	China
72	TUIFly	24	9,942	—	HF	Germany
73	Pakistan Intl Airlines	40	9,729	57.07%	PK	Pakistan
74	Sichuan Airlines	60	9,606	82.89%	3U	China
75	Frontier Airlines	59	9,526	83.30%	F9	USA
76	Monarch Airlines	30	9,399	85.21%	ZB	UK
77	ExpressJet	242	9,390	78.89%	XE	USA
78	Aer Lingus	44	8,836	77.84%	EI	Ireland
79	Hawaiian Airlines	36	8,675	85.46%	HA	USA
80	Copa Airlines	50	8,416	76.85%	CM	Panama
81	Gulf Air	32	8,326	—	GF	Bahrain
82	Air Transat	22	8,250	91.15%	TS	Canada
83	S7 Airlines	32	8,074	76.50%	S7	Russia
84	American Eagle	245	7,985	73.92%	MQ	USA
85	Avianca	60	7,930	78.34%	AV	Colombia
86	Ethiopian Airlines	46	6,840	72.73%	ET	Ethiopia
87	Spirit Airlines	35	6,625	82.05%	NK	USA
88	Royal Air Maroc	53	6,524	—	AT	Morroco
89	Transavia Airlines	29	6,374	78.43%	HV	Netherlands
90	CorsairFly	6	6,214	80.00%	SS	France
91	Sri Lankan Airlines	16	5,955	76.78%	UL	Sri Lanka
92	Iran Air	49	5,796	76.90%	IR	Iran
93	Atlantic Southeast Airlines	168	5,772	79.83%	EV	USA
94	Kenya Airways	32	5,528	69.20%	KQ	Kenya
95	Aerolenas Argentinas	40	5,468	—	AR	Argentina
96	Allegiant Air	54	5,212	90.76%	G4	USA
97	Onur Air	—	5,095	—	8Q	Turkey
98	Spanair	29	4,394	75.39%	JK	Spain
99	Mesa Airlines	74	4,073	79.04%	YV	USA
100	Middle East Airlines	17	2,263	64.18%	ME	Lebanon

Appendix E Aircraft Seat Capacity by Manufacturer

Manufacturer	Type	Seating configuration			Power plant
		3-class	2-class	1-class	
Boeing	747-100	366	452		4 × RB211-524B2, PW JT9D-7A/-7F/-7J
	747-200	366	452		4 × JT9D-7R4G2, CF6-50E2, RB211-524D4
	747-300	412	496		4 × PW JT9D-7R4G2 or GE CF6-80C2B1 or RR RB211-524D4
	747-400	416	568	660	4 × PW 4062 or GE CF6-80C2B5F or RR RB211-524G/H
	747-800	467	581		4 × GEnx-2B67
	777-200	305	400	440	2 × PW 4090, or GE90-94B, or RR 895
	777-300	368	451	550	2 × GE90-115B1
	767-200ER	181	224	255	2 × P&W PW4000-94, 2 × GE CF6-80C2
	767-300ER	218	269	350	2 × P&W PW4000-94, 2 × GE CF6-80C2
	767-400ER	245	304	375	2 × P&W PW4000-94, 2 × GE CF6-80C2
	757-200		200	234	2 × RB211, or PW2037, or PW2040, or PW2043
	757-300		243	280	2 × RB211, or PW2037, or PW2040, or PW2043
	707-300		141	189	2 × Pratt & Whitney JT8D
	717-200		106	117	2 × Rolls-Royce BR715-C1-30
	737-100		85	124	2 × Pratt & Whitney JT8D
	737-200		97	136	2 × Pratt & Whitney JT8D
	737-300		128	140	2 × CFM56-3B-1
	737-400		146	159	2 × CFM56-3B-2
	737-500		108	122	2 × CFM56-3B-1
	737-600		123	130	2 × CFM56-7B20
	737-700		140	148	2 × CFM56-7B26
	737-800		175	189	2 × CFM56-7B27
	737-900		204	215	2 × CFM56-7B27

Airbus	A318-100		107	132	2 × PW6000, or 2 × CFM56-5
	A-319		124	156	2 × CFM56-5
	A-320		150	180	2 × CFM56-5
	A-321		185	220	2 × CFM56-5
	A-300B4		266		2 × CF6-50C2 or JT9D-59A
	A-300-600R		266		2 × CF6-80C2 or PW4158
	A-300-600F				2 × CF6-80C2 or PW4158
	A-310-200		240		2 × PWJT9D-7R4 or CF6-80C2A2
	A-310-300		240		2 × PW4156A or CF6-80C2A8
	A-330-200	253	293	380	2 × PW4000
	A-330-300	295	335	440	2 × PW4000
	A-340-200	240	300	375	4 × CFM56-5C
	A-340-300	295	335	375	4 × CFM56-5C
	A-340-400	295	315	375	4 × CFM56-5C
	A-340-500	313	359	375	4 × RR Trent 500
	A-340-600	360	380	475	4 × RR Trent 500
	A-350-800	250	275	375	2 × RR Trent XWB
	A-350-900	314	366	420	2 × RR Trent XWB
	A-350-1000	350	412	475	2 × RR Trent XWB
	A-380	525	644	853	4 × RR Trent 970/B
Lockheed	L-1011-100	253			3 × RB.211-22
	L-1011-200	263			3 × RB.211-524B
	L-1011-300	234			3 × RB.211-524B

Appendix E *Continued*

Manufacturer	Type	Seating configuration			Power plant
		3-class	2-class	1-class	
McDonnell Douglas	MD-11	293	323	410	3 × PW 4462, 3 × PW 4460
	DC-10-10	255		399	3 × GE CF6-6D
	DC-10-40	255		399	3 × PW JT9D-59A
	DC-9-10			90	2 × PW JT8D-5 or -7
	DC-9-20			90	2 × PW JT8D-11
	DC-9-30			115	2 × PW JT8D−7, -9, -11 or -15
	DC-9-40			125	2 × PW JT8D−7, -9, -11 or -15
	DC-9-50			135	2 × PW JT8D-15, or -17
	MD-81		155	172	2 × PW JT8D-200
	MD-82		155	172	2 × PW JT8D-200
	MD-87		130	139	2 × PW JT8D-200
	MD-88		155	172	2 × PW JT8D-200
Bombardier	CRJ 100	50			2 × GE CF34-3A1
	CRJ 200	50			2 × GE CF34-3B1
	CRJ 700	70	66		2 × GE CF34-8C5B1
	CRJ 900	90	75		2 × GE CF34-8C5
	CRJ 1000	100	86		2 × GE CF34-8C5A1

Manufacturer	Model			Engines
de Havilland Canada	DHC-6-400	19		2 × Pratt & Whitney PT6A-34 turboprop
	DHC-6-300	22		2 × Pratt & Whitney PT6A-27 turboprop
	DHC-7-100	54		4 × Pratt & Whitney Canada PT6A-50 turboprops
	DHC-7-101	50		4 × Pratt & Whitney Canada PT6A-50 turboprops
	DHC-7-102	54		4 × Pratt & Whitney Canada PT6A-50 turboprops
	DHC-7-103	50		4 × Pratt & Whitney Canada PT6A-50 turboprops
	DHC-8-100	37		2 PW120A/PW121
	DHC-8-200	37		2 PW123C/D
	DHC-8-300	50		2 PW123B
	DHC-8-400	78		2 PW150A
Embraer	EMB 110	20	15	2 × Pratt & Whitney PT6A-20 com 579 hp
	ERJ 120	30		2 × Pratt & Whitney PT6A-34 com 750 hp
	ERJ 135	37		2 × RR AE3007
	ERJ 140	44		2 × RR AE3007
	ERJ 145	50		2 × RR AE3007
	ERJ 170	78	70	2 × GE CF34-8E
	ERJ 175	86	78	2 × GE CF34-8E
	ERJ 190	106	94	2 × GE CF34-10E
	ERJ 195	118	106	2 × GE CF34-10E

GLOSSARY

A

Airborne Collision Avoidance System (ACAS)   An ACAS is an aircraft system that operates independently of ground-based equipment and air traffic control in warning pilots of the presence of other objects that may present a threat of collision.

Air carrier   Any airline that undertakes directly, by lease or other arrangement to engage in air transportation.

Aircraft, crews, and maintenance insurance (ACMI)   A lease between two parties where the first party is a lessor with an Air Operator Certificate (AOC) responsible for the aircraft crews, maintenance, and insurance, and the second party is the lessee, usually with an AOC, who is responsible for schedules, flight charges, cargo handling, crew support, flight operations, ramp handling, and aircraft servicing and fueling.

Aircraft daily utilization   Aircraft hours flown (block-to-block) divided by aircraft days available.

Aircraft utilization   Aircraft utilization is calculated by dividing aircraft block hours by the number of aircraft days assigned to service on air carrier routes and presented in block hours per day.

Ancillary revenue   Revenue generated from non-ticket sources or services that differ from or enhance the main services or product lines of an airline such as baggage fees and onboard food and services.

Available seat kilometers (ASK)   A measure of a passenger airline's carrying capacity, calculated as

$$ASK = \text{Number of Seats} \times \text{Number of Kilometers Flown}$$

Available seat miles (ASM)   A measure of a passenger airline's carrying capacity, calculated as

$$ASM = \text{Number of Seats} \times \text{Number of Miles Flown}$$

Available ton miles (ATM)   A measure of a cargo airline's carrying capacity, calculated as

$$ATM = \text{Weight in Non-metric Tons} \times \text{Number of Miles Flown}$$

Average stage length (ASL)   The ASL is the average distance flown per aircraft departure, calculated as

$$ASL = \frac{\text{Plane Miles}}{\text{Departures}}$$

B

Bankruptcy   The inability of an airline to pay its creditor(s).

Block hour   Block hours are the airline industry's basic measure of aircraft utilization. A block hour is the time from the minute the aircraft door closes at departure of a revenue flight until the moment the aircraft door opens at the arrival gate.

Book value   The value of an aircraft stated on the airline's balance sheet, reflecting the original price reduced by accumulated depreciation.

Break-even load factor   The load factor that covers the necessary operating costs for scheduled traffic revenue, calculated as

$$\text{Break-Even}_{LF} = \frac{\text{CASM}}{\text{R/RPM}} = \frac{\text{CASM}}{\text{Yield}}$$

C

Cabotage   From the French word *caboter* (to sail along the coast); denotes the transport of passengers and cargo within the same country.

Capital lease   A financial lease that generally lasts for the life of the asset, with the present value of lease payments covering the price of the asset; the lease generally cannot be canceled.

Certified Air Carrier   An air carrier that is certified by the Department of Transportation (DOT) to conduct scheduled or non-scheduled interstate services. The certificate issued to the air carrier by the DOT is the Certificate of Public Convenience and Necessity.

Code-sharing   An arrangement where an airline may place its own code to another carrier's flight. The airline that is actually operating the flight is called the *operating carrier*, and the airline that is marketing the flight is called the *marketing carrier*. Both carriers may sell tickets for the flight.

Collateral   An aircraft may serve as collateral (security for a lender) and may be repossessed in a case of default.

Commercial service airport   An airport that is receiving scheduled passenger service and has 2,500 or more enplaned passengers per year.

Commuter air carrier   A passenger air carrier operating aircraft with 30 seats or less and performing at least 5 scheduled round trips per week. It operates for hire or compensation under FAR Part 135.

Cost of capital   The overall financial cost to an airline, expressed as a percentage taking into account its capital structure, the interest rate it pays on debt, and the cost of its equity.

Cost per available seat mile (CASM)   Represented in U.S. cents, calculated as

$$CASM = \frac{Operating\ Costs}{ASM}$$

D

D-check   Also known as a heavy maintenance visit (HMV), which more or less takes the entire airplane apart for inspection and overhaul.

Deregulation   Generally refers to the Airline Deregulation Act of 1978, which ended U.S. government regulation of airline routes and charges.

Dry lease   A leasing arrangement between two airlines where the first airline leases an aircraft from a second airline (lessor) to operate. Under a dry lease, the lessee pays for the crew, fuel, and maintenance.

E

Economy of scale   The increase in efficiency of production as the number of goods being produced increases.

Economy of scope   Average cost reduction as a result of increasing the number of different goods produced.

Eight Freedoms of the Air   The complete set of rights to carry passengers and cargo within a foreign country.

Elevators   On an aircraft, the elevators are a control surface usually on the trailing edge of the horizontal stabilizer to control pitch.

Enplanement   The boarding of scheduled and non-scheduled service aircraft by domestic, territorial, and international revenue passengers for intrastate, interstate, and foreign commerce, including in-transit passengers.

Equipment trust certificate (ETC)   A trust of investors that purchases an aircraft and then *leases* it to the operator, on condition that the airline will receive title upon full performance of the lease.

Extended-Range Twin-Engine Operations (ETOPS)   A rule that allows twin-engine aircraft (such as Airbus A300, A310, A320, A330, and A350; Boeing 737, 757, 767, 777, and 787; Embraer E-Jets; and ATR) to fly longer distance routes that were previously off-limit.

F

Federal Air Regulation (FAR)   Title 14 of the U.S. government's Code of Federal Regulations. FAR covers all the rules regarding aviation in the United States.

Federal Aviation Administration (FAA)   A U.S. government agency responsible for air safety and operation of the air traffic control system.

Finance lease   A capital lease that generally lasts for the life of the asset, with the present value of lease payments covering the price of the asset.

Financial leverage   A measure of the amount of debt used in the capital structure of an airline. An airline with high leverage is more vulnerable to downturns in the business cycle because the airline must continue to service its debt regardless of slow or stagnant business.

Financial risk   The risk that an airline may not have sufficient cash to meet its financial obligations.

Flight stage   The operation of an aircraft from takeoff to its next landing.

Form 41 data   Information derived from airline filings with the Bureau of Transportation Statistics (BTS). Airline financial data is filed with the BTS quarterly; traffic and employment numbers are filed monthly.

Freight   Any commodity other than mail and passenger baggage transported by air.

Freight ton mile   One ton of freight shipped one mile.

Frequent flyer program   A service in which an airline customer accrues points corresponding to the distance the person has flown on an airline. The points can be used for air travel discounts, increased benefits such as airport lounge access or priority bookings, and other products or services.

Future value   The value to which a current investment grows, within a given interest rate, over a specified period of time.

Future value of an annuity   The future value of a series of consultative equal payments.

H

Half-life condition   A component, like a jet engine, is in half-life condition when it is exactly midway between scheduled overhaul and replacement.

Hub and spoke   Many airlines designate an airport as a hub through which they transit passengers from spoke (origin) to spoke (destination).

I

Internal rate of return   The discount rate that makes the net present value of all cash flows from a project equal to zero.

J

Japanese leveraged lease   A lease arrangement under which the lessor borrows a large proportion of the funds needed to purchase the asset.

Japanese operating lease   A traditional tax structure with the investor taking 20% of the aircraft's value and borrowing the rest.

L

Launch customer   The carrier that places the first order for an aircraft.

Lease   A lease is a contract granting use or occupation of property during a specified period in exchange for specified lease payments.

Lessee   A person who leases a property from its owner (lessor).

Lessor   The owner of an asset who grants another party a lease to the asset.

Leverage   The use of debt to supplement investment.

Leveraged lease   A lease agreement wherein the lessor, by borrowing funds from a lending institution, finances the purchase of the asset being leased.

Liquidity   The ability of an asset to be converted to cash without significant loss of value.

Load factor   Load factor is the ratio of revenue passenger miles to available seat miles, representing the proportion of aircraft seating capacity that is actually sold and utilized, calculated as

$$\text{Load Factor} = \frac{\text{ASM}}{\text{RPM}}$$

M

Major airlines   Airlines earning revenues of $1 billion or more annually in scheduled service.

Maximum certificated takeoff weight (MCTOW)   The maximum weight at which the pilot of the aircraft is allowed to attempt to take off because of the aircraft's structural limitations.

Maximum Zero Fuel   The total weight of the aircraft and all its contents, minus the total weight of the fuel onboard.

Modified Accelerated Cost Recovery System (MACRS)   A method of accelerated asset depreciation that allows for more depreciation towards the beginning of the life of the capital asset so the tax-deductible depreciation expense can be taken sooner.

N

Narrow-body aircraft   Aircraft with a single aisle.

Net advantage to leasing (NAL)   Cost savings from leasing an aircraft compared to purchasing an aircraft.

Net present value (NPV) Equals the total present value of all cash inflows and outflows.

Net profit margin Net profit (or loss) after interest and taxes as a percent of operating revenues.

Non-scheduled service Revenue flights not operated as regular scheduled service, such as charter flights and all non-revenue flights.

O

Operating expenses Expenses incurred in the performance of air transportation, based on overall operating revenues and expenses.

Operating lease A short-term lease; for example, an aircraft that has an economic life of 30 years may be leased to an airline for 4 years on an operating lease.

Operating leverage A measure of the extent to which fixed assets are utilized in the business.

Operating profit margin Operating profit (operating revenues minus operating expenses) as a percent of operating revenues.

Operating revenues Revenues from air transportation and related, incidental services.

P

Par value The same as the face value; the principal value or maturity value of a bond. The par value is the amount of money the investor will receive once the bond matures.

Passenger load factor The ratio of revenue passenger miles to available seat miles, representing the proportion of aircraft seating capacity actually sold and utilized, calculated as

$$LF = \frac{RPM}{ASM} \times 100$$

Passenger revenue per available seat mile (PRASM) The average revenue received by the airline per unit of capacity available for sale, calculated as

$$PRASM = \frac{Revenue}{ASM}$$

Payback period The time that is required for recovering an initial investment.

Payload The part of an aircraft's load that generates revenue (freight and passengers).

Perpetuity A cash flow without a maturity date.

Preferred stock A hybrid security combining some of the characteristics of bonds and common stock that usually carries no voting rights.

Primary market The market for raising new capital for the first time.

Prime rate The rate that a commercial bank charges its most creditworthy customers.

Profitability ratios A group of ratios that are used to assess the return on assets, sales, and invested capital.

R

Residual value Describes the future value of an aircraft in terms of percentage of depreciation of its initial value.

Revenue passenger enplanement The total number of revenue passengers boarding aircraft, including origination, stopover or connecting passengers.

Revenue passenger load factor See also *Passenger load factor*. The ratio of revenue passenger miles to available seat miles, representing the proportion of aircraft seating capacity that is actually sold and utilized.

Revenue passenger mile (RPM) RPM is computed by multiplying the revenue aircraft miles flown by the number of revenue passengers carried on that route. RPM is a principal measure of an airline's turnover.

Revenue per available seat mile (RASM) The revenue received for each seat mile offered. RASM is computed by dividing operating income by available seat miles, and is not limited to ticket sales revenue.

Revenue ton mile (RTM) One non-metric ton of revenue traffic transported one mile.

S

Sale and leaseback Arrangement in which an airline sells an aircraft to a buyer and the buyer immediately leases the aircraft back to the airline.

Seat pitch The distance between one seat in the aircraft and the same point on another seat directly in front or behind.

Secondary market The markets for securities that have already been issued and traded among investors with no proceeds going to the company.

Small Certificated Air Carrier An air carrier holding a certificate issued under Section 401 of the Federal Aviation Act of 1958, as amended, that operates aircraft designed to have a maximum seating capacity of 60 seats or fewer or a maximum payload of 18,000 pounds or less.

Stage 2 Describes jets meeting certain noise parameters on takeoff and landing.

Stage 3 Describes the quietest jets in service.

Stage length The average distance flown per aircraft departure.

Straight-line depreciation A method of depreciation that is calculated by taking the purchase price of an asset less the salvage value divided by the total productive years the asset can be reasonably expected to benefit the company.

T

Traffic collision avoidance system (TCAS)   A system that monitors the air space around an aircraft for other aircraft equipped with a corresponding active transponder, which warns pilots of the presence of other transponder-equipped aircraft that may present a threat of mid-air collision.

U

United States Flag Carrier   One of a class of air carriers holding a Certificate of Public Convenience and Necessity issued by the U.S. Department of Transportation (DOT) and approved by the President of the United States, authorizing scheduled operations over specified routes between the United States and one or more foreign countries.

V

Variable cost   A variable cost is a cost that changes in proportion to a change in a company's activity or business.

W

Walk-away lease   A lease that allows the airline to return the aircraft at specified times without penalty.

Weighted average cost of capital (WACC)   The cost of each capital component multiplied by its proportional weight and then summing, calculated as

$$\text{WACC} = \frac{D}{A} \times k_d \times (1 - T) + \frac{E}{A} \times k_e$$

where

A = Market value of the company
E = Market value of the firm's equity
D = Market value of the firm's debt
k_e = Cost of equity
k_d = Cost of debt
T = Corporate tax rate

Wet lease   A leasing arrangement between lessor and lessee to acquire aircraft and crew from the second party that operates services on behalf of the first party.

White tail   An unsold aircraft that has been built by an aircraft manufacturer.

Wide-body aircraft   A commercial aircraft with two aisles.

Index

American Society of Appraisers
  (ASA), 254
appraisal company requirements,
  255
International Society of Transport
  Aircraft Trading (ISTAT), 254–5
Asia, commercial aircraft production
  in, 42–4
asset
  -backed securities, 215, 217
    cons of, 219
    pros of, 218-219*f*
  -based financing and leasing
    transactions, 339
  identification, 259
  rights, 188
  risk, 230
auto loans, 217
available seat kilometers (ASK), 236
available seat miles (ASM), 236
average seats per aircraft, 99–101
average stage length (ASL), 107–12,
  109–12*f*
  aircraft utilization by, 103, 106, 107*f*,
    108*f*
Aviation Capital Group (ACG), 294
Aviation Industry Corporation (AVIC)
  (China), 43
Aviation Working Group, 339
AVITAS
  *Aircraft Block Hour Operating Costs
    and Operations Guide*, 140

Babcock & Brown Aircraft Management
  (BBAM), 294
Bandeirante, 45–6
bankruptcy
  Delta Air Lines, 193
  Lockheed Aircraft, 18
  protection issues, 221–4
  Rolls-Royce, 19, 20
Barclays Bond Index, 215
Beech Aircraft Corporation, 46, 246

below-investment-grade bonds, 199
Bethune, Gordon, 135, 157
block hour(s), 201
  cargo revenue per, 145
  passenger revenue per, 144
  sensitivity
    of Airbus aircraft, 169–70, 170*f*
    of Boeing aircraft, 179
BNDES-Exim program, 336
Boeing, William, 5
Boeing aircraft, 2, 58–71, 186, 187, 200
  Boeing 737NG
    block hour cost of, 122–4, 123*f*,
      124*f*
    cost of available seat miles, 122–3,
      123*f*, 125, 125*f*
    cost structure of, 124–5, 124*f*
    operational characteristics of, 122,
      122*f*
  Boeing 777-200
    block hour cost of, 128, 129*f*
    cost of available seat miles, 128–30,
      129*f*
    operational characteristics of,
      127–8, 128*f*
  company, 5–12
  comparative analysis of, 69–71
  data selection, 141–2
  fleet composition, 98*t*
  fuel efficiency of, 116–18, 118*t*
  in-production fleet, 13*t*, 59–65
    general characteristics of, 60, 61*t*
    operational characteristics of,
      63–5, 64*t*
    physical characteristics of, 60,
      62–3, 62*t*
  leased vs. owned, 273*t*
  Next Generation (NG) program, 141
  out-of-production fleet, 12*f*, 13*t*
    general characteristics of, 65–7, 66*t*
    operational characteristics of,
      67–9, 68*t*
    physical characteristics of, 67, 67*t*